Rights, Wrongs, and Injustices

OXFORD PRIVATE LAW THEORY

Oxford Private Law Theory publishes leading work in private law theory. It commissions and solicits monographs and edited collections in general private law theory as well as specific fields, including the theoretical analysis of tort law, property law, contract law, fiduciary law, trust law, remedies and restitution, and the law of equity. The series is open to diverse theoretical approaches, including those informed by philosophy, economics, history, and political theory. Oxford Private Law Theory sets the standard for rigorous and original work in private law theory.

Rights, Wrongs, and Injustices

The Structure of Remedial Law

STEPHEN A. SMITH

OXFORD
UNIVERSITY PRESS

OXFORD
UNIVERSITY PRESS

Great Clarendon Street, Oxford, OX2 6DP,
United Kingdom

Oxford University Press is a department of the University of Oxford. It furthers the University's objective of excellence in research, scholarship, and education by publishing worldwide. Oxford is a registered trade mark of Oxford University Press in the UK and in certain other countries

First Edition published in 2019

Published in the United States of America by Oxford University Press
198 Madison Avenue, New York, NY 10016, United States of America

British Library Cataloguing in Publication Data

Data available

Library of Congress Control Number: 2019946482

ISBN 978–0–19–922977–2

For Jamie, Michael, and Jennifer

Preface

This book's origins lie in two puzzles. The first is pedagogical. In 2008, I agreed to teach a course on 'Private Law Remedies' for the first time. In anticipation, I assembled a list of materials based on topics typically discussed in such courses. When it became time to prepare lectures, I adopted my usual approach of trying to find a common thread—an overarching principle, concept, or question—to tie the materials together. I had no success. As a result, my initial view was that courses on remedies, as conventionally understood, were a hodgepodge of miscellaneous topics. The two groups of rules that were universally assumed to be the subject's core—those governing specific relief (e.g. specific performance, injunctions) and those governing damages awards—seemed to me to be radically different. The former appeared to be concerned exclusively with the availability of certain kinds of judicial rulings, while the latter appeared to be concerned exclusively with the substantive question of how much wrongdoers should pay their victims. From this perspective, the rules governing damages awards seemed similar to those that determine the content of substantive duties, such as the rules that establish the content of a contractual duty or a duty not to commit a nuisance.

In short, it seemed to me that, unlike the rules governing specific relief, the rules on damages awards were part of the 'substantive law': they established how individuals should treat each other in their day-to-day lives, and, in particular, what individuals should do after they breach a contract or commit a tort. Admittedly, both sets of rules could be described as broadly 'remedial'. However, they appeared to be remedial in entirely different senses: the rules governing specific relief determine when courts will assist claimants' efforts to ensure that defendants perform their substantive duties; by contrast, the rules governing damages awards determine what wrongdoers should do for their victims. Given my membership in a faculty that teaches both common law and civil law, it was difficult not to notice that civilian codes distinguish specific relief and damages awards in exactly this way.

The first puzzle, then, was why books and courses on remedies existed at all. The literature on remedies provided little help with this puzzle. Indeed, this literature rarely addressed or even acknowledged the puzzle. Textbooks on remedies simply did not raise the possibility that significant parts of their subject matter were comprised of substantive law rules. In particular, discussions of damages awards rarely made clear whether the rules under examination were rules for how citizens should act or rules for what courts should do—or whether the answer made a difference. Authors regularly referred to 'liabilities' to pay damages, but it was almost never made clear whether the liability in question was a liability to fall under a substantive duty to pay damages, or a liability to being ordered by a court to pay damages. The same observations apply to restitutionary orders, also discussed by most remedies textbooks.

As noted, my initial view was that there was no solution to the pedagogic puzzle: the subject matter of courses and books on remedies, as conventionally understood, seemed comprised of radically different rules. At the same time, reflection on these differences (and on Rafael Zakrzewski's groundbreaking book, *Remedies Reclassified*) led me to think that it might be possible to develop a coherent course on remedies by focusing on the rules governing specific relief. These rules seemed to me to be different from those that are the focus of substantive private law courses. Rather than telling individuals how to behave in day-to-day life, they direct courts to provide particular rulings in particular situations. Of course, all legal rules may be applied by courts. However, courts do not merely apply the rules governing specific relief; these rules tell courts how they should act. In particular, they tell courts what they should do when individuals come to them seeking their assistance. For example, they tell courts that they should not grant specific performance if the order would require the defendant to perform a personal service. To be sure, these rules also grant citizens legal powers to obtain remedies. Still, the duties that arise from the exercise of these powers are imposed on courts. The powers that such rules set out are held against the state; they provide individuals with powers to obtain rulings from the state. By contrast, the substantive rules of contract and tort law are fundamentally rules for citizens: they tell citizens how they should behave towards one another ('perform contracts', 'do not trespass', 'do not take others' property', and so on), and what they must do if they wish to change their legal relations with others (e.g. what they must do to make a contract).

As I prepared to teach my course, this distinction seemed important. It still does today. The question of what courts should do when citizens seek their assistance is different from the question of how citizens ought to treat one another. The former raises distinctive issues about, for example, the allocation of state resources, the administration of litigation, and the nature of judicial rulings. Most importantly, the question of how courts should respond to requests for relief raises distinctive issues of justice. Stealing, injuring, lying, and breaking promises are bad things to do, but they do not raise issues of justice: it is wrong to hit others, but we do not normally describe such actions as unjust (aside from special cases where the victim was unfairly selected from a group of potential victims). For the most part, issues of justice arise within private law when courts get involved—and the most direct way that courts get involved is by issuing rulings. It is unjust—not merely wrong—for a court improperly to refuse a plaintiff's request for specific relief. It is to the courts (and the 'justices') that citizens go when they seek justice, and getting justice in this context means getting the right ruling. For these reasons, it seemed that there was something distinctive—something that merited special treatment—about at least some of the rules that I was teaching in my remedies course. However, my initial view was that only a small portion of these rules—primarily those governing specific relief—fell into this category.

The second puzzle is philosophical. When I began teaching remedies, I was also teaching general jurisprudence. Unsurprisingly, I was curious as to what was said about judicial rulings in the jurisprudential literature. What I found was largely silence. This was not what I expected: after all, legal scholars, and especially scholars in common law jurisdictions, have long expressed a special interest in 'what courts do'. This interest is reflected in the common practice of beginning contract law courses by studying the rulings available to disappointed contracting parties. Some writers have gone so far as to argue that the law generally is nothing more than what courts do. However, it was apparent that this interest in rulings focused primarily on their availability and content (When is specific performance available? How are damages awards assessed? Is restitution available in kind or only in money?), or on the consequence of failing to comply with a ruling—that is, on sanctions. The concept of a ruling itself received little attention. In particular, there was nothing comparable to the extensive theoretical literature on rules and sanctions (the other main tools by which law attempts to impose itself on citizens). Indeed, it appeared that most writers assume that a ruling is either a mini-rule or a disguised sanction. Neither assumption seemed plausible. If rulings were mini-rules they would be, like regular rules, in the form of declarations of the defendant's legal duty ('the defendant has a duty to do X'). The vast majority of rulings are imperative, not declaratory: they command defendants to do or not do something. So too, if rulings were vehicles for imposing sanctions they would be in the form of instructions to officials. Some rulings are in this form, but, as just noted, most private law rulings simply instruct defendants to do or not to do something: in private law, legal officials impose sanctions only when rulings are unfulfilled.

The second puzzle, then, poses the question: why do courts issue rulings, and in particular why do courts issue rulings that require defendants to do or not do something. The answer was not obvious. Why bother telling defendants to do things ('pay the claimant £100') when the law has, or could have, substantive rules that appear to say the same thing ('everyone has a duty to pay their contractual debts') and sanctions that it can apply when the rules are not followed (e.g. seizing the defendant's property to pay the debt). Reflection on this puzzle led me to believe that we lack a satisfactory account of the nature and role of legal rulings; indeed, we seem unaware of the need for such an account. Further, as I thought about the ways that rulings differ from rules and sanctions, I concluded that understanding these differences is critical to understanding why courts make the particular rulings that they make. In short, the two projects—understanding private law remedies and understanding rulings—came together.

This book is the outcome of that merger. Its legal subject matter is the law governing judicial rulings, in particular, the law governing rulings that, as part of the resolution of private litigation, require defendants to do or not do something. To avoid making a long book even longer, I focus on awards arising out of disputes dealing with contracts, torts, and unjust enrichments. Thus, I examine injunctions, specific performance orders, damages orders, (some) restitutionary orders, orders for a sum due (debt), and orders for the recovery of land and other property. I do not discuss awards that, historically, were issued by the Chancery in its exclusive jurisdiction, such as awards for breach of trust or breach of fiduciary duties.

Although this book discusses a broad range of remedial rules, sometimes in detail, it is not a treatise on private law rulings. Rather, it is fundamentally an extended argument for taking its subject matter seriously. The argument has two prongs. The first is a response to the jurisprudential puzzle. The position I defend here is that rulings, or at least the 'directive' rulings that are my focus, are distinct from both rules and sanctions. Their distinctiveness lies not only in their form, but, critically, in the kind of authority they invoke to motivate their addressees. In contrast to rules and sanctions, directive rulings invoke the state's authority to command obedience. I further argue that this difference explains not only why courts issue orders, but also why, in certain cases, the law uses orders rather than rules to impose duties.

The second prong is a response to the pedagogical puzzle. Developing this response occupies most of the book, and illustrates what I have come to see as the considerable breadth of remedial law. Alongside the rules governing specific relief, I argue that the rules governing awards for a sum due and orders for the recovery of land or other property belong in remedial law. I offer a similar argument in respect of most of the law dealing with limitation periods, illegality, abuse of process, immunity, and a variety of other private law defences (and I provide a framework to explain how these and other remedial rules are related). Finally, but most importantly, I argue that most of the rules governing not only the availability but also the quantum of damages and restitution (narrowly defined) are part of remedial law. In other words, I defend a view that I had once thought heretical—namely, that there is no duty to pay damages or make restitution prior to being ordered by a court to do so.

As I hope is clear by now, I reject the idea that rights and remedies are just different sides of the same coin. To be sure, remedies frequently replicate existing duties. Specific performance orders, orders for a sum due, and most injunctions and orders for the recovery of land or other property are 'replicative' orders: they direct defendants to do things that they already had substantive legal duties to do. But other remedies create new duties. In some cases, these 'creative' remedies merely direct defendants to perform close monetary substitutes of replicative remedies ('substitutionary' remedies). However, in other cases, they create entirely new duties: most damages awards and the core instances of restitutionary awards are creative in this broader sense. Finally, in some cases courts refuse to issue a remedy at all, even where the defendant refuses to comply with a substantive duty owed to the claimant.

A large part of this book is devoted to demonstrating the importance of differentiating the grounds on which courts award different remedies. Replicative remedies are awarded because the relevant right is under threat from the defendant. In contrast, creative remedies typically are responses either to the infringement of a substantive right (as in the case of most non-compensatory damages awards) or to an injustice (as in the case of compensatory damages and a core group of restitutionary awards). In short, I argue that the common law recognizes three main private law 'causes of action': proof of a rights-threat, proof of a wrong, and proof of an injustice. Remedies are thus remedies either for rights-threats, for wrongs, or for injustices.

The idea that rulings are distinct from rules and sanctions, together with the idea that remedies are distinct from substantive rights, support this book's general theme that remedial law is distinctive and important. Further support for this theme takes the form of my inclusion of a topic that is not mentioned in most textbooks on remedies: the general part of remedial law. If there is such a thing as 'the law of remedies', some of this law must presumably be about remedies in general. Why discuss specific performance, damages, and so on in the same book unless they have something legally in common? Yet traditional remedies textbooks, which are organized exclusively around specific categories of remedies (e.g. 'rules about specific performance', 'rules about damages', and so forth), suggest that the various remedies have nothing in common. I try to rectify this omission. Two of this book's chapters are devoted to general remedial law rules and principles (Chapter 3 on 'Creation, Form, and Legal Effects' and Chapter 9 on 'Defences').

This book's title is slightly misleading. Although it focuses on remedial law's structure, this book is also concerned with the structure of the broader private law, or at least with the place of remedial law in that structure. Many of this book's arguments are about the place of rulings—and the law governing rulings—in private law's structure. I defend this approach in Chapter 1. Here, I merely note that, like most classificatory arguments in law, this book's classificatory arguments are closely connected to normative arguments. My argument for classifying the rules governing damages awards and restitutionary awards as remedial rests to a significant degree on arguments about why wrongdoers should pay damages and why individuals who have been unjustly enriched should make restitution. Similarly, my explanation of the reasons that the law gives us to comply with rulings rests on arguments about the nature of authority and legal obligation. These arguments raise fundamental questions about the nature of private law and, at times, about the nature of law generally. I hope that readers find my answers to these questions persuasive. However, even if they do not, I hope that they come to share my view that the questions are important. Fundamentally, this book is a plea for a subject: it is a plea to ask serious questions about what courts are doing when they issue rulings.

Acknowledgements

The intellectual debts that I incurred while writing this book are reflected in its themes and approaches. To the jurisprudential community in England, and particularly the community in Oxford—where I did graduate work and began my teaching career—I owe a debt for encouraging me to think seriously about the concept of a ruling, in particular the concept of an order. Although English theorists have written little about rulings directly, their work on the nature of rules and sanctions provided both inspiration for my study of rulings and the broader intellectual backdrop against which I pursued that study.

To the community of private law scholars in England, Canada, and the broader Commonwealth, I owe two debts. The first is for inspiring me to take private law seriously on its own terms. Throughout this book, I argue that we need to take seriously the language in which the law presents itself. In particular, we need to pay attention to the differences between orders and rules, duties and liabilities, and commands and declarations. Although I suggest that scholars have paid insufficient attention to some of these differences, the tradition of taking seriously the way in which the law presents itself is well established in the Commonwealth's private law literature. The second debt is for inspiring me to explore the philosophical commitments underlying the law's surface expression. An explanation of the law must account for the distinctive ways in which the law explains itself. For example, the law presents legal duties as genuine duties. Thus, to determine whether particular rules—for example, the rules governing the quantification of damages awards—are meant to impose duties on citizens, it is important to ask whether these rules could plausibly be thought to articulate genuine obligations. In exploring such questions, I have drawn inspiration and enlightenment from writers throughout the Commonwealth, and in particular from members of the remarkable community of Canadian private law theorists.

Finally, I owe an enormous debt to the Faculty of Law at McGill University. This book focuses on the common law, but it has been deeply influenced by the fact that I belong to a law faculty that teaches, in an integrated fashion, both the common law and the civil law. The idea that private law rulings may go beyond confirming substantive rights, for example by transforming such rights or even by creating entirely new rights, stands in opposition to a long tradition in civilian thinking. However, I hope that civilian scholars will recognize my concern for distinguishing between different kinds of rights. Further, I have attempted to develop, in civilian fashion, a 'general law' of rulings from what has traditionally been presented as heterogeneous groups of unrelated rules. My reflection on the clear and relatively simple civilian approach to the questions addressed in this book has also helped me appreciate the distinctive ways in which the common law deals with such questions. For example, my attempt to understand why this book's subject matter is not a significant legal topic for civilians, if indeed it is a topic at all, has helped me enormously in understanding why remedies play such a large role in how common law lawyers think about the law. Finally, while this book is not a work in legal history, its arguments are strongly influenced by my appreciation of the common law's distinctive roots and evolution, something that again may be traced to McGill. Perhaps the first lesson that I learned from teaching in an integrated programme is that legal systems cannot be understood without understanding the legal traditions in which they are situated.

Beyond the general debts just described, I have incurred a number of specific debts over the long period of writing this book. The Killam Foundation funded a Fellowship that gave me precious time, early in this book's genesis, to develop the ideas that eventually formed its core. The second debt is to my students at McGill, particularly those in my remedies and jurisprudence classes, with whom I first explored many of the book's themes and, more recently, early drafts. The third debt is owed to the research assistants (as they then were) who have worked with me during this book's long gestation, whether on the book itself or on essays that developed its arguments: Alexander Barroca, Karine Bedard, Andrew Brighton, Vanessa di Feo, Lisa Greenspoon, Aly Haji, Elena Kennedy, Jennifer Klinck, Nicola Langille, Jacqueline Madden, Zain Naqi, Tara Mrejen, Brodie Noga, John-Andrew Petrakis, and Leonid Sirota.

My final debt is to the many colleagues in Canada and abroad with whom I have discussed, in most cases over many years, my ideas about remedies. Special thanks (and apologies to anyone I have omitted) go to Allan Beever, Peter Benson, Ziv Bohrer, Alan Brudner, Hanoch Dagan, Helge Dedek, John Goldberg, Christopher Essert, Timothy Endicott, Andrew Gold, Scott Hershowitz, Daniel Jutras, Larissa Katz, Dennis Klimchuk, Rosalie Jukier, Adam Kramer, Robert Leckey, Ben McFarlane, Paul Miller, Jason Neyers, James Penner, Denise Reaume, Charles Rickett, Arthur Ripstein, Ruth Sefton-Green, Henry Smith, Zoe Sinel, Robert Stevens, Shauna Van Praagh, Stephen Watterson, Ernie Weinrib, and Benjamin Zipursky. I particularly want to thank three colleagues, each of whom spent countless hours discussing remedies with me, saved me from many errors, and, perhaps most importantly, inspired and encouraged me to finish the book: Evan Fox-Decent, Nicholas McBride, and Lionel Smith. I also benefitted greatly, in the final push to complete the book, by a workshop devoted to the draft manuscript, held in Toronto in January of 2019, and organized by Chris Essert and Lionel Smith. The workshop reminded me (though the reminder was hardly necessary) of two things: how many of my colleagues are not convinced by all of my arguments and, more importantly, how fortunate I am that the profession of law professor is one in which deep disagreement can sit happily alongside deep friendship.

Contents

1. Introduction 1
2. Historical Foundations 30
3. Form, Creation, Legal Effects 48
4. The Basic Structure 74
5. Philosophical Foundations 105
6. Rights-Threats 132
7. Wrongs 177
8. Injustices 223
9. Defences 273

Bibliography 323
Index 333

Contents

1. Introduction	1
A. Four Questions	1
i. What is a Remedy?	2
ii. Why Does the Law Provide Remedies?	4
iii. On What Grounds are Remedies Issued?	5
iv. What Kinds of Remedies are Available?	6
B. Four Answers	6
i. Remedies are Judicial Rulings	6
ii. Remedies Provide Distinctive Reasons for Action	8
iii. Rights-Threats, Wrongs, and Injustices	9
iv. Replicative and Creative Remedies	9
C. Why the Answers Matter	11
D. Private Law Orders and Other Rulings	14
E. Terminology	17
i. Remedies	17
ii. Orders, Rulings, Judgments	19
iii. The Conventional Labels	22
F. Jurisdiction	24
G. Methodology	25
H. Overview	27
2. Historical Foundations	30
A. Law and Equity	32
B. Remedial and Substantive Law	39
C. Looking Forward	46
3. Form, Creation, Legal Effects	48
A. Form	48
i. No Distinction in the Form of Legal and Equitable Rulings	51
B. Creation	56
C. Legal Effects	57
i. Court-Ordered Rights	58
ii. Substantive Rights and Action Rights	59
iii. Enforcement Rights	66
Direct Enforcement: Execution	67
Indirect Enforcement: Imprisonment, Fines, and Sequestration	70
Explaining Enforcement: Functional, not Historical	71
D. Conclusion	72

4. The Basic Structure 74
A. Classification in Terms of Rights 75
B. How are Remedies Related to Other Parts of the Law? 76
i. Substantive Rights 77
ii. Action Rights 80
iii. Court-Ordered Rights 82
iv. Enforcement Rights 84
v. Summary Chart 86
C. On What Grounds are Remedies Available? 87
i. Rights-Threats 89
ii. Wrongs 90
iii. Injustices 93
iv. Summary Chart 96
D. What Kinds of Remedies are Available? 96
i. Replicative Orders 97
ii. Creative Orders 98
Substitutionary orders 98
Wrong-responding orders 100
Free-standing orders 101
iii. No Order 102
iv. Summary Chart 103
E. Overall Summary Chart 104

5. Philosophical Foundations 105
A. Sanction-Based Explanations 106
B. Rule-Based Explanations 110
C. Orders as Commands 113
D. When: Grounds for Orders 126
E. What: Varieties of Orders 127
F. Who: Standing to Obtain Orders 129

6. Rights-Threats 132
A. The Concept of a Rights-Threat 133
B. Orders for a Sum Due 137
i. The *White & Carter* Exception 139
ii. Special Features of Orders for a Sum Due 140
iii. Are Orders for a Sum Due Replicative? 141
C. Orders for the Recovery of Land ('Ejectment') 142
D. Orders for the Recovery of Chattels ('Delivery Up') 144
E. Injunctions 146
i. *Quia Timet* Injunctions 147
ii. Injunctions to Take Care? 149
iii. Are Injunctions Always Replicative? 152
iv. Injunctions and Partial Defences 154
v. Substantive-Law Reasons for Refusing Injunctions 156

F. Specific Performance 162
i. Cause of Action and Content 162
ii. Restrictions on the Availability of Specific Performance 164
iii. Substantive-Law Reasons for Refusing Specific Performance 168
iv. The Vendor-Purchaser Constructive Trust 171
G. Substitutionary Damages 172
i. Are Substitutionary Damages Always Set at the Cost of Performance? 175
ii. Substitutionary Damages and Termination of Contract 176

7. Wrongs 177
A. Damages Law: Substantive or Remedial? 179
i. The Continuity Thesis 181
ii. Conceptual Objections 184
iii. Doctrinal Objections 188
B. The Positive Law: No Substantive Duty to Pay Damages 191
i. Language: Liabilities, Not Duties 192
ii. Doctrine 194
No Damages for Failing to Pay Damages 194
No Defence of Tender or Payment 196
Historical Note 196
An Unknowable Duty 197
iii. Theory: An Inchoate Duty? 199
C. The Duty-Creating View of Damages 202
D. Wrongs-Based Damages: Introduction 202
E. Wrongs-Based Damages: A Provisional Catalogue 206
i. Nominal Damages 208
ii. Exemplary Damages 209
iii. Vindicatory Damages: An Introduction 210
iv. User Damages 212
v. Waiver Damages 212
vi. Market-Price Damages 213
vii. Gain-Based Damages 214
viii. Non-Pecuniary Damages for Wrongs to the Person 216
ix. Miscellaneous 217
x. Pain and Suffering 218
F. The Variety of Wrongs-Based Damages 221
G. Compensatory Damages? 222

8. Injustices 223
A. Tertium Quid 223
i. Restitutionary Awards 224
ii. Compensation for Non-Wrongs 225
iii. Compensation for Wrongs 227
iv. The Concept of an Injustice 228
v. Why Orders? 232

B. Restitutionary Awards 237
i. Duty-Confirming or Duty-Creating? 238
ii. Language 239
iii. Doctrine 240
No Damages for Failure to Make Restitution 240
Interest Awards 241
Change of Position 241
Section 5(4) of the *Theft Act* 1968 242
iv. The Unknowability Objection 243
v. Restitution as a Response to an Injustice 245
C. Compensatory Damages 249
i. Rights-Based Theories 251
ii. Wrong-Based Theories 251
iii. The Assessment of Compensatory Damages 253
iv. The Availability of Compensatory Damages 256
Vicarious Liability 259
Rylands v Fletcher 259
Necessity 261
Non-Substitutionary Damages in Lieu of Specific Relief 261
Damages in Lieu of *Quia Timet* Injunctions 263
Innocent Misrepresentations 264
Wrongs to Third Parties 264
Summary 265
v. The Injustice-Based Theory 265
D. Other Injustice-Responding Remedies 269
i. Compensation for Detrimental Reliance (Equitable and Proprietary Estoppel) 270
ii. Property Transfer Injunctions 271

9. Defences 273
A. Remedial and Substantive Defences 274
B. Full Defences 277
i. Absence of Formalities 277
ii. Immunity 278
iii. Statutory Non-Actionability 280
iv. *Res Judicata* 282
v. Abuse of Process and *De Minimis* 282
vi. Limitation Periods 284
vii. Illegality 286
viii. Settlements and Exoneration Clauses 292
C. Partial Defences 294
i. Equitable Defences? 296
ii. Internal Partial Defences 299
Adequacy of Damages 299
Supervision 308
Personal Duties 309

iii. External Partial Defences 311
Delay (Laches) 312
Impossibility 314
Clean Hands 314
Hardship 316
Public Interest 318
iv. Discretion 319

Bibliography 323
Index 333

1
Introduction

The law imposes itself upon its subjects in three principal ways. First, lawmakers announce substantive rules: rules that stipulate general legal duties ('Everyone has a duty to perform their contractual promises') or that tell individuals what they must do to create or modify such duties ('A contract is created by an offer, acceptance, and consideration'). Second, courts issue rulings: they order individuals to do or not do specific things ('It is ordered that the defendant pay the claimant £100') or grant them specific powers or immunities ('Title to Blackacre is hereby vested in the claimant'). Third, legal officials impose sanctions: examples include imprisonment and the seizure of property.

Legal scholars have analysed the first and third of these ways—announcing rules and imposing sanctions—extensively. However, the second way—issuing rulings—has received little attention. This book seeks to remedy this neglect. Focusing on rulings that direct defendants in private litigation to do or not do something ('directive rulings' or 'orders')—for example, an order to pay a debt or damages, cease a trespass, or perform a contract[1]—I argue that orders are distinctive legal events, governed by distinctive legal principles. I further argue that appreciating this distinctiveness is critical not just for understanding why courts make orders, but also for understanding the broader private law. In short, this book is a sustained plea for taking the concept of a private law order—a 'remedy'—more seriously.

A. Four Questions

The suggestion that legal scholars have ignored remedies might be surprising. In the common law jurisdictions that are this book's focus, legal education and scholarship often seem preoccupied with rulings. Contract law courses frequently begin by examining the remedies available to disappointed contracting parties. There are entire common law treatises devoted to particular remedies, such as injunctions or damages, and even to subcategories of remedies, for example damages for personal

[1] In England today, each of these rulings is styled explicitly as an order ('It is ordered that the defendant pay the claimant £ . . . '). But formerly, and still today in many common law jurisdictions, some of the orders discussed in this book were styled as 'Judgments' of legally required states of affairs (e.g. 'It is adjudged that the claimant recover from the defendant £ . . . '). I discuss this terminology below and in Chapters 2 and 3. Briefly, I argue that my explanations of orders also apply, with small qualifications, to Judgments. To avoid constant qualifications, I describe rulings as orders if courts express them as such in England today.

Rights, Wrongs, and Injustices. Stephen A. Smith, Oxford University Press (2019). © Stephen A. Smith.
DOI: 10.1093/oso/9780199229772.003.0001

injury. More generally, there is a long tradition in the common law of thinking about private law in terms of judicial remedies. As I explain in Chapter 2, for most of the common law's history, private law was largely remedial law, broadly understood: private law consisted primarily of rules about judicial rulings. Learning the law meant learning how to get into court, how to plead in court, and what rulings a court might provide. The gradual recognition of rules governing how citizens should treat one another in ordinary life ('substantive law') occurred primarily through a process by which judges, lawyers, and scholars reasoned backwards from the rules governing rulings.[2] Common law lawyers described chattel property as 'personal' property because, unlike in the case of land ('real' property), courts rarely ordered defendants who had taken the claimant's property to return it.[3] The same process continues today: when common law lawyers seek proof that the law recognizes a particular substantive duty, they typically point to rulings that allegedly give effect to the duty. One reason lawyers widely assume that there is a legal duty to return mistaken payments is that courts are willing to order mistaken payees to reimburse these payments. Perhaps the most famous example of this way of thinking is Oliver Wendell Holmes' suggestion that we should define the law generally in remedial terms: 'Prophecies of what the courts will do in fact, and nothing more pretentious, are what I mean by the law.'[4]

Notwithstanding this preoccupation, common law scholarship has neglected the concept of a remedy itself. Specifically, four questions have received little attention.

i. What is a Remedy?

First, what is a remedy (and, relatedly, what is the subject matter of remedial law)? Some remedies textbooks do not address this question at all.[5] Others appear to adopt the everyday understanding of remedy according to which it is a cure for a problem of some kind or another.[6] This definition is impossibly broad (and textbooks never apply it seriously). Almost every legal phenomenon can be described as a cure for a problem of one kind or another. Law in general is a cure for the problems that arise in a world without law. With one notable exception, no textbook

[2] '[T]he common law (though there is no harder lesson for the stranger jurist to learn) began with the remedy and ended with the right': *Nocton v Lord Ashburton* [1914] AC 932, 964 (Lord Dunedin).

[3] Baker (2002) 380; Maitland (1909) 60–6. As remains the practice today (see Chapter 6), courts normally gave the defendant the option of paying the claimant a sum of money.

[4] Holmes (1897) 457. A judicial example of the confusion that may arise from conflating substantive and remedial law is Saville LJ's statement in *Law Debenture Trust Corporation v Ural Caspian Oil Corporation Ltd* [1995] Ch 152, 173 that 'An injunction is a discretionary remedy . . . [therefore] the right asserted by the plaintiff only arises when the court makes the order in question.'

[5] Spry (2014); Berryman et al. (2016).

[6] Andoh & Marsh (1997).

discusses the definitional question in depth.[7] It is true that in practice most remedies textbooks cover broadly similar terrain. Most of them focus on the same rules that this book examines. It is also true that definitions of legal fields are always imperfect. The concept of a 'contract' is familiar to every lawyer, but its boundaries remain a matter of controversy. Still, without serious reflection on remedial law's subject matter, it is impossible to know which rules should be discussed in remedies textbooks and, as importantly, what considerations we should be thinking about when we try to explain these rules.

One example suffices. Nearly every book on remedies discusses the rules governing the assessment of damages. Yet it is not obvious that these rules are a part of remedial law. Writers define 'remedy' in different ways,[8] but the most common usage (and the usage adopted in this book) equates remedies with judicial orders or at least with judicial rulings.[9] The law of remedies, in this definition, is comprised of rules about rulings. On one interpretation, the rules governing the assessment of damages satisfy this definition. According to this interpretation, there is no duty to pay damages prior to a judicial order to pay damages: there is merely a liability to being ordered to do so by a court. It follows, in this view, that the rules governing the assessment of damages are directed fundamentally at courts. Their basic role is to tell courts how they should assess damages. As such, they are rules about rulings.

For reasons that I explain in Chapter 7, I share this view. However, many commentators and at least some judges do not. In the best-known judicial pronouncement on this issue, Lord Diplock held that a breach of contract gives rise to a substantive duty to pay damages:

> Every failure to perform a primary obligation is a breach of contract. The secondary obligation on the part of the contract breaker to which it gives rise by implication of the common law is to pay monetary compensation to the other party for the loss sustained by him in consequence of the breach.[10]

Most authors who have addressed this issue hold a similar view about damages generally.[11] Yet if wrongdoers have substantive duties to pay damages, then the rules governing the assessment of damages are part of substantive law: they are rules that inform individuals what they should do if they have committed a legal wrong. In this understanding, an order to pay damages is like an order to pay a contractual debt; the order merely rubber-stamps the defendant's substantive duty to pay a sum of money. From this perspective, the rules on damages are no more a

[7] Zakrzewski (2005).
[8] Birks identified five meanings: Birks (2000a).
[9] See e.g. Zakrzewski (2005); Burrows (2004); Dobbs (2018); Rendleman (2006). Exceptions include Andow & Marsh (1997); Berryman et al. (2016).
[10] *Photo Production Ltd v Securicor Transport Ltd* [1980] AC 827, 847.
[11] See Ripstein (2007); Weinrib (2008); Raz (2004); Gardner (2011).

part of remedial law than are the rules that determine the existence and content of duties to pay contractual debts.

Against this background, we might expect that one of the central questions addressed in remedies textbooks would be whether the rules on damages are part of remedial law. Yet with rare exceptions, this question is not even raised.[12] The textbooks appear simply to assume that the law of damages is part of the law of remedies. They often make the same assumption in respect of the law governing restitutionary awards. Although many remedies textbooks discuss restitutionary awards in detail, the predominant view of restitution scholars (though, again, not my view: see Chapter 8) is that restitutionary awards rubber-stamp substantive duties to make restitution.[13] If this view is correct, then the rules governing the availability and quantification of restitution are not rules about rulings, and do not belong in remedies textbooks. Again, remedies textbooks almost never discuss this issue.

ii. Why Does the Law Provide Remedies?

The second neglected question is why courts issue directive remedies ('orders') at all. Legal scholars have discussed at length the roles of rules and sanctions; indeed, most of the theoretical literature on the nature of law focuses on rules, sanctions, or both.[14] In contrast, scholars have written very little about why courts issue orders. To be sure, scholars have discussed in detail why defendants should do the things that particular orders require them to do. For example, there is an extensive literature on the merits of requiring contract breakers to pay damages instead of performing their contractual promises. Yet scholars have said almost nothing about the merits of pursuing either of these requirements through judicial orders.[15] Nor is the answer self-evident. Why is the law not content merely with rules that stipulate how citizens should act (which might distinguish, for instance, between binding contractual promises and those for which promisees may substitute a money payment), together with rules providing that sanctions may be imposed on citizens who fail to follow the first set of rules? What do orders add to this picture? Legal systems need mechanisms to resolve disputes about what the substantive law requires in particular cases. However, except in the rare case of declaratory rulings, resolving such disputes is not the primary role of rulings, and it is certainly not the primary role of orders. An order simply commands a particular action.

12 A notable exception is Zakrzewski (2005).
13 See e.g. Birks (2005) 31.
14 See e.g. Austin (1832) (sanctions); Hart (1961) (rules).
15 Hart appeared to assume that rulings were ancillary to rules: Hart (1961) 21.

iii. On What Grounds are Remedies Issued?

Third, on what grounds do courts issue orders? Lawyers are of course familiar with the kinds of evidence that claimants must introduce to obtain particular orders. In common law jurisdictions, law professors often present private law primarily as a set of rules about such evidence. A typical question on a torts or contracts exam asks students to identify the legal actions arising from a hypothetical fact pattern. Students are expected to identify the remedies available to the parties and, crucially, to identify the facts that support those remedies. Yet scholars have made little effort to determine whether the common law's 'causes of action' (the facts that must be proven to obtain a particular remedy) have anything in common and, more broadly, if they reflect any general principles. Scholars sometimes suggest, or at least assume, that orders are always given in response to wrongs. However, this view cannot explain a variety of common orders, most obviously those that courts issue to prevent future rights infringements ('*quia timet*' orders), such as a future trespass or nuisance (see Chapter 6). A second suggestion is that courts issue remedies merely on proof that the defendant owes the claimant a substantive duty. But aside from its practical implausibility (why should courts get involved if the defendant may perform the duty anyway?), this suggestion fails to explain a variety of situations where courts refuse to issue remedies notwithstanding that the defendant clearly owes the claimant a substantive duty. An obvious example is a negative contractual duty, for example a duty not to compete with the claimant. No court will issue a remedy simply on proof that such a duty exists.

Relatedly, the literature on remedies has largely ignored the question of why courts sometimes refuse remedies notwithstanding that the relevant cause of action is satisfied. Defences such as illegality, immunity, the expiry of a limitation period, and the absence of a formality are well known, but the extent to which these defences are largely, if not wholly, part of remedial law has received little attention. Most textbooks on remedies do not discuss defences, let alone consider what makes a remedial defence remedial.

More generally, the common law lacks a theory of the relationship between orders and substantive duties. Most lawyers are familiar with the maxim 'for every right there must be a remedy' (*ubi jus ibi remedium*). But what does it mean? Assuming for argument's sake that 'right' refers to substantive rights and 'remedy' refers to judicial orders, does the maxim mean that all rights are protected by orders and that those orders always command compliance with the right? Or does the maxim merely suggest that for every right an order of some kind is available (with no guarantee that the order replicate the right)? And does it follow from the maxim that private law orders always confirm substantive duties or are at least a response to the existence of such duties? In other words, are 'free-standing' orders (orders unconnected to substantive duties) possible? Finally, is the maxim a description or a prescription? And if it is the former, is it meant to state a conceptual truth, or just an empirical fact? These questions have received little, if any, attention in the literature on remedies.

iv. What Kinds of Remedies are Available?

The fourth and final neglected question focuses on the kinds of orders that courts issue. There is a relatively well-established scheme for classifying private law orders. Nearly every remedies textbook distinguishes between injunctions, specific performance, damages, orders for a sum due, and so on. Sometimes the authors also draw a broader division between historically 'Equitable' remedies and historically 'Legal' remedies. However, both schemes are silent on the most important question about the content of a judicial order: what is its relationship to the claimant's substantive rights? Without an answer to this question, it is impossible to know whether the rules governing the order's content and availability are even a part of remedial law. Yet the literature on remedies almost never asks this question.[16] As I noted earlier, the typical discussion of damages awards and restitutionary awards does not even consider whether these awards confirm existing substantive duties or create new duties.

B. Four Answers

i. Remedies are Judicial Rulings

In brief, my answer to the first question ('what is a remedy') is that a remedy is a judicial ruling, and a private law remedy is a legal ruling that resolves a private law dispute. The most common private law remedies—and this book's focus—are remedies that direct defendants to do or not do something ('directive' remedies or just 'orders'). Examples include orders to cease a nuisance and orders to pay damages. Remedial law is the law governing such orders, specifically the law governing their creation, availability, content, and legal effects. This definition roughly fits conventional usage.[17] Textbooks on remedies invariably discuss the rules governing the availability of specific relief, and these rules are incontrovertibly rules about rulings. However, the main reason for adopting this definition is that it identifies a distinctive and important legal phenomenon. At the beginning of this chapter, I said that there are three main ways that the law imposes itself on its subjects, namely, by enacting rules, issuing rulings, and imposing sanctions. Each is distinct. Failing to comply with a private law ruling may lead to a sanction, but a private law ruling

[16] Exceptions include Birks (2000a); Zakrzewski (2005).
[17] See e.g. Burrows (2004); Dobbs & Roberts (2018); Rendleman & Roberts (2011).

itself is just words. A sanction is a physical interference with an individual's person, property, or liberty. Nor is a private law ruling a rule. Rules, or at least the substantive legal rules that are my present focus, are essentially statements about, and constitutive of, legal duties ('everyone has a duty to fulfil their contractual promises'), or statements about how individuals may create or alter legal relationships ('a contract is created by an offer, acceptance, and consideration'). In contrast, directive rulings are fundamentally commands. They command specific individuals to do specific things ('it is ordered that the defendant pay the claimant £100').

Of course, the practice of issuing rulings is governed by rules. But these rules are also distinctive. Rules about rulings ('remedial law') govern relations between courts and citizens. They provide citizens with powers to obtain rulings and they tell courts what they should do when citizens come to them seeking rulings. For example, the common law contains a remedial rule stating, roughly, that 'if a claimant establishes that the defendant has failed to pay a contractual debt, then (assuming no defence is available) the court must order the defendant to pay the debt'. In contrast, substantive-law rules govern individuals' interactions with each other. As the previous paragraph's examples illustrate, substantive rules tell individuals how they should treat one another in day-to-day life or how they can create or alter legal relationships with others. Like all legal rules, substantive rules may be applied by courts. But, unlike remedial rules, the guidance they provide is intended primarily for individuals.

Understood in this way, remedies are distinctive legal phenomena governed by distinctive rules. Indeed, this understanding suggests that remedial law is, in a sense, a part of public law: remedial law is comprised of rules governing relations between individuals and state officials. Another way of making this point is that the question of what courts should do when citizens seek their assistance (the subject of remedial law) is different from the question of how citizens should treat one another (the subject of substantive law). This difference explains why courts deciding remedial issues often take into account—to mention just one distinctive consideration—the cost, to the state, of issuing rulings. As we will see in Chapter 6, the difference explains, therefore, why courts consider whether their rulings are likely to lead to further litigation and whether, if defendants disobey their rulings, the rulings will be costly to enforce.

Defining remedial law as rules about rulings has far-reaching implications for the subject's scope. On the one hand, the definition excludes rules that are discussed in many remedies textbooks, such as those governing so-called 'self-help remedies' (e.g. recaption of property). Like other parts of substantive law, the rules governing self-help tell individuals what they may or must do in their everyday interactions with others, regardless of whether a court gets involved. On the other hand, the definition encompasses rules that most remedies textbooks ignore. It covers, for example, significant parts of the law governing defences (such as those governing limitation periods, formalities, immunity, statutory non-actionability, abuse of process, *res judicata*, and illegality). In most cases, the only effect of these defences is to prevent individuals from bringing actions (leaving their substantive rights intact). Finally, and as I mentioned earlier, this definition raises the possibility that almost none of the law of damages or restitution is remedial law (though this is not my view).

ii. Remedies Provide Distinctive Reasons for Action

The answer to the second question ('why does the law provide remedies') is that remedies, or at least the directive remedies that are this book's focus, provide distinctive reasons for action—reasons different from those provided by rules or by sanctions. In Chapter 5, I argue that duty-imposing rules are fundamentally statements about, and constitutive of, the existence of general duties ('everyone has a duty to fulfil their contractual promises'). It is impossible to obey or disobey such rules. These rules purport to state a fact (though, in some cases, a fact that they have brought into existence); in my example, that there is a duty to fulfil contractual promises. For the addressees of such a rule, the only question it raises is whether they should *accept* that what it says is true. Duty-imposing rules therefore rely for their force on what I call 'declarative authority'—the authority to declare that something is the case (here, that a duty exists).

In contrast, orders say nothing about the existence of legal duties. Orders are simply commands ('It is ordered that the defendant pay £100 to the claimant'). It is true that the law presumes that orders create duties to perform the acts they require. However, these duties arise indirectly by virtue of a presumed general duty to obey court orders. From a court's perspective, the reason that a defendant should comply with an order to pay £100 to the claimant is that the defendant has a duty to do whatever the court commands. The question facing the addressee of an order is therefore not whether to accept the order but whether to obey it. When courts issue orders, they rely on what I call 'directive authority'—the authority to command obedience.

As I explain in Chapter 5, declaratory and directive authority provide different reasons to perform the actions that they contemplate. A defendant who rejects the law's claim to declaratory authority may accept its claim to directive authority, and vice versa. And even for defendants who accept both claims, a judicial order may provide a new reason to do the thing required by a rule-based substantive duty. When defendants refuse to comply with orders they do not merely reject the law's view of their duties (as is the case when they reject rule-based duties), they disobey a court. Further, I argue that courts may use judicial orders to motivate defendants to perform actions that are not appropriately the subject matter of substantive rules. If duty-imposing substantive rules are propositions about the existence of duties, then it is appropriate to employ them only where it is reasonable to assume that individuals have duties to perform the specified action. Some of the actions that courts order defendants to perform fall outside this category. The clearest examples are actions that courts command for the purpose of punishing defendants, but there are other, more common examples (which I discuss in Chapters 7 and 8).

iii. Rights-Threats, Wrongs, and Injustices

Broadly, the answer to the third question ('on what grounds are remedies available') is that courts issue remedies when the claimant has established facts demonstrating that the reasons that the substantive law provides, or could provide, to perform the requested action are inadequate or inappropriate. In practice, this principle means that the common law recognizes three main private law causes of action: (1) proof that the defendant is unwilling to comply with the claimant's substantive rights (a 'rights-threat'); (2) proof that the defendant wronged the claimant (a 'wrong'); and (3) proof of an unfair loss or gain (an 'injustice'). In short, I argue that the common law's main causes of action—what claimants must prove to obtain a remedy—are rights-threats, wrongs, and injustices.

I defend these categories and explain which remedies each is associated with in Chapters 6 to 8. Briefly, I argue, first, that injunctions, specific performance orders, orders for a sum due, orders for the recovery of land or other property, and a small group of 'substitutionary' damages awards are responses to rights-threats. Second, the category of 'wrong-responding' orders includes exemplary damages, nominal damages, damages for pain and suffering, and a group of damages awards that I describe compendiously as 'vindicatory' (and individually as user damages, waiver damages, market-price damages, gain-based damages, and non-pecuniary damages). Third, and finally, the category of 'injustice-responding' orders includes orders to return benefits obtained from a defective transfer ('restitutionary orders') and damages for consequential pecuniary losses ('compensatory damages'). This scheme is novel in several respects, most notably in placing compensatory damages and restitutionary orders in the same category.

iv. Replicative and Creative Remedies

Finally, the answer to the fourth question ('what kinds of remedies are available') is complex. Many private law orders replicate substantive duties ('replicative orders'); examples include specific performance orders, most injunctions, orders for a sum due, and orders for the recovery of land or other property. However, other orders create new duties ('creative orders'), and they do this in different ways. In some cases, creative orders transform non-monetary substantive duties into closely related monetary duties ('substitutionary orders'). An example is an order to pay damages that is awarded in lieu of specific performance and where the reason specific performance is refused is that the relevant duty is to deliver fungible goods. In other cases, creative orders impose new duties on defendants because they have breached substantive duties ('wrong-responding orders'). This category includes exemplary damages, nominal damages, damages for pain and suffering, and the various vindicatory awards I mentioned in the previous section. And in yet other cases, creative orders impose duties on defendants who may neither owe the claimant a substantive duty, nor have breached such a duty in the past. Examples of the latter include some restitutionary orders and (with certain qualifications) compensatory damages awards. Finally, in some cases courts refuse to issue orders at all notwithstanding that the defendant breached, and perhaps continues to be in breach of, a substantive duty owed to the claimant.

The general lesson to draw from the answer to the fourth question is that the availability of remedies is only partly determined by the duties that the substantive law recognizes. To understand why courts make the orders they make we need a general theory, or at least a general explanation, of the relationship between orders and substantive rights. This book attempts to provide such an explanation.

In addition to addressing the above questions, this book seeks to fill another lacuna in the literature on remedies. The typical remedies textbook is a paradox. The existence of such textbooks suggests that their authors believe that the rules discussed within them have something in common. If there is such a thing as the 'law of remedies', some of this law must be about remedies in general. Yet the way that remedies textbooks are traditionally organized suggests otherwise. As I mentioned earlier, remedies textbooks typically present the law entirely or almost entirely in remedy-specific categories. There are chapters on specific performance, injunctions, damages, and so on—but, typically, no chapters dealing with rules or principles that apply to remedies generally. In contrast, this book argues that much of the law of remedies can be explained using general principles. For example, I argue that notwithstanding their historical origins in separate courts (the Chancery Court and the Royal Courts), the rules governing the creation, form, and enforcement of rulings reflect common concerns and apply common principles to address those concerns. Similarly, I argue that nearly all the reasons for denying a *prima facie* case for specific relief (e.g. adequacy of damages, supervision, clean hands, laches, and so on) are particular manifestations of principles that apply to rulings generally. The same rules and principles could have arisen in a unitary court system. A third, related, example is the broader law of defences: much of this law, I argue, is both general in application and concerned with exclusively remedial defences, that is, with reasons for refusing remedies.

Taken together, these answers provide the foundation for an understanding of remedies that takes the concept of a remedy seriously, that asks directly about the relationship between remedies and substantive rights, and that explains remedial law in terms of general principles, not historical categories.

C. Why the Answers Matter

Do these answers matter? Echoing Oliver Wendell Holmes, sceptics might argue that most people are not particularly concerned about their substantive rights, much less about the relationship between these rights and court orders. What people care about, it might be thought, is what the law will do for them if they become embroiled in a dispute, in particular, whether the law will invoke its coercive powers on their behalf or against them.[18] And judges might be thought to share this attitude, since what judges must decide is whether the facts satisfy the claimant's cause of action (not whether those facts establish a substantive right). More broadly, even legal theorists might suggest that this book appears uninterested in the most important question about orders: What is the purpose of doing the things that orders require defendants to do? Who cares whether an order to pay the claimant a sum of money replicates the defendant's substantive duty? What matters, surely, is whether making such a payment is a good thing, and why it is a good thing.

The short response to such observations is that this book's primary aim is not to reform the law or even to evaluate it, but simply to understand it. And to understand the law, it is necessary to make sense not just of its outcomes, but also the distinctive methods and reasons it employs in bringing about those outcomes. From this perspective, the distinction between rules, rulings, and sanctions is crucial. Indeed, it is crucial not just for understanding remedial law, but for understanding substantive law. An important consequence of the historical failure to distinguish remedial from substantive law is that it is frequently assumed that our substantive duties mirror those that arise from private law orders (or, what amounts to nearly the same thing, that private law orders always rubber-stamp substantive rights). In other words, it is assumed that we can identify our substantive rights simply by identifying the orders that courts are willing to make. In this view, if a court orders a claimant to return a sum of money paid by mistake, it follows that the claimant had a substantive duty to return the money prior to the order. This book rejects this assumption: as noted above, although I accept that some substantive rights are replicated in private law orders, I argue that others are transformed, and some are given no effect whatsoever. Further, some private law orders create entirely new duties. The complexity of this relationship has profound implications for our understanding not just of judicial orders, but also of the substantive law. For example, if orders to pay damages or to make restitution typically create new duties (as I argue), it follows that there is no substantive duty to pay damages or make restitution until a court makes the relevant order. This conclusion, in turn, has implications for the broader understanding of private law: most obviously, theorists

[18] Holmes (1897) 459–62.

must explain why the law does not impose a substantive duty to pay damages or make restitution. Many theories of substantive duties assume that such duties should (and do) exist.

The longer response must distinguish between the theorist and the Holmesian sceptic. To the theorist, the response is that it is difficult to say much about the law's normative foundations without having a clear picture of its structure. Indeed, having a clearer picture of remedial law's structure will help us to determine what normative arguments are appropriate in this field. Consider, for example, my argument that remedial law focuses upon the relationship between individuals and courts. As I mentioned earlier, this argument suggests that remedial rules are, in a sense, public law rules.[19] Claimants who satisfy the cause of action for an award of damages obtain the right to demand that the court—a state entity—perform a certain action, namely, to issue an order. The public law aspect of remedial law has obvious implications. The question of how citizens should behave towards one another (the primary subject matter of private law) is different from the question of how courts should behave towards citizens.[20] This is true even where the only thing claimants ask the court to do is to direct defendants to perform their pre-existing substantive duties. Indeed, the distinction would be critical even if it were the case that all private law rulings confirmed substantive duties and all substantive duties were enforceable by rulings. If the common law were like this, this book's subject matter would consist of a single rule that directed courts, on proof of an unfulfilled duty, to order defendants to perform that duty. It is not difficult to show that this picture is inaccurate. Yet even if it were accurate, we would still need to explain why courts make such orders, and this explanation would be different from the explanation of substantive private law rules. If the explanations were the same, there would be no point in making orders.

To the Holmesian sceptic, the longer response is that the distinctions drawn in this book are relevant in practice. It may be true that most citizens care about substantive rights only insofar as courts support those rights with orders (and insofar as sanctions back those orders). Still, there are undoubtedly citizens who treat substantive rules as sufficient reasons to perform the actions they stipulate.[21] For these citizens, it matters whether they have a substantive duty to pay money or merely a liability to be ordered to pay money. The distinction between substantive rights

[19] '[I]n a sense' because the rules governing private law orders are closely connected to core aspects of private law. Courts issue private law orders to resolve private law disputes, and the rules governing their availability and content invariably require judges to take account of substantive private law rules. To obtain an order of specific performance a defendant must prove the existence of a valid contract. Further, the primary legal consequence of issuing an order is that a private citizen—the defendant—falls under a duty to do what the order requires.

[20] Dan-Cohen (1984) distinguished, in a similar way, between 'conduct' rules and 'decision' rules in the context of criminal law rules. As I explain in Chapter 4, the rules governing availability of private law orders also grant individuals powers. However, these are powers to place courts under duties to issue orders. The duty-imposing part of remedial law imposes duties on courts.

[21] See generally Tyler (1990); Licht (2008).

and court orders is also practically important in litigation. Courts must sometimes determine whether a particular right correlates to a substantive duty owed by another citizen or whether it merely correlates to a court's duty to issue an order on proof of certain facts. This issue may arise, for example, in disputes concerning prejudgment interest, tender and settlement, the tort of procuring a breach of a legal duty, and the application of foreign law. More generally, the overall development of private law is affected by lawmakers' understanding of substantive duties, which in turn is affected by their understanding of the relationship between court orders and substantive rights. For example, if the reason that common law courts are reluctant to order specific performance of non-monetary contractual obligations is that such obligations are in reality disjunctive obligations to perform the relevant promise or to pay a sum of money, then it is inappropriate to treat deliberate refusals to perform non-monetary obligations as wrongs. It would also be inappropriate to apply different rules regarding remoteness of damages to deliberate contractual breaches or to contemplate ordering defendants in such cases to hand over their profits or pay exemplary damages. Similarly, if it is assumed that an order to pay damages for pain and suffering merely affirms an existing duty to pay such damages, then courts should be more concerned than they appear to be about ensuring that this duty's content is determinable in advance of a court ruling.

A final response to critics, Holmesian or otherwise, is that an exploration of the nature and role of judicial rulings is inseparable from an exploration of the nature and role of a concept that should be of special concern to lawyers: justice. When someone says that something is 'unjust', they often mean nothing more than that it is 'bad' or 'undesirable' and that the state, a court, or another authority should do something about it. In this understanding, a battery or nuisance or the breach of a contractual duty is an injustice. However, as I explain in more detail in Chapter 8, this way of describing batteries, nuisance, contract breaches, and other wrongs is atypical. We do not usually say that intentionally hitting someone is 'unjust'. It is more common—and more helpful—to describe batteries, nuisances, contract breaches, and so on simply as wrongs. We usually use the term injustice more narrowly, to describe actions or states of affairs that are in some sense unfair, typically because a loss or gain (broadly understood) has been unfairly allocated, distributed, or allowed to persist. Thus, we ask whether the tax system is just because we want to know whether it allocates the burden of taxation fairly. Similarly, we ask whether a particular punishment is just because we want to know the burden that it imposes is a fair response to the crime. And we ask whether a judicial decision was just because we want to know if the right party won.

It follows that while your neighbour wrongs you if he or she takes your property without your consent or imprisons you unlawfully, if a court does these things it does not merely wrong you, it acts unjustly. And the way that courts do such things is by issuing rulings. It is always appropriate, then, to ask whether a judicial ruling (or at least a ruling that resolves a private law dispute) is just. By definition, judicial rulings are allocative: one party wins and other law loses. This feature of judicial rulings helps to explain why judges are called 'Justices' and why claimants speak of going to court to 'obtain justice'.[22] In Aristotle's words, 'the judge wants to be, as it were, justice ensouled'. Of course, there are other parts of private law that raise issues of justice (although arguably the most important of these—the law governing unfair losses and gains—is also remedial law). However, the issuance of dispute-resolving rulings always raises issues of justice.

This observation does not mean that court rulings are more important than substantive rules. The point is merely—but importantly—that the law governing judicial rulings is the concern of a particular part of morality, and, moreover, a part of morality that should be of special concern to lawyers. Lawyers have no special insight into why it is wrong to lie, break promises, steal, or assault others. However, lawyers do, or at least should, have some insight into the nature of justice. And it is the remedial part of private law that raises issues of justice most clearly.

D. Private Law Orders and Other Rulings

This book's legal subject matter is rulings that courts issue as part of the resolution, permanent or temporary, of a private law action ('private law rulings'), and in particular the subcategory of such rulings that direct defendants to do or not do something ('private law orders'). More specifically yet, I focus on seven core examples of private law orders: orders to pay damages, orders for a sum due, injunctions, specific performance orders, (some) restitutionary orders, orders to recover possession of land, and orders to recover possession of chattels.[23] However, many of the book's arguments apply to other rulings. It may be useful, then, to say a few words about the rulings that I do not discuss, and why I do not discuss them.

As just noted, private law orders are a subcategory—though by far the largest and most important subcategory—of private law rulings. The other subcategories are declaratory rulings and constitutive rulings. A private law declaratory ruling ('declaration') is a judicial pronouncement, usually made as part of the final disposition of a private law action, which confirms a particular and nominative legal status, relationship, or duty.[24] An example is a judicial ruling stating 'IT IS DECLARED THAT the oil painting by . . . known as ". . . " is the sole property of the Claimant.'[25] Declarations are traditionally employed to confirm already-existing legal states of

[22] Aristotle (2009 reprint) V 4 (1132a 20–1).

[23] For reasons of space, I do not discuss remedies that trace their origins to the Chancery's exclusive jurisdiction, such as remedies for a breach of trust or breach of fiduciary duty (although many of my arguments can be applied to such orders). I also do not discuss dismissals of actions, or at least I do not discuss them separately. The law of dismissals is simply the other side of the law governing other rulings.

[24] Woolf (2011) 1–2.

[25] *Atkins Court Forms* (2014) Vol 23 (2) [461]

affairs; however, it appears that they can be used to declare the existence of a new legal state of affairs.[26] Confusingly, lawyers sometimes describe declarations as orders, but they are not orders in the ordinary sense. Declarations are authoritative statements of legal states of affairs.

Although declarations are both relatively rare and outside this book's strict concerns, I discuss them at various points. In particular, I discuss them when examining, in Chapter 7, the argument that orders to pay damages specify inchoate substantive duties (since this argument suggests that damages awards should be in the form of declarations). However, the primary reason for these discussions is to make clear how private law orders differ from declarations.

Private law constitutive rulings ('constitutive rulings') are judicial pronouncements that, by their issuance, immediately alter, terminate, or create a new legal right, status, or relationship. Examples include judicial pronouncements that vest a property right formerly held by the defendant in the claimant; impose a trust over property previously owned by the defendant; make the claimant a legal guardian of a minor; or dissolve a marriage, partnership, or other legal relationship.[27] Lawyers sometimes describe constitutive rulings as orders or, more narrowly, as 'constitutive orders',[28] but they are not orders in the ordinary sense because, again, they do not require anyone to do anything ('IT IS DECLARED AND ADJUDGED that the partnership mentioned in the claimant's particulars . . . was dissolved as from the date . . . '[29]). Constitutive rulings are self-executing: they bring about a judicially desired result through their issuance.

Constitutive rulings that create, alter, or dissolve a legal status or relationship (e.g. guardianship and divorce decrees) have little to do with private law orders; indeed, it is arguable that the responsibility for issuing such rulings should be shifted to administrative agencies. However, constitutive rulings that create or alter property rights are closely related both to private law orders and to substantive duty-imposing rules. In disputes over property, the judicially desired result can often be achieved by an order or a constitutive ruling. For example, instead of ordering a defendant to deliver or sign over property to the claimant, a court with the appropriate authority might simply decree that the claimant owns the property or that the defendant holds the property on trust for the claimant. Further, I argue in Chapter 5 that constitutive rulings are, in certain respects, the individualized

[26] An example is a declaration of a remedial constructive trust. Such rulings are generally understood to give rise to rights that did not exist prior to the declaration: see *Westdeutsche Landesbank Girozentrale v Islington London Borough Council* [1996] AC 669 (HL) 714–15; Swadling (2011). But note that England appears to no longer recognize remedial constructive trusts: *Re Polly Peck (No 2)* [1998] 3 All ER 812; Burrows (2011) 180–1

[27] Although not strictly self-executing, I include rulings that direct legal officials to execute conveyances or other legal documents in this category.

[28] Lawson (1980) 13.

[29] Form N303 Order for dissolution of partnership: *Civil Procedure Rules* (UK) ('*CPR*') Part 4 PD Table 3.

counterparts to duty-imposing rules. As I noted above, duty-imposing rules do not merely declare, but are also constitutive of, the existence of substantive duties, Thus, while constitutive rulings operate differently from orders, and so lie outside this book's strict bounds, they are again important when considering why courts issue certain kinds of orders.

Private law rulings generally are part of the broader category of remedial rulings ('remedies'). The other subcategory of remedial rulings is 'public law rulings', such as 'quashing orders' (nullifying a public decision), 'prohibitory orders' (forbidding a public action), and 'mandatory orders' (requiring a public action). No less than damages awards and specific performance, quashing orders, prohibitory orders, and mandatory orders satisfy this book's definition of a remedy as a ruling that a court issues as part of the resolution of a legal action. Not surprisingly, then, public law rulings raise many of the same issues that private law rulings raise; in particular, both public and private law rulings raise the general issue of their relationship to the parties' prior legal positions. This book focuses on private law rulings primarily for reasons of space. To say anything significant about particular examples of public law rulings would require a much longer book.

Finally, at the top level in the hierarchy of rulings, remedial rulings are different from criminal law rulings and procedural rulings. Criminal law rulings are sentences handed down in criminal trials (normally imprisonment or a fine), while procedural rulings are rulings that assist in the preparation and organization of a trial (e.g. search orders and disclosure orders) or that assist in the enforcement of previous orders (e.g. garnishee orders and contempt orders).[30] I mention criminal law rulings at various points in this book. For example, I argue, in Chapters 4 and 7, that certain private law orders are structurally similar to orders to pay fines. I also refer to criminal law rulings in Chapter 5's discussion of the difference between rules and orders. Finally, I discuss enforcement orders at numerous places, and a brief overview of the law governing such orders is set out in Chapter 3.[31] A general treatment of judicial rulings would examine both criminal law rulings and procedural rulings in detail. The main reason this book does not discuss them in detail is again pragmatic: to say anything useful about criminal law or procedural rulings would require an extended discussion of substantive criminal law and civil procedure.

Figure 1 summarizes the preceding discussion.

[30] See Zuckerman (2013) chs 10, 11, 14, 15, 23.

[31] In this book, 'enforcement orders' assist in the enforcement of earlier orders, and they do this by directing that a sanction be imposed on the defendant (e.g. seizure of assets, imprisonment). Of course, courts have the authority to issue sanctions-imposing orders even when no order has previously been issued. This is the normal practice in criminal trials. In theory, courts could make similar orders in private law cases. For example, on proof that the defendant committed a tort, a court could immediately order legal officials to seize the defendant's property. Contemporary English courts do not make such orders in private law cases, but as I explain in Chapter 2, it is arguable that courts in earlier times, while they did not strictly impose direct sanctions in private law cases, did at least authorize their imposition when they issued Judgments.

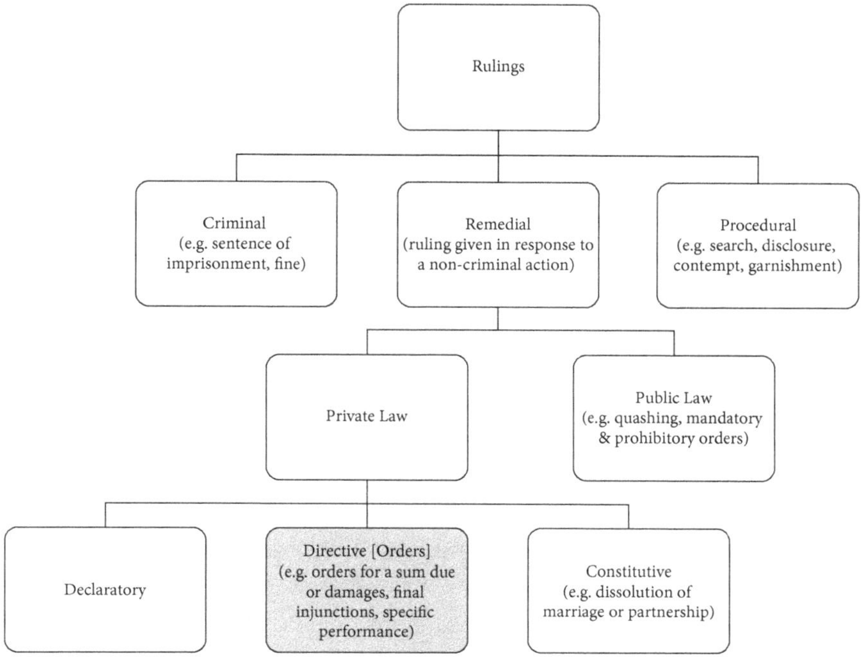

Figure 1 Classification of Rulings

E. Terminology

i. Remedies

This book raises a variety of terminological issues: three merit discussion here. The first concerns this book's title and, more broadly, its description of private law rulings as 'remedies'. Although most of the leading works on private law rulings adopt this label,[32] it is a potential source of confusion. Lawyers use the term remedy in different senses, and two of the most common senses apply only to some private law rulings; moreover, they also apply to things other than rulings.

In the first sense, a remedy is a cure for a past wrong, injury, or harm. It is this 'backward-looking' understanding of remedy that lawyers often intend when they say that an order to pay damages or an order to make restitution is a remedy: they describe the payment of damages or restitution as a remedy because

[32] See e.g. Burrows (2004) 2; Dobbs & Roberts (2018) 1; Laycock (2010) 1; Zakrzewski (2005) 44.

they regard the payment as a remedy for, respectively, a wrong or an unjust enrichment.

The backward-looking understanding of remedies differs significantly from the definition adopted in this book. In the backward-looking definition, it does not matter whether damages or restitutionary payments are paid pursuant to a judicial ruling. Any action that repairs, corrects, undoes, or otherwise cures a wrong or an unjust enrichment is a remedy, regardless of the source of the legal requirement to perform the action. In this view, then, remedial law includes, for example, the substantive rules that govern the validity of stipulated damages clauses or that govern the validity of clauses that require the return of deposits in the event of non-performance. And if there is a legal duty to pay damages following the commission of a legal wrong (as many writers believe), then the substantive rules governing this duty are also remedial. In addition, this definition would exclude from a work on remedies many familiar judicial rulings, such as orders to cease a nuisance or refrain from a trespass. The non-commission of a nuisance is not a cure for the harm caused by a past nuisance; it is merely the fulfilment of the general duty not to commit nuisances. In the backwards-looking sense of remedy, the only remedy for a nuisance or a trespass is the payment of damages or something similar.

A different sense of 'remedy' is intended when lawyers describe a ruling as a remedy because of the reason for issuing it (and not because of the ruling's content). In this usage, the label is meant to indicate that the issuance of the ruling itself is an attempt to cure the defendant's unwillingness to comply with a substantive duty. It is this 'forward-looking' meaning of remedy that lawyers often intend when they say that orders to do things like cease nuisances or refrain from trespasses are remedies. The actions that such orders require cannot cure the defendant's past nuisances or trespasses. However, these actions can cure the defendant's continuing refusal to comply with a substantive duty. Courts can also issue such orders to prevent a threat to commit a wrong from coming to fruition (even if no wrong was committed in the past). In the forward-looking understanding, a *quia timet* (preventative) injunction qualifies as a remedy.

The understanding of remedy adopted in this book is closer to the forward-looking than the backward-looking understanding. Like this book, the forward-looking understanding restricts the label to judicial rulings. However, the forward-looking understanding still differs from this book's usage. In particular, the forward-looking definition confines remedies to rulings that replicate substantive duties (because only such orders can cure a defendant's unwillingness to comply with a substantive duty). Many of the rulings discussed in this book, including restitutionary orders and orders to pay damages, do not replicate substantive duties, or so I argue.

A number of the orders discussed in this book are therefore not remedies in either of the senses just described, and some rules that are remedies in the first sense lie outside this book's scope. It might be asked, then, whether this book's approach of describing private law rulings as remedies is helpful. The question is difficult. On the one hand, regardless of how this book defines remedies, lawyers will continue to employ the term in other senses. The usages described above are well established and, when confined to the appropriate context, intelligible. On the other hand, regardless of how this book describes its subject matter, most readers will describe it as the law of remedies.

Against this background, the most useful approach is to retain the remedies label, but to insist on a definition that is stable, that identifies something important that remedies have in common, and that fits as nearly as possible with current usage and the ordinary meaning of the term. The definition of remedies as judicial rulings issued as part of the resolution of a legal action meets these criteria. To begin, it is relatively easy to identify remedies under this definition (though determining which rules are rules about remedies is often difficult). Second, the law governing legal rulings raises distinctive issues and, within that law, the rules governing private and public law rulings raise a subset of distinctive questions; in particular, they raise the question of the relationship between such rulings and the substantive rights enjoyed by the parties prior to litigation. Third, many leading authors on remedies adopt this book's definition (and authors who do not adopt it invariably treat all or nearly all private law rulings as falling within their definition). Finally, private and public law rulings are remedies in the ordinary sense of the word in that they are what courts do for claimants who come to them asking for help. They are the court's remedy for whatever problem brought the claimant to court.

ii. Orders, Rulings, Judgments

The second terminological issue is that lawyers sometimes use the word 'order' in a different sense than it is used here. In this book, an order is a judicial ruling that requires the defendant to do or not do something, that is, a directive ruling. However, there are three alternative meanings. In the first alternative, order is simply a synonym for a judicial ruling. When used in this broad sense, orders include rulings such as declarations, constitutive rulings, and dismissals of actions. It is useful to have a label that identifies the general category of legally operative judicial pronouncements, both directive and non-directive. However, the term 'order' is a poor choice precisely because it implies a directive: 'ruling' is a more transparent label for the actions intended by this first sense.

In its second alternative meaning, 'order' refers exclusively to rulings that courts issue prior to the final disposition of a lawsuit. In this understanding, the term order refers to judicial pronouncements such as interlocutory orders, interim injunctions, and time extensions. Authors who adopt this second meaning refer to final rulings—including the final monetary awards, specific performance orders, injunctions, and so on that are this book's focus—as 'judgments' (or more strictly as parts of judgments, since judgments are understood to include the court's reasons).[33] The distinction between final and non-final pronouncements is no longer legally significant in England, and the highly technical terminology associated with it (which this second usage reflects) has largely disappeared.[34] Thus, while 'judgment' continues to be used to refer to the entirety of a final decision (i.e. the reasons together with the ruling), it is normal practice for English lawyers and legislators to refer to judicial pronouncements generally, including the operative parts of judgments, as orders. This usage is adopted in this book, with the qualification that it understands orders as referring exclusively to directive rulings.

In the third and final alternative meaning, an 'order' refers to a directive pronouncement that traces its origins to the Chancery Court, such as an injunction or specific performance ('Equitable Remedies'). This usage, which remains popular amongst American lawyers, contrasts orders with 'judgments', where the latter refers to final rulings, directive or otherwise, that trace their origins to the Royal Courts ('Legal Remedies'). Important rulings that fall within the latter category include those requiring the payment of damages or a sum due under a contract, and rulings requiring the defendant to give up possession of land.

The historical background to this third meaning is that Equitable Remedies were originally understood, and styled explicitly, as personal orders ('... this Court doth order that an injunction be awarded to restrain the defendant, . . . from pulling down, or suffering to be pulled down, the house . . . ').[35] In contrast, Legal Remedies, save those of a constitutive or declaratory nature, were in the form of abstract statements of legally required results ('It is this day adjudged that the claimant recover against the defendant £100').[36] Further, the methods of enforcement differed as between 'Equitable Orders' and 'Judgments at Law'. Defendants who failed to comply with Equitable Orders were liable to be charged with contempt of court, and then imprisoned or fined. In contrast, the normal, and typically the only, consequence

[33] Kay, Sime, & French (2018) 1096–97. The historical explanation is that while Royal Courts described final rulings as Judgments, they described interim rulings (which prior to the *Judicature Acts* 1873 and 1875 were primarily procedural) as orders.

[34] Ibid 738; see also Zuckerman (2013) 1059 ('Already in the 19th century, the terms "judgment" and "order" began to lose their distinctive meaning'). This second meaning is still employed in parts of the *CPR*. Thus, Form N302 (PD 4), which sets out the form for specific performance orders, is labelled 'Judgment in Action for Specific Performance.'

[35] Lawrence & Hunter (1873) 296. A further complication is that 'final orders' from the Chancery Court were technically described not as 'orders' but as 'decrees': see Lawrence & Hunter (1873) 84–5. The precise terminology varied over time. One nineteenth-century book provides the following wording for a Chancery Court ruling: '. . . accordingly, it is ordered, adjudged, and decreed that . . . ' [111, Decree at the Hearing of the Cause Both Parties Being Present]: Great Britain, Court of Chancery (1828). I discuss this usage's history in Chapters 2 and 3.

[36] Chitty & Jacob (1965) no 688 (Judgment for Plaintiff for Debt or Damages and Costs after Trial by Judge Alone).

of failing to bring about the results contemplated by Judgments at Law was that the defendant's property could be seized and sold, or its wages garnished.[37]

The different labels, modes of expression, and means of enforcement associated with Equitable Orders and Judgments at Law continued in force in England after the nineteenth century merger of the court systems from which they originated. But since the passage of the *Civil Procedure Rules* 1998, all rulings in England other than declarations and constitutive rulings are styled explicitly as orders and subject to the same enforcement regime (albeit that regime functionally distinguishes between orders in a way that broadly replicates the old distinctions: see Chapter 3). The core provision of an ordinary ruling for payment of damages or a sum due under a contract from a contemporary English court reads: 'It is ordered that that the defendant do pay to the Claimant the sum of. . . .'[38] Similarly, the core provision of a ruling to recover possession of land reads: 'It is ordered that the defendant: give the claimant possession of the land described . . . .'[39] In short, contemporary English courts explicitly frame the rulings that are this book's focus as orders.

There remains the question of how to describe Judgments at Law when discussing earlier English rulings or rulings from other common law jurisdictions. The answer is not obvious. Judgments at Law are not strictly orders, as they do not state that the defendant or anyone else must do something. Nor are they declarations, much less constitutive rulings. A Judgment for damages does not say that the defendant has a legal duty to pay a sum of money, or that the defendant owes the claimant a sum of money, or even that the defendant should pay the claimant the sum of money. Nor does it transfer ownership in money or other property to the claimant. A Judgment at Law is simply an authoritative statement of a legally required future state of affairs. But rather than saying what ought to happen ('it is adjudged that the claimant should recover . . . '), Judgments at Law appear to say what will, necessarily, happen ('it is adjudged that the claimant recover . . . ')—without specifying how the desired state of affairs will come about, and presumably in awareness that it may not come about. I discuss this curious language and its historical origins in Chapter 2; for now, it is sufficient to note that there does not appear to be an ordinary English word to describe such rulings. It seems safest, therefore, to retain the traditional technical label, albeit capitalized to make clear that the term is used in a technical sense ('Judgment at Law' or just 'Judgment'). I adopt a similar approach when referring to rulings from the Chancery Court and from those contemporary courts (outside England) that continue to formally distinguish such rulings from Judgments (i.e. I describe them as 'Equitable Orders').

[37] Prior to the *Debtors Act* 1869, a defendant who failed to pay a debt could be imprisoned. In the case of a judgment for recovery of land, the defendant could be charged with obstructing the peace if he failed to vacate when the sheriff entered on the land. I discuss enforcement in Chapter 3.

[38] *CPR* PD 40B, 14.1.1, No 45 (Judgment after trial before judge without jury) (quoting the core provision only).

[39] *CPR* PD 4, Table 1, No 44 Part 24 (Judgment for claimant (summary)).

iii. The Conventional Labels

The third and final terminological issue concerns the labels for the various orders discussed in this book. There is no single set of labels appropriate for all contexts. For example, it is often useful to classify orders according to a single criterion, such as monetary/non-monetary, mandatory/prohibitory, or Legal/Equitable. The terms utilized in these and other single-criterion schemes are typically transparent. The difficulties arise when we move a step lower in the classificatory scheme and distinguish between different kinds of, for instance, non-monetary orders. Orders themselves do not come with labels attached. An order to pay £1000 by way of exemplary damages and an order to pay £1000 that is meant to fulfil a contractual debt are each written simply as orders to pay £1000. However, it is common and useful to describe such orders in terms that indicate, however roughly, their intended role. Exactly which labels are adopted depends on how fine a distinction is sought. However, for most purposes this book identifies the orders that are its focus as follows: (1) orders to pay damages; (2) specific performance orders (i.e. orders to perform contractual obligations); (3) injunctions (i.e. orders prohibiting a tortious or otherwise wrongful activity and orders mandating steps to prevent or end a wrongful activity); (4) orders for a sum due (sometimes known as orders to pay a debt or for an agreed sum); (5) orders for the recovery of land (sometimes known as 'ejectment'); (6) orders for the recovery of chattels (sometimes known as 'delivery up'); and (7) restitutionary orders (understood narrowly as orders to return property, or its value, that was obtained through a defective transfer).

These labels are familiar to lawyers, but they raise four potential sources of confusion. First, while it is common for lawyers to describe an order to perform a contract simply as 'specific performance', this description is traditionally limited to orders to perform positive contractual obligations. Lawyers typically describe orders to comply with negative contractual obligations as injunctions. Further, and more importantly, lawyers normally describe an order to pay a sum due under a contract as just that, not as specific performance. The explanation is historical. The term specific performance was traditionally restricted to orders to perform contractual obligations, and, as noted earlier, such orders were only available from the Chancery Court. However, the Royal Courts would issue Judgments at Law for sums due under contract. These rulings are now expressed as 'orders', but the historical practice of describing them as orders for a sum due (rather than as specific performance) continues.[40] Further, this practice matters

[40] The terminology is a minefield. It is responsible, inter alia, for the widespread misapprehension that the normal judicial response to a breach of contract is an award of damages and, more broadly, that common law courts rarely order contracting parties to perform their contracts ('The only remedy which the common law afforded for breach of contract was an award of damages. In equity, however, the due performance of the contract itself was in many cases enforced . . . ': McGhee, Baker, & Snell (2000) [40]–[41]). The most common remedy for breach of contract is not damages but an order for a sum due.

because the special preconditions historically associated with specific performance orders continue to apply to such orders and not to 'orders' that were formerly expressed as Judgments. A final complication in respect of 'specific performance' is that it was, and still is, possible to obtain specific performance of a contractual obligation to pay a sum of money.[41] While such orders were not common historically, they were sometimes granted; for example, they might be awarded in a case where the Chancery Court disallowed evidence that the Royal Courts would admit and that, once admitted, precluded the contract's enforceability.[42] As I explain in Chapter 6, courts today sometimes order specific performance of on-going monetary obligations (e.g. payments under an annuity) and in other specialized contexts. In principle, then, it may matter whether a claimant seeks an order for a sum due under a contract as opposed to specific performance of a monetary contractual obligation. However, in practice it may be difficult to maintain this distinction in a jurisdiction, like England, in which courts express both awards as orders.

Second, courts normally only award orders for the recovery of chattels ('delivery up') in cases where the claimant already owns the chattel. Thus, where the claimant seeks delivery of a promised chattel, and where title to that chattel has not passed to the claimant, the claimant must request specific performance. However, where title passed on contract formation (as commonly happens), the claimant has a choice of remedies.

Third, while lawyers typically apply the term 'injunction' to orders designed to prevent or stop an actual or potential tort or breach of a negative contractual obligation, the technical definition of an injunction is simply an order, of any kind, to do or not do something. Thus, authors occasionally describe orders to perform positive contractual obligations as injunctions. Lawyers also often describe procedural orders as injunctions. However, they never describe the first five of the orders listed above (damages, orders for a sum due, orders for the recovery of land or other property, and restitutionary orders) as injunctions. The explanation is again historical. Injunctions were the name given generally to the orders made by the Chancery Court, and the forerunners of orders (1) to (5) above were all Judgments from the Royal Courts. Again, these distinctions may matter in practice because special rules govern injunctions and specific performance.

Finally, the label 'restitutionary orders' raises a host of potential difficulties. This label is of recent origin and has yet to be adopted universally. It is usually understood to refer to a group of orders that were traditionally described in terms of the

Though originating in the Royal Courts, such orders are in substance specific performance. They direct defendants to perform a contractual obligation.

---

[41] See Spry (2014) 72, and the discussion of orders for a sum due in Chapter 6.

[42] Ibid 52–3.

forms of action under which they were sought (money had and received, money paid to the defendant's use, *quantum meruit*, and *quantum valebut*), and that are thought to require a giving back or returning of something or its value.[43] However, there is little agreement as to which orders fit within this category.[44] For example, some authors consider damages orders that courts assess at the value of the wrongdoer's gain as restitutionary. Other authors confine the label to orders that reverse unjust enrichments, and many of these authors (but not all) suppose that the previous orders fall outside this definition. At the same time, the traditional labels associated with the orders most commonly described as restitutionary are unhelpful. Partly to avoid these controversies and partly for convenience, this book uses the label 'restitutionary' in a narrow sense: it refers to orders that require defendants to undo defective transfers, such as orders to return payments induced by mistake, fraud, or force. Whatever other orders might properly be described as restitutionary, lawyers generally assume that this label is appropriate for orders to undo defective transfers.

F. Jurisdiction

The examples of private law orders discussed in this book originate from common law jurisdictions, typically England. Courts in civil law jurisdictions issue rulings that are broadly similar to those made in common law jurisdictions, and they do so in broadly similar circumstances. As is true of other legal fields, a study of the law governing court orders may profit from a comparative analysis. But while civilian ideas have influenced parts of this book, this book is not a comparative study. Such a task would be difficult at this stage in either system's understanding of court-order law. There are relatively few rules dealing with the content or availability of rulings in civil law systems (particularly in the civil law systems that I am most familiar with—those inspired by French law). Many of the issues that common law lawyers regard as determined by the law of damages, civilian lawyers treat as questions of fact. Further, they consider other rules discussed in this book as part of civil procedure (which rules vary greatly even across civilian jurisdictions). The other main hurdle to comparing the civil and common law is that much of the common law of remedies has been influenced by the jurisdictional distinction between the Royal Courts and the Chancery Court, or by that law's relationship to other institutional peculiarities of English law. More broadly, neither system has spent much time thinking about the concept of judicial rulings or about their relationship to substantive rights.[45]

43 See Zakrzewski (2005) 112.
44 See e.g. Stevens (2018); Penner (2018).
45 See generally Dedek (2010).

The orders examined in this book are found, with small variations, in all common law systems. However, the terms in which lawyers describe them and some of the technical incidents attached to them differ between jurisdictions. For example, in the United States (but not elsewhere), juries continue to play a significant role in assessing damages. More importantly, in England most of the traditional terminology and formal distinctions associated with the historical distinction between Legal and Equitable remedies were eliminated with the passing of the *Civil Procedure Rules* 1998. As mentioned above, England no longer recognizes a formal distinction between 'Equitable Orders' and 'Judgments at Law'—both are now just 'orders'. Other common law jurisdictions continue to employ the traditional terminology and continue to express rulings differently depending on their historical origins. These differences are not important for this book's larger themes. However, at the level of exposition, it is convenient to focus on a single jurisdiction. England is the best-known Commonwealth legal system. Further, the English law governing private law rulings is well developed, easily accessible, and has been extensively analysed. Finally, the relevant English law is unitary (it applies to all courts) and, following the above-mentioned reforms, is today expressed in relatively simple and transparent language.

G. Methodology

This book's focus on the relationship between remedial law and substantive law and, more broadly, on remedial law's structure, is unusual. Most of the literature on remedial law written over the past fifty or so years, and in particular the theoretical literature, has focused on its normative foundations.[46] For example, the primary aim of the vast law and economics literature on specific relief and damages awards has been to explain whether and how these awards promote utility. This literature almost wholly ignores structural questions.[47] Authors who adopt other theoretical approaches have more varied interests, but, for the most part, they also focus on normative issues, specifically on demonstrating that the law of damages can be explained in non-utilitarian terms.[48] It may be helpful, then, to say a few words about this book's approach.

As mentioned earlier, this book's primary aim is not to reform the law or even to evaluate it, but simply to understand it.[49] As is true of most explanatory legal

[46] See e.g. Goetz and Scott (1980) (1983); Craswell (1989); Coleman (1992) Ch 10; Friedmann (1995); Weinrib (2008); Ripstein (2007).

[47] An important exception is Calabresi & Melamed (1972), though this exception is also noteworthy for misunderstanding the relationship between substantive and remedial law.

[48] Important recent exceptions include Zakrzewski (2005); Zipursky (2002); Birks (2000a 2000b); and Stevens (2007). Doctrinal scholarship has long focused on categorizing legal rules. However, it rarely addresses the classificatory questions that are this book's focus.

[49] I discuss these issues in Smith (2004) ch 1. This book is 'interpretive' in the sense described in ch 1.

theories, explanatory theories of remedies can be categorized according to whether and how they answer two questions. The first question is normative (or 'justificatory'). This question asks what principles or values, if any, underlie remedial law. Common answers include social utility, individual rights, or a combination of utility and rights. The second general question is analytic (or 'classificatory'). This question asks how remedial law is like or unlike other parts of the law. As mentioned earlier, few scholars have attempted to answer this question, though in recent years some have addressed the parallel question in respect of damages awards. Amongst the answers that have been given to this question, the most important division is between those that suppose damages awards replicate existing substantive duties (the 'duty-confirming' view) and those that suppose damages awards create new duties (the 'duty-creating' view).

The normative and analytic questions overlap. To answer the normative question, it is necessary to have an idea of what one is trying to justify—which is the question that analytic theories seek to answer. For their part, answers to the analytic question are assessed partly by whether they are consistent with supposing that the law is justified or at least might plausibly be thought to be justified. The law presents itself as justified, so theories that explain how such a claim is intelligible are more persuasive than theories that cannot explain this feature. Nonetheless, the answer to the normative question does not determine the answer to the analytic question, and vice versa. Different combinations are possible. As I explain in Chapter 7, the deterrence-based account of damages favoured by many utilitarian theorists suggests that they regard damages awards as akin to criminal punishment, and so as creating new duties. Yet the suggestion defended in other utilitarian work that damages awards are effectively insurance for victims supports substantive duties to pay damages, and so supports the duty-confirming view of damages awards. Similarly, the rights-based literature on damages includes theories that defend duty-confirming views and theories that defend duty-creating views. Thus, it is common, and for most purposes perfectly appropriate, to approach the normative and analytic questions separately.

As should be evident by now, this book pays special attention to analytic questions, in particular to the core analytic question of the relationship between remedial law and substantive law. I have already mentioned one reason for this focus: the existing theoretical literature on damages focuses primarily on normative questions. A second reason is practical.[50] For the law to operate effectively, lawyers, judges, legal officials, scholars, and ordinary citizens must be able to understand it without excessive effort. And as is true of most academic fields, understanding in law is largely a matter of understanding whether and in what ways the law (or particular laws) is similar or different to other things (or other

[50] I explore this reason in Smith (2000a); see also Birks (2000b) xxxi–xxxii.

laws). Just as zoology students learn to distinguish vertebrates from invertebrates, law students learn to distinguish lies from broken promises. Knowledge is inseparable from classification.

It is true that classificatory inquiries cannot be separated entirely from normative inquiries. However, classificatory inquiries do not (or at least should not) require consideration of the kinds of comprehensive moral theories that are the focus of most contemporary normative scholarship, that is, theories like utilitarianism or (to take the best-known individual-rights theory) Kantianism. Classificatory inquiries can generally limit themselves to considering familiar, specific, norms such as 'keep promises', 'do not lie', 'do not injure others', and so on—norms that utilitarians, Kantians, and pretty much all contemporary moral theorists accept. Indeed, it would be a serious problem if it were not possible to understand the law without endorsing utilitarianism, Kantianism, or any similarly comprehensive moral theory. The success of contemporary legal systems depends in large part on their ability to guide individuals (including lawyers and judges) who may have radically different comprehensive moral views. The law's effective day-to-day operation requires, therefore, that individuals be able to use it without taking a position on the kinds of comprehensive moral theories advanced in most normative scholarship. In a similar way, if this book's arguments depended on the truth of utilitarianism, Kantianism, or any other comprehensive moral theory, their value would be severely limited.[51]

The final reason for this book's analytic focus is, paradoxically, normative. There is little agreement amongst scholars about the normative foundations of private law, or indeed if such foundations exist at all. However, nearly all legal scholars, not to mention nearly all judges and lawyers, agree on one normative proposition: like cases should be decided alike. Determining which cases are alike is primarily an analytic question.

H. Overview

This book is in four parts. The first part—Chapters 2–4—is an extension of the present introductory chapter. Chapter 2 describes remedial law's historical foundations. Although this book is not an historical study, it is difficult to understand the

[51] Closely connected to this second reason is a personal reason. Like most legal scholars, my legal training has (I hope) provided me with skills useful for answering analytic questions. Of course, legal scholars have made significant contributions to moral philosophy. But legal scholars are not typically experts in moral theory. Law students are introduced to moral puzzles, and they are taught how to use rules and make arguments to solve those puzzles. However, their training provides no special insights into the comprehensive moral theories that are the focus of normative legal theories. The main skill that law students are taught is how to draw distinctions, in particular how to distinguish like rules and cases from unlike rules and cases. One skill in which legal scholars can justifiably claim a comparative advantage is answering analytic questions.

contemporary law of remedies, and in particular to understand the contemporary misunderstandings of that law, without understanding its historical development. Chapter 3 explains how courts create private law orders, what they look like, and their legal effects. Though partly descriptive, Chapter 3 defends a particular understanding of the rules that it describes. It argues that these rules are part of the 'general' law of remedies. In practice, this means that Chapter 3 rejects the traditional approach of organizing and explaining these rules according to whether they originated in the Royal Courts or the Chancery Court. Instead, it explains the rules as reflecting general remedial law principles. Finally, Chapter 4 develops a general framework—or classificatory scheme—for expressing how private law orders differ from other legal phenomena, and how they differ amongst themselves. The framework is developed by considering three of the four questions that I raised earlier in this chapter, namely: (1) What is a remedy (and how are remedies related to other parts of the law)?; (2) On what grounds are remedies available?; and (3) What kinds of remedies are available? The answer to the first question distinguishes between substantive rights, rights to rulings ('action rights'), rights created by rulings ('court-ordered rights'), and rights to coercively enforce rulings ('enforcement rights'). The answer to the second question ('On what grounds are remedies available'?) argues that the common law recognizes three main causes of action: proof of a rights-threat; proof of a wrong, and proof of an injustice. Finally the answer to the third question ('What kinds of remedies are available?') distinguishes replicative orders from creative orders, and, within the latter category, distinguishes between substitutionary, wrong-responding, and free-standing creative orders. Chapter 4's scheme is preliminary because I explain and defend it only enough to show that the various categories it proposes are *prima facie* plausible. In principle, the framework developed in Chapter 4, which outlines positions defended in detail in Chapters 6 to 9, should appear at the book's end. However, it is easier to follow the subsequent arguments and to appreciate their significance with a map of the territory under discussion.

The second part of the book is comprised of a single chapter that focuses on the 'why orders' question. I argue that the best-known general theories of law ('law as a system of rules', 'law as a system of sanctions') fail to explain the distinctive features of orders and, more importantly, fail to explain why courts employ orders at all. The theory developed in Chapter 5 argues that orders differ from rules and sanctions not just in their form but also, critically, in the way that they are meant to motivate their subjects. I argue that orders are meant to invoke a distinctive kind of authority, different from that invoked by either rules or sanctions. At the end of Chapter 5, I also touch briefly on the theory's implications for when courts should issue orders, what kinds of orders they should issue, and who should be able to obtain orders.

The book's third and final part examines in detail the positive law governing when and in what form courts issue orders. Chapters 6 to 8 examine the rules governing the main private law orders discussed in this book: specific performance orders, injunctions, damages awards, orders for a sum due, orders for the recovery of land or other property, and restitutionary orders. These chapters are organized according to causes of actions, that is, according to the facts that claimants must establish to obtain remedies. Chapter 6 discusses orders issued on proof of a rights-threat (specific performance, most injunctions, orders for a sum due, orders for the recovery of land or other property, and substitutionary damages). Chapter 7 discusses orders issued on proof of a wrong (exemplary damages, nominal damages, damages for pain and suffering, and a variety of other damages awards that I describe as 'vindicatory'). Finally, Chapter 8 discusses orders issued on proof of an injustice (compensatory damages, restitutionary orders).

The book concludes with a chapter devoted to remedial defences. Chapter 9's main goals are threefold: (1) to demonstrate that remedial defences are practically important; (2) to explain how they illustrate some of this book's main themes; and (3) to demonstrate that they are governed by general principles—principles that cut across historical boundaries. In particular, and continuing an argument that I began in Chapter 3, Chapter 9 argues that most of the rules governing so-called 'Equitable' defences are best understood as a part of general remedial law.

Many of this book's arguments about specific orders are controversial, in particular, the argument that damages awards and restitutionary awards create new duties, and the argument that these awards share a common cause of action. It may be worth repeating, then, that the book's primary aim is not to convince readers to adopt a specific understanding of damages orders, restitutionary orders, or any other order. Its primary aim is to convince readers that the questions it asks about such orders are important. This book is fundamentally an extended argument for treating the rules governing damages awards, injunctions, specific performance orders, and so forth as constituting a distinctive and important body of law—a body of law focused exclusively on rulings.

2
Historical Foundations

In certain respects, this book is deeply ahistorical. It rejects ways of thinking about remedies that have developed over centuries and that are closely tied to remedial law's history. However, its explanations of why these ways of thinking arose, how they influenced contemporary views, and why they should be modified, draws heavily on an understanding of their historical origins. This chapter seeks to provide that understanding.

I focus on two features of remedial law's history. Each has given rise to views about contemporary remedies that, while widespread, this book rejects. The first feature is that the core rules governing damages, injunctions, specific performance, and so forth were developed during a period when England had two court systems: the Royal Courts (or 'Courts of Law') and the Chancery Court (or 'Courts of Equity'). Each of these systems had exclusive jurisdiction over certain rulings and each applied distinctive rules regarding their availability. For example, the most important monetary rulings, such as those that required the payment of a debt or damages, were issued exclusively by the Royal Courts and were said to be available 'as of right'—meaning that if certain facts were established (e.g. the existence of an unpaid debt), the order would necessarily be issued. By contrast, the majority of the rulings available in the Chancery Court ('Chancery') were non-monetary (e.g. injunctions, specific performance, constructive trusts), and were said to be available only in the court's discretion (which turned on issues such as the 'adequacy' of the remedy available from the Royal Courts, the hardship that the ruling might impose, and whether the claimant had acted reasonably). The Judicature Acts of 1873 and 1875 merged the two court systems, together with their respective rules. However, courts today continue, for the most part, to apply the special rules for each of these sets of rulings to their contemporary descendants. A consequence of this practice is that contemporary scholars continue to label, organize, and explain remedies according to whether they originated in the Royal Courts or the Chancery. Indeed, the organization of most remedies textbooks suggests that the most important thing to know about a remedy is its historical provenance; specifically, whether it originated in the Chancery or the Royal Courts.[1] The existence of books devoted to 'Equitable Remedies' and the inclusion of chapters on 'remedies' in books on Equity convey a similar message. In short,

[1] See e.g. Dobbs & Roberts (2018); Andoh & Marsh (1997); Rendleman (2006); Zakrzewski (2005); Burrows (2004).

Rights, Wrongs, and Injustices. Stephen A. Smith, Oxford University Press (2019). © Stephen A. Smith.
DOI: 10.1093/oso/9780199229772.003.0002

it appears to be assumed that it is impossible to understand contemporary remedies without understanding that they originated in different courts. Against this assumption, I argue (in subsequent chapters) that the remedies that exist today and the rules governing their content and availability could easily have arisen in a unitary legal system. Moreover, I argue that it is possible to describe and explain both (so-called) Legal remedies and (so-called) Equitable remedies on the basis of the same principles.

The second feature of remedial law's history examined in this chapter is its role in the broader history of private law. For most of the common law's history, 'private law' was primarily law about remedies, broadly understood. Medieval private law contained little in the way of rules stipulating how individuals ought to behave towards one another. Rather, it consisted primarily of rules stipulating on what grounds and in what ways courts could give rulings. Much of this law was procedural in the modern sense, but the remainder appears to have been largely rules about remedies. Contemporary 'substantive' law—the rules that express the duties individuals owe each other—was derived from, and so developed out of, this body of remedial law. Common law lawyers determined what rights individuals enjoyed by looking at the rulings that courts would provide and the conditions under which they would provide them. This practice has left its mark on how contemporary lawyers, judges, and scholars think about the relationship between rights and rulings.[2] It explains, for example, the common practice of starting courses on contract law by discussing the remedies available for a breach of contract: to understand contractual duties, the argument goes, you must first understand the remedies for breaking a contract. More broadly, it explains why common law lawyers often treat rights and remedies as two sides of the same coin: in this view, our rights are defined by the remedies we can obtain. This book also rejects this way of thinking about remedies. Indeed, one of its central themes is that the question of what rights individuals have is different from the question of what remedies they can obtain.

The chapter has two main parts, corresponding to the two features described above. The first part examines the historical relationship between different kinds of orders, in particular the relationship between orders originally available only from the Royal Courts and those originally available only from the Chancery. The second part examines the historical relationship between court orders and other parts of the law, in particular the relationship between court orders and substantive rules. The concluding section summarizes the challenges raised by the history of remedies law for Bontemporary attempts to understand that law, and briefly describes this book's response to those challenges.

[2] 'In England remedies tend to dominate lawyers' thinking because they have traditionally ascertained the substantive law not by reference to large principles but by examining what the courts actually do at judgment': Andrews (2003) 787.

A. Law and Equity

In England today, the rulings that are this book's focus are orders in the ordinary sense of the word: they literally command the defendant to do or not to do something. However, until the passing of the *Civil Procedure Act* 1998 (and still today in most other common law jurisdictions), many of these rulings were expressed not as orders but rather as abstract statements of legally required results. In particular, final private law orders that trace their origins to the Royal Courts (such as orders to pay damages, for a sum due, or for the recovery of land) were previously framed as 'Judgments' that the claimant 'recover', respectively, a sum of money or possession of land. Thus, an order to pay a debt might read: 'It is this day adjudged that the plaintiff recover £100 from the defendant'.[3]

Prior to the *Civil Procedure Act* 1998, the only awards explicitly framed as orders originated from the Chancery Court, such as specific performance and injunctions. For example, an injunction might read: 'It is this day adjudged and ordered that the defendant . . . before 1 o'clock in the afternoon of . . . pull down and remove . . . '.[4] Further, the methods of enforcing 'Judgments at Law' and 'Equitable Orders' (as they continued to be called notwithstanding the joinder of the Royal Courts and Chancery in the nineteenth century) were linked to the language in which they were expressed. With one exception (largely abolished in the nineteenth century),[5] indirect enforcement, such as imprisonment, fines, and sequestration, was reserved for defendants who failed to comply with Equitable Orders: imprisoning a recalcitrant defendant was a punitive response to the defendant's contempt of court. By contrast, direct enforcement, such as seizure and sale of goods, or the garnishment of wages, was confined to Judgments at Law: the results contemplated by the Judgment of a Royal Court could be brought about by authorized third parties.[6]

The traditional explanation for this difference in language and the associated differences in enforcement is that Judgments at Law ('Judgments') and Equitable Orders ('Orders') originated in court systems that had qualitatively different aims. According to this explanation, the Royal Courts' rulings were authoritative statements of what the law ('Law') required; by contrast, a ruling from the Chancery concerned itself solely with the defendant's behaviour. Consequently, the Chancery merely informed defendants how they should act in particular circumstances. Further, it commanded behaviour not on the basis of what the Law required, but on the basis of what 'conscience'—roughly, good morals—required. Further, the

[3] Chitty & Jacob (1965) No 688, Judgment for Plaintiff for Debt or Damages and Costs after Trial by Judge Alone.

[4] Chitty & Jacob (1965) No 1350, Judgment or Order for Injunction at Trial.

[5] The exception was imprisonment for failing to pay a debt, which the *Debtors Act* 1869 abolished for nearly all cases. Chapter 3 discusses enforcement in more detail.

[6] Again, there were important exceptions; for example, the Chancery could order the sale of sequestered goods to satisfy an unperformed order to pay a sum of money: Cook (1915) 110.

traditional explanation argues that this distinction explains important differences in the availability of Judgments and Orders. In particular, it is said to explain why Judgments were available automatically, or 'as of right', on proof of certain facts, while Orders were only available in the court's discretion—and why, in exercising that discretion, the Chancery considered a range of broadly 'moralistic' factors (such as 'clean hands', 'hardship', and 'delay').

As already mentioned, since the passing of the *Civil Procedure Act* 1998 courts frame all rulings other than declarations and constitutive rulings as, literally, orders. Thus, courts frame both rulings to pay damages (formerly Judgments to pay damages) and rulings commanding the execution of a trust of money (formerly Orders to execute a trust) explicitly as 'orders' that the defendant pay the claimant a sum of money. However, in other respects the rules and practices governing contemporary orders are broadly similar to those existing prior to the Act. The rules regulating enforcement are described differently today—there is little mention in the relevant legislation of 'contempt of court', let alone of 'Law' or 'Equity'—but their substance is, with a few exceptions, similar. As explained in Chapter 3, injunctions and specific performance are, for the most part, still enforced indirectly; while orders to pay sums due under contracts, damages, or to give up possession of land are, for the most part, still enforced directly. Further, and of particular importance, the rules governing the availability of rulings appear not to have been affected by the *Civil Procedure Act* 1998. For example, it is still said that courts enjoy a discretion to refuse specific performance and injunctions, and that damages awards are available as of right. It is perhaps not surprising, then, that many authors and judges continue to regard the historical distinction between Judgments and Orders as critical to understanding remedies. As mentioned, this work rejects this view. However, for the moment my concern is to explain why the distinction assumed such importance—and to do that, it is necessary to discuss its genesis.

Until late in the nineteenth century, England had two separate court systems—the Royal Courts and the Chancery—and two separate bodies of law administered by these courts, conventionally described as 'Law' and 'Equity'. The Judicature Acts of 1873 and 1875 eliminated this institutional bifurcation, establishing a largely unitary court system (similar acts occurred in most other common law jurisdictions, though in some cases only recently and not always in an identical fashion). At the same time, the Judicature Acts instructed judges in the new system to apply both the rules previously developed in the Royal Courts and those previously developed in the Chancery. Consequently, many of the rules and practices of contemporary English law, and of contemporary common law generally, evolved from rules and practices that were developed by the Royal Courts or the Chancery when they operated within a split system.

The origin of the Royal Courts (also called the 'King's' or 'common law' or just 'law' courts) is usually dated to the period of government reorganization that took place in the century or so following the Norman Conquest of 1066. The development of permanent courts with jurisdiction over the entirety of England—courts that administered a 'common' law (and which, in time, crowded out other forms of law)—was a major achievement; but, like any court system, it did not satisfy everyone. Powerful interests often overawed the judges or juries on whom the Royal Courts relied. The Royal Courts' strict and highly technical rules governing procedure, evidence, and proof were also unsuitable for many cases. Further, and of particular significance, the Royal Courts would only hear a limited range of disputes. To gain access to the Royal Courts, one needed a writ (roughly, a letter from the Chancellor that outlined the claimant's demand or complaint and that commanded a sheriff to bring the defendant to court),[7] and writs were only available for disputes in which the Sovereign had an interest, which, at first, meant mostly disputes dealing with land, status, and forcible wrongdoing. New writs might be issued (or sympathetic judges might permit new actions under old writs), but there was always a concern—familiar to lawyers of any age—about opening too wide a gate or stretching a fiction too far. Individuals who could not obtain appropriate redress from the Royal Courts usually had the option of going to one of the many local or manorial courts that continued to exist in England long after the conquest. However, these courts had limited powers, and often a geographically limited jurisdiction.

Unsurprisingly, individuals who were unhappy with the results they obtained or were likely to obtain from the Royal Courts would sometimes petition the Sovereign personally to intercede on their behalf. Such interventions were not, at that time anyway, perceived as raising a conflict between the Royal Courts and the Sovereign. It was the Sovereign's role to ensure that justice was done, and if the Royal Court could not ensure this, the Sovereign could step in.[8] It was understood that the machinery and procedures of the Royal Courts were suitable only for certain disputes. Of course, the Sovereigns could reform their courts (e.g. they could direct that courts make more writs available), but fine-tuning a large bureaucracy raises its own challenges, and, as I explain below, the Royal Courts worked well for most cases. It was often easier for the Sovereign to deal individually with cases that the official machinery of the Royal Courts handled poorly. In short, the Sovereign's interventions were regarded as complementary to the work done by his courts.[9]

[7] Where the claimant's action was intended to bring about compliance with an existing substantive right (such as a property right or a contractual right), the sheriff was instructed to bring the defendant to court only if the defendant failed to comply. In contrast, where the claimant sought redress for a wrong, that is, a trespass, the defendant had no option but to come to court: Baker (2002) 60. As I explain in Chapter 7, this distinction is important for understanding damages awards.

[8] See ibid 98.

[9] '. . . Chancellors did not regard themselves as administering a system of law different from the law of England. They were reinforcing the law by making sure that justice was done in cases where shortcomings in the regular procedure, or human failings, were hindering its attainment by due process. They came not to destroy the law, but to fulfill it': ibid 102.

The practice of bringing special petitions to the Sovereign was popular, and in time the Sovereign delegated authority to the Chancellor, who, in turn, shared authority with a group of officials that came to be known in its official capacity as the 'Chancery' (or 'Equity') Court. Over the course of many centuries, the decisions rendered by the Chancery ceased to be extraordinary interventions. By the seventeenth century, the Chancery had developed settled and, in some cases, highly rigid rules. Its decisions were reported and, in this way, gave birth to a body of precedents—of law—that is today associated with important substantive legal doctrines (e.g. unconscionability), institutions (e.g. the equitable charge), and entire legal subjects (e.g. trusts).

Alongside these developments in substantive law, the Chancery also gave birth to distinctive forms of rulings. The most important such rulings—injunctions and specific performance (hereafter 'injunctions')[10]—were expressed as orders commanding the defendant to do or not do something. There are two ways of explaining this development. As I explain below, these ways line up roughly with two ways of explaining the relationship generally between rules that originated in the Chancery and rules that originated in the Royal Courts—and hence of explaining the contemporary significance of this development.

The first explanation is that the Chancery developed injunctive relief purely as a practical response to the unavailability of injunctive relief in the Royal Courts. At a relatively early stage in their history, the Royal Courts confined themselves to issuing Judgments.[11] As mentioned earlier, Judgments are not strictly orders but rather abstract statements of legally required results. Further, they only specify results that third parties can bring about. Thus, while it was possible to obtain a Judgment stipulating that a piece of land 'shall be partitioned' (because court officials could bring about the partition), it was not possible to obtain a Judgment stipulating that a contract 'shall be performed' (since only contracting parties can perform contracts). The only relief Royal Courts offered to disappointed contracting parties were Judgments stipulating that the claimant shall recover a sum of money (whether by way of a sum due under a contract or damages for non-performance).

It does not appear that this limitation was based on any deep principle. In their early years, the Royal Courts occasionally issued what we would now call orders.[12] There appear to be two reasons that the practice died out. The first is that it was impractical for juries (which were only used in the Royal Courts) to stay seized of a case following judgment.[13] If a monetary judgment was issued, it

[10] This label is for convenience, but it is accurate as specific performance orders are in substance no different from mandatory injunctions.

[11] Baker (2002) 557 provides an early example of the language adopted: 'Therefore it is awarded that the same Isot do recover her aforesaid damages against the aforesaid John son of John' (*Bellhouse v Clavering* (1341) translation)). The Royal Courts also issued constitutive rulings, as for example where they declared a previously married couple to be divorced or where, after adjudging that a property should be divided, they instructed the sheriff to make a partition.

[12] See Milsom (1981) 90, 247; Baker (2002) 58.

[13] Stein (1984) 46–7.

was unnecessary for the jury to remain involved as a sheriff or other official could determine if payment had been made. The second, related, reason is that orders were difficult to enforce. The only way to induce compliance with an order is to threaten the addressee with punishment. And regardless of the claimant's interest in compliance, a punitive response would have been thought necessary to uphold the court's authority—a failure to comply with an order was a direct challenge not just to the Royal Court but to the Sovereign. Yet, punishment was costly, as were the trials that would need to take place prior to any punishment. Further, the very cases where the defendant's personal involvement would be most sought (e.g. in a personal service contract), were also the cases where disputes over compliance would be most likely to arise. These obstacles were not insurmountable: the Royal Courts punished criminal wrongdoers, and the Chancery enforced its orders in this way. But as was true of other apparent gaps in royal justice, the effort required to fill this gap probably did not seem worth the effort. The vast majority of disputes heard by the Royal Courts involved land, status, or forcible wrongs. The scope of both tort and contract law was narrow, and contracts themselves were relatively unimportant in medieval economies. Further, it was usually too late in cases involving torts or contracts for an injunction, and even when it was not, most claimants were content with monetary relief. Finally, the widespread practice of attaching conditional bonds (broadly, contractual penalty clauses) to contracts provided an effective means to compel contractual performance. In short, Judgments provided satisfactory relief for most disputes brought before the Royal Courts. Moreover, Judgments had the advantage that it was relatively easy for legal officials to determine whether the contemplated result (payment of money, recovery of land) was achieved, and, if necessary, to employ third parties to bring about those results (e.g. by seizure and sale)—and to do both these things largely without the court's (or jury's) further involvement. Bailiffs or sheriffs can enforce Judgments, and they were (and to a significant extent still are) essentially private actors, not government officials.

Against this background, the Chancery's willingness to issue injunctions appears to be a straightforward instance of filling a gap in the justice available from the Royal Courts. Not bound by the writ system, and with considerable resources at its call,[14] the Chancery could offer exceptional forms of relief in the rare cases where the usual forms were unsatisfactory. Had this issue first surfaced at a later stage in the Royal Courts' evolution (say in the fifteenth century), when the rules on issuing writs were loosened, the Royal Courts might have responded by developing injunctions themselves. However, by the fifteenth century the pattern was set: each court system had its own jurisdiction—and the associated fees from applicants—and attempts to move into the other's terrain were unwelcome. From

[14] See Ogilvie (1978) 35; Walsh (1930) 17.

this perspective, and limiting our attention to final private law injunctions, the Chancery's rulings appear noteworthy only for the extent to which they support the view that the Chancery functioned primarily as a practical complement to the Royal Courts. Consistent with this interpretation, the actions required by the final private law injunctions issued by the Chancery fully supported the legal principles applied in the Royal Courts. The Royal Courts' practice of issuing damages awards presumed that nuisances, trespasses, contract breaches, and so on were wrongs. Similarly, the Royal Courts' willingness to award Judgments for sums due under contracts presumed a duty to perform contractual obligations. The Royal Courts could not have had any objections, therefore, to ordering defendants to perform contracts or to refrain from committing torts. They merely lacked the machinery to make such rulings themselves.

The second way of explaining the Chancery's development of injunctive relief presumes that there was a general and qualitative difference between how the Chancery and the Royal Courts—or Equity and Law (the terms preferred by those adopting this explanation)—dealt with disputes.[15] This explanation begins with the observation that the Chancery employed orders generally, not merely in cases where damages awards were deemed an inadequate response to a wrong. Stated differently, the Chancery used orders in cases falling within its exclusive jurisdiction (such as disputes over trusts), and not merely in cases where it had concurrent jurisdiction (such as contracts and torts cases). Thus, where the Chancery determined that a trustee had, in breach of trust, failed to pay a sum of money to a trust beneficiary, it would issue a ruling ordering the trustee to make the payment. In such a case, it was not possible to argue that the issued order filled a gap in the rulings available from the Royal Courts. Rather, the order appeared to fill a gap in the substantive law—namely, the Royal Courts' refusal to recognize trusts at all. Had the Royal Courts recognized trusts, a Judgment at Law allowing the beneficiary to recover the relevant sum would presumably have been a perfectly adequate remedy.

Viewed from this perspective, injunctions are just one example of the Chancery's general practice of resolving disputes by issuing orders rather than Judgments. But why did the Chancery employ orders? The short answer, in this second view, is that they employed orders to avoid a conflict with the Royal Courts. If the Chancery had issued Judgments (or anything similar), the Royal Court could have accused it of infringing its jurisdiction. A Judgment, in this view, stated what the law required, and the law was within the Royal Courts' sole authority. By restricting themselves to issuing orders, the Chancery could leave this authority unchallenged, at least in theory. In this view, orders said nothing about what the law required: orders were

[15] 'Equity is no part of the law, but a moral virtue which qualifies, moderates and reforms the rigour, hardness and edge of the law': *Dudley v Dudley* (1705) Prec Ch 241, 244 (Lord Chancellor Cowper).

merely personal directions telling individuals how they should deal with their legal rights.[16]

If the Chancery was not dealing with the law, the question then arose as to the source of its authority: what was the Chancery's positive justification for, inter alia, issuing orders? It is in response to this question that the idea developed, around the fifteenth century, of the Chancery as a court of 'conscience'.[17] It is not easy to say what this idea signifies, but at the time it seems to have been broadly understood to mean that the Chancery was concerned not just with outcomes but also, indeed primarily, with motives or 'conscience'. In this view, the Royal Courts' focused on the external manifestations of behaviour—that is, on results. What mattered to the Royal Courts was whether the debtor paid the creditor or whether a landowner enjoyed possession; the 'Law' was unconcerned with why the creditor was paid or why the landowner had possession. Consistent with this approach, Judgments stipulated results, not actions. So long as the creditor was paid and the debtor provided the funds, justice was served and the Royal Courts were satisfied.

In contrast, the Chancery, in this view, was concerned primarily with the parties' behaviour, including their motives. In particular, the Chancery's main concern was to prevent unconscionable conduct—conduct that shocked its 'conscience'. Personal directions, or orders, are then said to fit naturally into this story since their goal is not so much to bring about particular results, but particular behaviours. Orders inform defendants as to how a person of good conscience would behave. It might be asked whether orders backed by the threat of imprisonment spoke more to defendants' self-interest than to their conscience, but on the surface anyway, such orders could be understood merely as directions as to what good conscience required. The Chancellor could not change defendants' motives, but he could try to ensure that they acted in the way that a defendant with the right motive would act.

These two explanations of the Chancery's practice of issuing injunctions—the 'institutional' and the 'moral'—are obviously in tension. The institutional explanation views the practice as a gap-filler, introduced to address an exceptional need that, for essentially practical reasons, the Royal Courts were unwilling to fulfil. In contrast, the moral explanation views injunctive relief as one manifestation of the broader idea that the Chancery was concerned with a distinctive aspect of morality.

As I explain in Chapters 3 and 6, these contrasting explanations have contemporary counterparts. Admittedly, few contemporary scholars would go so far as to suggest that the rules that originated in the Chancery are not 'law' in the

[16] 'The decrees [from the Chancery] operated in personam; they were binding on the parties in the cause, but were not judgments of record binding anyone else': Baker (2002) 88–9.

[17] 'We are to argue conscience here, not the law': *Subpoena*, (1452) Mich 31 Hen VI, Fitz Abr, pl 23 (Fortescue CJ); 'The office of the chancellor is to correct men's consciences for fraud, breaches of trust, wrongs and oppressions of whatever nature . . . ': *Earl of Oxford's Case* (1615) 1 Ch Rep 1, 6 (Lord Ellesmere).

ordinary sense of the word; that view fell out of fashion long before the Judicature Acts. However, the idea that contemporary legal rules that trace their origins to the Chancery, including the rules governing injunctions, are qualitatively different from those that trace their origins to the Royal Courts has many defenders.[18] I do not examine this broader debate further here, but it may be useful to note in passing some features of the contemporary rules governing injunctions that appear to align naturally with one side of this debate or the other. The rule that courts will not grant specific relief except where damages awards are inadequate fits neatly with the institutional, or gap-filling, explanation. If specific relief is an alternative means of achieving the same justice that damages awards seek to achieve (albeit by a more costly, or at least more complex, method), then it is appropriate only where damages awards are inadequate. The adequacy rule appears to assume that damages awards and specific relief share a common aim or foundation. Conversely, the various 'equitable bars' to injunctive relief (clean hands, hardship, delay, and so forth), together with the 'bundle of factors' way in which these bars are traditionally considered, appear to align with the idea that specific relief is one aspect of a broader concern with unconscionable conduct. The equitable bars appear to invite courts to assess, in a global fashion, the parties' behaviour.

B. Remedial and Substantive Law

Alongside the division between Legal and Equitable Remedies, a second noteworthy feature of remedial law in common law jurisdictions is its prominent role in how lawyers and legal scholars think about private law generally. There are entire treatises devoted to particular orders (such as damages awards), and most law faculties have courses ('remedies') that are organized around different types of rulings. Further, and of particular importance, discussions of individuals' 'rights' in books and courses ostensibly devoted to substantive private law topics frequently frame these discussions partly or wholly in terms of rights to rulings. Contract courses frequently begin by examining the rules governing specific relief and damages awards. Similarly, discussions of causation, remoteness, and fault in tort law are typically presented in terms of what needs to be proven in order to obtain a court ruling. More broadly, substantive duties are invariably described at least partly in terms of what courts will do for claimants: 'A contract is an agreement enforced by law . . . ';[19] 'tort law is a collection of causes of action, each made up of three main components: an interest protected by the law, conduct affecting that interest which

[18] 'Equitable principles have above all a distinctive ethical quality, reflecting as they do the prevention of unconscionable conduct': Spry (2014) 1; 'Equity . . . restrains injustice by stopping the unconscionable conduct of a particular person': Virgo (2018) 5.

[19] Treitel (2000) 3.

the law sanctions, and a remedy by which the interest is protected and the conduct sanctioned'.[20]

It may be that such propositions are, in effect, propositions about substantive law: their authors may assume that court rulings necessarily rubber-stamp substantive duties. However, this seems unlikely given that most authors distinguish rights and rulings in at least some contexts; for example, it is trite law that limitation periods extinguish the remedy (i.e. the ability to get a ruling), not the right. Similarly, most lawyers, judges, and scholars, at least in England, assume that contractual duties are duties to do what contracting parties promise to do, regardless of whether courts will specifically enforce such promises. In any event, for the moment it is sufficient to note that, while lawyers seem to assume a close relationship between substantive rights and rulings, the nature of that relationship is rarely spelled out. Textbooks on contracts and tort are replete with references to 'liabilities' to pay damages, but it is almost never said whether the liability in question is a liability to fall under a substantive duty to pay damages or merely a liability to the possibility of being ordered by a court to pay damages—or whether the difference even matters.

Briefly—a complete explanation is beyond this book's scope—it seems clear that a large part of the explanation for the importance of remedial law in how common law lawyers think about the broader private law is that private law was, and largely still is, developed in the context of litigation. This explanation has a short and a long version.

The short version is that rulings and rules about rulings are important in the common law because litigation is ultimately about rulings: claimants go to courts to obtain rulings. Of course, courts today typically discuss substantive law when reaching their decisions; indeed, sometimes they discuss little else. However, it is common for litigation to focus primarily, if not exclusively, on the appropriate judicial response to an admitted breach. Further, even where the primary issue before the court is a matter of substantive law—for example, where the issue is whether the defendant breached a contract—the court must always determine what ruling to issue in response to its resolution of the substantive issue. At the same time, the blurring of the distinction between rules that govern how individuals should treat one another (substantive law) and rules that govern what courts should do when individuals ask them for relief (remedial law) is consistent with this story because the distinction is rarely important in litigation. It is irrelevant to the outcome of litigation whether the court refuses to order specific performance of a personal service because there is no substantive duty to perform personal services or because, although there is a duty, the courts will only enforce it indirectly (by ordering damages). In either case, the result is an award of damages. More generally,

[20] Davies (2000) 408.

it is irrelevant whether claimants seeking rulings must establish a particular fact in order to show that their substantive rights were infringed or, instead, to show that, their rights having been breached, the ruling they seek is appropriate. In either case, the fact in question is just another element in the relevant cause of action. In short, the litigation context in which the common law developed helps to explain both why common law lawyers think rulings are important and why they frequently blur the distinction between remedial and substantive law.

The longer version of this explanation argues that the special, albeit uncertain, place of remedial law within the broader private law is a consequence of the close relationship between remedial and substantive law in the latter's development. For much of the common law's history, the very idea of substantive law—substantive in the sense of rules stipulating how individuals should treat each other—was absent. The first attempt to provide anything like a comprehensive account of the common law in terms of individuals' rights and duties vis-à-vis one another was Blackstone's *Commentaries*, written in 1765–69. For most of the common law's history, 'law' largely meant rules about getting rulings.[21]

Leaving aside the special case of rules governing title to property and status,[22] early English private law consisted primarily of three kinds of rules: (1) rules governing the mechanisms by which one might bring a dispute to trial; (2) rules governing the rulings litigants might obtain at trial; and (3) rules governing the conduct of trials.[23] The first category governed the complaints and requests that the courts would hear. In the Royal Courts, this category included the law governing writs, later augmented by rules governing jury directions.[24] Throughout most of the common law's history, individuals who wanted to bring an action in the courts had to obtain a writ from the Chancellor.[25] Writs came in a limited number

[21] 'The dichotomy [between substance and procedure] was fathered by Jeremy Bentham in a 1782 work entitled *Of Laws in General, sub nom* the distinction between substantive law and adjective law. Bentham there makes clear that he believes he is drawing a new distinction in the descriptive organization and analysis of the concept of law, and an examination of the leading pre-Bentham sources on English legal theory supports his claim': Risinger (1982) 191. See also Glenn (2014) 278, who argues that substantive law did not fully emerge until the nineteenth century.

[22] The substantive law governing property and status developed much earlier than the substantive law of obligations. Thus, it was possible to write a book on the substantive law of property in the fifteenth century: see Littleton's *Tenures* (first published 1481).

[23] Baker describes the twelfth-century textbook on the 'laws and customs of England', traditionally attributed to Glanville, as 'primarily about how to gain access to those courts [the Royal Courts] and what to do when there' (14), adding later that '[t]he forms of action were the first object of legal study. The two earliest treatises on the common law, *Glanville* and *Bracton*, were essentially books about writs and the procedures generated by them': Baker (2002) 56.

[24] We can tell a broadly similar story about the Chancery. Procedures in the Chancery were different—for example, the Chancery did not use the writ system—but the first rules developed by the Chancery concerned the kinds of rulings available from the Chancery and the procedures for obtaining them.

[25] A writ was essentially a letter to the sheriff commanding him to bring the defendant to court (which was sometimes conditional on the defendant not complying with a request, for example to vacate the claimant's land). Writs were not formally abolished until 1980, but most of the substantive restrictions on the kinds of writs available were eliminated in the nineteenth century: see Baker (2002) 68.

of standard forms, corresponding to specific complaints or demands, for example, a demand that the defendant give up possession of land to the claimant or a complaint that the defendant injured the claimant. The Chancellor sometimes created new writs, but there were always a limited number of writs corresponding to a limited number of officially recognized demands or complaints (never more than about sixty in total).

The second category of law was rules about the kinds of rulings that courts might award. The writ system, understood broadly, placed limits not just on the actions that courts were willing to hear but also on the relief that they were willing to give. For example, it was established relatively early on that writs were not available for parties who sought injunctive relief from the Royal Courts. The third and final category consisted of rules governing the procedures by which requests for rulings were expressed, argued, and decided. This category included the law governing pleading, evidence, and the various ways of reaching a final decision, such as trial by battle, oaths, or juries.

It was only relatively late in the common law's history that legal textbooks said much about rules governing how individuals should treat one another. For most of the common law's history, learning the law (which happened in apprenticeships, not universities) was primarily a matter of learning how to bring a dispute before the courts, how to present arguments in court, and what rulings courts were able to give. As mentioned earlier, the first serious attempt to explain the law in substantive terms was Blackstone's *Commentaries*, published at the end of the eighteenth century. The authors and judges responsible for developing the substantive law process did not purport to be creating new law. They presented the substantive law as implicit in the existing law, in particular as implicit in the first two categories of rules mentioned above. The process by which they made such implications appears, in broad outline anyway, to be relatively straightforward. If the Chancellor would issue writs compelling individuals who were alleged to have forcibly injured claimants to come to court, and if courts were willing to issue rulings requiring losing defendants in such cases to pay damages, one might surmise that there was a substantive duty not to forcibly injure others.[26] Similarly, if the Chancellor would issue writs requiring individuals to pay debts, and if courts were willing to issue rulings requiring losing defendants in such cases to pay their debts, one might surmise that there was a substantive duty to pay debts.[27] Admittedly, it is unlikely that

[26] Hence Lord Dunedin's classic statement '. . . the common law (though there is no harder lesson for the stranger jurist to learn) began with the remedy and ended with the right': *Nocton v Lord Ashburton* [1914] AC 932, 964. Dunedin understands 'remedy' in the traditional sense of a procedural route to get one's case before a jury: Glenn (2014) 242. And this procedural route (rather than procedure in the modern sense of rules of evidence, and so on) is what Henry Maine was referring to when he famously observed that, in the common law's early days, substance was 'secreted' in the 'interstices' of procedural law: Maine (1883) 389.

[27] These examples are not random. They illustrate what was for centuries the most basic division within what is now called private law—and one that assumes some importance in this book—namely,

common law lawyers understood the law in this way, at least originally. Lawyers no doubt thought it was wrong to injure others and that debts should be paid, but they would not have thought it was the law's business to tell individuals how to go about their day-to-day lives.[28] The law's business was to resolve disputes. Exactly how it first came to be thought that the law concerned itself with telling people how to lead their lives is not easy to explain. But once this step was taken, the process of deriving substantive rights from the rules governing writs and rulings would seem natural.

In practice, however, the process was far from straightforward. For much of the common law's history, there was not much law of any kind for scholars to work with. Writs often said little more than that the claimant had suffered an injury, was owed a debt, or had title to a particular plot of land. In many cases, even this limited information was unhelpful because of the widespread tolerance of fictional writs. For example, courts might allow claimants to plead that a blacksmith had intentionally injured their horse when the reality was that he had done a poor job shoeing the horse.[29] The rules governing the range of available rulings did not provide much more information. If a debt or a title to land was established, the court would rule that the debt must be paid or title respected, but like the writs, these rulings gave little clue as to the legal basis of the debt or title. Damages awards were available if the claimant proved a wrong, but juries determined the amount. The court's reasons might have provided more information, but they were often reported inaccurately. In any event, the reasons typically said little about the substance of the action because the court's role was not to decide the case but to control the procedure. In the beginning, success in getting one's complaint heard meant that one obtained a 'trial' by battle, ordeal, or oath taking. Juries gradually replaced these methods, and they no doubt had their reasons for their decisions, but those reasons were not announced, let alone recorded.

As the use of the relatively formless writ of trespass on the case became more common (beginning, but slowly, around the fifteenth century), and as courts began issuing ever more detailed instructions to juries, the law governing rulings filled out, providing a broader basis from which substantive rights might be derived. Yet no matter how detailed the law governing rulings eventually became, there remained two major obstacles to deriving substantive rights from this law. The first is that the rules about rulings often left it unclear whether a ruling was intended

the division between writs that complained of a wrong (*ostensuruas quare* writs) and writs that demanded compliance with a right (*praecipe* writs).

[28] 'In the fourteenth century there was no law of England, no body of rules complete in itself... There were justice and right, absolute values; but it was not yet the lawyer's business to comprehend them in the sense of knowing what was the just and right result upon these facts and those. His business was procedural, to see that disputes were properly submitted to the appropriate deciding mechanism': Milsom (1981) 83.

[29] See *De Rook v de Hauleye* (1352), discussed in Ibbetson (1999) 45.

to ensure that the defendant fulfilled a pre-existing duty. This uncertainty arose, for example, where the writ was in the form of a complaint that the defendant had wronged the claimant, say by injuring or defrauding him ('*ostensurus quare*' or 'trespass' writs). In cases involving such writs—from which most of the modern law of contract, tort, and, to a lesser extent, unjust enrichment originated—the ruling, if the claimant was successful, was a Judgment to pay damages. Where the court issued such a ruling, it might be presumed that the defendant had a substantive duty not to do the thing that amounted to the wrong. However, it was unclear whether the defendant should also be presumed to have had a substantive duty to pay damages following the wrong's commission. The existence of such a duty, which the civil law has long recognized explicitly, is consistent with the practice of issuing damages awards. However, this practice is also consistent with the contrary view that the duty to pay damages is remedial; in other words, with the view that a damages award creates, rather than confirms, a duty.

The same difficulty could arise in cases where the ruling appeared to affirm the very right demanded by the claimant ('*praecipe*' writs). Suppose that the claimant's writ demanded that the defendant pay a debt, and suppose further that in the ensuing litigation the court awarded the claimant a Judgment for the claimed debt. It might be presumed in such a case that the court's ruling replicated an existing substantive duty. But this presumption could not always be made. As already mentioned, many writs were outright fictions. Because of the limited number of writs, and because of procedural difficulties associated with certain writs, courts frequently allowed claimants to squeeze their demand or complaint into a writ that, on the surface, it plainly did not fit. To take just one example, claims for the return of money paid by mistake or under compulsion were often framed as claims for failing to perform a promise to pay a debt.[30] It may well have been the case that the rulings in such cases replicated existing duties to return the money, even if those duties were admittedly not duties to perform a promise. However, it is also possible (as I argue in Chapter 8) that the defendant had no duty of any kind prior to the ruling. Once it is admitted that a writ's factual basis may be a fiction, the only thing that can be said with certainty about the rulings given in response to this writ is that they will be given on proof of certain facts. Those facts might establish an existing duty, but they might equally establish nothing more than the appropriateness of creating a new duty by issuing a ruling.

The second difficulty is that even when it is clear that the availability of a particular writ and the associated ruling implicitly recognizes a particular substantive right (e.g. a substantive right to payment of a debt or damages), the circumstances in which that right arises (or disappears) cannot typically be fully specified. Consider again the example of a writ demanding that the defendant pay a debt.

30 See Baker (2002) 370–1.

From this writ's availability, one might surmise a substantive duty to pay debts. However, suppose, as eventually happened (following legislation), that courts would not issue rulings to pay debts in cases where the debt was due more than six years earlier. From this rule, one might conclude that the substantive duty to pay the debt expires after six years. However, the rule is equally consistent with the conclusion (which the law adopted) that the passage of time only extinguished the court's willingness to assist the claimant; in other words, that the substantive duty lives on. Similar questions arise in respect of the Chancery's practices. Consider, for example, the rule that the Chancery would not order specific performance of a contract if damages awards were adequate. From this rule, one might argue that there is no duty to perform a contractual undertaking except where damages awards are inadequate. Oliver Wendell Holmes, amongst others, made this argument.[31] However, one might equally suppose (as most lawyers do) that this rule is merely about the availability of remedies, and therefore that it tells us nothing about the parties' substantive duties. The general lesson to take from these examples is that it is often not obvious whether the facts that must be proven to obtain a particular ruling go towards establishing that the defendant had a substantive duty to do what the ruling requires or, instead, merely establish the appropriateness of issuing that ruling—or some combination of the two.

A possible response to these observations is that it is easier to derive substantive rights from rulings than my examples suggest because substantive rights are conceptually linked to rulings. In particular, it might be argued that rulings necessarily replicate substantive duties and, further, that courts must always issue rulings on proof that a substantive duty has not been fulfilled. If this view is accepted, then the process of deriving substantive law from rulings law—and vice versa—is straightforward. Much of the remainder of this book is devoted to explaining why this view is mistaken. However, for the moment I merely note that there is no evidence that such a view was accepted, let alone uniformly adopted, by the judges, lawyers, and scholars who developed the common law's understanding of substantive rights. For example, judges, lawyers, and scholars have long assumed that limitation periods extinguish remedies, not rights (and thus they have assumed a substantive duty to pay a debt even where the limitation period has expired). Similarly, they have long assumed that contractual duties are duties to do what contracting parties promise to do, even if courts will not order them to do these things. Neither of these assumptions would be widespread if our notion of substantive rights assumed that rulings necessarily replicate rights, and vice versa.

Against this background, it might be asked how the substantive law was developed in those cases where the existing law—the remedial law—allowed for more than one interpretation of the substantive law. To begin, it should not be assumed

[31] Holmes (1897) 462.

that the common law has actually developed a substantive law, or at least not a fully formed substantive law. Even today, it is normal for lawyers to describe the common law partly or wholly in terms of 'causes of action' rather than substantive rights. Closely related to this language is the practice of describing the law in terms of the 'liabilities' that it imposes. As I have noted before, courts and commentators regularly describe the rules governing damages awards as imposing liabilities to pay damages. These descriptions typically do not say whether this liability is a liability to fall under a substantive duty to pay damages or, instead, a liability to a court order to pay damages. We can read such statements either as propositions about substantive law or as propositions about rulings law.

However, to the extent that the common law has developed a concept of substantive law, the judges, lawyers, and scholars who brought about this concept filled the gaps in the above picture in the only way they could—by relying on external sources. They drew on philosophical concepts, religious ideas, civil law learning, legal theories, and common-sense morality, to name but a few.[32] Of course, the difficulty with external sources is that writers disagree about which ones to use and about their content. Such disagreements help to explain why even today we can find radically different views about the existence and content of the common law's substantive rights and duties. As mentioned above, most lawyers, or at least most English lawyers, would say that contracting parties have substantive duties to perform their contractual promises. Yet Oliver Wendell Holmes—a well-known jurist and judge—famously argued that a contractual duty is merely a disjunctive duty to perform or pay damages. Such divergent views regarding the nature of a contractual obligation are possible because each is broadly consistent with the common law rules governing relief for breach of contract.

In summary, remedial law has had a prominent, but complex, role in the common law's history. As the main form of early law, remedial law was the foundation on which substantive private law was built. However, that foundation was unstable because it is rarely possible to derive substantive rights directly from remedies. In most cases, the rules regarding the availability and content of particular remedies are consistent with more than one interpretation of our substantive rights and duties.

C. Looking Forward

The fact that remedial law developed prior to substantive law, and that it originated in a bifurcated system, has profoundly influenced how contemporary common law lawyers think about private law. It explains why writers continue to organize and

[32] Once the process of identifying substantive rights began, it could build upon itself; that is, once some substantive rights were recognized, other rights could be recognized by analogy.

explain remedial law in largely historical terms, and why they rarely distinguish remedial law clearly from substantive law. However, the question for this book is whether we should rest content with this historical legacy. The answer, as I have already suggested, is that we should not. Thus, I argue, in Chapters 3 and 9, that the historical distinction between Legal and Equitable Remedies should largely be ignored when organizing and explaining contemporary remedial law. These chapters firmly support the 'institutional' explanation of the emergence of specific relief. In addition, I argue throughout this book that it is crucial to distinguish between remedial and substantive law and, in particular, that it is important to be clear about the different ways that remedies are related to substantive rights. In short, I will argue that the main lesson to take from this chapter is that the peculiar history of remedies in the common law has impeded our understanding of their contemporary role and importance.

3
Form, Creation, Legal Effects

The core subject matter of the law of private law remedies is judicial rulings that require defendants to do or not do something ('directive rulings' or 'orders'). Yet while remedies textbooks invariably discuss the rules governing the availability and content of orders, they rarely examine the legal aspects of orders themselves. This chapter discusses these aspects. It has two main aims. First, it provides an overview of the law governing the form, creation, and legal effects of private law orders. Although this book is not a textbook, many of its arguments turn on specific ways that courts express, create, and give legal effect to orders. Some of these ways may be unfamiliar. A court's reasons normally indicate whether and what kind of order will be issued, but they do not include orders themselves (and orders are not otherwise published in the law reports). Most law students never see the wording of a private law order. Even textbooks on remedies rarely discuss the form, creation, or legal effects of orders.[1] Procedure courses sometimes explore the means of enforcing orders, but for the most part enforcement is something that lawyers learn about on the job.

The chapter's second aim is to explain the above law, in particular to explain why the relevant rules should be understood as part of the 'general law' of private law rulings. In substance, this explanation is a sustained critique of the traditional approach of organizing and explaining these rules according to their historical origins, that is, according to whether they originated in the Royal Courts or the Chancery Court. I argue that the rules discussed in this chapter reflect general remedial-law principles, principles that could have easily developed in a unitary legal system.

Taken together, these aims are an important part of this book's broader project of taking seriously the idea of remedies as a legal subject. If remedies are judicial orders, then the rules governing their form, creation, and effects are an important part of remedial law. And if remedial law merits its title, those rules ought to have common foundations.

A. Form

As understood in this book, private law orders are judicial pronouncements that direct defendants to do or not to do something, and that are issued,

[1] A notable exception is Zakrzewski (2005), upon which this chapter draws heavily. I also draw heavily on two civil procedure texts: Zuckerman (2013) ch 23 and Kay, Sime & French (2018) chs 63, 79.

Rights, Wrongs, and Injustices. Stephen A. Smith, Oxford University Press (2019). © Stephen A. Smith.
DOI: 10.1093/oso/9780199229772.003.0003

typically together with reasons, as part of the resolution of a private law dispute.[2] Statistically, the most common private law orders are for payments of a specified sum of money, typically a sum due under a contract.[3] Other common examples are orders to give up possession of land, to perform a contract, or to refrain from a tortious activity.[4]

There are prescribed forms for orders,[5] although these may be varied as circumstances require.[6] The typical language used in the operative parts of the orders mentioned above is as follows:

1. An order to pay money:
   'It is ordered that the defendant: pay the claimant the sum of £ . . .'[7]
2. An order for the recovery of land:
   '[T]he Court orders that: the defendant give the claimant the possession of . . . on or before . . . '[8]
3. An order to perform a contract ('specific performance'):
   'It Is Ordered That the contract dated . . . referred to in the Particulars of Claim . . . be specifically performed.'[9]
4. An order to refrain from an activity ('injunction'):
   'The Court ordered that [the defendant] is forbidden to . . . '[10]

[2] In rare cases, orders may be issued by court officers on application from the claimant (e.g. where the defendant has admitted liability to pay a sum of money or failed to provide a defence: *CPR* 14.1, 14.4, 14.5, 14.6, 14.7, 14.9).

[3] In 2016, there were 1,802,248 claims before the county and magistrates' courts in England and Wales, of which 1,374,039 were for specified sums: see *Civil Justice Statistics Tables: October to December 2016:* https://data.gov.uk/dataset/163c7366-0988-44f8-9803-6d3124311716/civil-justice-statistics.

[4] For a comprehensive listing of orders currently issued by English courts, see Atkins (2019).

[5] These forms are set out in the *CPR* PD 4, and in Atkins (2019).

[6] 'A form may be varied by the court or a party if the variation is required by the circumstances of a particular case': *CPR* 4(2).

[7] See e.g. Forms No 45, No 46 which *CPR* PD 40B, 14.1 refers to as general forms of a trial judgment. The standard wording is slightly different in the Queen's Bench ('It is this day adjudged that the Defendant do pay the Claimant £ . . . ') and in the Chancery Division ('It is ordered that the Defendant do pay the Claimant the sum of £ . . . '): Atkins (2014), Vol 23(2) [454]. In the case where the sum is ordered as damages, this fact may be mentioned in the order; and in the case of damages for personal injuries, the order must specify the amounts attached to different categories of damages, for example, pain and suffering or future loss. Examples of the formulae adopted for all the orders discussed in this work can be found in Zakrzewski (2005) 106, 107, 113, 115, 116, 122, 134, 135, 143, 147–9, 154, 158, 159, 167, 183, 185, 190, 197, 201, 208, 209, 213. The wording used prior to the introduction of the *CPR* in 1998 is discussed below.

[8] *CPR* PD 4, Form N26, Table 1. This form is used where the claimant seeks possession from a known defendant who initially acquired possession lawfully. In other cases, such an order is, uniquely, directed to persons unknown: '(Enter name of Judge) ordered that the applicant do recover possession of the land mentioned in the originating application and interim possession order in this matter, namely (description of premises)': *CPR* PD 4, Table 3, Form N136 (Possession Order).

[9] Atkins (2015) Vol 37 (1) [159].

[10] *CPR* PD 4, Table 3, Form N138 (Injunction Order): Atkins (2016) Vols 23 (1) [60].

It is common to describe orders in terms that indicate the legal nature of the stipulated act: thus, authors (including myself) frequently refer to orders to 'pay damages', 'pay a debt', 'cease a trespass', or 'perform a contract'. However, as the above examples indicate, orders themselves typically do not come with such labels, or otherwise indicate the legal nature of the stipulated act. The wording of a monetary order does not say if the sum is meant to represent damages, a sum due under a contract, restitution, or something else. Similarly, an order to refrain from an action (a 'prohibitory injunction') typically does not indicate if the prohibition is meant to give effect to a contract or to prevent a tort—and if the latter, what kind of tort. An order to perform a contract ('specific performance') is an exception, though courts could write such orders without mentioning the contract; for example, an order to perform a contractual duty to deliver specified goods could simply order that the specified goods be transferred (in which case the order would be described as a 'mandatory injunction').

Aside from operative words of the kind described above, the only formal requirement for a valid private law order is that in the case of orders to perform positive, non-monetary acts the court must specify a date by which the act must be performed.[11] Monetary orders need not specify a date, but the law implies a default period of fourteen days.[12] By contrast, in the case of negative ('prohibitory') orders, the order is effective immediately unless a date is stipulated. In practice, non-monetary orders typically include a 'penal notice' informing defendants that they may be imprisoned or fined if they do not comply.[13] Although not strictly required, a penal notice is necessary if a subsequent court wishes to imprison or fine the defendant for failing to perform the order.[14] A subsequent court may also refuse to commit, fine, or otherwise enforce an order if its directions are vague or ambiguous. Courts therefore seek to frame orders in precise terms, and sometimes refuse to issue an order on the ground that they cannot frame it in sufficiently precise terms.

The operative part of many orders, in particular monetary orders, may be no more than a few words in length, but there is no limit to the number or complexity of their terms. In practice, courts usually specify complex directions by incorporation via a

[11] *CPR* PD 40B, 8.1. Orders must also indicate the date, judicial title of the person who issued them, and they must be sealed: *CPR* 40.2. In practice, orders will include, inter alia, the parties' name and a brief mention of the evidence.

[12] *CPR* 40.11. In the case of monetary orders consequent to a default judgment or upon an admission, payment is due immediately in the absence of a specified time; *CPR* 12.5(2); *CPR* 14.5(9).

[13] *CPR* PD 40B, 9.1. The Practice Direction specifies the wording: 'If you the within-named [] do not comply with this order you may be held to be in contempt of court and imprisoned or fined, or [in the case of a company or corporation] your assets may be seized'.

[14] If the notice is missing, a court can issue a new order that includes a notice, which can then be enforced in the ordinary way.

'Tomlin' order, in which they stay the proceedings on agreed terms that are set out in a schedule.[15]

i. No Distinction in the Form of Legal and Equitable Rulings

From an historical perspective (and from the perspective of other common law jurisdictions), the most striking feature of the form of the rulings examined in this book is that it is uniform. In England today, all rulings that contemplate a future state of affairs ('directive rulings') are expressed as 'orders'. Until recently (and still today in other common law jurisdictions), directive rulings appeared in two different forms, and the difference between these forms was thought by many writers—and is still thought by many writers today—to reflect a fundamental difference in the nature of the relevant rulings.

As we saw in Chapter 2, directive rulings that originated in the English Chancery Court ('Chancery'), such as injunctions and specific performance, were traditionally expressed as personal orders ('Equitable Orders') commanding the defendant to do or not to do a certain act: 'It is this day adjudged and ordered that the defendant John Jones, before 1 o'clock in the afternoon of Jan 1, 2015, pull down and remove the structure located . . . '.[16] By contrast, directive rulings that originated in the Royal Courts, such as rulings to pay damages, a sum due under a contract, or to recover land,[17] were traditionally expressed as impersonal pronouncements ('Judgments at Law') that a certain state of affairs 'shall happen'. Typically, this meaning was expressed by stating the claimant 'shall recover' money or property: 'It is this day adjudged that the claimant shall recover £100 from the defendant.'[18]

This difference in the form of directive rulings continued after the nineteenth-century merger of the Chancery and the Royal Courts, ending only with the passing of the *Civil Procedure Act* 1998. Today, courts in England express all directive rulings as orders: an award of damages literally orders the defendant to pay a sum of money. Nonetheless, for many authors the distinction between Equitable Orders (hereafter 'Orders') and Judgments at Law (hereafter 'Judgments') remains fundamental to understanding the nature of remedial rulings, even in jurisdictions

[15] See Zuckerman (2013) 1083–4; *White Book* (2006) 40.6.2. Because the agreed terms are not part of the order, strictly defined, they can only be enforced if a court subsequently orders their performance (which courts will do if the terms are not fulfilled). Strictly interpreted, a Tomlin order is closer to a declaration than a private law order.

[16] Chitty & Jacob (1965) No 1350 (Judgement or Order for Injunction at Trial).

[17] Many orders that would today be described as 'restitutionary' (e.g. a ruling requiring the payment of money transferred by mistake) also originated in the Royal Courts. The form and content of these awards is the same as that of awards to pay a sum due under a contract; indeed, though the practice has changed, many restitutionary awards were traditionally described as awards for a sum due under a contract.

[18] Chitty & Jacob (1965) 'Forms' (n 5) at No 688 ('Judgement for Claimant for Debt or Damages and Costs after Trial by Judge Alone').

where the distinction is abolished.[19] Two propositions are usually advanced in support of this view. The first, which I discuss (and reject) later in this chapter, is that the difference in the forms of Orders and Judgments explains important differences in their legal effects and modes of enforcement. The other proposition, which I discuss immediately below, is that this difference reflects a fundamental difference in the relationship of Orders and Judgments to the substantive law.[20]

According to what I will describe as the 'formal-separation thesis,' a Judgment was a declaration or statement of the litigants' legal situation. In this view, a Judgment that the claimant 'shall recover £100 from the defendant' was fundamentally a judicial declaration that, as a matter of law, the defendant owes the claimant £100. By contrast, an Order requiring that the defendant 'deliver the cow Charlie to the claimant' said nothing, in this view, about the parties' legal rights and duties. The Order was simply an expression of the Chancellor's (or his contemporary representative's) view that the defendant ought, as a matter of morality (or 'conscience'), deliver the cow to the claimant. According to the formal-separation thesis, an Order was fundamentally an act of the executive, which left the parties' legal relationship unaffected. In its extreme version, the thesis supposes that Orders had nothing to do with the 'law',[21] strictly defined.[22]

The suggestion that Orders were fundamentally non-legal fits neatly with a common understanding of the Chancery's historical evolution. In this understanding, the Chancery issued Orders (not Judgments) to ensure that its rulings did not conflict with the Judgments issued by the Royal Courts. However, as an explanation of the contemporary law, the formal-separation thesis is vulnerable to two serious objections. The first, which strictly speaking applies only to England, is the already mentioned fact that contemporary English courts express all directive rulings as orders. If expressing a ruling in the form of an order indicates that the ruling has nothing to do with the law, then rulings to pay damages, a sum due under a contract, or recover land—each of which originated in the Royal Courts—have nothing to do with the law in England today. This objection cannot be avoided on the ground that the described

[19] See e.g. Spry (2014) 27–37, 333; Dobbs (2018) 5–6, 12–13, 61–3.

[20] See e.g. Spry (2014) 27–37, 333; Dobbs (2018) 5–6, 12–13, 61–3. I discuss the historical background to this view in more detail in Chapter 2.

[21] The reference here is to 'law' (not Law) because in the view under consideration the Chancery did not merely try to avoid rulings that conflicted with those available from the Royal Courts; they did not concern themselves with law at all in the contemporary sense of this word. However, I place quotation marks around this usage because it sounds strange, today, to say that the rulings from the Chancery had nothing to do with law. These rulings (or their descendants) are taught in common law faculties everywhere.

[22] See Dobbs (2018) 62–3 ('The difference between the Judgment at law, which declared rights in things—*in rem*—and the decree in equity which commanded the defendant's conscience to act—*in personam*—was thus a very considerable one. The chancellors used it constantly to explain why they could be apparently contradictory systems at work on English soil, yielding different results: one was law, the other was merely a personal matter').

change is merely formal since the formal-separation thesis is based on differences in the form of rulings.

At present, England is the only common law jurisdiction to adopt a uniform terminology for directive rulings. However, the significance of the English reforms extends beyond their strictly legal effects. With little fuss or fanfare, England overturned a distinction that, if the thesis were correct, lay at the common law's core. Contrary to what the thesis might have predicted, the adoption of a personal form for all directive rulings appears to have been regarded merely as part of a general cleaning-up of archaic language.[23]

This observation leads to the second objection to the formal-separation thesis: the traditional difference in the form of Judgments and Orders can be explained without adopting the formal-separation thesis or any similar thesis. The states of affairs contemplated by Judgments and Orders were, in each case, states of affairs that ordinary legal rules—the law developed by the Royal Courts—assumed were legally required. Both an Order to deliver goods due under a contract and a Judgment stipulating that a sum of money due under a contract shall be recovered contemplated the satisfaction of an ordinary contractual duty—a duty first recognized in the Royal Courts. A claimant who obtained an Order 'not to trespass' and, at the same time, a Judgment for damages for losses arising from past trespasses, received the latter because the defendant did the very thing that the Order forbade. It is true that Orders, unlike Judgments, could be issued before a breach had occurred ('*quia timet*' Orders), but the states of affairs that such Orders contemplated—for example, not trespassing or causing a nuisance—were still legally required.[24] The actions required by an Order not to trespass were the same regardless of whether the defendant trespassed in the past: in each case, the required action was 'not trespassing'. The suggestion that Orders were somehow outside of the law or that they did not deal with the law must therefore be rejected: the states of affairs contemplated by Orders had the same relationship to the substantive law as those contemplated by Judgments.

It is true that the states of affair contemplated by Orders differed from those contemplated by Judgments in one important respect. They differed in the means by which they could be realized if defendants failed to bring them about. In principle, legal officials could bring about the states of affairs contemplated by Judgments without the defendant's participation. For example, execution against the defendant's assets could achieve the transfer of money contemplated by a Judgment to pay a debt or damages. By seizing the defendant's property, selling it, and then transferring the appropriate sum to the claimant, a third party (or even

[23] The main evidence in support of this conclusion is the absence of evidence for the contrary view. As far as I am aware, the change has not been discussed in legal journals. More generally, scholars and lawyers seem unaware of the change.

[24] I discuss some exceptions in Chapter 7.

the claimant) could bring about the result contemplated by a monetary Judgment. Similarly, the state of affairs contemplated by a Judgment for the recovery of land could be brought about by the claimant taking possession. In either case, the defendant might obstruct the attempt to bring about the desired result. And in the case of a monetary Judgment, the defendant might lack the assets needed to satisfy the Judgment. However, in principle the states of affairs contemplated by Judgments could be brought about without the defendant's participation.

This feature of the states of affairs contemplated by Judgments explains the traditional difference in the forms of Judgments and Orders.[25] Judicial pronouncements stating that claimants 'shall recover' money or land were a natural (albeit linguistically awkward) way to make clear that it is not strictly necessary that the defendants themselves hand over the relevant money or land. Admittedly, if it were important that defendants should personally bring about the states of affairs contemplated by Judgments, this locution would require further explanation. However, there is no evidence that such a principle existed. Nor is there any reason that it should have existed. Defendants who fail to pay debts, commit wrongs, or take possession of another's land, have by definition failed to follow the guidance provided by the substantive law. The question for a court contemplating a ruling in such cases is how to bring about the desired state of affairs. In cases where that state of affairs can be brought about by either the defendant or a third party, a judicial ruling declaring that this state of affairs 'shall happen' makes clear that either method is acceptable.

In contrast, third parties usually could not bring about the states of affairs contemplated by Orders, or at least not easily. Short of throwing defendants in jail, the only way to stop defendants from trespassing, causing nuisances, or breaching restrictive covenants is for the defendants themselves to decide not to trespass, commit a nuisance, and so forth. Similarly, an Order to convey title to land could not be fulfilled unless the defendant decided to sign the necessary documents. The states of affairs contemplated by Orders to tear down buildings or deliver specific goods could in theory be brought about by third parties, but not easily and not without the risk of violence. Courts seeking to bring about the states of affairs contemplated by traditional Orders therefore had an obvious reason to seek the defendant's assistance. And the obvious way to try to obtain this assistance was to command the defendant personally to bring about the desired state of affairs.

The conclusion suggested by these observations is that the distinction between Judgments and Orders should not be seen as a distinction between rulings that stipulate what the law requires and rulings that stipulate what equity requires.

[25] The explanation that follows applies exclusively to the Orders that are this book's focus, that is, Orders made in Equityfours 'auxillary' jurisdiction, such as specific performance orders and injunctions prohibiting torts. It does not apply to Orders made in Equity's 'exclusive' jurisdiction, such as orders for the enforcement of trusts and orders for equitable compensation.

Rather, it is a distinction between rulings stipulating states of affairs that can be brought about or 'executed' by third parties ('executable rulings') and rulings stipulating states of affairs than cannot be so executed ('non-executable rulings'). Naturally, some rulings lie on the borderline. Examples include rulings contemplating the tearing down of a building or contemplating the transfer of specific goods in the defendant's possession. As noted, third parties can achieve the states of affairs contemplated by such rulings in principle, but for practical reasons it is generally preferable for the defendant to bring them about. In such cases, current English law generally provides that courts should in the first instance order defendants to bring about the desired state of affairs, but it also gives claimants the option of enforcing the order by third-party execution.[26]

Admittedly, some Orders that fall within this book's scope cannot be explained in this way. One example is an Order directing a purchaser to pay the price in a contract for the sale of land.[27] There does not appear to be any reason for a court seeking a monetary—and so executable—result to employ an Order in preference to a Judgment.[28] However, in general the distinction between executable and non-executable rulings lines up with the traditional distinction between Judgments and Orders. In legal systems that continue to employ both Judgments and Orders, courts generally use Judgments to stipulate executable state of affairs, while they generally use Orders to stipulate non-executable state of affairs. It is not necessary to assume that Judgments and Orders have different relationships to the substantive law to understand this distinction.

The way that the English reforms described earlier were introduced and received further supports the above explanation. As we have seen, the explanation supposes that the difference in form between Orders and Judgments was largely a matter of administrative convenience. Judgments and Orders are alternative routes to the same result, and it is that result—for example, the payment of a sum of money—that matters, not how courts bring it about. Seen in this light, the English reforms reflect nothing more than the mundane decision that even in cases where it is not strictly necessary for the defendant to personally bring about the desired result, it is generally preferable if the defendant does so (if for no other reason than to avoid involving third parties), and therefore that this preference should be made explicit. Admittedly, there will be cases where it is clear that the defendant is unlikely to

[26] See *CPR* Sch 1 RSC Ord 45, r 4(1), 5, 8.

[27] See *Johnson v Agnew* [1980] AC 367. The explanation (not justification) for such Orders appears to have been the idea that it would be inequitable if only one contracting party's obligations were specifically enforceable ('positive mutuality'). While there might have been some practical justification for mutuality of specific performance in these particular circumstances and in the time prior to the Judicature Acts (see Berryman (2013) 186), the idea has never been applied widely and is today largely discredited: Berryman (2013) 235–39; Burrows (2004) 459.

[28] The explanation appears to be historical, namely, that an action for the price in a contract for the sale of goods or land could not generally be brought until title had passed; see Peel (2015) 1223–4. As I explain below, today such a ruling can be enforced by execution against property.

comply with an order to bring about an executable state of affairs, and thus where issuing such an order would have little point; but in such cases judges can set a short time period for compliance. Under the old system, judges dealt with the parallel situation (cases where Judgments were issued notwithstanding that the defendant was willing to bring about the result voluntarily) by restraining third-party execution until the defendant had time to act. The main advantage of the contemporary English system is uniformity and simplicity of expression. It is not surprising, then, to find that the English changes attracted almost no attention: far from disrupting the common law's foundations, they were a matter of housekeeping.

These observations are not meant to deny that the traditional distinction between Orders and Judgments arose in a dual system and that at least part of the reason it arose was to avoid a conflict between those systems. The fact that the Chancery issued Orders, not Judgments, is an important part of English legal history. But whatever the distinction's historical genesis, its contemporary significance is best understood in non-historical terms. Impersonal directives—Judgments—are a natural (though not inevitable) way to try to bring about states of affairs that do not require the defendant's participation. Personal directives—Orders—are a natural way to try to bring about states of affairs that require the defendant's involvement. Both forms could easily have arisen in a unitary legal system.

B. Creation

The creation of private law orders is usually a simple and informal process. This informality may be surprising given that the main purpose of most litigation is to obtain a ruling. However, it is consistent with the general role of judicial orders. In most cases, orders are means to the ends that they contemplate. If those ends could be otherwise achieved (e.g. by a judge physically removing money from a defendant's pockets), orders would be unnecessary. This understanding of the role of court orders is defended in Chapter 5. However, I have already provided one piece of supporting evidence. The fact that the recent transformation in England of 'Judgments' into orders passed with little notice suggests that courts and commentators view both Judgments and orders as means of bringing about legally desired states of affairs. Whether it is the claimant, the sheriff, or someone else who undertakes the required action is primarily a matter of practical convenience. For similar reasons, it does not particularly matter that (as will be discussed) orders are not published or that they are sometimes drawn up by the parties themselves.

The final disposition of a lawsuit may consist of nothing more than an order (or a dismissal or other ruling), although judges normally provide reasons, which are usually published in law reports. The way that courts make and record orders varies slightly between courts, but in general judges write orders after their reasons and they record them on a separate document that is sealed and filed with court officials. It is not uncommon for one or both of the litigating parties to assist in drafting the order or to actually draft it (especially where it involves complex directions, as in the case of the agreed terms in a Tomlin order), subject in the latter case to confirmation by the court.[29] An order may also leave certain matters to be determined by a master or district judge; for example, an order for damages may be for an unspecified amount, simply stating 'damages and interest to be assessed'.[30] The order is not reproduced in the published law reports, though its basic terms will be clear from the reported reasons. For example, the reasons might conclude by stating 'Judgment for claimant against first defendant in sum of £15,464,106 plus costs',[31] or, where the reasons already mention the relevant sum, they may simply end by saying 'Judgment for the claimant'. Filed orders are available to the parties, though if the court has prepared the order it will normally have sent the parties copies.

C. Legal Effects

The legal effects of private law orders consist primarily in the rights that they create, eliminate, or otherwise affect. As I explain in more detail in Chapter 4, these rights fall into four categories: substantive rights, action rights, court-ordered rights, and enforcement rights. For this chapter's purposes, it is sufficient to define these categories briefly, focusing on how they differ from one another. These differences reflect distinctions regularly made or assumed by lawyers and judges: they should be familiar, therefore, even to readers who query their existence (including readers who believe that all legal rights are ultimately enforcement rights).

A substantive right, as understood in this book, is a right held by individuals (or other legal persons) that other individuals do, or not do, certain things. Substantive rights arise because the right-holder resides in the jurisdiction (e.g. as in the case of my right not to be assaulted) or because of the occurrence of an event other than a judicial ruling (e.g. as in the case where I enter a valid contract). If I have entered a valid contract to deliver goods to you, then you have a substantive right that the goods be delivered and I have a substantive duty to deliver the goods. To say that I have a 'duty' to deliver the goods is just to say that, as a matter of law, I ought to deliver them. And to say that you have a right to the goods is to say that you can legitimately demand that I make the delivery and also, exceptional cases aside, that you can waive my duty to deliver.

[29] 'I am grateful to both counsel for their clear and efficient exposition of their cases. I invite them to draft an order to give effect to these conclusions': *Nationwide Building Society v Dunlop Haywards Ltd* [2010] 1 WLR 258 [84]. This practice, which is authorized by *CPR* 40.3, varies slightly depending on the court: see Blackstone (1979) 749.

[30] O'Hare & Browne (2017) 283.

[31] *Nationwide Building Society v Dunlop Haywards Ltd* [2010] 1 WLR 258 [84].

An action right is a right to a legal ruling. Individuals obtain action rights if they initiate litigation and satisfy the cause of action for the rulings they seek. If I prove in court that I delivered goods to you under a valid contract and that you failed to pay the contractual price, then I will normally obtain a right—an action right—to a ruling requiring you to pay me the money. Action rights are therefore rights that individuals hold against courts. The court's duty is to issue the appropriate ruling. Action rights are distinct from the legal powers to obtain such rights. Although lawyers sometimes say that the victim of a contractual breach has a right to damages, until the breach is established in court the victim only has a legal power to obtain a right to an order that the defendant pay damages.

Court-ordered rights are the rights that arise from court orders. If a court orders you to pay me a sum of money, then you have a duty, born of the order, to pay me the sum of money. Importantly, your duty to comply with the order is owed to the court, not to me: duties to follow orders are owed to those who issue the orders.

Finally, enforcement rights are rights that orders be enforced by the state or that they be enforced with the state's assistance or at least authorization. Typical methods of enforcement include seizing and selling the defendant's goods or imprisoning the defendant. Enforcement rights typically arise if an order remains unfulfilled and the claimant has taken certain procedural steps, such as requesting a legal officer to enforce the ruling. Again, an enforcement right is distinct from a legal power to obtain such a right. Your failure to comply with an order directing you to pay me a sum of money, does not strictly lead to me obtaining a right that the order be enforced. Rather, it leads to me obtaining a power to acquire such a right. The right itself arises only after I have made an application for enforcement and satisfied the requirements of that application.

The legal effects of court orders are conveniently explained by considering the relationship between orders and the four categories of rights described above.

i. Court-Ordered Rights

Court orders impose legal duties on defendants to perform the acts that they command. In the same way that individuals have legal duties to comply with validly issued commands of traffic wardens or police officers, individuals have legal duties to comply with validly issued judicial orders. And as I explain in Chapter 4, because this duty is born of the order, it is owed to the court, not the claimant. This feature of orders explains why litigants who wish to have an order varied or waived must seek permission from a court.[32]

The creation of court-ordered duties is the most important legal consequence of court orders: from a strictly legal perspective, creating this duty is the reason that court orders are made. Of course, many defendants comply with orders only

[32] *Austins of East Ham Ltd v Macey* [1941] Ch 338.

because they fear the consequences that may befall them if they do not comply. Still, what is distinctive, legally, about orders is that they create a duty to do what the order requires. If courts issued orders merely to threaten defendants, orders would be in the form of threats (and if they were issued to facilitate enforcement, they would be in the form of orders to legal officials). However, there is little more that can be said here about the nature or justification of court-ordered duties without entering into the classificatory and philosophical debates that are the focus of Chapters 4 and 5. For the moment, it is sufficient to note that court orders impose legal duties to perform the actions that they require.

ii. Substantive Rights and Action Rights

Claimants who obtain orders typically focus their subsequent attention on the rights born of those orders and the means by which they can enforce them. However, in some cases claimants may wish to reassert in a court the same substantive rights that they earlier asserted to obtain the original order. For example, in cases where a defendant does not comply with an injunction to refrain from committing a nuisance, the plaintiff may wish to bring an action for damages with respect to losses suffered subsequent to the injunction. The common law allows such actions in most—but not all—cases. Explaining when the common law allows such actions and, more importantly, why it allows them is complex. The main source of this complexity is that the rules in this area have traditionally been explained in terms of the now largely obsolete (or so I argue) distinction between Equitable Orders ('Orders') and Legal Judgments ('Judgments').

Imagine that you fail to pay me a sum of money due under a valid contract. Assuming that I have not terminated the contract,[33] you remain under a legal duty (a 'substantive' duty) to pay me the sum you owe me and I have a legal right (a 'substantive' right), correlative to your duty, to the payment of the sum. The duty and correlative right exist because the common law contains a substantive rule to the effect that 'everyone has a duty to perform their contracts' and because you entered, and thus far failed to fulfil one of your obligations under, a still valid contract. It is trite law that if I sue you for the money owed, and the court agrees to order you to pay me the owed money, that I cannot sue you again for the same debt. The principle of *res judicata* means that my right to bring an action—my 'action right'—disappears with the ruling.[34] If I wish to reassert the same rights, my only option is to appeal the ruling.[35] But suppose that having obtained a ruling in

[33] The victim of a serious breach of contract generally has the option to terminate the contract, and thereby to terminate the other party's unfulfilled obligation (while leaving untouched the victim's power to obtain damages); however, it is rare that this option is taken up with respect to monetary obligations.

[34] See Zuckerman (2013) 1246–52.

[35] A mistake in the expression of an order may be corrected without a new hearing. Orders obtained by fraud may also be set aside: Zuckerman (2013) 1067–80.

my favour, I do not receive the payment by the date specified in the ruling. This result may arise if you refuse to pay and if it not possible to execute the ruling immediately on non-payment, for example by seizing and selling your property. In these circumstances, it may be asked whether I can bring an action to recover damages with respect to losses that I suffered as result of the post-ruling delay in payment (such as a loss arising because I was forced to borrow money at a high rate in the interim[36]). More specifically, can I bring an action with respect to either (1) losses arising from your failure to comply with your court-ordered duty to pay me or (2) losses arising from your continued failure to comply with your substantive duty to pay me? Further, if I am precluded from the latter action, what is the reason? Is it that my substantive right to payment disappeared with the ruling? Or is the reason that my ability to assert my substantive right in court disappeared?

The law's answer to the first question (is it possible to bring an action with respect to losses arising from the failure to comply with a court-ordered duty?) is a clear 'no'. As I explain below, the only action that can be taken upon a ruling is an action to enforce the ruling through seizure of property, and so forth. In theory, this principle might be justified on various grounds, but the most straightforward is that the claimant is the wrong litigant. The only person who can bring an action for losses arising from the breach of a legal duty is the person to whom the duty is owed, which in the case of a court-ordered duty is the court.

The law's response to the second question (is it possible to bring an action with respect to losses arising from a post-ruling failure to comply with the substantive duty whose breach gave rise to the ruling?) is more complex. The orthodox common law answer is that the possibility of obtaining such damages depends on the original ruling's historical provenance. Specifically, it is traditonally said that claimants may bring post-ruling actions for damages only if the original ruling was an Order issued by the Chancery or the contemporary descendent of such a ruling. Thus, it is said that claimants who obtain specific performance orders or injunctions may bring subsequent actions for damages with respect to losses arising from defendants' post-ruling failures to comply with their substantive duties.[37] By contrast, it is traditionally said that a claimant who obtained a Judgment from the Royal Courts or who obtained a ruling that is the contemporary descendant of such a Judgment cannot bring a post-ruling action for damages. Thus, it is said that a claimant who obtains an award of damages or an award for payment of a debt may not recover damages for losses arising from the defendant's post-ruling failure to pay the damages or debt.[38] The traditional explanation for this difference

[36] Interest is normally awarded on money awards: *Senior Courts Act* 1981, s 35A; *Sempra Metals Ltd v Inland Revenue Comrs* [2007] UKHL 34, [80]. However, a delay in paying an award may still lead to a loss, as for example where claimants must borrow money at a rate higher than the statutory interest rate.

[37] See *Austins of East Ham Ltd v Macey* [1941] Ch 338, 341.

[38] See *In Re European Railway Co, Ex Parte Oriental Financial Corporation* (1876) 4 ChD 33, 37–8. Claimants today are normally awarded interest on monetary rulings, but their losses from delayed payment may exceed this award: see note 36.

is that Orders create new or additional rights to performance, leaving untouched the claimant's original substantive right to performance.[39] In contrast, Judgments are said to extinguish the original right and replace it with a right born of the order itself (which right can then be enforced through execution and the like but cannot be used to found a new action).[40] The theoretical foundation of this explanation, in turn, is the idea (discussed in Chapter 2) that Judgments are statements of the law as it applies to the parties, while Orders are merely personal commands from the Chancellor or his contemporary representative.

As mentioned above, the judicial practice in England since the *Civil Procedure Act* 1998 is to express all directive rulings, regardless of their historical provenance, as orders. Given this practice, it is not entirely clear how the traditional rule—and, in particular, the traditional explanation of that rule—can be applied to contemporary rulings. However, it is unnecessary to pursue this question because the traditional rule, or at least the traditional understanding of that rule, is unpersuasive. The traditional understanding fails to distinguish between a ruling's effect on the claimant's substantive rights and its effect on the claimant's action rights (i.e. rights to a ruling). Regardless of how they are, or were, expressed, directive rulings never extinguish substantive rights, though they may affect claimants' ability to assert those rights before a court.[41]

The traditional view that Orders left substantive rights unchanged is easily explained. Courts expressed orders as commands, not as statements of substantive law, and as already mentioned the duty to comply with a command is owed to the authority that issued it, not the beneficiary. Orders said nothing about the defendant's substantive duties, and, with one qualification, there is no reason to think that they implicitly affect such duties. It is true that this view assumes that the performance of a single physical action, for example delivering goods to a purchaser, can simultaneously fulfil both a court-ordered duty (to deliver the goods) and a substantive duty (to pay the goods). However, the law regularly recognizes overlapping duties: for example, an employer's provision of holiday pay typically fulfils a statutory duty and a contractual duty.[42]

[39] See Zakrzewski (2005) 137–8, citing, respectively, *Austins of East Ham Ltd v Macey* [1941] Ch 338, 341 and *Singh (Sudagar) v Nazeer* [1979] Ch 474, 480.

[40] Thus, with respect to Judgment to pay a debt, Bramwell, JA said that the Judgment becomes 'the sole debt between the parties . . . [T]he original debt is gone, *transit in rem judicatam*, a fresh debt is created with different consequences': *Re European Railway Co, Ex Parte Oriental Financial Corporation* (1876) 4 ChD 33, 37–8. See generally Zakrzewski (2005) 108–9, 169–70.

[41] The relationship between rulings and substantive rights following the 1998 Act does not appear to have been addressed directly (or at least consciously) by courts or writers. However, consistent with the position defended below neither Zuckerman (2013) 1059 nor *Halsbury's Laws of England* (2015) mention the traditional distinction. Further, the only comment in *Halsbury's* concerning the effect of a ruling on the claimant's substantive right is that a subsequent claim may be brought with respect to new circumstances: '[A claimant is allowed to bring a new claim] where, though the causes of action in the first and the second claim have a common origin, they are not the same, as in the case of a continuing trespass or of successive breaches of the same contract': Vol 12A (2015) [1594].

[42] The one qualification, which is still accepted by the courts, is that in cases where an Order is meant to affirm a substantive duty the Order defines the duty's content. For example, where a court orders

The conclusion that Orders left claimants' substantive rights unchanged does not mean that courts would have been acting incoherently if they had prohibited claimants from seeking damages for post-Order infringements of their substantive rights. The common law limits individuals' powers to obtain rulings in support of their substantive rights in a variety of situations (e.g. where a limitation period has expired). Indeed, I argue below that the common law limits the powers of beneficiaries of Judgments for debts in just this way. However, the important point is that while the courts would not have been acting incoherently in denying such powers, they had good reasons to deny them. Future trespasses, nuisances, and so on, are as real and as meritorious of redress as prior ones (if anything, they are more meritorious as the defendant cannot plead ignorance). If the beneficiaries of Orders had the power to enforce them immediately, and so had the power to limit the harm arising from future breaches, then a case might have been made for limiting beneficiaries' post-Orders powers to the power to seek enforcement. However, beneficiaries did not have the power to enforce Orders immediately: the only practical method of enforcing Orders was by relatively slow quasi-criminal actions for contempt of court.

The orthodox view of the legal effect of Orders (and their contemporary descendants) on claimants' substantive rights is therefore perfectly understandable. The complexities arise when we turn to the traditional view that Judgments eliminate substantive duties. This view confuses substantive rights with action rights, or more strictly with the powers to obtain action rights. The directive Judgments that are our present concern were judicial pronouncements stating, roughly, that the defendant 'shall recover' a sum of money or possession of land. Like Orders, these Judgments said nothing about the parties' substantive rights and duties.[43] Nor is there any other reason to suppose that Judgments eliminated substantive duties. Judgments may well have provided new reasons for defendants to do what their substantive duties required (as well as removing doubts as to the existence or content of these duties), but the reasons that defendants had to perform their substantive duties continued to apply after a Judgment was handed down. Defendants owe

the defendant to deliver goods on the basis that the defendant had a contractual duty to deliver the goods, compliance with the Order automatically counts as compliance with the substantive duty: *Singh (Sudagar) v Nazeer* [1979] Ch 474, 480. When, as was typically the case, courts used Orders in this way, they also made clear the court's view of the content of the defendant's substantive duty. The principle of *res judicata* applies to that view.

[43] As I explained in Chapter 1, the ordinary language meaning of a 'shall recover' ruling is not transparent. However, none of the obvious candidates supports the conclusion that such rulings explicitly or implicitly eliminated substantive duties. If Judgments were meant to direct defendants to do or not do something, then they are equivalent to Orders, and so should have had the same legal effect. Alternatively, if they were meant to direct or at least authorize officials to seize the defendant's property, and the like, then, again, they are similar to Orders (albeit directed at officials, not defendants). Finally, if Judgments were authoritative statements of the parties' legal relationship, then they are effectively declarations, and as such should have left unchanged the right and duties that they were declaring.

substantive duties to claimants—not courts—and exceptional cases aside, these duties should remain binding unless the claimant has consented to waive them. There may well be reasons to prohibit the beneficiaries of enforceable rulings from bringing subsequent actions on the basis of the same substantive rights that were the basis of the earlier ruling (as I argue below). However, such a prohibition is consistent with the continued existence of the claimant's substantive rights. As I mentioned a moment ago, common law courts regularly refuse to allow individuals to bring actions in support of valid substantive rights.

The traditional view also finds little support in the positive law. With one exception, claimants were not actually precluded from reasserting their substantive rights in court following a Judgment. For example, claimants who obtained Judgments for damages were allowed to bring subsequent actions for damages if the defendant committed the same wrong again. Thus, if the defendant trespassed on the claimant's property after the claimant had obtained a Judgment for damages in respect of an earlier trespass, the claimant could bring a new action for damages. Such claimants were in the same position respecting future claims for damages as were claimants who obtained injunctions against trespassing.[44] It is true that claimants who obtained Judgments for damages could not sue for losses arising from the defendant's post-Judgment failure to pay those damages. However, the explanation for this rule is not that the Judgment extinguished the defendant's substantive duty to pay damages; the explanation is that there is no substantive duty to pay damages in the first place. As I explain in Chapter 7, the only duty to pay damages that the common law recognizes is the duty to comply with a judicial ruling to pay damages (a duty that defendants owe to the court). It is because there is no substantive duty to pay damages that it was not, and still is not, possible to obtain damages for a failure to pay damages prior to a ruling.[45] The explanation for why beneficiaries of Judgments for restitution could not bring actions for damages with respect to losses arising from post-Judgment delays is the same: there is no substantive duty to make restitution (see Chapter 8). As in the case of non-payment of damages, the non-payment of restitution is not a ground for a damages award regardless of whether it happens before or after a ruling. Finally, the traditional view is also misleading with respect to Judgments for the recovery of land. Claimants who obtained such Judgments were not prevented from bringing actions for damages for losses caused by the occupier's post-Judgment failure to quit the property (including actions for loss of profits or rents).[46] It is true that if the defendant

[44] The same is true of claimants who obtained a Judgment for damages for breach of contract (although in such cases the contract was normally terminated by the time of the Judgment, thereby precluding any further action).

[45] Alternatively, the exclusionary rule with respect to damages could be explained on the same basis as the exclusionary rule with respect to duties to pay debts is explained in the next paragraph. The same is true of the exclusionary rule with respect to restitution, discussed next.

[46] See Elvin & Karas (2002) 4-017, 4-022; *Ministry of Defence v Ashman* [1993] 2 EGLR 102.

remained on the land the claimant could not bring a new action for recovery of the land; but the claimant was in the same position as the beneficiary of an Order (or any other ruling): the victim of a continuing trespass cannot bring repeated requests for an injunction. The victim's recourse in each case is to seek enforcement of the ruling.

The only Judgments for which a special rule was applied were Judgments for debts. As the traditional view assumes, creditors could not bring actions for losses arising from post-Judgment failures to pay debts notwithstanding that there undoubtedly was (and still is) a substantive duty to pay debts.[47] However, it is not necessary to suppose that Judgments for debt eliminated the defendant's substantive duty to explain this rule. Until relatively recently, it was a clear rule of English law that damages were not available generally for the failure to pay a sum of money, regardless of when the action was brought.[48] This rule was much criticized, particularly in times of inflation, but while it was in force it fully explained the court's refusal to award post-Judgment damages for failing to pay a debt. Post-Judgment delays were treated the same as pre-Judgment delays.

The rule precluding damages for pre-Judgment delays in payng debts has never been officially overturned, but following a series of decisions in the latter half of the last century[49] it came to be generally accepted (prior to the 1998 Act) that such damages are available.[50] The apparent survival of the rule precluding damages for post-Judgment failures may be due merely to a delay in applying the changes to the general rule to the case of post-Judgment failures. However, the explanation may be that the rule precluding damages for post-Judgment delays has a different basis than the (former) rule precluding damages for pre-Judgment delays. Specifically, the post-Judgment rule can be explained—and defended—on the ground that, while Judgments for debt did not extinguish defendants' substantive duties, they extinguished claimants' powers to bring actions on the basis of those duties.

As mentioned earlier, the law limits individuals' powers to obtain rulings in a variety of situations, notwithstanding that their substantive rights may have been infringed or threatened. Examples include where a limitation period has expired, where the defendant is the Crown or a foreign diplomat, or where the action is an abuse of process. In these cases, the law accepts that the claimant's substantive rights have been infringed or threatened, but then concludes, essentially for policy reasons, that the claimant should not be allowed to bring litigation on the basis of those rights. The rule that precluded creditors from obtaining damages from debtors with respect to post-Judgment failures to pay is explicable on similar grounds. This rule prevented repeat litigation in situations where

[47] *In Re European Railway Co, Ex Parte Oriental Financial Corporation* (1876) 4 Ch D 33, 37–8.
[48] *London, Chatham and Dover Railway Co v South Eastern Railway* Co [1893] AC 429.
[49] See *Wadsworth v Lydall* [1981] 1 WLR 598.
[50] Burrows (2004) 154–5.

the law provides claimants with other, less costly, ways of protecting themselves. The simplest way to protect claimants in cases where defendants were unlikely to pay promptly or where a delay could be harmful was to give defendants little or no time to satisfy the Judgment. Claimants could then protect themselves from post-Judgment delays by promptly enforcing their Judgments.[51] The courts could (and still can) further reduce the risk of claimants being prejudiced by a delay in payment by awarding interest on the Judgment.[52] In most cases, the only foreseeable loss from a delay in payment is the time-value of money. Against this background, the rule precluding creditors from obtaining damages for post-Judgment delays appears to be a relatively uncontroversial limitation on individuals' powers to obtain rulings.

To summarize, properly understood, neither Orders nor Judgments affected claimants' substantive rights. However, in one case—a Judgment for debt—the issuance of a Judgment precluded claimants from later asserting their substantive rights in court. Judgments for debt had this effect not because they extinguished the parties' substantive rights, but because they extinguished creditors' powers to obtain action rights. Here as elsewhere in the law, the failure to distinguish substantive rights from action rights is a source of confusion.

Returning to the current law (where all directive rulings are styled as 'orders'), there is even less reason to suppose that a subcategory of today's directive rulings extinguish claimants' substantive rights. The explanation for why Orders do not affect substantive rights applies equally to present-day judicial orders to pay damages or debts. At the same time, the explanation of the effect of Judgments for debt on claimants' subsequent powers to obtain rulings also applies to present-day orders to pay a debt. That explanation turned on how Judgment debts were enforced, and on the possibility of obtaining post-Judgment interest. As I explain below, a present-day order to pay money, including money owed as a debt, is enforced in the same way as Judgments to pay debts were enforced, and interest continues to be awarded on monetary rulings.

To conclude: there is no difference between how Equitable Rulings (and their contemporary descendants) affect substantive rights and how Legal Rulings (and their contemporary descendants) affect substantive rights. In the single case of Legal Rulings to pay a debt, there is a difference between how such rulings affect claimants' powers to obtain action rights and how other rulings affect such powers. But the explanation for this difference has nothing to do with the historical origins of actions for debts. The explanation lies in the nature of the performances that such orders require and in the means available to enforce them.

[51] The defendant might lack the assets to satisfy the Judgment, but, in this case, an additional Judgment for damages would be of no value.

[52] See *Judgments Act* 1838, s 17; *County Courts Act* 1984, s 74.

iii. Enforcement Rights

In practical terms, the most important legal consequence of a private law order is that it gives claimants the option, if the order is unfulfilled, of enlisting the state's coercive machinery to impose sanctions on the defendant. The practical importance of this consequence helps to explain why legal scholars often describe orders as sanctions[53] and, more generally, why it is common to describe private lawsuits as a means of 'enforcing' one's rights. However, these descriptions are misleading. Sanctions are physical actions undertaken or authorized by state officials in response to something that individuals did or failed to do and which deprive individuals of their property or liberty, or inflict pain upon them, for example, by seizing their goods or placing them in prison. Orders are just words. Moreover, in the case of private law orders they are words addressed to defendants rather than to bailiffs, sheriffs, or anyone else with the authority to impose a sanction.[54] The only relationship between orders and sanctions is that non-fulfillment of the former gives rise to the possibility of the latter. Still, this relationship is practically important. As far as civil wrongdoers are concerned, the non-fulfillment of orders is the only ground for imposing sanctions. Criminal wrongdoers may be imprisoned directly on proof of their criminal wrongdoing, but civil wrongdoers are only liable to sanctions if a court has ordered them to do something and they have failed to do it.

As was true of the traditional explanation of the effect of rulings on substantive rights, the traditional explanation of enforcement rights drew a sharp distinction between Equitable Orders and Legal Judgments. Judgments, it was said, were enforced by 'executing' the ruling, that is, by bringing about the very result contemplated by the ruling. By contrast, Orders were enforced by contempt of court procedures. The traditional explanation for this difference was that failing to comply with an Order was a direct affront to the Chancellor's authority (or the authority of his modern-day representative). In contrast, Judgments were not affronts to the King's or anyone else's authority because they did not direct anyone to do anything. However, Judgments did state what the law required, and as such authorized the use of coercive measures to bring about that result. On this basis, a sharp divide was drawn between, on the one hand, the enforcement of injunctions and specific performance orders and, on the other hand, the enforcement of awards for damages, sums due under contracts, restitution, and the recovery of land.

The contemporary English law of enforcement is not organized according to the historical provenance of rulings. Although the range of enforcement methods following the *Civil Procedure Act* 1998 is broadly similar to the range that was available

[53] See e.g. Lawson (1980) 12–14. Many authors also misleadingly describe orders and other rulings as the means by which the law 'enforces' legal duties: see e.g. Calabresi & Melamed (1972).

[54] As I explained in Chapter 1, it is arguable that Legal Judgments were different in this last respect. Although Judgments were not specifically directed to legal officials, they might be interpreted as indirectly authorizing legal officials to impose sanctions to bring about the contemplated result.

beforehand, the availability of those methods does not turn on whether the ruling was traditionally described as an 'injunction' or 'damages' or, more broadly, on whether the ruling traces its origins to the Royal Courts or the Chancery. Instead, it turns primarily on the content of the order, in particular whether the order is monetary in nature.

As we will see, the methods of enforcing the contemporary descendants of Orders and Judgments are roughly similar to the methods that were available before the 1998 Act and, indeed, to those available before the Judicature Acts (though they are not identical). This similarity might be thought to show that the historical divide between Law and Equity continues to underlie the contemporary law of enforcement. However, I argue that the opposite lesson should be taken from this similarity. What the similarity demonstrates is that the best way of understanding the earlier law is through the broadly functional distinctions that are used to organize the contemporary law. Stated differently, I argue that there were compelling functional reasons that the rulings handed down by the Royal Courts were enforced as they were, reasons that had nothing to do with the fact that they were expressed as Judgments or that they were issued by the Royal Courts. The same is true of the rulings issued by the Chancery. There are exceptions, but in general it is not necessary to know that, for example, an injunction was originally available only from the Chancery or that damages were originally available only from the Royal Courts to understand why these rulings are, and were, enforced using different methods. As I explain below, the way that the contemporary law is organized assists in understanding the earlier law.

The common law employs two basic methods of enforcing private law orders: 'direct' and 'indirect'. Although I describe both as methods of 'enforcing' orders, this label should be used carefully as only the first method can bring about the actual result contemplated by the order. In England, the terms in which the relevant rules are expressed, and some of their technical details vary slightly depending on whether the order is issued by the High Court or a County Court, but in substance the methods are similar in both courts. I describe each method below. Following these descriptions, I explain why the 'historical origin' explanation of enforcement should be rejected in favour of a broadly functional explanation.

Direct Enforcement: Execution

Execution is the process by which a bailiff, enforcement officer,[55] or other authorized person directly brings about, or attempts directly to bring about, the result stipulated in an order. With rare exceptions, execution is the only way of enforcing a monetary order, such as an order to pay a debt or damages. In such cases, execution typically involves a bailiff or enforcement officer (hereafter 'enforcement

[55] In contrast to bailiffs, who are employed by the Crown, enforcement officers (who are used in respect of High Court proceedings) are private contractors.

officer') seizing the defendant's property, and then transferring the proceeds of its sale—to a maximum of the ordered sum—to the claimant. Other methods of executing monetary orders include attachment of earnings (directing an employer to pay some or all of the defendant's wages to the claimant), charging orders (giving the claimant a charge over the defendant's property that is enforceable on non-payment), and third-party debt orders (directing a debtor of the defendant to make payment to the claimant).

Execution is also available for certain non-monetary orders (though unlike in the case of most monetary orders, execution is not the only enforcement method). Broadly speaking, execution is available for non-monetary orders if their content is such that someone other than the defendant can bring about the desired result. Examples include orders to recover possession of land, orders to convey title or otherwise complete a document, orders to deliver specific goods (including in this and the previous example cases in which the courts formulate the order as an order to specifically perform a contract), and orders to remove a building or other property from the claimant's land. The means of execution in these cases vary. An order for recovery of land is executed by an enforcement officer taking the steps necessary to ensure that the claimant obtains possession of the land (e.g. changing locks, arresting trespassers). An order to complete a document is normally executed by authorizing a judicial official to complete the document in the defendant's name. An order of specific delivery is executed by an enforcement officer seizing and transferring the relevant chattel. In addition, where practicable courts can direct that an act required under an order to specifically perform a contract may be done by the claimant or another party, with the cost borne by the defendant.[56] These methods of execution are often described in terms of the particular 'writs' (or 'warrants') associated with them; the writ being the specific direction to the enforcement officer. For example, a claimant who seeks the return of a chattel will request a writ of 'specific delivery'.

The methods of execution described above are all initiated, though not usually carried out, by the claimant.[57] The claimant initiates the process by making a request for execution to a court (though it is not typically necessary to appear before an actual judge).[58] The process is usually not complicated—where the claimant

[56] *CPR* Sch 1 RSC Ord 45, r 8.

[57] However, these methods remain distinct from so-called 'self-help' remedies. As usually understood, self-help refers to methods that individuals can use in support of their substantive rights that do not require them first to go to court. Examples include landowners' powers to retake their land, landlords' power to seize tenants' goods, secured creditors' powers to take or hold on to secured property, and so on. The rules governing self-help are part of substantive law.

[58] For example, an order to deliver goods or hand over a sum equal to their value may be enforced by a writ of delivery which can be given without judicial permission (*CPR* Sch 1 RSC Ord 45, r 4(2)(a)); in contrast, a writ of specific delivery, if used to enforce the same order, requires judicial authorization: *CPR* Sch 1 RSC Ord 45, r 4(2)(b) (but authorization is not required if the same writ is employed to enforce an order of specific delivery). Obtaining a writ for execution of a monetary order does not normally require authorization: Lafferty & Jarvis (2008) 7.

seeks the seizure and sale of goods, little more is required than to identify the writ sought and the order that was made[59]—although in the case of monetary orders, the County Court (unlike the High Court) will not issue a warrant without the defendant first being sent a notice giving them a further seven days to pay.[60] As previously mentioned, most orders carry either an express or a statutorily implied date for compliance; enforcement before this date is not possible.[61] In the relatively rare cases where no date is given or implied (as sometimes happens with orders to recover possession of land), execution may be initiated immediately following the order's issuance. Of course, if the defendant is willing to comply with the order, then, even if a writ authorizing execution is issued, compliance will be voluntary. Further, defendants may always apply for a stay of execution, which is typically granted if defendants demonstrate that they are willing and able to perform the order in the near future.[62] In general, writs of execution are granted as a matter of course, assuming the order has not been fulfilled by the relevant date, but they can be refused if the application is considered overdue. And as I explain in Chapter 9, some parties enjoy immunity from writs, notably (with some qualifications) the Crown and foreign diplomats.

As mentioned above, execution itself is normally undertaken by an enforcement officer or other judicial official, who will have been directed to, for example, seize and sell goods,[63] seize and deliver goods,[64] cause the claimant to obtain possession of land,[65] or execute a document.[66] In other cases, the court may direct a third party to assist in execution, as where it directs an employer or third-party debtor to pay money owed by the defendant to the claimant.[67] Finally, the court itself may impose a charge over property.[68]

There is no guarantee that enforcement by execution will succeed in achieving the desired result. In the case of monetary orders, the defendant may lack sufficient assets. In the case of specific delivery, the defendant may have destroyed or

59 According to r 6 (b), the writ cannot be issued unless '(b) the court officer authorised to seal it is satisfied that the period, if any, specified in the judgment or order for the payment of any money or the doing of any other act there under has expired'.

60 *CPR* Sch 2 CCR Ord 26, r 1(4): 'Where a warrant is issued for the whole or part of the said sum of money and costs, the court officer shall, unless the district judge responsible for execution of the warrant directs otherwise, send a warning notice to the person against whom the warrant is issued and, where such a notice is sent, the warrant shall not be levied until 7 days thereafter'.

61 Non-monetary mandatory orders must include a date for compliance. It is not strictly required that monetary orders include a date for performance, but the *CPR* 40.11 sets a default period of fourteen days and, more generally, the need for a date is implicit in the concept of an order.

62 *CPR* Sch 1 RSC Ord 47, r 1; *CPR* Sch 2 CCR Ord 25, r 8.

63 *CPR* Sch 1 RSC Ord 46, 47; *CPR* Sch 2 RSC Ord 26.

64 *CPR* Sch 1 RSC Ord 45, r 4(1).

65 *CPR* Sch 1 RSC Ord 45, r 3. At common law, the owner may enter and take possession of the land provided no force is used.

66 *Senior Courts Act* 1981, s 39; *CPR* Sch 1 RSC Ord 45, r 8.

67 *CPR* 72 (third party debt); *CPR* Sch 2 CCR Ord 27 (attachment of earnings) (not available in the County Court, but a High Court Private law order can be enforced in the CC: *CPR* 70.3)

68 *CPR* 73.10.

transferred the relevant chattel. And in the case of orders for the recovery of land or other property, the defendant may refuse to cooperate (though non-cooperation may lead to a finding of criminal contempt, and then committal, which—at least in the case of recovery of land—will achieve the desired result indirectly). The only case where execution is guaranteed to be successful is where it involves nothing more than a court official completing a document.

Indirect Enforcement: Imprisonment, Fines, and Sequestration

Indirect enforcement[69] refers to the action of imprisoning,[70] fining,[71] or sequestering the property of defendants[72] who refuse to comply with private law orders. Unlike the various forms of enforcement by execution described above, imprisonment, fines, and sequestration cannot directly bring about the result desired by the order. However, they may reasonably be regarded as a means of indirect enforcement because their primary aim is to provide incentives to comply with orders. In the past, courts regularly imprisoned recalcitrant defendants to an indefinite term that terminated only when the defendant agreed to perform the order.[73] Indefinite imprisonment is no longer possible,[74] but courts can and do release defendants if they comply with an order or show a willingness to comply,[75] and they may suspend an order to enable performance.[76] Conversely, courts may recommit defendants after their release if they continue to refuse to comply. Courts also often impose fines for each day of disobedience.[77] Finally, sequestration—detaining the defendant's property until performance occurs—is by definition an incentive to comply because the sequestered property is released upon compliance.

It is true that courts frequently say that imprisonment and fines for non-performance of orders have a public policy element. Courts often justify these sanctions in part as a response to a straightforward criminal contempt or wrong—namely, the wrong of refusing to comply with a court's orders.[78] However, the conventional understanding is that the overriding aim of these sanctions is not to

[69] See generally, Miller & Perry (2017) chs 2, 8; Arlidge et al (2017) chs 3, 12.

[70] *CPR* Sch 1 RSC Ord 52, r 1; *CPR* Sch 2 CCR Ord 29, r 1. Imprisonment is limited to two years. Committal is the most common method of indirect enforcement, though it is still rare in comparison to the methods of direct enforcement described above. In 2009, the County Courts issued 236,293 warrants of execution, but only 1,103 warrants of committal: *Judicial and Court Statistics 2009* (Ministry of Justice, UK).

[71] *CPR* Sch 1 RSC Ord 52, r 9.

[72] *CPR* Sch 1 RSC Ord 46, r 5. Sequestration involves seizing and holding the defendant's property until compliance with the order is achieved. Fines and sequestration are commonly used when the defendant is a corporation.

[73] See *Contempt of Court Act* 1981, s 14.

[74] Ibid s 14(1).

[75] See Miller & Perry (2017) 40–1.

[76] See ibid; *CPR* Sch 1 RSC Ord 52, r 7.

[77] See e.g. *AMIEU v Mudginberri Station Pty Ltd* (1986) 161 CLR 98.

[78] '[There is] an element of public policy in punishing civil contempt, since the administration of justice would be undermined if the order of any court of law could be disregarded with impunity': in *AG v Times Newspapers Ltd* [1974] AC 273, 308 [Lord Diplock].

punish but to induce performance. This understanding explains why they are traditionally described as sanctions for civil (not criminal) contempt of court.

In principle, any order may be indirectly enforced, but since the passage of the *Debtors Acts* of 1869 and 1878 imprisonment is no longer available with respect to monetary orders, with a few exceptions (e.g. maintenance orders, orders to make payments to the Crown).[79] More generally, indirect enforcement is rarely sought, or awarded, if there is a practical means of direct enforcement available, such as execution of documents or execution against goods. In practice, therefore, indirect enforcement is typically only used in respect of orders to perform contracts and orders to refrain from torts.

As with direct enforcement, claimants initiate the process of indirect enforcement,[80] but legal officials or third parties authorized to act on their behalf carry it out. As might be expected in light of its potential consequences (e.g. imprisonment), this process is more complicated than direct execution: the defendant must be given a hearing, and proof of contempt must be established beyond a reasonable doubt. The court may also refuse to impose a sanction if the defendant did not know the facts that made its actions a breach of the order, if the breach was purely technical,[81] or if sequestration of the defendant corporation's property would harm innocent third parties.[82] It is also assumed that a coercive sanction is normally not appropriate, at least as an initial response, following a failure to comply with an order for the possession of land, delivery of goods, conveyance of title to property, or for family matters generally.[83] In these cases, courts will usually require the claimant first to attempt direct means of enforcement, through either a writ of possession or delivery, or an order authorizing that a conveyance be executed by a legal official.[84]

Explaining Enforcement: Functional, not Historical

As we have seen, the contemporary English rules regarding enforcement are not organized according to the historical division between Legal and Equitable Rulings. Indeed, this division does not figure explicitly at all in the current law, which is organized in terms of broadly functional distinctions. The most important of these distinctions is between orders whose contemplated results can occur without the defendant's participation ('executable' orders) and orders whose contemplated results require the defendant's participation ('inexecutable' orders).

[79] *CPR* Sch 1 RSC Ord 45, r 5; *CPR* Sch 2 CCR Ord 29; *Administration of Justice Act* 1970, s 11. See generally Miller & Perry (2017) 515.

[80] There are exceptions: see *Churchman v Joint Shop Stewards' Committee* [1972] 3 All ER 603; Miller & Perry (2017) 43–44. The *Protection from Harassment Act* 1977, s 3(6) makes it a criminal offence to breach an injunction not to harass.

[81] See Kay, Sime & French (2018) 1498–9.

[82] See Arlidge et al (2017) 1037.

[83] Ibid 898, 901.

[84] As permitted by the *Senior Courts Act* 1981, s 39; *CPR* Sch 1 RSC Ord 45, r 8.

This distinction broadly overlaps with the distinction between Equitable Orders and Legal Judgments (and their historical descendants), but it is not identical. For example, specific performance orders and mandatory injunctions are sometimes executable (as in the case of an order to specifically perform a contractual obligation to deliver goods). Another difference is that, in principle, indirect enforcement is possible with respect to all orders, subject only to a bar on imprisonment for failing to comply with most monetary orders. Thus, a defendant who fails to comply with the contemporary version of a Judgment for the recovery of land—namely, an order to give up possession of land—may be imprisoned.

Given these differences, it seems evident that the current law is not grounded in the traditional distinction between Legal and Equitable Rulings. Indeed, once the decision was made to express all directive rulings as orders there was no obvious way to give that distinction legal effect in the current law. The contemporary equivalent of an Order to specifically perform a monetary contractual obligation looks the same as the contemporary equivalent of a Judgment for debt: each is expressed as an order to pay a sum of money.

The more difficult question is whether the rules that applied when England distinguished between Judgments and Orders (or the rules that apply today in jurisdictions that maintain the distinction) should be understood in historical terms. Briefly—a full response is outside this work's scope—I argue that they should not. Whatever the original explanation for why Orders were enforced by punishment and Judgments by execution, the most straightforward explanation for why that distinction was (or has been) maintained for so long is functional. As far as enforcement is concerned, the distinguishing feature of Equitable Orders is that the states of affairs they contemplated could not generally be brought about without the defendant's participation. The only way to induce that participation was the threat of punishment. In contrast, the distinguishing feature of Judgments is that the states of affairs they contemplated could generally occur without the defendant's participation, for example, by execution against the defendant's property. In short, the reason courts 'executed' Judgments, and not Orders, is that they could. And the reason courts punished failures to comply with Orders, but did not punish failures to comply with Judgments, is that they had no obvious alternative way to enforce the former. There are a few exceptions—the historical distinction would not be a 'distinction' if it meant nothing—but the general explanation for why Legal and Equitable Rulings were enforced differently is that their subject matters were different. The same enforcement regime could have arisen as easily in a unitary legal system.

D. Conclusion

If remedial law is the law of judicial orders (as I have argued), then taking remedial law seriously means taking seriously the rules governing the form, creation, and effects of orders. This chapter has taken up that challenge. In addition to describing the relevant rules, it has argued that these rules reflect general remedial-law principles—principles that apply to judicial orders generally. It might be thought obvious that such principles exist: if there is such a thing as remedial law, it would seem to follow that there are general principles of remedial law. However, it is rare to find such principles discussed in remedies textbooks (and even rarer to find a discussion of general principles dealing with the form, creation, and effects of rulings).

In contrast, this book argues that there are general principles of remedial law, and this chapter begins that argument. Specifically, I have argued that the traditional account of the rules governing the form, creation, and effects of judicial orders—an account that focuses on these rules' historical origins—is not only unnecessary, but also misleading. To the extent that rulings that originated in the Royal Courts are created, expressed and given effect in a different way from rulings that originated in the Chancery, the explanation lies in practical differences in the states of affairs that the respective rulings are intended to bring about. The most general and important of these differences is between states of affairs that can be brought about without the defendant's participations ('executable' rulings) and states of affairs that require the defendant's participation ('inexecutable' rulings).

4
The Basic Structure

Understanding the law is in large measure a matter of determining how the parts one seeks to understand are like or unlike other parts of the law. In the case of private law orders, this inquiry is primarily a matter of determining, first, how orders differ from rules and sanctions, and, second, how orders differ from one another. At present, we lack such an understanding. Indeed, we lack a stable terminology for expressing such an understanding. This chapter attempts to fill these gaps: it develops a preliminary framework for expressing how private law orders differ from other legal phenomena, and how they differ from one another.

The framework is preliminary because its categories are incompletely filled-in and because my illustrative examples are only lightly defended. I cite few authorities. This chapter aims to say just enough to show that the framework is *prima facie* plausible, leaving its detailed defence for later. My arguments consist largely of showing that the framework's categories are implicit in judges', lawyers', and scholars' conventional understandings of what courts are doing when they issue orders. These understandings might be wrong. The conventional understanding may be so conceptually confused that it fails to qualify as an understanding at all. Or it may be that it fails to fit the rules that it purports to understand. Chapter 5 defends the framework's conceptual foundations, while Chapters 6 to 9 defend its descriptive accuracy. In principle, this chapter should appear after those chapters. However, it is easier to follow the arguments in Chapters 5 to 9 and, in particular, to appreciate their significance with a map of the territory in hand.

Substantively, the framework expresses two of this book's main themes. The first is that while court orders are connected in important ways to substantive rules and sanctions, they are, in the end, qualitatively different from both. The second theme is that the relationship between court orders and rule-based ('substantive') rights is complex: although some orders replicate existing substantive duties, others create new duties—and they do this in different ways and for different reasons.

The framework is organized around three questions: (1) how are remedies related to other parts of the law; (2) on what grounds are remedies available; and (3) what kinds of remedies are available? In theory, these questions should be preceded by a definitional question—what is a remedy?—but that question was answered in Chapter 1: a remedy is a legal ruling. This chapter explores the implications of that definition. I begin, however, by saying a few words about the terms and concepts employed in answering the above questions.

Rights, Wrongs, and Injustices. Stephen A. Smith, Oxford University Press (2019). © Stephen A. Smith.
DOI: 10.1093/oso/9780199229772.003.0004

A. Classification in Terms of Rights

My answers to the above questions are expressed in terms of the rights created or recognized by orders and related phenomena. Substantively similar answers could be developed using concepts such as 'duties', 'rules', 'powers', or 'legally significant events'. The choice of 'rights' is primarily a matter of terminological convenience, though it also reflects the central role of rights in contemporary legal discourse.

This chapter adopts a relatively thin and, I hope, uncontroversial definition of a legal right. As understood here, legal rights are correlative to legal duties: rights are rights that others do or not do certain things.[1] To say that I have a contractual right that you pay me a sum of money is equivalent to saying that you have a legal duty to pay me that sum of money. Legal duties, in turn, are propositions about what, legally, ought to happen. More specifically, they are propositions about what ought to happen categorically (or 'all things considered'). They are meant to pre-empt whatever other reasons we might have to do or not to do the stipulated action.[2] And the normal ways that the law creates such duties is by enacting a duty-imposing legal rule (e.g. a rule stating that 'everyone has a duty to perform their contractual promises') or issuing a judicial ruling (e.g. an order directing the defendant to pay the claimant a sum of money).

Legal rights are related to, but distinct from, legal powers. [3] The latter are capacities to create, change or extinguish legal rights, duties, liabilities, or other legal relations. For example, individuals have legal powers to make contracts and wills. In practice, the distinction between rights and power is often elided because rights frequently arise from the exercise of powers. Indeed, the three kinds of specifically 'remedial rights' recognized in the common law (action rights, court-ordered rights, and enforcement rights) are all created through the exercise of legal powers. Action rights (roughly, rights to the issuance of court orders) are created by individuals exercising their legal powers to initiate litigation and then satisfying the cause of action associated with the ruling that they seek. Similarly, court-ordered rights (roughly, rights that defendants do what a court has ordered them to do) arise from courts' powers to issue orders. Finally, enforcement rights (roughly, rights that a sanction be imposed on a defendant who failed to comply with an order) arise from claimants' powers to enforce rulings through applications to courts or legal officials. Most of what I say below about remedial rights and their relation to substantive rights could be reframed as an account of remedial powers and their relation to substantive rights.

[1] 'A duty is merely the obverse of a right': *Letang v Cooper* [1965] 1 QB 232, 247 (Lord Diplock).

[2] Raz (1999) 39.

[3] See Hohfeld (1913).

The above definition is neutral on most of the difficult questions about the nature of rights.[4] However, it may be controversial in one respect. The definition assumes, contrary to some views,[5] that a legal right may exist notwithstanding that the right-holder cannot call on the state's coercive powers to enforce the right. Nothing in the substance of this chapter's arguments turns on this assumption. The main reason it is adopted is that it is widely accepted. The common law clearly recognizes 'unenforceable rights': for example, it is orthodox law that substantive rights (e.g. the substantive right to performance of a contract) normally survive the expiry of a limitation period, notwithstanding that the expiry precludes the possibility of bringing a legal action to enforce the right. Similarly, the tort of inducing a breach of contract can be committed in respect of an unenforceable contract.[6]

B. How are Remedies Related to Other Parts of the Law?

'Other parts of the law' is a broad category. In answering this first question, my primary focus is the relationship between remedies and substantive rights. Further, my interest is not strictly with remedies themselves (i.e. judicial rulings), but rather with the rights most closely associated with remedies. 'Remedial rights', as I will describe them, fall into three categories: (1) rights that remedies be granted ('action rights'); (2) rights created by remedies ('court-ordered rights'); and (3) rights that remedies be enforced ('enforcement rights'). The question I consider in this section is how these rights are related to substantive rights.

My focus on substantive rights reflects their central role in our understanding of private law. In most cases, the explanations of particular action rights, court-ordered rights, and enforcement rights assume that substantive rights exist. Action rights most often arise on proof that a defendant breached or is threatening to breach a substantive right, court-ordered rights are usually judicial responses to such breaches, and enforcement rights are rights to enforce these responses. At the same time, it is difficult to identify substantive rights without understanding their relationship to remedial rights. In a legal system in which the law develops through

[4] In particular, it takes no position in the debate between the 'interest' and 'will' theories of rights. According to the 'interest' theory, rights necessarily protect the interests of individuals or other legal entities: individuals have rights, in this view, when the law mandates behaviour in order to serve their interests: Raz (1986) 166. Thus, a defender of the interest theory would say that I have a right not to be defamed because the rules that prohibit others from defaming me exist to serve my interest in my reputation. By contrast, the 'will' theory supposes that rights protect individuals' capacities to choose or to control their environment: Hart (1982) 183. Thus, a defender of the will theory would say that I have a right not to be defamed because the law gives me control over other people's ability to defame me; specifically, I can waive my right not to be defamed. Both the interest theory and the will theory are able to explain most instances in which lawyers and judges say that rights exist; however, neither theory fits conventional usage perfectly. The rights examined in this book satisfy both theories.

[5] Kelsen (1961) 51; Austin (1832) 23.

[6] *Lumley v Gye* (1853) 2 E & B 216.

judicial decisions, and in which those decisions are fundamentally decisions about rulings, the understanding of substantive rights is closely tied to the understanding (conscious or not) of the relationship between substantive rights and remedial rights. For example, lawyers who believe in the rubber-stamp view of court orders (according to which orders always confirm substantive rights) must believe that there is a substantive duty to pay damages. By contrast, lawyers who reject the rubber-stamp view might reach the opposite conclusion.

In the discussion below, I explore substantive rights, action rights, court-ordered rights, and enforcement rights separately. This approach anticipates my conclusion that none of these categories is fully determined by, or can be collapsed into, one of the other categories.

i. Substantive Rights

As understood here, a legal right is substantive if it refers to a legal relationship in which one person (or persons or a 'legal person') owes another a duty to do or not do something, and if the right exists because individuals enjoy it generally or because of the occurrence of an event other than a judicial ruling. Examples include debtors' rights to be paid, landowners' rights to exclusive possession of their property, and everyone's right not to be assaulted.

The label 'substantive' is admittedly uninformative. Substantive rights are the most basic private law right; they might equally be called 'non-adjectival rights' or just 'rights'. They are substantive only in the sense that, unlike the other rights that I discuss, they can be explained without reference to litigation, rulings, or anything else that occurs in court. It is true that in the common law the usual ground for concluding that a substantive right exists is that the courts have said it exists. However, this feature is common to all legal rights. A right is substantive not because of the way it is validated, but because of the facts that give rise to it. Those facts are about who citizens are, or what they have done, in their day-to-day lives.

Specific substantive rights arise either because the right-holder resides in a jurisdiction where such rights apply generally or because an 'ordinary' right-creating event has occurred (as opposed to a judicial event, such as an order). For example, my right not to be assaulted exists because I reside in a jurisdiction that recognizes that citizens generally enjoy such rights. By contrast, my right to receive my salary arises because I entered a valid contract with my employer and satisfied the conditions for payment under that contract. As these examples illustrate, other legal persons typically owe the duties to which substantive rights correlate.

How do we know what substantive rights we enjoy? The short answer is that we enjoy a substantive right if there is a legal rule, recognized by the courts, stipulating that such a right exists, and if the pre-conditions mentioned in the rule are satisfied. If the Supreme Court says there is a legal rule that debtors must pay their debts, then creditors have substantive legal rights to such payments. When I want to stress this feature of substantive rights (which is not shared by court-ordered rights), I will describe them as 'rule-based rights'.

The longer answer is more complex. In common law jurisdictions, courts do not normally look to statutes or codes to determine citizens' private law rights. When asked for proof that the legal system recognizes a particular substantive right, courts typically point to cases that are said to recognize the right. Manufacturers have a legal duty to take care that their products do not injure consumers because the House of Lords said so in *Donoghue v Stevenson*.[7] This method of establishing substantive rights raises an immediate difficulty. Judicial decisions are not strictly decisions about the substantive rights that citizens generally enjoy, or even decisions about the substantive rights that particular litigants enjoy (or enjoyed). In a typical case, the fundamental question for the court is whether to issue the requested ruling. Declarations aside, the rights that are the focus of judicial decisions are the 'court-ordered rights' that (as I explain below) are created by court orders. A typical tort action is an action for damages; the court's task is to determine whether to order the defendant to pay damages, and, if so, in what amount.

Of course, courts often affirm the existence of substantive rights in their reasons for judgment. For example, courts will normally only award damages on proof that the defendant infringed a duty owed to the claimant; it follows that in adjudicating claims for damages courts must normally determine whether the defendant infringed one of the claimant's substantive rights. Yet, even in such cases, the court's reasons may provide limited guidance about the claimant's substantive rights. The majority of the court, if one exists, must agree on the ruling, and they must express the ruling clearly and briefly. However, the majority does not need to agree on the reasons for making the ruling, much less to state those reasons clearly or briefly. More importantly, courts are normally not required to distinguish claimants' substantive rights from their rights to rulings. To obtain rulings, claimants must normally prove certain facts (the 'cause of action'). These facts often (though not always) include facts that are meant to show that the defendant failed to comply with a substantive duty. Yet (as we saw in Chapter 2) it is generally immaterial to the result whether a particular fact goes towards proving the existence of a substantive duty or, instead, is a separate aspect of the cause of action. If the claimant proves the required facts, the result is usually the same: the ruling is issued.[8] For

[7] [1932] UKHL 100.

[8] There are exceptions. For example, the distinction in conflict of laws rules between substantive and procedural law roughly parallels the distinction between substantive and (what I call below) 'action' rights. Other rules that arguably require courts to distinguish substantive rights from action rights are found in the law governing damages and interest for late payments, restitution for mistaken transfers, tenders and settlements, set off, assignment, and limitation periods. However, none of these rules draws clear and consistent distinctions between substantive rights and action rights. The relevant case law is often inconsistent (e.g. the conflicts rules and the rules on interest for late payments), and the rules rarely appear to be based on considered views about our rule-based rights (see the rules on prejudgment interest). Furthermore, the rules can often be explained on alternative grounds: see Smith (2008) 50–2.

example, courts will not order damages in respect of pain and suffering in negligence cases unless the claimant proves that, in addition to breaching a duty of care, the defendant's actions caused pain and suffering. The latter requirement is consistent with the view that defendants in such cases had substantive duties, arising from the moment the pain and suffering occurred, to pay the claimant a sum of money because of the pain and suffering. But it is also consistent with the view that a duty to pay damages for pain and suffering only arises when a court orders the defendants to pay such damages.

Against this background, it is not surprising that writers in common law jurisdictions often draw conclusions about substantive rights based on what courts do (rather than what they say); in particular, they often draw such conclusions based on the rulings that courts make. For example, most authors assume that there is a duty to make monetary restitution following a defective transfer (see Chapter 8). If asked for evidence of this duty, and, further, for evidence that it is merely a monetary duty (as opposed to a duty to return property *in specie*), many of these authors would point to the practice of courts ordering restitution on proof of a defective transfer and, further, to the practice of ordering monetary restitution.

As we saw in Chapter 2, this way of deriving rights from remedies (the 'rubber-stamp' conception of remedies) has a long pedigree in the common law. But it is rejected in this book. I also reject the view's close cousin—the 'remedial' conception of substantive rights—which holds that substantive rights exist only if courts are willing to order defendants to do what the alleged right requires. Against both of these views, I argue that the availability of remedies is just one factor to consider when determining our substantive rights. Other factors include what courts say, what makes moral sense, and, of course, what fits with the rest of the law. Chapters 6 to 8 defend this view by exploring a number of core common law orders. This chapter limits itself to offering a few examples to show that the everyday assumptions that judges, lawyers, and legal scholars make about rights and remedies are incompatible with both the rubber-stamp conception of remedies and the remedial conception of rights.

I begin with the rubber-stamp conception of remedies. It is undeniable that many rulings merely rubber-stamp ('replicate') substantive rights. For example, an order for a sum due replicates the defendant's substantive duty to pay the same sum. However, counter-examples abound. Courts regularly say, or assume by other things they say, that we have rights to the performance of contractual promises made to us. Yet courts also regularly refuse to order defendants to perform such promises even when they have proof that the defendant is unwilling to perform voluntarily. Particularly in the case of non-monetary contractual promises, courts typically order defendants to pay damages rather than perform. The courts take a similar approach to duties to return another's property (or at least to duties to allow individuals to retrieve their property). 'Converting' another's property is a legal wrong, yet the typical remedy for conversion, even where the defendant retains the relevant property, is an order to pay a sum of money or to return the property. Another counter-example is an order to pay exemplary damages. An order to pay exemplary damages does not replicate a substantive duty to pay such damages (see Chapter 5). Punishment is only punishment if a court or other authority has ordered it. Moreover, it would be impossible for wrongdoers to determine the content of such a duty prior to the court order: the rules governing both the availability and quantum of exemplary damages give courts considerable discretion. If there were a substantive duty to pay exemplary damages, it would be a duty that those subject to it could not determine.

As for the remedial conception of rights, it is trite law that courts frequently refuse to issue an order—any order—notwithstanding that they have found that the defendant is in breach of a still-valid substantive duty. For example, it is orthodox law that the expiry of a limitation period does not extinguish the defendant's substantive duty, but merely precludes a court from making an order—any order—in support of that duty. As I explain in Chapter 9, the failure to comply with the necessary formalities for a contract often has the same result. Similarly, the Crown, foreign states, and individuals involved in legal proceedings are often immune from liability for clear breaches of substantive duties. Litigants who have been involved in illegal activities or who abuse the legal process may also be denied any form of redress regardless of the substantive merits of their claims.

Other examples of non-replicative rulings and unenforceable rights are discussed below and in Chapters 6 to 9. However, these examples are sufficient to show that judges', lawyers', and legal scholars' ordinary understanding of the relationship between substantive rights and remedies is inconsistent with both the rubber-stamp conception of remedies and the remedial conception of rights. That understanding assumes that it is not possible to determine our substantive rights simply by evidence of the orders that courts are willing to make, and vice versa.

ii. Action Rights

A 'cause of action' is the set of facts that a claimant must prove to obtain a court order,[9] and a cause-of-action right (hereafter 'action right') is the right to the order that claimants enjoy once they prove the required facts. For example, if it is established in court that the defendant owes the claimant a sum of money, the court normally has no choice but to issue an order directing the defendant to pay the money. The duty correlative to an action right is a duty to issue an order; accordingly, this duty is imposed on the court, the institution responsible for issuing the order (and

[9] '[A cause of action is] every fact which it would be necessary for the plaintiff to prove, if traversed, in order to support his right to the judgment': *Read v Brown* [1889] 22 QBD 128, 131 (Lord Escher). See also *Letang v Cooper* [1965] 1 QB 232, 242–3.

prior to litigation, the claimant has a power, correlative to a liability on the court—not on the defendant—to put the court under a duty to issue an order). Claimants typically go to court to obtain orders, and their arguments are normally intended to show that the court is legally bound to grant them an order. When claimants make such arguments, they are asserting their action rights.

I discuss the various actions rights recognized in the common law in my answer to the next question ('on what grounds are remedies available?'). Here, I limit myself to four general comments. First, attempts to establish action rights are subject to remedial defences. I explore these defences in Chapter 9, but as the very idea of a remedial defence is novel it may be useful to mention here that they are numerous and practically important. They include, inter alia, some or all of the defences associated with limitation periods, formalities, immunities, and illegalities. They also include, I argue, 'adequacy of damages' and 'supervision', as well as so-called 'equitable defences', such as laches, clean hands, and hardship.

The second comment is that while action rights are typically rights to the issuance of specific orders—for example, a right to an order for a sum due or to an order for the recovery of land—in certain cases action rights are effectively rights to obtain one of two possible orders. Such rights can arise when claimants seek orders that originated in the Chancery Court, for example, an injunction or specific performance ('specific relief'). These orders are traditionally said to be available only in the court's discretion. Claimants seeking specific relief have to establish certain facts, but there is no guarantee, at least in theory, that the court will grant specific relief even if the necessary facts are established. I discuss the nature of this discretion in Chapter 9. For the moment, I merely note that it is heavily qualified (which explains why it is possible to appeal decisions to refuse specific relief), and that when a court refuses specific relief in the exercise of this discretion, it usually grants damages in lieu. It is not obvious how to describe the legal situation of claimants who have established a set of facts that allow—but do not require—a court to grant specific relief. It is perhaps simplest to say that such claimants have an action right that the court consider granting specific relief and, if the court does not grant specific relief, that they award damages.

The third comment is that action rights are not coercively enforceable. Although civilian legal systems sometimes allow citizens to bring legal proceedings against the state or even against specific courts for losses suffered because of a court's failure to issue a proper ruling,[10] in the common law the only recourse to a disappointed claimant is an appeal to a higher court. It follows that if it is assumed that for a right to exist it must be capable of being coercively enforced, action rights are

[10] See Cappelletti (1989) 65–7, 78–88. In theory, if the English court system fails to protect a citizen's rights, the citizen may now bring an action under Article 6(1) of the *European Convention on Human Rights*. However, the remedy in such a case would not be a sanction per se, but rather a declaration that the English state failed to uphold the relevant rights.

not rights. However, as mentioned above, this assumption is not part of the conventional understanding of legal rights. Claimants who have proven before a court that the defendant owes them money have an action right to an order commanding payment because courts consistently say that they must order payment on such proof. If a lower court wrongly refuses to grant the order, an appellate court will not hesitate to correct the mistake.

A final observation is that most of remedial law can be explained in terms of action rights. The core of remedial law is a body of rules that govern when, and in what form, courts make orders: the subject matter of these rules is action rights. To say that courts will rubber-stamp creditors' rights to payment is to say that on proof of a debt creditors obtain action rights to orders directing that the debt be paid. In contrast, to say there is no right to rulings requiring payment of time-expired debts is to say that creditors have no action rights in these circumstances. Propositions about when, and in what form, courts issue orders are propositions about action rights. Still, it is useful to distinguish action rights from the 'court-ordered rights' that arise when action rights are fulfilled. The fact that a claimant enjoys an action right does not guarantee that the court will issue the relevant order. Further, we have just seen that some action rights are rights not to particular orders, but to either of two possible orders. Finally, it is useful generally to separate the question of why an order should be issued from the question of what kind of order should be issued. Proof that a defendant has failed to fulfil a contractual obligation to deliver goods is usually a sufficient reason to issue an order, but the question of what kind of order should be issued—for example, whether it should be an order that the defendant deliver the goods or, instead, merely pay a sum of money—raises different considerations. Similarly, while proof that the defendant wronged the claimant may be sufficient reason to issue an order, the question of what kind of order should be issued (and in what amount) raises, again, new considerations.

iii. Court-Ordered Rights

The second category of remedial rights—court-ordered rights—is comprised of rights established by judicial orders. It seems clear that such rights exist: by definition, orders should be obeyed. When a court orders a defendant to pay the claimant £100, the defendant henceforth has a duty, born of the order, to pay the sum. Court-ordered rights are the rights correlative to such duties. The main question raised by such rights is who holds them? To whom is the duty to comply with orders owed?

The few authors to have addressed this question appear to assume that claimants hold these rights.[11] This assumption would be correct if the rulings under

[11] See Zakrzewski (2005) 78–81; Birks (1997b) 19.

consideration were declarations. When courts declare that a defendant is bound by a particular duty, the duty in question is typically a duty owed to the claimant. For example, the duty contemplated in a ruling that states 'It is declared that the defendant has a contractual duty to pay the claimant £100' is self-evidently owed to the claimant. In this respect, declarations are effectively mini-substantive rules: like substantive rules, they affirm the existence of substantive rights and duties, albeit the rights and duties of particular persons.

Orders, however, are not declarations, they are commands ('It is *ordered* that the defendant pay the claimant £100'). The duties that commands create are owed to whoever issued them, which in the case of judicial commands is the court or, more generally, the state. In this respect, a defendant's duty to comply with a judicial injunction against trespassing is similar to a motorist's duty to comply with a police officer's order to stop driving. The purpose of the police officer's order may be to benefit another individual, for example, another driver, but the motorist's duty to comply with the order is owed to the police officer. Stated differently, the duty imposed by an order is to obey the order. And since it is courts that issue orders, it is to courts that this duty is owed. Whether citizens are morally bound to obey judicial orders, and if so why, is a separate, and more difficult, question (see Chapter 5); for the moment, it is sufficient to note that the legal duty imposed by a court order is owed to the court.

This interpretation of court orders is broadly consistent with legal practice. It is true that judges sometimes describe monetary orders as creating 'judgment debts'.[12] This language seems to imply that, as in the case of ordinary legal debts, the claimant has a right to payment. However, courts do not present orders as statements of rights or duties (or of debts), and failing to comply with an order is not treated in the same way as, for example, failing to perform a contractual obligation owed to the claimant or trespassing on the claimant's land. As we saw in Chapter 3, failure to comply with an order is not a tort or any other recognized species of private law wrong. Claimants cannot obtain damages from defendants, or any other form of redress, with respect to losses that arise from the defendant failing to comply with an order. To be sure, claimants can take steps to enforce unfulfilled orders. However, this option confers a power, not a right, and the power is to call on the state's coercive machinery. Further, if claimants held the rights born of orders they ought to be able to waive or reduce these rights unilaterally. Yet judicial orders cannot be varied or waived except by the court, and even then, only in rare circumstances.[13] Courts may even issue orders against the parties' wishes once the order has been drafted (but not issued) and possibly at any time after the closing of

[12] *In Re European Central Railway Co, Ex Parte Oriental Financial Corporation* (1876) 4 ChD 33, 37–8 (Bramwell J).

[13] Zuckerman (2013) 1072–80.

arguments.[14] Of course, litigants can agree, post-order, that the claimant will not seek to enforce the order, but such agreements say nothing about the order's validity or the duties that it creates.

Court-ordered rights differ from substantive rights in two further respects. First, court-ordered rights may be coercively enforced. In contrast, failing to comply with a substantive duty merely leaves one liable to being subject to a court order. Proof that a defendant failed to comply with a substantive private law duty is normally a sufficient basis upon which to grant an order, but it is not a sufficient basis for seizing the wrongdoer's property, imprisoning the wrongdoer, or imposing any other private law sanctions.

The other respect in which court-ordered rights are distinctive is simply that courts create them while acting in their official capacities. A court's decision to issue an order or other ruling differs in several ways from an individual's decision to exercise a substantive legal power (such as the power to make a will or a contract). Courts have legal duties to issue the orders that they issue. Further, courts intend these orders, in broad terms, to reflect a reasoned decision as to what is required in order for justice to be done between the parties. Finally, a court's decision order may be appealed to a higher court. In short, when courts create court-ordered rights, they are fulfilling a fundamentally public function.

iv. Enforcement Rights

The final category of remedial rights—enforcement rights—are rights that the state's coercive machinery be employed to enforce an order. In a typical case, enforcement rights come into existence when claimants who have obtained an order make an application to a court, bailiff, sheriff, or other enforcement officer, and then satisfy certain conditions, the main one being proof that the defendant failed to comply with the order. For example, where a defendant fails to comply with an order to pay the claimant a sum of money, the claimant, on application to an enforcement officer, normally obtains a right that the officer seize and sell the defendant's assets to satisfy the order. The duties correlative to enforcement rights are therefore duties imposed on the state or its agents to employ the state's coercive machinery against the subject of a judicial order. I discussed the rules governing such applications and the various means of enforcement available to private law litigants in Chapter 3.

[14] Ibid 812–13; *Three Rivers District Council & Ors v The Governor & Company of the Bank of England* [2006] EWHC 816.

As was true of action rights, enforcement rights arise from the exercise of legal powers, in this case claimant's powers to call upon the state's coercive forces. However, even more than in the case of powers to obtain action rights, powers to obtain enforcement rights are commonly described as rights themselves. Lawyers regularly say that successful claimants have rights to enforce the orders that they obtain. It is difficult to avoid such language, but, strictly speaking, a right to enforcement only arises once a claimant has made the appropriate application to an enforcement officer.

If a defendant fails to fulfil an order, the state typically has no discretion to refuse to enforce the order following a proper application (though it may have the discretion to refuse certain methods of enforcement). In such cases, the claimant has a right to enforcement in the ordinary sense of the word. However, in some cases the claimant obtains something short of a right, strictly speaking. Specifically, where defendants fail to comply with non-monetary orders—for example where they fail to comply with injunctions—the only enforcement right that claimants can normally acquire is a right that the court consider finding the defendant in contempt of court and, on this basis, further consider imprisoning or fining the defendant, or sequestering the defendant's property. Courts are not bound to find recalcitrant defendants in contempt nor, if the defendants are found in contempt, to punish them. For example, if the defendant has a plausible excuse for not having complied with the original order, the court may refuse to impose a sanction. In this respect, the enforcement rights associated with non-monetary orders are similar to the action rights that the beneficiaries of such orders enjoyed prior to the orders being issued: they are rights that the state consider certain actions.

Claimants' powers to obtain enforcement rights does not guarantee that the results contemplated by judicial orders will be achieved. In the case of non-monetary orders, the normal means of enforcement (imprisonment, fines, sequestration of property) may provide incentives for compliance, but they cannot bring about the result sought by the order. In the case of monetary orders, while the normal means of enforcement (seizing and selling the defendant's property) can in principle bring about the result contemplated by the order, in practice the contemplated result is often thwarted because the defendant is insolvent.

Finally, it bears repeating that enforcement rights can only be obtained if a court has already issued an order in the claimant's favour. Criminal cases aside, courts will not command or authorize sanctions merely on proof that the defendant committed a wrong. In private law cases, such proof gives rise at most to a right to an order directing the defendant to do or not to do something. The court orders that are this book's focus are necessary, but not sufficient, conditions for the existence of enforcement rights.

v. Summary Chart

Substantive Rights

- Rights held by individuals (or other legal persons) that other individuals do or not do something.
- Substantive rights arise because individuals enjoy them generally or because of an event other than a judicial ruling (e.g. a contractual agreement).
- Examples include debtors' rights to be paid and landowner's rights to exclusive possession.

⇩

Action Rights

- Rights held by claimants that a court issue a requested order.
- Action rights arise where claimants establish certain facts (the 'cause of action') before a court. (Below, I argue that these facts must demonstrate a rights-threat, wrong, or an injustice).
- Examples include rights to orders that the defendant cease a nuisance or pay damages.

⇩

Court-ordered Rights

- Rights held by courts that defendants perform actions required by orders.
- Court-ordered rights arise from the issuance of court orders.
- Examples include rights that the defendant pay damages to the claimant or that the defendant not trespass on the claimant's land.

⇩

Enforcement Rights

- Rights held by claimants that the state impose a sanction on a defendant.
- Enforcement rights arise on proof before a court or other legal body that the defendant failed to comply with a court order.
- Examples include rights that a legal official seize and sell the defendant's assets (to satisfy a monetary order) or that the defendant be imprisoned.

Figure 1 Substantive and Remedial Rights

Two lessons may be drawn from the chart shown in Figure 1. First, the substantive rights that citizens enjoy vis-à-vis one another as part of their day-to-day lives are not the same as the rights that they may enjoy, following litigation, to court rulings—and neither of these rights is the same as the rights that rulings create or the rights that the beneficiaries of those rulings may obtain to their enforcement by the state. Second, substantive rights, action rights, court-ordered rights, and enforcement rights relate to one another in different ways. In some cases, the linkage is relatively simple. For example, the breach of a substantive duty often gives rise to a power to obtain a ruling requiring the defendant to do the very thing required by the original duty, and, further, in many of those same cases the law backs up the ruling by making its coercive powers available to help bring about the result that the ruling stipulates. But in other cases the breach of a substantive duty does not give rise to power to obtain an order or gives rise only to a power to obtain an order with a content different from that of the breached duty. Further, and as I explain in more detail below, courts sometimes issue orders notwithstanding that the defendant has not breached or even threatened to breach a substantive duty. Finally, the means of enforcing orders may not bring about anything like the results required by the order, let alone the results required by the defendant's substantive duty. The overall lesson, then, is that explaining court-ordered rights is different from explaining substantive rights, action rights, or enforcement rights.

C. On What Grounds are Remedies Available?

This question has attracted little attention from legal scholars. Scholars have discussed in detail the availability of particular types of remedies; for example, the availability of specific performance orders or orders to pay exemplary damages. But there appear to have been only two attempts to generalize from these discussions. Although neither generalization fits the law, each captures part of the truth.

The first generalization, often associated with Blackstone,[15] supposes that remedies are always responses to wrongs. This view neatly fits the ordinary understanding of 'remedy' as a cure for a problem. The most obvious kind of legal problem, it might be thought, is a legal wrong. Nonetheless, this suggestion cannot explain a variety of ordinary orders. The most obvious counter-examples are *quia timet* ('preventative') orders, which are available in cases where the defendant is likely to infringe the claimant's rights in future but has not yet done so. For example, a court might issue a *quia timet* injunction to cease construction of a building that, if completed, would infringe the defendant's right to light. Courts also issue remedies in cases where the defendant has not even threatened to commit a wrong. The clearest examples are legislative in origin. For instance, many common law jurisdictions have legislation authorizing courts to issue orders dealing with maintenance and the division of matrimonial property following a marriage breakdown. In England, the relevant legislation provides that courts may make 'an order that either party to the marriage shall pay to the other such lump sum or sums as may be so specified'.[16] There is no suggestion in the legislation that claimants must show that the defendant had a duty to do what the order requires prior to the order's issuance, much less that the defendant breached this duty. To obtain an order the claimant must merely show that, broadly speaking, it would be fair in the circumstances to issue it. Restitutionary orders are another example. If you mistakenly transfer money into my bank account, you can normally obtain an order requiring me to return the money. It does not

[15] Blackstone, (1979 reprint) Book I 137, Book III 115–16.

[16] *Matrimonial Causes Act* 1973, s 23(1) (c).

matter that, as will usually be the case, I am an entirely innocent beneficiary of your mistake. Other counter-examples are discussed in Chapters 6 and 8 (and in Chapter 8 I conclude that relatively few remedies are responses to wrongs).

The second generalization supposes that private law remedies are always responses to substantive rights. According to this view, if claimants establish that they enjoy a substantive right vis-à-vis the defendant, courts will uphold this right by ordering the defendant to comply with the correlative duty. For example, on proof that the defendant has a contractual duty to pay the claimant a sum of money, the court will order the defendant to fulfil this duty. Peter Birks is the best-known contemporary defender of this view.[17]

The suggestion that courts would agree to issue orders merely on proof that the defendant is bound by a substantive duty owed to the claimant is implausible on its face. Unless the claimant's right has been infringed or is under threat, why should a court—a publicly funded institution—get involved? The suggestion also does not fit the law. As I mentioned when discussing the closely related 'remedial conception of rights', courts will not order defendants to comply with negative contractual duties (or issue any other kind of order) merely on proof that the duty exists. The same observation applies to the negative rights against trespasses, batteries, slanders, defamations, carelessly caused injuries, and so forth that lie at the heart of tort law. Courts only issue orders supporting these rights on proof that the right has been infringed or is about to be infringed. Nor can this suggestion explain the matrimonial property orders discussed above or the earlier example of orders to pay exemplary damages. In neither case does the defendant have a duty to do what the order requires prior to its issuance, and thus in neither case can the order be a response to that duty's existence.

The law governing causes of action is more complex than Blackstone and Birks' suggestions assume. Below, I argue that the common law recognizes three main causes of action: rights-threats, wrongs, and injustices. The first two are related to the causes of action identified in Blackstone and Birks' work, but the third—injustices—is not present in either writer's work.

Of course, courts and lawyers' descriptions of causes of action are typically more detailed than the one-word descriptions given above. A lawyer seeking an order directing the defendant to comply with a contractual non-competition covenant might explain to her client that she will need to prove that the parties created a valid contract, the non-competition covenant is valid, the covenant prohibits the defendant from engaging in certain behaviour, and the defendant is engaging in this behaviour or intends to do so in the near future. However, viewed broadly, what the lawyer in this example is seeking to prove is that her claimant's rights are under threat, or so I argue. The terms 'rights-threats', 'wrongs', and 'injustices' are summary descriptions of the facts that claimants must establish to obtain remedies.

[17] Birks (2000b) xxxvi–xxli.

i. Rights-Threats

The most commonly invoked cause of action in the common law is a rights-threat. In Chapter 6, I argue that a rights-threat is the cause of action for specific performance orders, injunctions, orders for a sum due, orders for the recovery of land or other property, and substitutionary damages.

The above orders are generally available on proof that the defendant is unwilling to comply with a substantive duty—in other words, on proof that the relevant substantive right is under threat from the defendant.[18] In most cases, claimants establish rights-threats by showing that the defendant is engaged in an ongoing breach of a substantive duty owed to the claimant; for example, by showing that the defendant is causing a nuisance, committing an ongoing trespass, or is overdue on a contractual debt. Courts rightly regard an ongoing infringement as strong evidence that the defendant will not respect the claimant's rights in future. However, and subject to certain practical considerations, claimants can also establish unwillingness by showing that, while the defendant has yet to infringe their rights, it is likely to do so in the near future. For example, a claimant can establish a rights-threat by demonstrating that the defendant is constructing a building that, when completed, will constitute a legal nuisance. If claimants establish a rights-threat in either of these ways, the court will normally order the defendant to comply with the relevant substantive duty. In cases where the defendant is not yet in breach, the order is described as preventative or '*quia timet*', but in substance it is the same as the orders issued in cases where the defendant is in breach.

By definition, defendants who are engaged in ongoing rights-infringements have committed wrongs. It might be thought, then, that in these cases the claimant's cause of action must be a wrong. However, while proof of a wrong is indeed a cause of action (and will normally support a separate order to pay damages: see below), it is not the cause of action for the orders under consideration here. For claimants seeking injunctions, specific performance, orders for a sum due, and so forth, proof that the defendant wronged them is merely evidence that the defendant is likely to continue wronging them. The defendant's ongoing wrong is evidence of the threat to the claimant's rights. It is because the courts' underlying concern is the threat, not the wrong, that they are willing to issue *quia timet* versions of the above orders.[19] The focus on the threat also explains why courts refuse to issue injunctions when there has been a past wrong, but no threat of a future wrong—for

[18] What I call a 'rights-threat' is therefore more accurately (though also more awkwardly) described as a 'right under threat'. To prove a rights-threat the claimant does not need to show the defendant communicated an explicit threat ('your money or your life'); it is sufficient to show that the defendant is likely to infringe or continue infringing the claimant's rights in the future.

[19] Although it is not strictly possible to obtain *quia timet* orders for a sum due or for the recovery of land or other property, substantively similar orders are available (as I explain in Chapter 6) under other names.

instance, where the wrong was a one-off accident. For similar reasons, courts also deny specific relief in cases where it is impossible for the defendant to comply with the order—for instance, courts will not order defendants to deliver goods that they no longer own or possess. In these cases, the defendant has committed a wrong, but there is no threat to the claimant's substantive rights. More generally, specific performance, injunctions, orders for a sum due, and orders for the recovery or land or other property are prospective rulings. They cannot erase, undo, or compensate for something that happened in the past. The only thing that these orders can do is to try to prevent future wrongs. And preventing future wrongs is just another way of saying 'responding to rights-threats'. The only reason to issue an order to prevent a future wrong is that the court thinks there is a significant risk that, absent the order, the wrong will happen—in other words, that the claimant's rights are under threat.

Finally, it may be useful to mention that, with one exception, a rights-threat is not the cause of action for either damages awards or restitutionary awards (the exception, which I discuss below, is substitutionary damages). I mention this exclusion because some authors and judges believe that the common law recognizes substantive duties to pay damages, as well as substantive duties to make restitution. If this belief is warranted, orders to pay damages and restitutionary orders are similar to orders for a sum due (and to the other orders discussed above): they merely order defendants to do what they already had substantive duties to do. In this book's classificatory scheme, the cause of action for these orders would therefore be the same as the cause of action for orders for a sum due: a rights-threat. If we have substantive duties to pay damages and to make restitution, then the only reason to order us to do these things is that we are unwilling to do them voluntarily.

I explain my reasons for rejecting the 'duty-confirming' view of damages awards and restitutionary awards in Chapters 7 and 8. Briefly, these reasons include: (1) courts and commentators rarely describe wrongdoers or recipients of defective transfers as having duties to pay money to the claimant—what they say, instead, is that wrongdoers and recipients are liable to make such payments; (2) relatedly, courts invariably describe the rules governing the assessment of damages and restitution as rules directed at them, that is, as rules that tell courts, not defendants, how to assess damages and restitution; (3) damages are not available for failing to pay damages or failing to make restitution and, more generally, neither of these events is recognized as a legal wrong; and (4) if there were substantive duties to pay damages or make restitution they would be unknowable duties: the facts that determine the existence and magnitude of such a duty are in the claimant's hands.

ii. Wrongs

The second cause of action recognized in the common law is proof of a wrong. The clearest example of an award for which the cause of action is a wrong is exemplary (or 'punitive') damages. Exemplary damages are only issued on proof of a wrong, and they are issued because of the wrong. Their quantum is determined according to the wrongfulness of the defendant's action (which takes into account both the wrongdoer's motivations and the action's consequences). As I mentioned a moment ago, some authors believe that wrongdoers have substantive duties to pay damages. But, whatever the plausibility of this view in respect of other damages awards, it is wholly implausible in the case of exemplary damages. Courts enjoy considerable discretion with respect to both the availability and the assessment of exemplary damages. If there were a substantive duty to pay exemplary damages, it would be a duty that the party subject to it could not ascertain, and so could not plausibly be expected to fulfil. More broadly, when courts assess exemplary damages they never suggest that they are trying to determine what the defendant should have done prior to judgment. Instead, what they say, broadly, is that they are trying to determine what they—the court—should do in order to condemn the defendant's actions and vindicate the claimant's rights. In any event, punishment is only punishment when it is meted out by a court or other authority. A substantive duty to punish one's self would be incoherent (see Chapter 5).

A second clear example is nominal damages. Proof of a wrong is both a necessary and sufficient basis for an award of nominal damages. And as in the case of exemplary damages, courts have considerable discretion regarding the magnitude of nominal damages. Nominal damages are also similar to exemplary damages in that courts clearly understand themselves to be sending a message when they issue them, in this case a message that the defendants infringed the claimant's rights. For this message to be communicated, the duty to pay must arise with the order. If a substantive rule imposed the duty, the duty would carry no message other than that the payment ought to be made.

The classification of exemplary and nominal damages as 'wrong-based' remedies is, I hope, uncontroversial. The difficult question is which other remedies belong in this category. It might be thought that the obvious answer is 'all other damages awards'. But I defend a different answer. I argue that the core damages awards, namely, awards of compensatory damages (roughly, awards set at the value of the claimant's consequential pecuniary losses), are responses to injustices, not wrongs. This interpretation is controversial. It is orthodox law that to obtain compensatory damages, the claimant must prove a wrong. And if there is no substantive duty to pay damages, it might be thought that there is no possible reason, aside from a wrong, to order a defendant to pay for consequential losses. I once held this view. My primary reasons for rejecting the 'wrong-based' view of compensatory damages, which I set out in Chapter 8, are twofold. The first is that the rules for assessing compensatory awards limit compensation in a myriad of ways that are inconsistent with a wrongs-based view. A wrongful loss is no less wrongful because it was mitigated, offset by a collateral benefit, caused partly by the victim or a third party, excluded by agreement or, more generally, not reasonably foreseeable. As the courts consistently affirm, the justification for these limitations is that it would not be 'fair', 'just', or 'reasonable' to attribute the losses they exclude to the defendant. Of course, wrong-based theories do not suppose that courts should issue unfair damages awards. But if courts are seeking to respond to the defendant's wrongdoing, the question is not whether its fair to hold the defendant responsible for the relevant loss. The question is what is the appropriate response to the defendant's wrongdoing. And insofar as the court is considering the significance of the claimant's losses, the only thing that matters is whether the relevant loss was a consequence of the wrongdoing.

The second reason is that compensatory damages awards are available in respect of actions that are not wrongs, or at least are not wrongs in a sense that could merit a wrong-based response. Examples include compensatory awards for loss caused by the escape of something brought onto one's land (*Rylands v Fletcher*), in a state of necessity, or by an innocent misrepresentation. Other examples include damages awards issued against vicariously liable employers, in lieu of *quia timet* (preventative) injunctions, for wrongs committed against third parties, and in cases where the award is issued in lieu of specific relief and for reasons based on the substantive undesirability (typically the exorbitant cost) of the requested action. In all these cases, courts award compensation notwithstanding that the action that caused the loss was permissible, if not positively desirable. It is possible, of course, that these awards are unrelated to the compensatory awards that are issued in those cases, by far the majority, where the defendant has committed a wrong. However, the law does not distinguish between damages for non-wrongs and ordinary damages: both are simply 'damages'. More importantly, the assessment process is identical. Damages for injuries caused by the escape of water collected on your land are the same whether you are liable because the escape was your fault or because, under the doctrine of *Rylands v Fletcher*, landowners are strictly liable for the escape of water collected on their land. If the claimant's cause of action differed depending on whether the defendant committed a wrong, we would expect that the courts' response would also differ.

With compensatory damages relegated to the third category, it might be thought that the category of wrong-based remedies is limited to exemplary and nominal damages. But, again, that is not my view. In Chapter 8, I argue that exemplary damages and nominal damages are just two examples of a broader group of damages awards that, being neither compensatory nor substitutionary, are best understood as wrong-based. These awards include damages for pain and suffering and a variety of damages awards I describe compendiously as 'vindicatory damages' and individually as user damages, waiver damages, market-price damages, gain-based damages, and non-pecuniary damages for wrongs to the person. Like exemplary and nominal damages, these awards are not set at the amount of the plaintiff's loss. Indeed, most of these awards are available where the claimant has not suffered a loss at all. These awards represent the defendant's wrong by attaching a monetary figure to it. And like nominal and exemplary awards—and wrong-based awards generally—there is no formula for determining what that figure should be (although the courts adopt conventional measures, where feasible, such as the market price). The main difference between these awards and awards of nominal or exemplary damages is the seriousness of the wrongs to which they are a response. Broadly, the wrongs to which these awards respond are more serious than the wrongs to which nominal damages respond and less serious than the wrongs to which exemplary damages respond.

iii. Injustices

The last of the three main causes of action recognized in the common law is an injustice. As understood here, an injustice is, roughly, an unfair loss or gain that has arisen from a transaction between the claimant and defendant. In Chapter 8, I argue that an injustice is the cause of action for orders to make restitution following defective transfers ('restitutionary orders') and orders to pay damages for consequential pecuniary losses ('compensatory orders'). However, there are almost certainly other injustice-responding remedies, some of which I mention in passing (one example is the matrimonial property orders, mentioned above).

The idea of 'injustice-responding orders' is novel. Even more novel is the suggestion that restitutionary and compensatory orders share a common cause of action. It may be helpful to mention, then, that Chapter 8's original motivation was not a particular understanding of the meaning or importance of the concept of justice. It was motivated by my view, briefly defended above, that restitutionary and compensatory orders are not plausibly interpreted as responses to either rights-threats or wrongs. If this view is accepted, the main question is how to describe the missing category. The term 'injustice' is apt. Courts and commentators already explain restitutionary orders using a cognate concept ('unjust enrichment'), and, as we have seen, courts regularly invoke justice when they explain and apply the rules governing compensatory orders. More importantly, the subject matter of justice is the same as the subject matter of the rules governing restitutionary and compensatory damages: the allocation of gains and losses. The adjective 'unjust' is characteristically used to describe states of affairs in which a loss or gain has been unfairly imposed, distributed, or allowed to persist. We ask whether the tax system is just because we want to know whether it allocates the burden of taxation fairly. The focus of restitutionary and compensatory orders is the fairness of the outcomes that they modify.

It might be thought that the concept of an injustice is too broad to do any explanatory work. The explanation for why the outcome that triggers a restitutionary order is unjust is very different from the explanation for why the outcome that triggers a compensatory order is unjust. 'Transferring money by mistake' has little in common with 'carelessly causing pecuniary losses'. However, the concept of an injustice is sufficiently explanatory for this book's aims. At the level at which this book's classificatory scheme operates, the concept of an injustice is no broader than the concept of a wrong or a rights-threat. The facts that must be proven to establish the wrong of battery are radically different from those that must be proven to establish a breach of contract or a defamatory statement or the breach of a statutory duty. And the explanations for why these actions are wrongs are similarly diverse. The concept of a legal wrong is unified not by the tests that the law employs to establish wrongs; it is unified by the characterization of the relevant event as a wrong, that is, as something that ought not to happen. If we ask why the event is a wrong, the explanations are very different. The same is true of injustices. The main difference is that the concept of a wrong is used to identify undesirable behaviour, while the concept of an injustice is used to identify undesirable consequences of behaviour.

The argument for classifying restitutionary awards as responses to injustices is relatively simple. Restitutionary awards are not responses to wrongs. Although some defendants in the defective transfer cases that are my focus are wrongdoers, most are innocent. If you transfer money by mistake into my bank account, you can obtain an order that I return the money regardless of whether I had anything to do with the transfer. Such an order also cannot be explained on the ground that I agreed, even implicitly, to return the money to you (and thus that I am engaged in an ongoing breach of a duty to return the money). The money simply showed up in my bank account. Substantively, claimants seeking restitutionary orders following a defective transfer must show that the defendant obtained title to property (usually money) and that the claimant's autonomy was impaired because of a mistake, fraud, duress, compulsion, necessity, or something similar.[20] The natural explanation for why you should not be able to keep something in such circumstances is that it is unfair to keep it. This explanation is of course entirely orthodox. Courts and commentators standardly describe the outcome of a defective transfer as an 'unjust enrichment'. My classification of restitutionary orders accepts that description at face value. As the term is ordinarily understood, an unjust enrichment is the same as, or is at least included within, what I have described as an injustice. To say that something is an unjust enrichment is just another way of saying that it is an injustice, and both are just ways of saying that a gain or loss (in this case a gain) has ended up in the wrong hands.

Compensatory awards are in certain respects the mirror image of restitutionary orders. In each case, the court responds to an unjust outcome by ordering the advantaged party to correct the outcome. The main difference between restitutionary and compensatory awards is that while the former are responses to unjust gains,

[20] Burrows (2011) 201–317.

the latter are responses to unjust losses. It is true that lawyers traditionally classify compensatory damages, and indeed damage awards generally, as responses to wrongs. And in most cases in which compensatory awards are issued, the defendant has committed a wrong, and the claimant has to prove this wrong to obtain the award. However, I argue that in these cases the wrong is a condition of the award, not the reason for issuing it. If the wrong were the reason, the rules for assessing compensatory damages and for determining when compensatory awards are available would be different. As in the case of restitutionary awards, the law's fundamental concern is not the wrongfulness of the defendant's behaviour; its fundamental concern is the fairness of the relevant transaction's outcome. The wrong is merely a reason (and not the only possible reason) for holding the defendant responsible for an unfair outcome.

Under what conditions, then, is it fair to hold defendant responsible for losses that they have caused? I do not provide a comprehensive answer to this question. However, I do argue that the various conditions under which courts grant compensatory damages are consistent with both the ordinary and theoretical understanding of responsibility. The most obvious and important sufficient condition is that the defendant's action was a wrong. If you incur a loss because of my wrongful action, it is fair to hold me responsible for that loss. If I should not have done the action, you should not have suffered the consequences you suffered. And, since it was my choice to commit the wrongful action, it is fair to hold me responsible for those consequences. Responsibility for the consequences of one's wrongful actions is probably the most basic form of legal responsibility.

However, it is not the only form. For example, it is fair to hold an individual responsible for losses that they have caused in a state of necessity. In *Vincent v Lake Erie Transportation Co*,[21] the defendant moored his ship, without permission, to the claimant's dock to prevent it being destroyed in a violent storm. The court held that although the defendant acted reasonably (there was no other way to save the ship and crew), he must nonetheless compensate the claimant for damage caused to the dock. Because the defendant chose to use the claimant's property, it is fair to hold him responsible for the claimant's loss. Similarly, it is fair to hold individuals responsible for losses that they have caused while engaged in a dangerous activity. It is on this basis, I argue (together with many others), that the defendant in *Rylands v Fletcher*[22] was held responsible for the losses caused by the escape of water from his dam, notwithstanding that the dam was built with due care. Some dangerous activities are simply banned outright. However, others are permitted because their benefits are thought to outweigh the risks. At the same time, it is fair to hold individuals who choose to engage in such activities responsible for the harm

[21] [1910] 109 Minn 456.
[22] [1868] LR 3 HL 330.

they may cause. Individuals who engage in dangerous activities expose others to unusual risks, risks that go beyond the ordinary risks that are properly regarded as part of the ordinary vicissitudes of life (and for which there is ordinarily no liability without wrongdoing). Broadly similar explanations account, I argue, for the liability of employers for the torts of their employees. It also accounts for liability for losses that arise because the defendant is permitted to engage in an act or omission that, while normally a wrong, is not a wrong in the circumstances because its value far outweighs the harm that it causes. Indeed, courts and commentators typically explain these liabilities in just these terms. This book's main contribution to the literature on responsibility and damages is to locate these familiar explanations in a general account of remedies.

iv. Summary Chart

The chart shown in Figure 2 summarizes the above discussion.

RIGHTS-THREATS	WRONGS	INJUSTICES
Definition: defendant unwilling to fulfil substantive duty owed to claimant.	Definition: tort or breach of contract.	Definition: unjust loss or gain arising from a transaction between the parties.
Rights-Threat-Responding Orders:	Wrong-Responding Orders:	Injustice-Responding Orders:
• Specific performance • Injunctions • Ordersfor a sum due • Ordersfor the recovery of land or other property • Substitutionary damages (damages in lieu of specific relief in cases where specific relief is refused for remedial reasons, e.g. cost of supervision)	• Exemplary damages • Nominal damages • Vindicatory damages (user damages, waiver damages, market price damages, gain-based damages, non-pecuniary damages for wrongs to the person) • Damages for pain and suffering	• Compensatory damages • Restitution (following a defective transfer)

Figure 2 The Common Law's Primary Causes of Action

D. What Kinds of Remedies are Available?

The final structural question about remedial law concerns the kinds of remedies available from courts. Although remedies textbooks rarely address this question directly, they indirectly answer it in their tables of contents, which are typically organized according to different categories of remedies—a chapter on specific performance, a chapter on injunctions, and so on. Insofar as the authors intend such schemes to reflect deeper principles, the principles are usually historical. Thus, textbooks often distinguish between remedies that originated in the Royal Courts and those that originated in the Equity Courts.

It is unsurprising that textbooks would focus on this distinction given its historical importance. But history aside, it has little to recommend it in a general discussion of remedial law. For anyone with a general interest in remedial law, the most important things to know about remedies are (1) when they are awarded (the focus of the previous question) and (2) how they relate to the parties' substantive rights and duties. The second question flows from the basic justification for studying remedial law, namely, that it is a distinctive body of law, in particular, a body of law distinct from substantive law. As far as the contents of court orders are concerned, the most important thing to know is whether and how they vary from the content of substantive duties. Bluntly, do remedies merely rubber-stamp substantive duties, or do they do something different, and, if so, when?

The answer defended here is that while some remedies confirm substantive duties ('replicative' remedies), others create new duties ('creative' remedies). Further, creative remedies are creative in different ways.

i. Replicative Orders

Replicative orders direct defendants to do things that they already had substantive duties to do.[23] A relatively uncontroversial example is an order directing the defendant to refrain from contravening a contractual non-competition clause. This order directs the defendant to do the very thing that the defendant had a substantive duty to do—namely, not to compete with the claimant. A second relatively uncontroversial example is an order directing the defendant to pay an outstanding contractual debt: the content of this order replicates the content of the defendant's substantive duty to pay the debt.

As I mentioned above, some authors appear to assume that all orders are replicative (the 'rubber stamp' theory of court orders). This book rejects the rubber-stamp theory, in particular it rejects the view that damages orders and restitutionary orders are replicative. However, it accepts that most private law remedies are replicative. Specific performance orders, most injunctions, orders for a sum due, and order for the recovery of land or other property are all replicative: the content of these orders replicates the content of the defendant's substantive duty. Indeed, the

[23] Zakrzewski (2005) introduced the term 'replicative order'. The concept of replicative orders raises two technical questions. The first is whether it is possible, even in theory, to issue a replicative order in respect of an already-breached, time-specific, positive obligation. The second is whether an order can replicate duties that are owed by everyone in the world (e.g. the duty not to trespass on the claimant's property). I defend affirmative answers to these questions in Chapter 6.

category of 'replicative' orders and the category of 'orders issued in response to rights-threats' overlap almost perfectly.[24]

ii. Creative Orders

As suggested by their label, 'creative' orders bring new rights into existence, rights that differ from whatever substantive rights the claimant enjoyed vis-à-vis the defendant prior to the order. Described in terms of duties, creative orders direct defendants to do things that are different from what their substantive duties required.

In contrast to replicative orders, the very idea of creative orders is controversial. Many authors regard creative orders as undesirable and some regard them as conceptually impossible. Chapters 6 to 8 examine these views in the context of particular orders. For the moment, I merely note that it seems clear as a matter of positive law that common law courts issue creative orders. The question is how many orders are like this and how 'creative' they are. The classification adopted below distinguishes, in ascending order of creativity, three categories of creative orders.

Substitutionary orders

As understood here, an order is 'substitutionary' if it directs the defendant to perform a close substitute—invariably a close monetary substitute—of a still-valid substantive duty. In practice, substitutionary awards are monetary substitutes for specific relief. An example is an order to pay damages that is given in lieu of specific relief, where the reason specific relief is refused has nothing to do with the desirability of the requested action but instead reflects administrative or other concerns associated with the form of specific remedies.[25] For example, a court will normally refuse a request to order specific performance of a contractual duty to deliver fungible goods even where the claimant proves that the defendant is in breach of this duty. Instead, the court will order the defendant to pay damages set at the cost of hiring a third party to deliver the goods. This award is substitutionary because the

[24] 'Almost' because, as I explain below, courts sometimes respond to rights-threats by ordering defendants to perform monetary substitutes for non-monetary duties. In addition, *quia timet* mandatory injunctions sometimes direct defendants to do things that, while not strictly required by a substantive duty, are intended to prevent or cure the breach of such a duty. An example is an order that the defendant cease construction of a building that, once completed, will qualify as a nuisance. Constructing a building that could become, but is not yet, a nuisance is not a tort. These 'prophylactic' orders are close cousins of replicative orders. They are responses to rights-threats and, like replicative orders, they direct defendants to perform actions that, in the court's view, are necessary to ensure that the defendants comply with their substantive duties. Still, strictly speaking, prophylactic orders belong in their own sub-category within creative orders. However, as they are rare and substantively similar to replicative orders, I discuss them alongside replicative orders.

[25] The usual reason that courts award substitutionary damages is that they are easier to express, supervise, and enforce than non-monetary awards. But as I explain in Chapter 9, there are other reasons, such as a concern for ordering the performance of personal duties or for assisting wrongdoers.

reason that the court refuses specific performance has nothing to do with the desirability of the defendant delivering the goods or, more generally, with the existence or force of the rights-threat. As I explain in more detail in Chapter 9, courts refuse specific performance in such cases for primarily administrative reasons: monetary orders are easier to express, supervise, and enforce than non-monetary orders. Further, in such cases, the claimant can purchase almost-equivalent performance from a third party. Thus, rather than directly requiring the defendant to perform the relevant duty, the courts indirectly require performance by directing the defendant to pay for the cost of performance by a third party. The cause of action for such orders is the same as that of the replicative orders for which they are substitutes, namely, a rights-threat.

Substitutionary awards are relatively rare. For an award to be substitutionary, it must be possible, at the time of trial, for the defendant to perform the relevant substantive duty. It follows that damages awards are not substitutionary if courts award them in respect of terminated contractual obligations or in respect of past injuries to the claimant's person or property. Further, it is only where the court refuses specific relief for administrative or similar reasons that damages 'in lieu' of specific relief are substitutionary. If the court refuses relief for substantive reasons—for example, because the cost of performance is out of all proportion to its value—the damages are compensatory. In such cases, the court has already made clear that it is not interested in performance.

The existence of substitutionary orders (and indeed of creative orders generally) is implicitly rejected by authors who adopt an 'enforcement' view of legal duties, that is, by authors who assume that substantive duties exist only insofar as they are supported directly by court orders. For such authors, the courts' unwillingness to order defendants to perform promises to deliver fungible goods means that there is no legal duty to fulfil such promises. Adopting this view, Oliver Wendell Holmes famously described the duty to keep a contract at common law as 'a prediction that you must pay damages if you do not keep it,—and nothing else'.[26] However—and notwithstanding that Holmes was a judge in addition to a scholar—this view finds little support in the positive law. As I mentioned earlier, judges regularly say that contracting parties have duties to perform their contractual promises, and when they say this they do not distinguish between promises that courts will specifically enforce and promises that courts will not specifically enforce. Damages for breach of contract are described as just that—damages for breach. More concretely, the doctrine of frustration would be meaningless if contracting parties' only duties were to pay damages, since it is almost never impossible to pay a sum of money. Similarly, the tort of inducing breach of contract assumes that contracting parties have duties to perform their contractual promises, since it is inducing the breach

[26] Holmes (1897) 462.

of such promises (and not the breach of a supposed duty to pay damages) that constitutes the tort. Nor can the Holmesian view explain why courts regularly order defendants to perform their contractual promises, whether by ordering specific performance or, more commonly, by ordering payment for a sum due under a contract. Finally, this view cannot explain why specific performance is most commonly awarded when damages are inadequate in the sense that it is not possible to purchase substitute performance. In short, whatever theoretical arguments might be offered to support the Holmesian view, it finds little support in the positive law.

Wrong-responding orders

The second category of creative orders—wrong-responding orders—is comprised of orders that impose new duties on wrongdoers and that are issued in response to the defendant's wrongdoing. The label 'wrong-responding' does not tell us anything about the contents of the orders it identifies. It refers to a cause of action. However, there is almost nothing that can be said, at least in general terms, about the contents of wrong-responding orders. Wrong-responding orders are unique in this respect. For other orders, the cause of action and the judicial response are tightly linked. The natural and logical response to proof of a rights-threat is to order the defendant to comply with the threatened right (which is what courts do); similarly the natural and logical response to proof of an injustice is to order the defendant to correct the injustice (which, again, is what courts do). But as I explain in Chapter 8, there is no natural or logical response to a wrong. Like the law's response to criminal wrongs, the law's response to private wrongs is a matter of choice and convention. Not surprisingly, the content of wrong-based awards varies widely. Nominal damages are typically small, exemplary damages are typically large. In neither case is there a simple relationship between the infringed right and the amount of the award.

For the same reason, wrong-responding orders cannot realistically be regarded as a subcategory of replicative orders. Although wrong-responding orders are only issued on proof that the defendant breached a duty owed to the claimant, their content is radically different in both form and substance from the breached duty and from any of the defendant's other substantive duties. Further, in most cases it is too late for the defendant to perform. For example, most contractual obligations that are the subject of litigation were terminated long before the parties came to court.

As I mentioned in the discussion of causes of action, relatively uncontroversial examples of wrong-responding orders include orders to pay exemplary or nominal damages. Other examples, admittedly more controversial, include damages for pain and suffering and the variety of awards that I described above as vindicatory damages. Some of these awards are 'at large' (or 'discretionary') in the same way that exemplary damages are at large. However, for others the courts have adopted, primarily for rule of law reasons, a conventional measure, which is typically the market price of the right that was infringed. A defendant who wrongfully uses the claimant's land is liable to pay the market rental rate for the land, even if the claimant was not harmed by the use, and even if the claimant would not have rented the land to the defendant or anyone else. Defendant must pay simply because of the wrong that they committed.

Free-standing orders

The most 'creative' creative orders are free-standing orders. Free-standing orders are neither replicates nor substitutes for substantive duties; nor is their content a response to the breach of such duties. The clearest examples are orders that can be obtained without proving a wrong or a threatened wrong. The matrimonial property orders, mentioned earlier, satisfy this definition. Section 23 of the *Matrimonial Causes Act* 1973 authorizes courts to issue orders, following the breakdown of a marriage, that direct one of the parties to pay a sum of money or transfer specific property to the other party. Claimants seeking such orders do not need to prove that the defendant breached or threatened to breach a legal duty: it is sufficient to show that, in the circumstances, it is fair to issue the requested order. Closer to this book's main concern, restitutionary orders are similarly available without proof of a wrong or even a threatened wrong. The same is true of some (but not all) compensatory damages awards. As I noted above, this sub-group includes compensatory awards for loss caused by the escape of something brought onto one's land (*Rylands v Fletcher*), in a state of necessity, or by an innocent misrepresentation; as well as awards issued against vicariously liable employers, in lieu of *quia timet* (preventative) injunctions, for wrongs committed against third parties, and in cases where the award is issued in lieu of specific relief and for reasons based on the substantive undesirability of the requested action.

More controversially, I also argue that the remaining compensatory damages awards (the majority) are free standing, notwithstanding that they are conditional on proof of a wrong. As I explained in my account of wrong-responding orders, while a standard compensatory award (e.g. damages for negligence) is conditional on proof of a wrong, the wrong is a condition, not the reason, for the award. The reason for an ordinary compensatory award is the same as the reason for restitutionary awards, matrimonial property awards, and the other free-standing awards mentioned above: an injustice.

Because all of the above awards are responses to injustices, their content is the same in every case, at least in general terms. In every case, the order directs the defendant to correct the relevant injustice (e.g. by compensating a loss or returning a mistaken payment). However, it is useful to retain the label 'free standing' (rather than describing them only as 'injustice-correcting orders') as this label identifies what is distinctive and controversial about the content of these remedies. It also seems possible that there exist free-standing remedies that do not correct injustices.[27]

iii. No Order

A refusal to issue an order is not itself a court order or a judicial ruling. However, to understand the relationship between substantive rights and court orders, the possibility that some substantive rights are not supported in any way by court orders must be considered.

The qualification 'in any way' is important. As explained in the discussion of rights-threats, courts will generally refuse to make an order—any order—in support of a substantive right except on proof that the defendant is unwilling to comply with that right. For example, courts will not order performance of a contractual duty to pay for goods prior to the date specified for payment. Similarly, courts will not award injunctions to protect property without proof of an actual or threatened infringement of the defendant's property rights.

It is also clear that some substantive rights are never directly supported by court orders in the sense that courts never order performance of the correlative duty. Many contractual rights are like this; for example, courts are generally unwilling to order employees to comply with their contractual duties to show up for work. Similarly, courts do not order defendants to take care not to injure others' persons or property, or to refrain from assaulting others. However, these and similar substantive duties are supported indirectly in that courts will order defendants who have breached them to pay damages. The question addressed here is whether there exist substantive rights that are not supported in even this indirect fashion. In Chapter 9, I discuss (and reject) the argument that such rights are a conceptual impossibility. For the moment, I merely note that courts accept the possibility of rights without remedies. We see this acceptance—to return to a familiar example—in the conventional understanding of limitation periods. Although the expiry of a limitation period normally extinguishes the claimant's ability to seek redress before the courts, it leaves unaffected the relevant substantive right. Thus, while English courts will refuse to issue an order in a case where the claimant is suing upon a contractual debt that was due more than six years earlier, they insist that the defendant remains under a duty to pay the debt.

Chapter 9 describes other examples of 'unsupported' substantive rights. However, it should be kept in mind that in every case the substantive rights in question are rights whose breach normally gives rise to a liability to a judicial order.

[27] Possible examples includes rulings under s 23 of the *Access to Neighbouring Land Act* 1992 (allowing landowners to enter a neighbour's land to do work on their property); s 84 of the *Law of Property Act* 1925 (discharging of restrictive covenants on land); and s 39 of the *Consumer Credit Act* 1974 ('reopening' unfair credit agreements). None of these rulings is straightforwardly directive, that is, none are straightforwardly 'orders'.

For example, while it is not possible to obtain an order in support of the substantive right to payment of a debt after the limitation period has expired, creditors can in general obtain rulings directing that defaulting debtors pay their debts. The rules governing limitation periods describe specific circumstances in which it is not possible to bring actions of a kind that, in general, can be brought with respect to the duty in question. The question arises, then, whether the common law recognizes legal duties that are not supported even in this way. Does the common law recognize duties that defendants can disregard in all instances with impunity? The answer, at least insofar as we limit ourselves to private law duties, appears to be no. To this extent (but no more), the maxim that 'for every right a remedy' appears to be true in the common law.

iv. Summary Chart

A summary of the kinds of remedies available is shown in Figure 3.

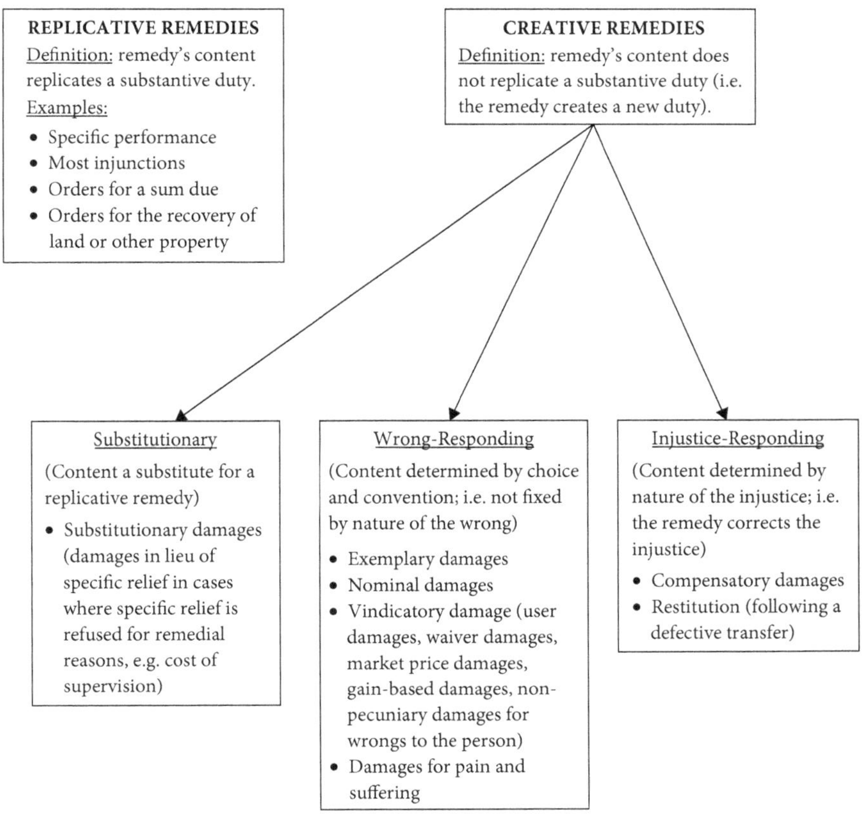

Figure 3 The Kinds of Remedies Available

E. Overall Summary Chart

An overall summary is provided in Figure 4.

Substantive Rights

- Rights held by legal persons that other legal persons do or not do something.
- Substantive rights arise because individuals enjoy them generally or because of the occurrence of an event other than a judicial ruling (e.g. a contractual agreement).
- Examples include debtors' rights to be paid and landowners' rights to exclusive possession.

⇩

Action Rights

- Rights held by claimants that courts issue a requested order.
- Action rights arise where claimants establish, before a court, that the defendant threatened one of their substantive rights ('rights-threats'), infringed one of their substantive rights ('wrongs'), or benefitted from an unfair gain or imposed an unfair loss vis-à-vis the claimant ('injustices').
- Examples include claimants' rights to orders that the defendant cease a nuisance or pay damages.

⇩

Court-ordered Rights

- Rights held by courts that defendants perform actions required by orders.
- Court-ordered rights arise from the issuance of court orders.
- Some court orders replicate substantive duties (e.g. orders not to trespass and orders to fulfil contractual promise).
- Other orders give rise to new duties. Certain of these 'creative' orders are close-substitutes for substantive duties (in particular, 'substitutionary damages', e.g. an order to pay damages issued in lieu of a requested order that the defendant perform a contractual duty to deliver fungible goods). However, other creative orders create entirely new duties (e.g. most damages awards and most restitutionary awards).

⇩

Enforcement Rights

- Rights held by claimants that the state impose a sanction on a defendant subject to a court order.
- Enforcement rights arise on proof before a court or other legal body that the defendant failed to comply with a court order.
- Examples include rights that the state sell the defendant's assets or imprison the defendant.

Figure 4 Overall Summary Chart

5
Philosophical Foundations

Enacting rules is an obvious way for authorities, legal or otherwise, to guide behaviour and set standards for large numbers of people. Imposing sanctions, in turn, is an obvious way to help ensure compliance with rules, either by directly bringing about the outcomes they require (e.g. by taking money from me and giving it to you) or by providing incentives for compliance. The role of judicial orders is less obvious. What is the point of ordering defendants to do things when the law has, or could have, rules that tell individuals to do the same things and sanctions that it can impose when rules fail to motivate?

This question has received surprisingly little attention from legal scholars. In comparison with the extensive literature examining the roles of rules and sanctions—the literature on general jurisprudence typically focuses on one or the other (or both) of these concepts—relatively little has been written about orders.[1] Discussions of legal authority often introduce examples that involve orders, but the orders in question are rarely judicial and, further, are rarely distinguished from examples that do not involve orders. Most legal theorists appear to assume (though they rarely make this assumption explicitly) that a court order is either a type of sanction or a mini-rule, or at least that it is a supplement to a sanction or a rule. According to this view, or more strictly according to this pair of views, the role of court orders is to do what sanctions or rules do, or at least to assist sanctions or rules in performing their functions.

The first step in understanding the nature of court orders is to grasp why these views should be rejected, at least insofar as they are intended to provide a general justification for court orders. That task is the focus of this chapter's first two sections. In the remainder, I develop an alternative explanation of the role of court orders. The theme of this explanation is that orders provide distinctive reasons to perform the actions they stipulate, reasons that differ in kind from those provided by either rules or sanctions. Like duty-imposing rules—but unlike sanctions—orders purport to give rise to duties to perform the actions they describe. However, the explanation of how such duties arise differs as between rules and orders. Stripped to their essentials, duty-imposing rules are propositions about, and constitutive of, the existence of duties. The legal rule that 'everyone has a duty to perform their

[1] Hart famously critiqued the suggestion that laws are 'coercive orders', but he said little about judicial orders. Hart's model order was a gunman's command, which, as I explain below, is different in important ways from a judicial order (not least that no one thinks they have a duty to obey gunmen): Hart (1961) 20–6.

Rights, Wrongs, and Injustices. Stephen A. Smith, Oxford University Press (2019). © Stephen A. Smith.
DOI: 10.1093/oso/9780199229772.003.0005

contractual promises' both describes and, in its first articulation, creates the basic duty recognized by the law of contract. In subsequent articulations, courts authoritatively affirm the rule's existence. When courts or other lawmakers assert such duty-imposing rules, they presume that they possess what I call 'declarative authority'—the authority to declare that, by virtue of the assertion (or 'declaration'), something is the case, here that a certain duty exists.

In contrast, orders say nothing directly about legal duties. Orders are imperative statements: they *command* the performance of particular actions ('It is ordered that the defendant pay £100 to the claimant'). Insofar as orders give rise to duties to perform the actions they stipulate, they do so indirectly, by virtue of a presumed general duty to obey orders. In presuming that this general duty exists, the law invokes 'directive authority'—the authority to command obedience. Of course, in practice the law may possess neither declarative nor directive authority. However, for the purpose of understanding why courts make orders, what matters is that declarative and directive authority are plausible and distinct.[2] It is because they are distinct that orders provide new reasons to do things that rules already require. And as we will see, the distinction also explains why orders can provide reasons to do things that are not a proper subject matter for rules.

A. Sanction-Based Explanations

Authors often describe court orders as sanctions or as the means through which the law 'enforces' rights.[3] This terminology is misleading. A sanction is an interference with an individual's liberty, person, or property: common sanctions include seizing goods, garnishing wages, or imprisonment. Orders are just words.

However, orders are undoubtedly connected to sanctions. The question is the nature of that connection. In what follows, I argue that the issuance of an order is merely a pre-condition to imposing sanctions. I defend this position by considering three possible, but ultimately unpersuasive, grounds for linking orders more closely to sanctions. Each of these grounds supposes that even if orders are not literally sanctions, they are issued in support of, or as an aspect of, sanctions.

The first possibility is that orders are directions to, or at least authorizations for, officials to apply sanctions. Individuals who seek private law orders presumably believe that the law's substantive rules are insufficient to bring about the states of affairs contemplated by those orders. Claimants come to court with complaints about

[2] Explaining the law is largely a matter of making it intelligible. The practices of enacting rules and issuing orders are intelligible if the law's claims to declarative and directive authority are plausible. And these claims are plausible if they are the kinds of claims that sincere lawmakers and courts could make (even if they turn out to be wrong): see Smith (2004) ch 1.

[3] See e.g. Lawson (1980) 12–14.

the status quo. If courts find these complaints justified, it might seem natural for them to respond by attempting to change the status quo directly. The most obvious way to do this is to command or authorize a sanction. For example, a court might order a legal official to seize money held by the defendant and then to transfer the money to the claimant to satisfy a contractual debt.

The suggestion that judicial orders command or authorize sanctions is appealingly straightforward, but it does not explain the orders that are this book's focus. Courts do not express 'final private law orders' ('this book's focus') as authorizations, much less directions, to state officials to impose sanctions. As we saw in Chapter 3, final private law orders are addressed to defendants, telling them what *they* must do ('It is ordered that the defendant pay the claimant the sum of . . . '). Sanctions are only possible in the case where the defendant fails to fulfil the order, and following a separate procedure which the claimant must initiate and which may involve an entire trial. Moreover, the sanction's content may be different from the order's content: the typical sanction for failing to comply with specific performance orders and injunctions is imprisonment or a fine. Finally, if the defendant complies with a judicial order, the law has no further interest in the dispute. From the law's perspective, paying a contractual debt because there is a rule that individuals must pay their contractual debts and paying a 'Judgment debt' because the court has ordered its payment lead to the same result: the debt is extinguished, and no sanction will be imposed. These observations do not deny that courts have the authority to direct or authorize officials to impose sanctions directly. Courts regularly authorize officials to impose sanctions when they sentence criminal wrongdoers to imprisonment. The suggestion is merely, but importantly, that final private law orders are not directions or authorizations to impose sanctions.

A second possibility is that orders are threats to impose sanctions. As we have just seen, defendants who fail to comply with orders are liable to be sanctioned. It might be thought, then, that issuing an order is effectively a threat to impose a sanction, specifically a threat to impose a sanction in the case that the defendant fails to fulfil the substantive duty that, in this explanation, is mentioned in the order. Of course, it is not strictly necessary for courts to issue personalized rulings if they wish to make such threats. The law could threaten to impose sanctions against individuals who fail to comply with substantive duties simply by making it clear, through a general rule, that defendants who have infringed substantive duties are liable to have sanctions imposed on them immediately. Courts in criminal law cases frequently impose sanctions at the end of the original trial (typically by ordering that the defendant be incarcerated); in principle, there is no reason that courts adjudicating private law disputes could not adopt a similar practice. Still, it might be thought useful, at least in a private law context, for courts to issue individualized threats prior to imposing sanctions. Generalized threats may fail to motivate potential wrongdoers because wrongdoers might assume that their wrongdoing will remain undetected or, even if it is detected, that they will never be brought to trial. In contrast, an individualized threat (i.e. a threat communicated by a ruling) is difficult to ignore.

There is no doubt defendants often view orders as threats and, further, that many of them alter their behaviour in response to orders because they fear the sanctions that may be imposed if they fail to comply. However, the suggestion that orders are threats does not explain why courts express orders as orders. Nor does it explain why the sanctions imposed for failing to comply with orders are often identical to the content of the defendant's substantive duty. Informing recalcitrant debtors that if they fail to pay their debts their bank accounts will incur a debit equal to the amount of the debt is hardly a threat: the content of the sanction is the same as the content of the substantive duty. Finally, this suggestion cannot explain orders that direct defendants to do things that they had no prior duty to do. The usual response to proof that the defendant breached a still-valid non-monetary contractual duty (e.g. a duty to deliver goods) is not to order the defendant to perform the duty, but, instead, to order the defendant to pay a sum of money by way of damages. Indeed, all damages awards and restitutionary orders create new duties, or so I argue. This observation is fatal to the suggestion that orders are threats, since the suggestion supposes that orders are meant to induce actions that the defendant already had a rule-based duty to perform. Admittedly, there is nothing stopping courts from ordering defendants to perform actions not required by substantive rules and, at the same time, threatening them with sanctions if they fail to perform those actions. But, in this scenario, the intent to threaten does not explain why courts make the initial order.

A final possibility is that orders are effectively warnings that sanctions may be imposed imminently. According to this suggestion, the purpose of orders is not so much to threaten defendants as to ensure that they have fair notice of the circumstances that may lead to their being sanctioned. It might be thought reasonable for courts to provide such warnings. As is true of rules generally, the rules describing individuals' substantive duties may be unclear in their application to particular cases. It might be thought, therefore, that even if it is appropriate in principle to impose sanctions immediately on proof of a failure to comply with a substantive duty, in practice it would be unfair to do so without first warning defendants that if they fail to perform a specified act they are liable to be sanctioned. The role of orders, in this view, is to provide such warnings.

The most obvious objection to this final suggestion is, again, that courts do not express orders as warnings.[4] A second objection is that it hardly seems necessary to provide warnings in cases where the sanction for non-compliance is identical

[4] However, specific performance orders and injunctions typically have warnings attached to them. The *Civil Procedure Rules* 1998, *PR* PD 40B, 8.1 stipulate that courts may not imprison or fine defendants for failing to comply with such an order unless it specifically mentions this possibility.

in content to the original duty (as in cases where the original duty is monetary). A final objection is that, like the previous suggestion, this suggestion cannot explain creative orders. If an order creates a new duty, its purpose can hardly be to ensure that defendants have fair notice that their behaviour is liable to lead to a sanction. To be sure, such orders could be construed as implicitly warning defendants that they are liable to be sanctioned if they fail to comply with the just-created duty—but, like the previous suggestion, this interpretation leaves unexplained the reason for making the order in the first place.

The suggestion that courts issue orders to impose or threaten sanctions or to warn defendants about the risk of sanctions fails to explain why orders are orders. In each of its iterations, this suggestion leaves unexplained the basic fact that orders command individual defendants to perform specified actions. This conclusion does not deny that orders are closely connected to sanctions. The only sanctions that the law imposes in connection with private law disputes are for failing to comply with court orders. Further, in many cases, the nature and magnitude of the sanction is determined by the order; for example, the normal sanction for failing to fulfil a monetary order is that the sum stipulated in the order is taken from the defendant. However, these connections do not establish that orders are sanctions or that they threaten or warn of sanctions.

Finally, although contemporary English private law orders are not sanctions, certain of their ancestors are plausibly interpreted as authorizing officials to impose sanctions. As I explained in Chapters 2 and 3, private law rulings that trace their origins to the Royal Courts (such as rulings requiring the payment of damages or debts, or those requiring the defendant to give up possession of land) were until recently framed as 'Judgments'. Such rulings were abstract statements that something 'shall' happen ('It is this day adjudged that the plaintiff shall recover X money/X property from the defendant'). Judgments do not strictly say anything about sanctions, and no sanction is possible following a Judgment if the defendant satisfies the ruling voluntarily. Yet by stating that a certain outcome 'shall happen', without specifying how it will happen, Judgments might plausibly be interpreted as implicitly authorizing officials to bring about the stipulated outcome. This interpretation is broadly consistent with how Judgments operated in practice. Once a Judgment was issued, the defendant could generally take the Judgment to an enforcement officer and, assuming the Judgment was immediately effective (which was often the case) and that the defendant could not convince the officer that it would satisfy the judgment voluntarily, the officer would normally proceed to 'execute' the Judgment by, for example, seizing and selling the defendant's goods and then handing over the relevant sum to the claimant. Thus, while Judgments did not specifically require that a sanction be imposed, they could be construed as authorizing sanctions and, further, as being equivocal as to whether the stipulated outcome was brought about by the defendant's actions or by officials imposing a sanction.

B. Rule-Based Explanations

The conclusion that sanction-based explanations fail to account for the fundamental fact that orders direct individuals to perform actions leads naturally to the suggestion that the role of orders is to supplement or support substantive rules, in particular to supplement or support duty-imposing substantive rules. There are three ways that orders might fulfil this role: (1) as rule-reminders; (2) as rule-substitutes; and (3) as rule-specifications. I describe these ways below then evaluate them jointly.

The suggestion that orders are rule-reminders flows from the observation that (as I explain in more detail below) substantive legal rules are abstract propositions, addressed to the population at large ('everyone has a duty not to defame others'), and that they are typically established on the basis of an evolving and often complex body of judicial decisions. A consequence of these features is that individuals may be unaware of their private law duties or, even when they are aware of them, may find it easy to ignore them or to rationalize that they do not apply to their situation. Against this background, it might be thought that orders are intended to provide vivid and difficult-to-ignore reminders to defendants of their legal duties.

A second way that orders might be thought to supplement rules is by serving as rule-substitutes in situations where, for practical reasons, rules cannot effectively guide behaviour. In particular, it might be thought that orders are useful in cases where the behaviour desired by the law is triggered by circumstances that potential defendants cannot reasonably be expected to ascertain. Suppose that lawmakers want tortfeasors to compensate their victims for any harm they have suffered by the tortfeasor's actions. An obvious way to try to achieve this outcome, it might be thought, would be for the lawmakers to enact a rule-based duty that requires wrongdoers to compensate their victims. However, as I explain in Chapter 8, there is a practical hurdle to using a substantive rule to establish this duty: wrongdoers cannot reasonably be expected to know or obtain the facts that trigger the duty in advance of litigation. Every damages claim potentially includes a claim for damages for consequential losses. By definition, the facts on which such claims depend—such as whether the plaintiff has lost profits and, if so, how much—are in the victim's hands. Indeed, in many cases, the facts that establish whether a wrong has occurred at all, and so whether the defendant should pay damages in any amount, will be known only to the victim. A vendor who delivers defective goods may not know that the goods are defective. Further difficulties arise in cases where victims can elect between different remedies and where lawmakers want wrongdoers to compensate victims for their pain and suffering: even victims could not reasonably be expected to quantify such awards. In short, even if it is thought that tortfeasors ought to, in principle, have a duty to compensate their victims, it seems impractical to impose such a duty through a substantive rule. Further, it might be thought that the obvious solution to this hurdle is to specify that wrongdoers' duties to pay compensation arise only when courts specify these duties. The second suggestion, then, is that courts employ orders as rule-substitutes in situations of this kind.

Finally, it might be thought that orders are intended to supplement rules by serving as rule-specifications.[5] Because rules are by definition general propositions, they are frequently indeterminate in their application. Even where the relevant facts are known to the relevant parties, it may be uncertain how a rule applies to those facts: reasonable people may disagree over the behaviour required by a rule. Further, even where it is obvious what the law requires in a particular case, it must be the law—not the affected individuals—who are the ultimate judges of what the law requires. It is part of what it means for something to be a legal system that it provides mechanisms for determining the law's existence and content.[6] It might be thought, then, that the role of court orders is to provide legally authoritative specifications of defendants' substantive duties.

There is a grain of truth in each of these suggestions. There is no doubt that orders are sometimes employed to motivate compliance with substantive rules or used in situations where substantive rules would be impractical. And, in practice, orders often indirectly provide authoritative specifications of defendants' duties (or at least they make clear that the defendant breached a duty). However, none of these suggestions explains more than a subset of the currently available range of orders. Defendants who have failed to pay their debts or refused to vacate a claimant's property rarely need judicial reminders that they ought to do these things. Nor can the idea of rule-reminders explain orders that create new duties: orders cannot remind a defendant of a duty that does not yet exist. The suggestion that orders are rule-specifications is vulnerable to the same objection: it cannot explain creative orders. More generally, insofar as courts wish to provide authoritative determinations of legal duties they can, and in practice do, provide such determinations in their reasons for judgment (which is why law students are assigned to read reasons, not orders). The suggestion that orders are rule-substitutes avoids these objections, but it cannot explain the many orders that do nothing more than replicate substantive duties. An order that replicates the content of a rule is not a substitute for that rule. Finally, none of these suggestions can account for substitutionary orders (orders that direct defendants to perform monetary equivalents of still-valid non-monetary obligations). An order to pay damages that a court awards in lieu of ordering the defendant to perform a contractual obligation is not a reminder, or specification, of that obligation; nor does it attempt to fill a gap in the substantive law.

Beyond these specific objections, there is a general objection to the suggestion that orders are rule-supplements. If orders were rule-supplements they would not be 'orders': they would be declarations. A declaration is a judicial pronouncement

[5] See Ripstein (2009) 168–76.
[6] Raz (2009) 108–15.

about the existence of a legal duty (or power, immunity, status, and so forth): 'It is declared that [the claimant is] . . . entitled to payment from the defendant on January 1 of the sum of £300'.[7] If a court wants to provide a reminder or specification of a rule-based duty, the obvious and appropriate way to do this is by issuing a declaratory ruling ('It is declared that the defendant has a duty to . . . '). In cases where courts want their rulings to serve as rule-substitutes, declarations are arguably inappropriate (as declarations are usually understood to confirm *already-existing* duties); however, in these cases the appropriate ruling would be a 'constitutive' ruling. Closely related to declarations, constitutive rulings give effect, by their issuance, to a new legal state of affairs (the usual example is a divorce decree: see Chapter 3). In short, the individualized counterpart to a duty-imposing rule is not an order: it is a declaratory or constitutive ruling.

Of course, there is nothing stopping courts from using orders as substitutes for rules or from using orders to specify rule-based duties, and it is likely that orders sometimes fulfil these functions. But it is unlikely that courts would routinely issue orders for these reasons. Aside from the fact that orders say nothing directly about duties, employing orders in cases where the desired duty is either unspecified (because the relevant rule is vague) or does not exist at all (because there is no rule) makes nonsense of the idea of a legal duty. If the relevant duty is vague or nonexistent prior to the order, then by definition the defendant could not reasonably be expected to act on it prior to the order. Issuing orders in such circumstances wrongly implies—without any proof—that the orders' subjects are unwilling to comply voluntarily with their legal duties.[8] As the rules governing the availability of *quia timet* (preventative) injunctions demonstrates, common law courts are loathe to order defendants to comply with legal duties without clear proof that the defendant is unwilling to comply voluntarily. As I explain in Chapter 6, *quia timet* injunctions are only available where there is an imminent risk that the defendant will breach the relevant duty. The suggestion that orders specify previously unspecified rules, or are substitutes for rules, implies that courts issue pre-emptive orders routinely.[9]

[7] *Rajbenback v Mamon* [1955] 1 QB 283, 287.

[8] The above objection cannot be avoided on the ground that issuing declarations or constitutive rulings might lead to additional litigation. A declaration or constitutive ruling stipulating that the defendant has a duty to pay a sum states as clearly as a monetary order that the defendant must pay the sum. In practice, such rulings could function—so far as enforcement is concerned—exactly as orders to pay damages currently function in English law. Courts would need to give the defendant a period of time—though it could be very short—to do what the ruling required. Once the period expired, the plaintiff could apply to legal officials to enforce the duty affirmed by the declaration. The plaintiff would need to establish that payment had not yet happened, but the current procedure also requires this step. This procedure would not require the claimant to seek an order prior to enforcement, but for reasons explained below, the only justification for orders in such cases—namely, the practical one that they might serve to motivate recalcitrant defendants—carries little weight. A defendant who fails to comply with the actions required by a declaration or constitutive ruling is unlikely to comply with an order.

[9] There are also practical reasons for announcing legal duties in advance of ordering them or authorizing their execution. To the extent that the law presents paying damages as a legal duty, citizens predisposed to view their legal duties in the way the law wants them viewed—as all-things-considered

These observations are consistent with believing that courts sometimes issue orders to motivate defendants to perform rule-based substantive duties. As I explain below (and in more detail in the next chapter), one of the main reasons for issuing orders is precisely to provide defendants who have failed to act in accordance with substantive rules new reasons to do what those rules require. However, this role differs from the role that is assumed by the idea of orders as rule-reminders, rule-substitutes, or rule-specifications. Orders are not reminders of defendants' substantive duties for the simple reason that they say nothing about such duties. The only duty they invoke is the duty to obey orders. For the same reason, orders are not substitutes for, or specifications of, duty-imposing rules for the simple reason that they do not provide a substitute for, or specification of, the core feature of such rules, namely, that they affirm the existence of duties.

It remains only to add that the suggestion that the primary role of final private law rulings is to supplement rules fares no better when applied to the (formerly available) rulings that were expressed as 'Judgments' that the claimant 'shall recover' money, land, or other property. This older formulation is even more inconsistent with the idea that final rulings supplement rules because under the former law it was possible to obtain coercive execution immediately following the putative fixing of the defendant's duty.

Sanction-based and rule-based attempts to explain orders must therefore be rejected. However, the reasons for rejecting these suggestions point us in the right direction. In each case, the explanation fails to explain orders as *orders*. Each explanation ignores the distinguishing feature of orders, indeed their only real feature: orders command their addressees to perform an action.

C. Orders as Commands

At one level, there is no mystery as to why courts issue orders: they issue orders to motivate defendants to perform the actions described in the orders.[10] Nor is there any mystery, at least in general terms, as to why orders might be thought an appropriate way to provide such motivation: courts presumably assume that issuing an

duties—will approach such actions differently than they would if courts merely ordered them to perform these actions. For law-respecting citizens, settlements made in advance of litigation will not be regarded as akin to plea-bargaining deals, but rather as attempts to determine, so far as practical, how they should act. Similarly, law-respecting citizens will regard post-litigation payments as fulfilling a genuine obligation, not merely as something that courts have forced onto them. For these citizens, there will be a stigma attached to attempts to avoid payment (for instance, by hiding assets) that would not exist if the only reason for making payments were that the law commanded them.

[10] I adopt the description 'orders as commands' with hesitation because 'command' is sometimes incorrectly understood, following Austin, to refer an order that is combined with the threat of a sanction for non-compliance: Austin (1832) 21–2. Non-compliance with a command need not attract a sanction. The concept identified by Austin is closer to a threat: 'give me your money or else'.

order gives the defendant a reason to fulfil the order. In other words, courts presume that they have the authority to issue binding orders. The mystery is the basis of this authority; more specifically, the mystery is how this authority differs from the authority that courts (or other lawmakers) assert when they enact rules.[11] If the authority is the same, orders seem superfluous.

The first step in unravelling this puzzle is to identify the kind of authority that courts invoke when they enact duty-imposing rules. It is often assumed that it is the authority to be obeyed. Discussions of legal authority are frequently presented as attempts to answer a single question: 'Is there an obligation to obey the law?'.[12] As I explain below, this approach is appropriate when considering the courts' authority to issue orders. But it is misplaced when considering the authority on which courts rely when they enact duty-imposing private law rules.

An example may be useful. Stripped to its essentials, the main (if not the only) duty-imposing rule recognized by the law of contract holds, roughly, that 'everyone has a duty to perform their contractual promises'. When a court, legislature, or other law-making body with the appropriate jurisdiction enacts a rule of this kind it is both describing the content of a legal duty and providing the grounds for its existence. Like constitutive rulings—for example, a divorce decree or the declaration of a constructive trust—duty-imposing rules are self-executing. By their communication, they give rise to, or at least affirm the existence of, the legal duties that they describe. If the Supreme Court says that 'everyone has a duty to perform their contractual promises', then it is automatically the case that everyone has such a duty.[13]

Of course, most judicial statements of this kind refer to duties that courts have already recognized. If, tomorrow, a court says 'everyone has a duty to perform their contractual promises', the duty which the court is asserting is one that already exists. The court's statement might be thought, therefore, to do nothing more than to describe the law, similar to a writer's description in a textbook. Some judicial statements about duties undoubtedly fit this pattern. If the statement is obiter or if it is made by a court that lacks the authority to modify or extinguish the duty in question, it has no legal significance (at least in theory), and so must be merely descriptive. But if the statement is part of the ratio of a judgment issued by a court that has jurisdiction to modify or extinguish the relevant duty, then the statement is not merely descriptive. If the Supreme Court says that a particular duty exists then, even if the duty already existed, the Supreme Court's statement authoritatively

[11] For convenience, I generally describe courts and other lawmakers as 'enacting' rules, though it is sometimes more accurate, depending on the context, to describe them as announcing, promulgating, asserting, issuing, or affirming rules.

[12] See e.g. Wasserstrom (1963); Smith, M.B. E. (1972); Raz (1984).

[13] Such statements are therefore examples of what Austin famously described as 'performative utterances': Austin (1979). However, the distinction that I draw between duty-imposing rules and orders does not turn on this feature of duty-imposing rules because, as Austin recognized, orders are also performative utterances.

confirms the duty's existence. Subsequent judgments will point to the Supreme Court's statement as proof that the duty exists. In this sense, even statements about the existence of already-existing duties are constitutive: if the Supreme Court says, 'everyone has a duty to perform their contractual promises', then by definition everyone has such a duty.[14] And, of course, where the duty in question did not previously exist or existed in a different form, the Supreme Court's statement that the duty exists, and in such and such a form, is even more clearly constitutive: the duty comes into being because the Supreme Court says that it exists. In short, a lawmaker's statement to the effect that 'everyone has a duty to do X' may merely describe the law, but it may also create an entirely new duty, modify an existing duty, or authoritatively affirm the existence of a duty.

Some of the clearest examples of authoritative statements of legal duties that resemble my example of 'everyone has a duty to perform their contractual promises' are found in civil law codes. Article 1458 of the *Civil Code of Québec* states that 'Every person has a duty to honour his contractual undertakings'.[15] In common law systems, similar pronouncements abound, even in the case of judge-made law (though they are rarely expressed as clearly as Article 1458). For example, in *Heaven v Pender*[16] (the precursor to *Donaghue v Stevenson*) Brett MR stated that 'If one man is near to another or is near to the property of another, a duty lies upon him not to do that which may cause a personal injury to that other, or may injure his property'. Similarly, in *Hedley Byrne v Heller*[17] (the case that established the tort of negligent misrepresentation) Lord Devlin held that 'wherever there is a relationship equivalent to contract there is a duty of care'. It should also be kept in mind that courts frequently assert the existence of duties indirectly. In particular, they frequently assert duties by stating that individuals 'must' do something. For example, in *Donaghue v Stevenson*[18] Lord Atkin famously held that: 'You must take reasonable care to avoid acts or omissions which you can reasonably foresee would be likely to injure your neighbour.' In such cases, it is generally clear from

[14] The analogy between constitutive rulings and constitutive rules breaks down at this point because constitutive rulings always create, modify, or extinguish a legal state of affairs (see Chapter 3). The ruling equivalent to an authoritative judicial affirmation of an already-existing duty is a declaration. Although the usage is not entirely consistent, declarations are generally employed to affirm the existence of an already-existing legal duty, right, or other legal state of affairs. Possible exceptions include declarations of remedial constructive trusts, which are generally understood to give rise to rights that did not exist prior to the declaration: see *Westdeutsche Landesbank Girozentrale v Islington London Borough Council* [1996] AC 669 (HL) 714–15. England appears to no longer recognize this form of constructive trust: *Re Polly Peck (No 2)* [1998] 3 All ER 812; Burrows (2011) 180–1.

[15] Other examples include: 'A person who obtains something as a result of the performance of another person or otherwise at his expense without legal grounds for doing so is under a duty to make restitution to him' *BGB* (German Civil Code) s. 812 (official translation); 'Any human action whatsoever which causes harm to another creates an obligation in the person by whose fault it occurred to make reparation for it' *French Civil Code* 2016, Art. 1240 (translation).

[16] [1893] 1 QB, 497.

[17] [1963] 2 All ER 575 611.

[18] [1932] All ER Rep 1, 11.

the surrounding text that the phrase 'must do X' is another way of saying 'there is a duty to do X'. Lord Atkin clearly understood 'must' in this sense because on the same page that the above quotation appears, he described the court's task as one of determining whether a duty exists in the alleged circumstances: 'We are solely concerned with the question whether as a matter of law in the circumstances alleged the defender owed any duty to the pursuer to take care.'

If duty-imposing rules are of the form 'everyone has a duty to X'—as I have argued—then the question of whether to obey them does not arise. It is not possible to obey or disobey a statement that something exists. For the addressees of duty-imposing rules, the question that they raise is whether they should be *accepted*. Specifically, the question raised by duty-imposing rules is whether to accept that they do what they purport to do, namely, to create or affirm a valid duty. Of course, if a duty-imposing rule is enacted by a lawmaker with the appropriate jurisdiction and following the appropriate procedures, then by definition the duty it asserts is a valid *legal* duty. However, the question facing the subjects of a duty-imposing rules is not (merely) whether the asserted duty is a legal duty, but whether it is an 'all-things-considered' (or 'moral' or 'unqualified') duty. The question, in other words, is whether to view legal rules as the law presents them, namely, as unqualified standards for behaviour.[19] It is not possible to obey a standard; a standard is either accepted or not accepted.

The law presumes, of course, that the duties that it asserts are genuine. Expressed in the language of authority, the law presumes that it has the authority to enact duty-imposing rules. This authority is probably most accurately described as 'declarative-constitutive' authority. As we have seen, the statement of a duty-imposing rule by an appropriate court or other lawmaker both authoritatively affirms, or declares, the existence of a legal duty and, at the same time, is constitutive of the duty's existence. However, for convenience, I will describe this form of authority simply as 'declarative authority'.[20] It only needs to be kept in mind that this

[19] From the law's perspective, legal duties are also all-things-considered (or 'moral') duties: Raz (2009) 3–33; (1994) 210–37. Indeed, it is difficult to think what else legal officials could mean when they say that there is a duty to do X. Unless one makes clear that one is using the word 'duty' in a restricted sense, to say that 'there is a duty to do X' is just to say that there is a moral duty to do X. Stated differently, if doing X were not thought to be a moral duty, why bother describing it as a duty at all? If the law wishes merely to inform individuals that failing to do X may lead to a sanction, the language of duty is redundant and misleading. This explanation applies even where the legal duty is a response to a coordination problem, such as which side of the road to drive on. We have moral reasons to do whatever is reasonably necessary to solve coordination problems. Of course, it does not follow that because the law views a particular action as obligatory that individuals in fact have an obligation to perform the action. The law may be wrong.

[20] The literature on authority commonly distinguishes theoretical (or 'epistemic') authority from practical authority. The former is authority in regards to what we should believe, while the latter is authority in regards to how we should act. At first impression, declarative authority appears a form of theoretical authority since it applies to statements that appear merely to say that something is the case ('everyone has a duty . . . '). But as we have seen, duty-imposing rules do not merely describe duties: they also create or affirm them. Nor is declarative authority the same as practical authority. Although a duty-imposing rule is meant to provide a reason for action, it does not direct its addressees to do anything. Rather, it affirms that they have a duty to do something. Declarative authority is distinct from both theoretical and directive authority. Directive authority, which I discuss next in connection with orders, is a form of practical authority.

authority extends beyond the authority to affirm a duty's existence to include the authority to create or modify a duty.

Whatever label we give to the above authority, it is different from the authority that courts rely upon when they issue orders. Orders say nothing about the existence of legal duties. They are simply commands: orders command their addressees to perform specified actions ('It is ordered that the defendant pay £100 to the claimant'). It is true that the law presumes that court orders give rise to duties to perform the acts they require. However, the explanation of such duties is different from the explanation of rule-imposed duties. In the latter case, the duty exists, or at least the law presumes it exists, because the relevant rule says that it exists ('everyone has a duty to perform their contractual promises'). In contrast, the presumed duty to perform the acts contemplated by orders arises indirectly, by virtue of a presumed duty to obey court orders. From the court's perspective, the reason that a defendant should comply with an order to pay £100 to the claimant is that the defendant has a duty to do whatever the court commands. The question facing the addressee of an order is thus precisely that of whether to obey it. Orders call for obedience, not acceptance.[21] This feature explains why orders must be communicated directly to defendants, why defendants are bound by order-based duties, and why (as we saw in Chapter 4) defendants owe these duties to courts. In contrast, anyone can owe rule-based duties, including lawmakers, and these duties can be owed to anyone, including private citizens. We all have a duty not to trespass, which we owe to anyone who owns property. In short, the authority on which courts rely when they issue orders is the authority to command obedience. I describe this authority as 'directive authority' because it is an authority to direct actions.

The authority on which courts rely when they issue rulings is different, then, than the authority on which they (or other lawmakers) rely when they enact rules. It is because of this difference that ordering a defendant to do X can provide a new reason to do X even where the defendant already has a rule-based duty to do X. A defendant who rejects or is otherwise unmotivated by the court's claim to declaratory authority may accept its claim to directive authority. Of course, if the grounds on which the courts' claims to declaratory and directive authority are based are identical, then wherever rules fail to motivate, orders will similarly fail.[22] If the justifications are identical, whatever justification defendants might have

[21] The distinction between accepting duty-imposing rules and obeying orders could be collapsed by interpreting the question raised by an order as that of whether to accept the rule that there is a duty to obey orders. However, the distinction would reappear in a different form. As I explain below, the kinds of reasons that could support accepting the law's authority to enact a duty to obey courts are different from the kinds of reasons that could support accepting the law's authority to enact private law duties.

[22] I refer to the courts' 'claims' to declaratory and directive authority to make clear that I do not assume that courts actually possess either kind of authority. As I have mentioned before, to explain the practice of issuing orders (or any other legal practice), it is sufficient to show that the practice is intelligible, and to be intelligible it is sufficient that the practice might plausibly be thought to be justified. It is not necessary that the practice actually be justified. I explain below why both declaratory and directive authority might plausibly be thought to be justified.

for obeying an order would also justify accepting a substantive rule. However, it is highly unlikely that these justifications are identical. The ordinary practices of courts and other authorities, and of those subject to them, assume that the justifications differ. The clearest example is the practice that is this chapter's focus, namely, ordering defendants to do things that they already have rule-based duties to do. This practice presumes that orders provide reasons for action that differ from those provided by rule-based duties. There would be no point in issuing orders if the reasons were identical. And if the reasons are different, then the authority that they presume must be different. Three other examples are discussed below.

First, consider how the law attempts to motivate individuals to do things that are intended as punishment. Imagine that a city's lawmakers want to impose a fine of £1000 on anyone who dumps waste into a local river. In theory, the lawmakers could pursue this aim by enacting a legal rule stipulating that anyone who dumps waste immediately incurs a duty to pay £1000 to the city. If such a rule were passed, it would be unnecessary to bring offenders before the courts in order to 'impose' the £1000 fine: the rule would make it clear that offenders must pay. Of course, many offenders would ignore this rule unless the threat of an additional fine or other punishment accompanied it. However, such a threat would be easy to add. In the same way that legislatures provide that intentionally failing to pay taxes is a criminal offence, the city could pass a statute specifying that failing to pay the £1000 fine is a criminal offence. However, lawmakers never impose fines by rules; they always impose fine by individual orders, which are issued by courts (or their delegates). To be sure, legal systems invariably have rules governing who can impose fines, when they can impose them, and in what amounts. But fines themselves are imposed by orders. Why?

The explanation lies in the duty-declaring nature of duty-imposing rules. A rule that attempted to inflict punishment on the polluters in my example would read something like 'anyone who dumps waste has a duty to pay £1000 to the state'. As far as its form and content are concerned, this rule is unremarkable. The rules that ground duties to pay taxes are expressed in a similar fashion ('anyone who earns X income has a duty to pay Y sum to the state'). However, such a rule appears distinctly odd in cases where the duty's rationale is to punish the addressee. It appears odd because the idea of a duty to punish one's self is odd (if not incoherent). If such a duty existed, we would have to conclude, implausibly, that whenever wrongdoers fail to punish themselves they are committing an additional wrong. More generally, whatever justification exists for punishment (retribution, deterrence, and so forth) is a justification not for wrongdoers punishing themselves, but for the state imposing punishment on wrongdoers.

Indeed, if lawmakers enacted a rule stating that anyone who dumps waste has a duty to pay £1000 to the city, their efforts would almost certainly be self-defeating. The rule would be interpreted as imposing a tax or fee rather than a fine. This interpretation would be adopted because it is the only interpretation that makes sense of the duty contemplated by the rule. A duty to self-punish is unintelligible, but a duty to pay a tax or a fee is perfectly intelligible. This feature of duty-imposing rules explains why lawmakers who want to fine wrongdoers pursue this end by giving courts (or their delegates) the authority to order wrongdoers to pay fines. The only message carried by an order that the defendant must pay a sum of money is that the courts want the defendant to pay this sum. It is true that courts presume that wrongdoers have duties to pay the fines that they impose. However, these duties arise not because the court asserts a duty to pay a sum of money, but because courts assume that there is a general duty to obey their orders, whatever their content or purpose. The duty to pay a court-ordered fine is a particular manifestation of the general duty to obey courts—and the latter is clearly not a duty to punish one's self or anything similar. In short, the law imposes fines by orders, and only by orders, because it rightly recognizes that it makes no sense to suppose that we could have substantive duties to punish ourselves.

The difference between declarative and directive authority also explains why authorities frequently issue orders in situations where rules have failed to motivate. I argue below that this explanation accounts for the availability of legal orders that direct defendants to do what they already had rule-based duties to do ('replicative orders'). For the moment, I merely note that the same explanation accounts for many non-legal orders. Consider parents who have established a rule to the effect that 'at Christmas everyone in the family must visit our relatives'. If one of the children is unwilling to comply with the rule, the parents might well respond, at first anyway, by trying to explain why the rule expresses a valid obligation. Thus, the parents might explain that Christmas is the only time that the family can get together with relatives or that spending time with relatives is part of what it means to be a family, and so on. The parents might also respond by explaining that by virtue of their age and experience they are particularly well placed to understand family obligations (i.e. that they are authorities as to the existence of family obligations). Parents offer such explanations in the hope that the child will accept that the rule does what it purports to do, namely, to state a valid obligation. But if the child continues to refuse to comply with the rule, the parents will often switch to the different kind of authority embodied in orders: 'Get in the car!' At this point, the parents are invoking their presumed right for the child to obey them, regardless of the merits of the stipulated action. This switch to a different kind of authority is often made explicit when parents issue orders: 'Fine, I don't care what you think [of this rule]: just get in the car!' (And if the order also fails to achieve its purpose, parents, like the law, may well resort to physical sanctions—such as picking up the child and placing him or her in the car).

Finally, the distinction between declarative and directive authority helps to explain why individuals often accept the law's authority to issue orders while denying its authority to enact rules—and vice versa. An example of the first category is 'conscientious objectors' who publicly refuse to obey a rule-based duty (such as a rule-based duty not to smoke marijuana), and yet, at the same time, willingly submit to whatever punishment the courts order for that refusal (e.g. by extending their arms for handcuffs as they smoke marijuana on the courtroom steps). The conscientious objector denies the law's declarative authority (at least with respect to a specific rule's subject matter), but accepts its directive authority to impose punishments. An example of the second category is the protestor who, seeking to overthrow an evil government, makes every effort to avoid being caught and punished—but who nonetheless complies with the government's substantive rules regarding, for example, traffic safety. The protestor denies the law's directive authority, but accepts, at least with respect to the subject matter of certain rules, the law's declarative authority.

As these examples illustrate, the distinction between declarative and directive authority is familiar to lawyers and non-lawyers alike. But what is its basis? Why do we assume that orders may motivate when rules do not, and vice versa? Strictly speaking, it is not necessary for my purposes to answer this question. It is sufficient if there is a difference between declarative and directive authority, whatever its explanation. However, I will offer some brief and preliminary observations.

As I mentioned earlier, the literature on authority is largely silent on this question. Although theorists have devoted considerable attention to the concept of an 'order backed by a threat',[23] the concept of an order itself, and the related question of how orders are related to rules, are little discussed. For the most part, it appears to be assumed that accounts of the authority of rules apply equally to orders, and vice versa. Duty-imposing legal acts are typically described as 'directives' or 'norms,' and it is assumed that these categories include both duty-imposing rules and orders.[24] However, when the literature on authority is examined with the distinction between declarative and directive authority in mind it becomes apparent that most theories of authority are theories of either declarative or directive authority—but not of both. It is not possible to defend this sweeping claim here. The literature on authority is vast, as is the variety of theories of authority. However, it is possible to show that two of the most influential such theories are theories of, respectively, declarative and directive authority.

Perhaps the best-known contemporary theory of authority—Joseph Raz's 'service' conception—is a theory of declarative authority.[25] According to Raz, the normal way of justifying authorities is by showing that they help their subjects to act on reasons that already apply to them. Authorities are justified, in this view, when their subjects are more likely to comply with reasons that already apply to

[23] Austin famously argued that this concept explained law generally: Austin (1832) 21–2. Austin's argument was one of HLA Hart's main targets in the *Concept of Law* (1961).

[24] See e.g. Raz (2006) 1012.

[25] Raz (1985). Although I cannot defend this suggestion here, my comments on the service conception would appear to apply also to theories that ground authority in the duty to support just or otherwise

them if they follow the authority's 'pronouncements' (to use a neutral term) than if they try to act on those reasons directly. For example, if the authority is an expert on pollution, then by following the authority's pronouncements regarding acceptable levels of pollution, individuals are more likely to comply with the reasons that (it is assumed) they already have to avoid polluting than if they try to work out for themselves the acceptable levels. Similarly, if the authority is able to solve coordination problems (e.g. which side of the road to drive on), then by following the authority's pronouncements (e.g. to drive on the left) individuals are more likely to comply with the reasons that already apply to them (in this case, reasons to avoid accidents) than if they try to solve the coordination problem by themselves (for instance, by flipping a coin). More generally, following the law's pronouncements may be rational because those pronouncements arise, at least in theory, from a reasoned, dispassionate process: in contrast, when people try to work out for themselves the best course of action, the exigencies of the moment may sway them improperly, particularly in emergencies. In short, 'follow the law' is often good advice for someone who wants to do the right thing.

The service conception is a compelling account of authority. However, as critics have noted, it has difficulty explaining how there could be an obligation *to obey* the law.[26] The service conception explains why a rational individual might have good reasons to follow the pronouncements of an expert authority or a coordination problem-solving authority, but not why such an individual would feel obliged to obey the authority. It is generally a good idea to follow the advice of experts, but people do not say that they have an obligation to follow such advice. For example, if I want to make a soufflé, I would be well advised to follow the advice of a soufflé-making expert. The reasons that I have to make a good soufflé (e.g. to please my family) will more likely be satisfied if I follow the expert than if I try to work out by myself how to make a soufflé. However, it would be odd to conclude from this observation that I have a duty to 'obey' the soufflé-making expert. To obey another is not merely to do what that person thinks you should do, but to do so with a particular attitude—broadly, one of fidelity—towards the other. The service conception, which views authority in entirely practical terms, cannot explain such an attitude.[27]

However, this objection is easily avoided insofar as the service conception is employed to explain the declarative authority invoked by duty-imposing rules. As we

valuable institutions (respectively, Rawls (1999) 293–01; (Finnis (1980) 245–52), as well as theories that justify authority on the ground that the state acts on behalf of its subjects: Ripstein (2009) 190–5.

[26] See e.g. Darwall (2013) 143–50.

[27] To be clear, the objection just described does not deny that individuals who obey a particular authority might better comply with reasons that apply to them than if they refuse to obey. The point is that insofar as those individuals comply with the authority's directives for this reason their compliance would not be described as obedience.

have seen, it is not possible to obey (or disobey) duty-imposing rules. Thus, the fact that the service conception cannot explain how individuals might have duties to obey duty-imposing rules is not an objection to the service conception. The question raised by duty-imposing rules is whether to accept them, specifically, whether to accept that the duty that the rule says exists does in fact exist.[28] The service conception of authority provides a straightforward answer to this question: it says that individuals should accept rule-declared duties when by doing so they will better comply with reasons that already apply to them. And since individuals will often better comply with reasons that apply to them if they follow legal rules (or at least lawmakers can plausibly believe that individuals will better comply), the service conception can explain the law's claim to declarative authority. The service conception renders the law's claim to declarative authority intelligible. Indeed, it is difficult to imagine any other conception of authority that could render this authority comprehensible: the only reason to accept the law's statement that you have a duty to do X is that you have good reasons for believing that if the law says you have a duty to do X, that you actually ought to do X.

However, the above objection is fatal to the service conception insofar as it is employed to explain directive authority, that is, to explain the authority on which court orders rely. As we have seen, the question raised by orders is precisely whether to obey them. To explain the authority that courts invoke when they issue orders, we need to explain how there might be an 'obligation to obey' the courts. For the reasons just given, the service conception cannot provide such an explanation.[29]

The literature on authority provides a variety of alternatives to the service conception of authority. Probably the best known of these theories, or more strictly the best-known group of such theories, are what I will call 'relationship' theories of authority. Relationship theories ground the law's authority in the relationship between the law (or the state more generally) and its subjects. The best-known relationship theories are consent theories. Strictly interpreted, such theories hold that the state is a legitimate authority insofar as its subjects have consented to obey it. However, the category of relationship theories also includes, to name three examples, theories that argue it is sufficient if the subject authorizes the state to act on its behalf,[30] identifies with the state in a meaningful way,[31] or benefits from the state's actions.[32] These theories differ in significant respects, but in broad terms

[28] This point is another way of making Hart's point that rules differ from commands in their 'internal' aspect, that is, that they differ in that they are meant to serve as standards for behaviour and that the ultimate test of whether they achieve this end is not whether they are followed but whether they are accepted: Hart (1961) 82–91.

[29] Punitive orders illustrate this limitation. The service conception cannot explain obligations to obey punitive orders because such orders do not even purport to be based on reasons that apply to the subject.

[30] Hobbes (1994 reprinted) chs 16–18.

[31] See e.g. Raz (1986) 54–6, 97–100; Raz (2006) 1028–9.

[32] See e.g. Hart (1955). See also Simmons (1979) 323–4, who restricts the duty to support the law to 'participants' (who do not merely receive benefits, but also accept them).

they explain authority as arising from interactions (broadly defined) that have occurred or could in future occur between the subject and the authority. Further, they are alike in that they cannot explain why individuals should treat lawmakers' declarations of duties as authoritative. The fact that an individual has a particular relationship to an authority provides no reason for that individual to accept the authority's declaration that 'everyone has a duty to do X'. The declaration is a statement of what is the case, and what is the case is independent of one's relationship to whoever made the statement. I can agree to act *as if* I had accepted that duty-declarations impose duties on me, but I cannot agree to accept that they actually impose such duties. Imagine that I tell you that 'I agree that I will accept that I am bound by whatever duties you say that I am bound by'. The next day you tell me that I have a duty to kill a close friend. Clearly, I would not actually accept that I have such a duty. And the fact that I apparently agreed to accept it is irrelevant. The act of 'accepting' that a duty exists requires that I have a certain mental attitude towards the duty's existence. I must actually accept, in my mind, that it exists. My apparent agreement cannot bring about this state of mind. At most, it could give me a reason to act as if I had this state of mind. In short, relationship theories of authority cannot explain declarative authority.

However, relationship theories are capable, at least in principle, of explaining the law's claims to directive authority. To explain directive authority, we need to explain how individuals could plausibly be thought to have an obligation to obey the law, and in particular to obey judicial orders. Relationship theories provide just this kind of explanation. If I have consented to obey legal officials then, exceptional circumstances aside, I have a duty to obey courts when they issue orders. This duty exists with respect to orders that do not even purport to be based on reasons that apply to me—for example, punitive orders. Similarly, if I ought to support the law because of the benefits it provides, an obvious way to support it is by obeying what legal officials ask me to do, that is, by obeying orders. It is not coincidental, therefore, that relationship theories typically present themselves not merely as theories of authority, but specifically as theories of obligations to obey the law.[33] It is a different question, of course, whether the law's claims to declaratory and directive authority are justified. My own view is that these claims are only justified in a limited range of circumstances. However, for present purposes, it is sufficient if these claims are plausible.[34] If they are plausible, then we can explain why courts issue orders. They issue them because they plausibly presume that the authority on which orders rely is different from the authority on which duty-imposing rules rely.

The distinction between declarative and directive authority explains, therefore, why courts might issue orders notwithstanding that the law can, and does,

[33] Nor is it coincidental that the typical examples of authoritative communications discussed in such theories are orders: see e.g. Hershowitz (2012).

[34] See note 2; Smith (2004) Ch 1.

contain duty-imposing rules. Orders and rules rely on different kinds of authority, and so can provide different reasons for performing the actions they contemplate. However, this explanation leaves one question remaining. Why do courts issue orders against recalcitrant defendants rather than simply imposing sanctions? For example, if the defendant has failed to comply with the rule-based duty to pay her debts, why does the court not immediately order the seizure of the defendant's property to pay the debt? Why bother going through the step of ordering the defendant to pay the debt?

In broad terms, the explanation is that there are practical advantages to employing orders in advance of possible sanctions. As I explained in Chapter 3, the nature of these advantages varies, in most cases, according to whether the order is monetary or non-monetary. In the case of non-monetary orders, orders are practically useful because it is generally not possible for third parties to bring about the outcomes contemplated by such orders.[35] Short of incarcerating defendants (which is inappropriate on various grounds, not least the cost to the state), third parties cannot bring about the execution of negative orders (e.g. an injunction to restrain a nuisance or a trespass). And in the case of positive non-monetary orders, even incarceration will not bring about the desired result. With rare exceptions, the only way to bring about the result contemplated by a positive non-monetary obligation is for the defendant to perform the obligation. And for reasons that I have just explained, the obvious way for courts to motivate such performance is to order the defendant to perform the relevant action. Another way of making this point is that in cases where courts want to bring about non-monetary states of affairs (e.g. the cessation of the defendant's nuisance or the tearing down of a building on the defendant's property) and where the defendants are unwilling to comply with rule-based duties to bring about these states, the only means left to the courts to try to achieve the desired state of affairs is to order the defendant to bring it about.

In the case of monetary orders, the answer is different because in principle third parties can bring about the results contemplated by such orders (for instance, through the seizure and sale of assets). In such cases, the explanation for employing orders in advance of sanctions is convenience. In principle, there is no reason to order a defendant who owes money to make the payment if third parties can obtain the money as easily for the claimant. Courts issue orders to bring about specific results, not to provide standards of behaviour, and if other means are available to achieve those results just as easily, there is no reason to employ orders. However, in practice the other means available to courts (such as employing bailiffs to seize and sell the defendant's property) are costly and often give rise to further disputes

[35] There are exceptions, such as where the unfulfilled non-monetary duty merely involves transferring title to property. Not surprisingly, courts sometimes authorize legal officials to make such transfers in the defendant's name rather than ordering defendants to transfer title themselves: *Senior Courts Act* 1981, s 39; Zuckerman (2013) 1101–2.

(e.g. disputes over the value of seized property). Given that defendants are often willing to pay voluntarily once courts order them to pay, there is an obvious practical advantage to issuing orders prior to resorting to sanctions. Consider again the example of orders to pay fines. In principle, it would be acceptable for a judge contemplating such an order to reach into the defendant's pocket and remove a sum equal to the fine. However, in practice defendants usually do not have sufficient money in their pockets and directing officials to seize their assets—from their pockets or elsewhere—is costly and may lead to violence. Given that defendants often pay fines voluntarily, it is more convenient, at least as a first step, for judges to issue orders commanding defendants to pay fines. If the order fails to motivate the defendant, sanctions may then be employed. The same principle applies to monetary private law orders.

The above observations do not deny that defendants often comply with orders for reasons that have nothing to do with the courts' presumed directive authority. For instance, they often comply with orders because, prior to the order, they were mistaken or uncertain about the existence or content of the duty that the order confirms. Or, more commonly, defendants may comply with orders because they fear the sanctions that are likely to follow if they do not comply. The above explanation does not suppose that the court's directive authority always motivates an order's addressee. It merely supposes that the distinctive thing that orders do—the thing that neither rules nor sanctions do—is to call upon the addressee's assumed allegiance to obey legal officials. Understood in this way, it is not mysterious that courts will order defendants to do the same thing that they were already required to do by substantive rules. Such orders are exactly what we should expect from an institution that regards itself as a directive authority.

It remains only to add that this explanation is consistent with the practice, in former times (and still today in some common law jurisdictions), of framing rulings that originated from the Royal Courts in the form of abstract 'Judgments'. Judgments are similar to orders in that they state what must happen rather than declaring a defendant's legal duty. The main difference between orders and Judgments is that the latter do not specify how the stipulated action should happen. A Judgment to pay a sum of money does not say whether payment should be made voluntarily (by the defendant) or involuntarily (by the coercive actions of third parties). This indifference is consistent with the above explanation. Orders are a means to bring about particular outcomes. In cases where either the defendant's voluntary actions or a third party's actions could achieve the desired outcome (as is true of monetary outcomes), the choice between them is a matter of convenience. In principle, there is no reason that courts must give defendants the chance to bring about the outcomes contemplated by final private law rulings (though, as noted above, it is usually convenient in practice to provide this opportunity). England's decision to frame rulings that were formerly expressed as Judgments in the form of orders (as set out in the *Civil Procedure Act* 1988: see Chapter 3) passed largely without comment because it signified nothing more than a decision that, for practical reasons, it is generally preferable if the outcomes stipulated in Judgments are brought about voluntarily. Under the former regime, courts typically gave defendants time to comply with a Judgment. The replacement of Judgments by orders merely formalized this practice.

D. When: Grounds for Orders

I have argued that rules and orders rely on different kinds of authority and so provide different reasons for performing the acts that they contemplate. The task of demonstrating that this distinction helps to explain the specific circumstances in which courts issue private law orders and the particular orders they issue must await Chapters 6 to 9 (though Chapter 4 provided a summary preview). However, the basic features of these explanations should be clear from the preceding discussion.

If orders invoke a distinctive kind of authority, then (like the parents in my example) we might reasonably expect courts to employ orders to motivate defendants who appear unwilling (but able) to comply with their rule-based duties. Indeed, it is difficult to think of any other reason to issue what I have described as 'replicative' orders. There is no point—and there is a significant waste of public resources—in issuing a replicative order if the defendant will in any event comply with the substantive duty that the orders replicates. Nor is there any point in issuing the order if it is impossible for the defendant to comply. The only circumstances in which issuing a replicative order can possibly make a difference is where the defendant is able, but unwilling, to comply with the relevant substantive duty. It should not be surprising, then, to find that (as I argue in Chapter 6) courts normally grant orders directing defendants to comply with their substantive duties on proof that the defendant is likely to breach, or to continue breaching, that duty in future—in other words, on proof that the claimant's substantive rights are under threat from the defendant. Examples of such orders, I argue, include injunctions, specific performance orders, orders for a sum due, orders for the recovery of land or other property, and most orders to pay damages in lieu of specific relief.

The other situation where this chapter's arguments suggest that courts might be expected to issue orders is where they want individuals to do things that are not an appropriate subject matter for a rule-based duty. An order to pay exemplary damages, which I discussed earlier in this chapter, falls into this category. The reason the law does not recognize a rule-based duty to pay exemplary damages (or, indeed, rule-based duties to pay fines or do any other action that is intended as punishment) is, roughly, that duties to punish ourselves are incoherent. For punishment to be punishment is must be imposed by a court or other authority.

Exemplary damages are relatively unusual and are regarded by many authors as an anachronism. However, in Chapters 7 and 8 I argue that all damages awards (as well as most restitutionary awards) are similar to exemplary damages in that they direct defendants to do things that are not appropriate subject matters for substantive rules.

E. What: Varieties of Orders

This chapter's arguments also provides some hints as to what kinds of orders we might expect courts to issue. Most obviously, we might expect courts to issue replicative orders, that is, to issue orders that direct defendants to do the very things that they have substantive duties to do. The fact that orders rely upon a distinctive kind of authority is not just a reason to make them available in cases where the claimant's rights are at threat, but, as well, for courts to respond to such threats by ordering defendants to comply with the claimant's rights. Orders provide new reasons for defendants to do what the substantive law requires them to do.

In addition, courts might be expected to issue orders to do things that, like paying exemplary damages, are not appropriate subject matters for substantive rules. By definition, such orders are not replicative. Rather, they will be what I described in Chapter 4 as creative orders. The addressees of orders to pay exemplary damages did not have duties, prior to the order, to pay exemplary damages: the order created the duty. In Chapter 8, I argue that both compensatory and restitutionary awards are creative in the same way.

Finally, but importantly, it would not be surprising to find that courts sometimes refuse to issue orders, or at least certain kinds of orders, in some cases where the claimant's rights are under threat from the defendant. To begin, there are practical reasons that courts might reasonably be expected, in certain circumstances, to refuse to order defendants to perform non-monetary duties (e.g. a contractual duty to build a house) and, instead, to order them to perform monetary substitutes (e.g. to pay the claimant a sum equal to the cost of hiring a third party to build the house). Briefly—Chapter 6 provides a more detailed explanation—monetary orders impose fewer costs on the legal system. The risk of litigants returning to court is generally higher where courts award claimants non-monetary as opposed to monetary orders. Monetary orders are also typically enforced by the relatively inexpensive (and largely paid for by the parties) means of third-party seizure and sale of assets. In comparison, the normal method of enforcing a non-monetary order is by the expensive (and paid for by the state) means of a subsequent trial and imprisonment. Finally, and crucially, in many cases monetary orders are, in substance, close substitutes for non-monetary orders. The money that the claimant receives under a 'substitutionary' order can be used to purchase the goods or services that would have been the object of a non-monetary order.

It might be argued that financial considerations should be irrelevant when courts are considering what kinds of orders to issue. Surely, part of what it means to possess a right is that the correlative duty is binding notwithstanding that it may be costly or otherwise inconvenient to satisfy. A contractual duty 'to build a house' is not a disjunctive duty 'to build a house or pay the cost of someone else building a house': it is a duty to build a house. This objection confuses the rights that citizens enjoy against one another (substantive rights) with their rights (or more strictly 'powers') to obtain court orders. It is no doubt true that the cost of building a promised house should generally have no bearing on the contractual duty to build that house (a substantive duty). However, a court's decision to issue a substitutionary order for financial reasons of the kind just described says nothing about the content or validity of such a duty. The court's ruling is a decision about the kind of assistance that the court—the state—should provide to claimants. That decision is determined, in part, by what is required to achieve justice between the parties, but also, in part, by the costs of providing justice. Justice is an important good, but so are hospitals, schools, and roads. Precisely how the costs and benefits of providing better justice should be balanced against the costs and benefits of providing better hospitals, schools, and the like is a difficult question. However, it seems clear that these costs must be balanced: no one supposes that in the battle for the state's resources, courts should always trump hospitals. That premise accepted, it is a small step to accept that one relatively simple way to reduce the cost of providing justice is to allow courts to substitute monetary for non-monetary orders.

Broadly similar considerations also explain why, in a narrow range of cases, we might also expect courts occasionally to refuse to issue any order at all in support of a claimant's substantive rights, even if the claimant can establish a clear threat to, or infringement of, those rights. Possible examples (which I explore in more detail in Chapter 9) include where the claimant's action is based on a trivial rights infringement, where the claimant's failure to initiate an action in a timely fashion means that evidence has become less reliable, and where the claimant has failed to comply with a formality that would provide clear proof of a disputed transaction. Refusing a remedy—any remedy—in such cases is at least prima facie defensible on the ground that citizens who seek the court's assistance may reasonably be asked to take steps to minimize the cost of this assistance. The courts are rightly cautious about acting on this principle. If it is normal to support substantive rights with rulings, a decision to refuse a ruling will normally be interpreted to mean that the claimant had no substantive right in the first place. However, once it is recognized that the process of issuing orders raises considerations that are not raised by a decision to recognize a substantive right, the possibility that it may be appropriate in some cases to refuse a remedy entirely must be entertained.

F. Who: Standing to Obtain Orders

Private law orders are only issued if claimants have requested them and if those claimants have introduced evidence that satisfies the cause of action for the requested order. Further, courts will not issue orders at the request of just any claimant: claimants must have 'standing' to request the relevant order. Briefly, claimants seeking replicative or substitutionary orders establish standing by showing that the defendant owed them a corresponding substantive duty. For example, to obtain an order to pay a debt, the claimant must be owed a debt by the defendant. In a similar way, claimants seeking what I describe as wrong-responding orders must show that they were the victim of the relevant wrong. For example, to obtain exemplary damages, the claimant must be the victim of the wrongdoing that the award is meant to punish. Finally, claimants seeking injustice-correcting orders (such as compensatory damages and restitutionary orders) must show that they suffered the injustice that the order is intended to remedy. For example, claimants seeking an order directing the recipient of a mistaken payment to return the payment must show that they made the payment.

The main question raised by the rules on standing is why courts grant standing to these, and only to these, just-described individuals. In particular, the main question raised by these rules, is why the state is denied standing to request private law orders. The state's willingness to authorize its courts to issue orders directing that rights be respected, wrongs redressed, and injustices corrected, presumably shows that it believes the actions contemplated by such orders ought to happen and, more broadly, that courts have good reasons to issue the orders they issue. Why, then, may the state not seek orders on its own initiative? If the state is willing to announce, on its own initiative, a general duty not to trespass, why are the state's courts not permitted, on their own initiative, to order particular individuals not to trespass? Similarly, if the wrong of trespassing involves breaching a state-recognized duty, why are the state's courts not permitted to require redress for that breach? The reasons for issuing these orders would seem to be reasons for the state to act.

The explanation is that while the state may well have an interest in the actions required by orders, it has this interest only insofar as the citizens who are 'directly affected' (in the ways identified by the just-mentioned standing rules) also have this interest. The rights that we enjoy are our rights and, as such, may be waived or ignored if we choose. If I give you permission to cross over my land, then your crossing is not a trespass. More generally, if I do not care whether you cross over my land—even if I have failed to give you express permission—there is no reason for the state to care either. Legal duties may be 'legal' because the state recognizes them as such, but it does not follow that the interests these duties serve are those of the state. As their name suggests, private law duties are meant to serve private interests. The contractual promiser owes the duty to perform a contractual promise to the contractual promisee—not to the state. Similarly, private law wrongs are wrongs to private individuals and private law injustices are injustices suffered by private individuals. Restricting private law actions to those directly affected by the relevant rights, wrongs, or injustices ensures that these actions serve the interests of those whom the rights are meant to protect. Of course, some private wrongs are also public wrongs: for example, most torts are crimes if they are committed deliberately. In these cases, the state may initiate proceedings against the wrongdoer. But the state brings such proceedings to obtain criminal law orders.

If there were a simple method by which courts could determine, prior to issuing orders, whether the parties directly affected desired those orders, it might be acceptable in principle to allow the state or anyone else to bring a private law action. The courts could simply refuse to issue a requested order if it determined that the directly affected party did not desire the order. However, no such method exists or is practically feasible. And even if there was such a method, there are practical reasons for limiting standing to directly affected parties. Access to the courts is a scarce, publicly funded, service. Indeed, the public cost of running the courts explains why even claimants who satisfy the standing rules and the relevant cause of action may be denied an order if the harm that they have or will suffer is trivial. Limiting standing to directly affected parties helps to prevent wasteful or unnecessary litigation.

These reasons for refusing standing to seek orders to anyone not directly affected by those orders are, at the same time, part of the explanation for why courts grant standing to those who are directly affected. The individuals who satisfy the standing rules are precisely those whose rights are at threat or who have suffered wrongs or injustices. Of course, these reasons do not explain why courts bother to issue orders at all, even to directly affected parties. Orders may well provide distinctive reasons for action, but sanctions are nearly always a more effective method of bringing about the results contemplated by an order. Rather than ordering a defendant to pay the claimant a sum of money or to stay off the claimant's land, why not simply take the money (or other assets) from the defendant or throw the defendant in jail until he or she agrees to stop trespassing? As I explained above, the answer to this question turns on the practical advantages of orders. Sanctions raise the risk of violence and (partly because they raise the risk) are relatively costly; ultimately, the threat of imprisonment backs up all sanctions, at the state's expense. There are obvious advantages, for all concerned, if defendants can be convinced to do voluntarily what private law sanctions attempt to achieve involuntarily. Orders are a means of trying to achieve this result.

A final question is why the law is willing to do anything, whether by way of imposing sanctions or issuing orders, to protect rights, redress wrongs, and correct injustices. After all, even the practice of providing orders (let alone sanctions) is costly. Why do anything? A proper answer to this question, which would require a general theory of the role of the state, is outside this book's scope. Briefly, however, it can at least be said that the answer is not that it is part of what it means for a right to be 'legal' that the state must protect it through orders and sanctions, much less that orders or sanctions must be available to redress legal wrongs or correct legal injustices. As we have already seen (and as I explain in more detail in Chapter 6), courts regularly and openly refuse to do each of these things. The answer must point to the value, not the logical necessity, of these practices. My own view—though I will not attempt to defend it here—is that the availability of orders and sanctions is defensible on two grounds. First, their availability is part of the quid pro quo for the state's prohibition on the use of private coercion to protect rights, redress wrongs, and correct injustices.[36] The state does not merely impose substantive duties on its citizens: it also prohibits citizens from using force to ensure that others comply with those duties and that others redress their wrongs and undo the injustices from which they have benefitted. In short, fairness demands that the state provide what may be called, compendiously, 'justice services', in exchange for what it has taken away. The second, complementary, reason is simply that justice is inherently valuable.[37] Justice is a good, and it is a good that the state is particularly well situated to provide. For the same reason that the state should build roads, hospitals, playgrounds, and schools, it should provide justice.[38]

[36] I draw here on the work of Goldberg and Zipursky; see eg Goldberg (2005) 541–4; Zipursky (1998) 82–5.

[37] See Finnis (2011) 161–4; Gardner (2012) 238–69.

[38] For those who prefer to explain the practice of granting remedies in terms of the practical benefits it provides (as opposed to the value of justice), a similar story could be told in terms of the inherent value of 'welfare' and of the law's role in promoting welfare.

6
Rights-Threats

This chapter and the following two chapters explore the main 'causes of action' (the facts that claimants must prove to obtain remedies) recognized in the common law. This exploration has two main aims. The first is to explain when, why, and in what form, courts issue private law remedies. My general views on these questions should be clear from earlier chapters. However, as those chapters are organized around topics in remedial law (not categories of remedies), their discussion of individual remedies is dispersed and incomplete. In addition, I made claims about the nature of particular remedies in those chapters that rest on undefended assumptions about the positive law. For example, my classification of damages awards and restitutionary awards as duty-creating remedies assumed that the common law does not recognize substantive duties to pay damages or to make restitution. Chapters 6 to 8 defend this and related assumptions.

The second aim is to provide further support for the broader classificatory and normative arguments introduced in Chapters 4 and 5. Chapters 6 to 8 are organized around grounds for awarding orders. However, these chapters also provide further support for the idea that directive rulings ('orders') provide distinctive reasons for action, different from those provided by either rules or sanctions. This second aim connects closely to the first, since the broader themes both reflect and shed light on the rules governing individual orders.

The present chapter focuses on orders for which the cause of action is a rights-threat. Chapters 7 and 8 focus on orders for which the cause of action is, respectively, a wrong or an injustice. Taken together, these chapters argue that there are three main grounds on which courts issue private law remedies. In other words, they argue that remedies can be classified according to whether they are responses to rights-threats, wrongs, or injustices. There are other ways of classifying orders. In particular, orders can also be classified in terms of their content, specifically in terms of the relation between their content and the content of the parties' substantive rights and duties. Adopting this approach, orders can be distinguished (as we saw in Chapter 4) according to whether they are replicative or creative orders, and, within the category of creative orders, further distinguished according to whether they are substitutionary, wrong-responding, or free standing. If I were to give equal weight to each of these classificatory schemes, Chapter 8 would be followed by chapters on 'replicative orders' and 'creative orders'. However, aside from making a long book even longer, it is convenient to discuss the 'when' and the 'what' question about remedies at the same time. The content of the remedies discussed in this

Rights, Wrongs, and Injustices. Stephen A. Smith, Oxford University Press (2019). © Stephen A. Smith.
DOI: 10.1093/oso/9780199229772.003.0006

chapter and in Chapter 8 are almost fully determined by their causes of action. The remedies discussed in Chapter 8 are different in this regard, but considering the when and what questions about these remedies together helps us to understand why they are different. In any event, nothing substantive turns on the decision to organize these chapters in terms of causes of action rather than content. The same arguments and explanations would appear in a content-based scheme.

A final preliminary comment is that a traditional remedies textbook would almost certainly discuss the 'remedial defences' (to adopt my label) of adequacy of damages, difficulty of supervision, personal duties, laches, clean hands, impossibility, hardship, and public interest at the same time that it discusses injunctions, specific performance, and orders for the recovery of chattels (each of which I discuss in this chapter). But while I mention these defences in this chapter, they are discussed primarily in Chapter 9. Notwithstanding that in practice these defences apply only to requests for injunctions, specific performance, and, orders for the recovery of chattels ('specific relief'), I argue that they reflect general remedial-law principles—principles that courts should consider, at least in theory, when contemplating requests for any kind of remedy. It follows, as I explain in Chapter 9, that these defences belong (together with other remedial defences) in the 'general' part of remedial law.

A. The Concept of a Rights-Threat

A rights-threat is the most basic private law cause of action. It is possible to imagine legal systems in which courts have the authority to issue orders, but where they do not recognize wrongs or injustices as causes of action. However, it is difficult to imagine order-issuing legal systems that do not recognize rights-threats as causes of action.

As understood here, a rights-threat arises when one of the claimant's substantive rights is under threat from the defendant. More specifically, a rights-threat arises whenever it is likely that, if the defendant's plans do not change, the defendant will infringe one of the claimant's substantive rights in future (or continue infringing them).[1] On proof of a right-threat, courts normally respond by ordering the defendant to comply with the correlative substantive duty (in which case the remedy is 'replicative') or to comply with a close monetary substitute for that duty (in which case the remedy is 'substitutionary'). For example, if the claimant proves that the defendant is threatening to trespass over its land (or to continue trespassing), the

[1] Strictly speaking, a threat requires a communication of the form 'do X or I will do Y': see e.g. Nozick (1969). As I use the term, rights-threats typically arise without such communications. What I call a 'rights-threat' is probably more accurately (though more awkwardly) described as a 'right under threat' or, more accurately yet, as a 'right that is at significant risk of being infringed in future'.

court will normally order the defendant not to trespass. The explanation of such orders is straightforward. From the law's perspective, defendants should comply with their substantive duties: if the defendant has a substantive duty not to trespass on the claimant's property, then by definition, the defendant should not trespass. And if the defendant is unwilling to comply with this duty, then, again by definition, the reasons that the substantive law provides for such compliance must be insufficient. The court issues a remedy to provide the defendant with a new reason to do what the substantive law requires.

I argue that a rights-threat is the cause of action for orders for a sum due under a contract ('for a sum due'), orders for the recovery of land ('ejectment'), orders for the recovery of chattels ('delivery up'), injunctions, specific performance orders, and some (but not all) orders to pay damages that are issued in lieu of injunctions ('substitutionary damages'[2]). For convenience, I refer to these orders collectively as 'replicative orders' (although, as we will see, in two cases—substitutionary damages and a small subset of injunctions—they are not strictly replicative).

The usual way that claimants establish a rights-threat is by demonstrating that the defendant is engaged in an ongoing rights-infringement, such as an ongoing trespass or an ongoing breach of a contractual duty. Courts properly regard ongoing breaches as strong evidence that the defendant is unwilling to respect the claimant's substantive rights, and so likely to continue infringing those rights in future. Accordingly, courts will grant remedies in such cases, typically by ordering the defendant to respect the relevant right. For example, if the defendant is committing a nuisance, the court will normally order the defendant to cease the nuisance: 'Injunctions are given to prevent wrongs which are threatened.'[3]

By definition, defendants who are engaged in ongoing rights-infringements have committed legal wrongs. However, replicative orders are not responses to wrongs *qua* wrongs. So far as the activity of 'trespassing' or 'paying debts' is concerned, the only thing that orders not to trespass or orders to pay debts can do is to help ensure that, in future, defendants do not trespass and that they pay their debts. Defendants ought to do these things regardless of whether they have failed to do them in the past. For courts contemplating replicative orders, evidence of defendants' prior wrongdoing is merely evidence of their unwillingness to comply, in future, with their substantive duties.

Perhaps the clearest proof that the cause of action for replicative orders is a rights-threat, not a wrong, is that courts will issue such orders notwithstanding

[2] As understood here, damages are 'substitutionary' if they are given in lieu of specific relief and if the reason the court does not award specific relief is broadly administrative (as opposed to a reason based on the desirability of the action contemplated by the order). For example, in *Cohen v Roche* [1927] 1 KB 169 the claimant brought an action for delivery up of a set of 'ordinary Hepplewhite chairs'. The court refused delivery up, instead awarding damages set at the chairs' market value. This award was substitutionary. I discuss substitutionary awards at the end of this chapter.

[3] *Leeds Industrial Co-Operative Society Ltd v Slack* [1924] AC 851, 859 (Viscount Finlay).

the defendant has yet to commit a wrong. In these cases, the order is described as preventative or '*quia timet*', but in substance it is the same as an ordinary replicative order. For example, on proof that the defendant is intending to infringe a valid restrictive covenant in the imminent future, a court will normally issue a *quia timet* injunction directing the defendant to comply with the covenant.[4] A court will issue the same order on proof that the defendant is already breaching the covenant.

Further evidence that the cause of action for replicative orders is a rights-threat, not a wrong, is that courts refuse to issue such orders where the defendant has committed a wrong, but the wrong is unlikely to be repeated.[5] Thus, courts will not issue injunctions in response to one-off trespasses or nuisances. Indeed, even where defendants are engaged in ongoing wrongs, courts may refuse replicative orders if they are persuaded that the defendant's behaviour will change (e.g. because the defendant has given an undertaking to this effect to the court[6]). Courts also refuse specific relief if it is impossible for the defendant to comply with the order.[7] For example, courts will not order the delivery of goods that no longer exist. In such cases, although the defendants have committed wrongs, they are not threatening to commit a wrong in the future: so far as the claimant's right to delivery is concerned, the future is fixed.

Finally, it is difficult to think of any reason that could justify courts issuing replicative orders other than that the claimant's rights are under threat. Peter Birks, drawing on civilian scholarship,[8] held that the cause of action for replicative orders is simply proof that the defendant has a substantive duty to do what the order requires.[9] In this view, the cause of action for replicative orders is proof of a right, not a rights-threat. If the claimant enjoys a right vis-à-vis the defendant, then the court will support this right with an order to do what the right requires. Birks' view cannot account for *quia timet* orders. Nor can it explain the rules governing orders to perform negative duties. Courts will not order defendants to comply with negative contractual duties—for example, a duty not to compete with the claimant—merely on proof that the duty exists. The same is true of duties not to trespass, not to cause nuisances, not to commit conversions, and so on. To obtain a negative injunction, the claimant must show that the defendant is in breach of the relevant duty or is about to breach it.

However, the most fundamental objection to Birks' view is that it supposes courts will issue orders regardless of whether this serves any practical purpose.

4 *Lumley v Wagner* (1852) 21 LJ Ch 898. As I explain below, although it is not strictly possible to obtain *quia timet* orders for a sum due, ejectment, or delivery up, substantively similar orders are available under different names.

5 *Graigola Merthyr Co v Swansea Corporation* [1928] Ch 235, 244 (aff'd [1929] AC 344).

6 *Evans Marshall & Co Ltd v Bertola SA* [1973] 1 WLR 349.

7 Spry (2014) 419–22.

8 Dedek (2010) discusses the civilian scholarship.

9 Birks (2000a) 6, 15–16, 36; (2000b) xxxvi–xlii.

What is the point of ordering defendants to do things that they are already willing to do? If the existence of a substantive duty were sufficient reason to issue a replicative order, a defendant bound by a contractual duty to pay a debt 'within thirty days' could be subjected on day one to a court order requiring such payment. It would not matter that the debtor fully intended to make the payment on day two. Issuing an order in these circumstances is a waste of scarce judicial resources. Orders, or at least the trials that precede them, are costly. It is also insulting to defendants to order them to comply with duties that they were going to comply with anyway. Indeed, such orders are arguably inconsistent with the concept of a substantive duty. When the law states that 'everyone has a duty to do X', it is affirming that everyone has a reason to do X. There is little point in affirming such reasons unless individuals have the opportunity to act on them. Why tell individuals that they ought to do something unless they will be given the opportunity to do that thing, and for that reason?

It might be thought that a similar objection applies to the suggestion that replicative orders are responses to rights-threats. What is the point of ordering defendants to comply with their substantive duties if they have already shown themselves unwilling to comply? I addressed this question in Chapter 5. Briefly, the answer is that orders provide additional, and qualitatively different, reasons for action from those provided by substantive rules. Substantive rules rely on the law's presumed 'declarative authority'—the authority to declare that something is the case (in this case, that a particular duty exists). In contrast, orders rely on the court's presumed 'directive authority'—the authority to command obedience. Because these forms of authority are different, orders provide defendants with new reasons to do what the substantive law requires. Of course, some defendants will be unmoved by the law's claims to authority of any kind. Still, sanctions should be a last resort. Sanctions are costly and intrusive. Given that it is simple to impose sanctions if an order fails in its purpose, it is appropriate to reserve sanctions for such cases.

The main question raised by orders issued in response to rights-threats is not whether they exist, but whether they are the only kind of remedial order. As I have mentioned before, courts and commentators often assume that remedies always replicate substantive duties. If this view—the 'rubber-stamp' view of remedies—were correct, then there would be only one cause of action in the common law: a rights-threat. Against this view, I argue in Chapters 7 and 8 that restitutionary orders and (most) damages awards create new rights and, accordingly, are not responses to rights-threats. For the moment, it is sufficient to keep in mind that while rights-threats are the most common private law cause of action, they are not the only cause of action.

The remainder of this chapter examines, individually, the main categories of private law orders issued in response to rights-threats.

B. Orders for a Sum Due

An order for a sum due is the most common private law order.[10] It is probably also the simplest example of an order issued in response to a rights-threat. With rare exceptions, an order for a sum due is available automatically on proof that the defendant failed to pay the relevant sum when it was due. The rights-threat is established by the defendant's ongoing failure to comply with its contractual duty to pay. The courts' response, unsurprisingly, is to order the defendant to perform the duty. In principle, *quia timet* versions of such orders are also available (albeit under a different name); however, they are rare in practice, for reasons explained below.

The addressees of orders for a sum due have usually failed to pay for goods or services, but orders for a sum due are available in respect of any unfulfilled monetary contractual obligation. The order in the famous case of *Carlill v Carbolic Smoke Ball Company*,[11] directing that the defendant pay a sum it had promised to pay to anyone who fell ill after using its 'smoke-ball', was for a sum due. Other examples include orders for a sum specified in a stipulated damages clause,[12] orders to pay indemnities,[13] and orders to return deposits. In common with the

[10] In 2016, there were 1,802,248 claims before the county and magistrate's courts in England and Wales, of which 1,374,039 were for specified sums (the overwhelming majority of which would have been for sums due under a contract): see *Civil Justice Statistics Tables: October to December 2016* (https://www.gov.uk/government/statistics/civil-justice-statistics-quarterly-october-to-december-2016). The status of orders for a sum due in American law is unclear. Neither Laycock (2010) nor Rendleman (2006) mention them. In a discussion of monetary awards that are not damages, Dobbs & Roberts (2018) refer to the situation 'when the plaintiff recovers the price due on an account or on a contract of sale', as well as to an action to recover a sum due on an indemnity (214). However, this reference is a single paragraph in a discussion of damages, and Dobbs & Roberts do not refer to the remedy in their table of contents or index. Finally, s 2-709 of the *Uniform Commercial Code*, entitled 'Action for the Price', which is in force is most American states, appears to contemplate what an English lawyer would describe as an action for a sum due in the context of sale contracts. The section distinguishes between the action for the price and a claim for incidental damages. Overall, it appears that in many if not all situations where English claimants would bring an action for a sum due, American claimants bring actions for damages. In practice, the result will usually be the same. Ironically, Article 2 of the *Uniform Commercial Code* precludes a claim for consequential damages for non-payment of money. Such a claim is possible in the UK as part of a separate action for damages for consequential losses. Note, finally, that lawyers sometimes describe orders for a sum due as orders to pay a debt/an agreed sum/the price.

[11] [1893] 1 QB 256.

[12] Stipulated damages clauses are invalid if they are not genuine pre-estimates of loss. This rule is part of substantive law. From the perspective of remedial law, stipulated damages clauses are the same as other monetary contractual clauses contracts: if the clause is valid and payment is overdue, the court will order the defendant to make the payment.

[13] Oddly, the traditional common law view is that an insured's claim under a typical insurance contract is for damages. The doctrinal basis for this view is that the 'hold harmless' clauses found in traditional insurance policies are promises 'to prevent the indemnified person from suffering damage', and, accordingly, the insured's action is an action for losses suffered from the breach of this promise: *Firma C-Trade SA v Newcastle P & I Assn* [1991] 2 AC 1, 35 (Lord Goff). This interpretation is a fiction: courts clearly do not expect the typical insurer to do anything to prevent the insured from suffering a loss. In any event, it is not possible to promise that someone will not suffer

other orders discussed in this work, an award of a sum due is expressed literally as an order by UK courts: 'It is ordered that the defendant: pay the claimant the sum of £ . . . '.[14]

Notwithstanding their practical importance, orders for a sum due receive little attention in most contracts and remedies textbooks. Some writers seem unaware of their existence ('[t]he only remedy which the common law afforded for breach of contract was an award of damages'[15]). This neglect may have contributed to the popular view that the civil law and common law have radically different approaches to breach of contract. According to this view, the primary remedy for breach of contract in the common law is damages (not specific performance), while the civil law adopts the reverse position. Yet, if 'primary' means the most common remedy, the primary remedy in both the UK and continental Europe is an order for a sum due. Further, while an order for a sum due is not technically a form of specific performance (because the order originated in the Royal Courts, not the Chancery Court) it is, in substance, what most lawyers mean when they refer to specific performance. It is an order to do the very thing that the defendant contractually promised to do. If one asks civil law lawyers to identify the most common specific performance order in their jurisdiction, they will name an order for a sum due under a contract.

It is not entirely clear why scholars have neglected orders for a sum due. Part of the reason may be that the law governing such orders is extremely simple. Save for cases where the defendant is able to raise a remedial defence, if the claimant proves that a sum due has not been paid the court will automatically order that the sum be paid.[16] With one exception (discussed next), the only question that courts contemplating requests for orders for a sum due must consider is the substantive-law issue of whether the relevant sum is indeed due. Almost the entirety of the remedial law governing orders for a sum due can be summarized in one sentence: if the claimant establishes that the defendant has failed to pay a sum due, the court will order the sum to be paid.

a loss. In the typical case, the only promise that insurers could plausibly be understood as making is a promise to indemnify the insured in the case of loss. Contemporary insurance contracts often include explicit clauses to this effect (though they also typically include 'hold harmless' clauses); accordingly, actions by insureds under such policies are sometimes (though not always) treated as actions for a sum due: *Caledonia North Sea Ltd v British Telecommunications Pls and Others* [2002] 1 Lloyd's Rep 553, 572.

[14] See e.g. *CPR* PD 4 Forms N45, N46. Traditionally, and still today in other common law jurisdictions, courts express an award of a sum due as a judgment that the claimant shall 'have and recover' the sum due: see Chapter 3.

[15] McGhee, Baker, & Snell (2000) [40-01]. This sentence was revised in the 2015 edition to read: 'the primary remedy which the common law affords for breach of contract is an award of damages' (McGhee, Bridge, & Snell (2015) [17-001]). The revised sentence remains inaccurate if 'primary' means 'most common'.

[16] *Jervis v Harris* [1996] Ch 195, 202–3.

i. The *White & Carter* Exception

The famous case of *White & Carter (Councils) Ltd v McGregor* introduced the sole exception to the above rule.[17] The Councils agreed to display advertisements for McGregor's garage on their litterbins for three years. Later the same day, McGregor informed the Councils that they no longer wanted the advertisements. The Councils nonetheless placed the advertisements and then sued McGregor for the sum due under the contract. The House of Lords ordered McGregor to pay the sum. However, Lord Reid added the qualification that in a case where the claimant had 'no legitimate interest' in performing the contract rather than claiming damages, the claimant should be limited to damages (which claim would then be subject to the rules on mitigation).[18] Subsequent courts have confirmed this exception, albeit stressing that it applies only in rare cases.[19]

The *White & Carter* exception is controversial because it appears to allow parties unilaterally to terminate valid contracts. However, the exception is not as anomalous as might be thought. As I explain below when examining specific performance, the law treats many ordinary contract breaches as effectively terminating the contract, regardless of the innocent party's wishes. If I fail to deliver promised goods to you, your only remedy, in most cases, is damages, and the court will assess those damages as if you had sought substitute performance (even if you insisted on delivery). Further, there are many cases where the law effectively ignores rights-threats for reasons similar to those that animate the *White & Carter* exception. As I again explain below (and in more detail in Chapter 9), courts sometimes refuse both specific relief and substitutionary awards when the cost of the defendant complying with the claimant's alleged right is disproportionate to its value. In such cases, the claimant is limited to compensatory damages notwithstanding the defendant's apparent failure to comply with a substantive duty. The *White & Carter* exception reflects the same principle: the exception precludes parties from insisting on their right to performance when the cost of compliance is out of proportion to its value. The special feature of the *White & Carter* exception is that the means by which the claimant insists on performance is by performing her own obligation and then demanding payment. The suggestion that rights may be lost when the cost of complying with them is disproportionate to their value is, of course, controversial, even if (as turns out to be the case), its application is narrowly confined. However, for the present the important point is that this idea has been accepted

[17] [1962] AC 413.

[18] Lord Reid did not explain why the claimants had a legitimate interest in performing the contract. Unless they had already done the work (which seems unlikely), the only possible interest would seem to be that by displaying McGregor's advertising on their bins they were advertising the possibility of putting advertising on bins—an interest that would have been difficult to quantify.

[19] See e.g. *Attica Sea Carriers Corporation v Ferrostal Poseidon Bulk Reederei GMBH (The Puerto Buitrago)* [1976] 1 Lloyd's Rep 250, 254–6; *Clea Shipping Corporation v Bulk Oil International Ltd (The Alaskan Trader)* [1984] 1 All ER 129.

(though sometimes covertly) in a range of cases and, further, that it is essentially a substantive-law principle. When courts preclude claimants from insisting on their substantive rights because they regard the cost of complying with those rights as excessive, their concern is not for the form of the claimant's remedy. Their concern is the desirability of the action required by the substantive right itself.

ii. Special Features of Orders for a Sum Due

Aside from the *White & Carter* exception, the law governing orders for a sum due is interesting primarily for what it does not allow, or at least for what it appears not to allow. To begin, claimants cannot obtain compensation for consequential losses caused by a delayed payment as part of an order for a sum due. However, in practice compensation for the loss of use of money is available on other grounds. By virtue of s 35A of the *Senior Courts Act* 1981, claimants can obtain interest on monetary awards generally. In addition, if claimants suffer further losses they can bring an ordinary action for damages in addition to their action for the sum due.[20] The result is that claimants seeking orders for a sum due are in the same situation as regards obtaining compensation for delayed performance as claimants seeking specific performance. A purchaser who obtains specific performance of a vendor's contractual duty to convey title to land can obtain damages for losses arising from the delay in conveyance. This similarity in treatment is consistent with interpreting orders for a sum due as, in substance, specific performance.

A second feature of orders for a sum due is that they are not available in *quia timet* versions. This rule follows from the definition of an order for a sum due: if the order were *quia timet*, the sum would not yet be due. At first impression, the unavailability of *quia timet* orders for a sum due appears to count against their classification as responses to rights-threats. However, this impression is misleading as *quia timet* versions of orders for a sum due are available, albeit under a different label—namely, as *quia timet* orders for the specific performance of contractual duties to pay money.[21] *Quia timet* orders to perform monetary duties are admittedly rare. In part, this is because it is difficult to prove an intent to breach a monetary duty prior to the due date. The other reason such orders are rare is that the remedies available for the breach of monetary duties (namely, orders for a sum due and/or damages) reduce considerably the risk that a mistaken refusal to issue a *quia timet* monetary order may cause the claimant significant harm. As I explain

[20] *Wadsworth v Lydall* [1981] 1 WLR 598.

[21] Though not typically described as such, orders to perform contractual duties to make periodic payments are *quia timet* insofar as they apply to payments that are not yet due: see e.g. *Beswick v Beswick* [1968] AC 58. Both monetary specific performance orders and *quia timet* specific performance orders are rare, so the combination is particularly uncommon: see note 82 and related text.

below in the general discussion of *quia timet* orders, similar considerations generally (and appropriately) limit the availability of *quia timet* orders.

A final noteworthy feature of orders for a sum due is that they are not subject to the partial remedial defences, such as adequacy of damages, supervision, personal duties, clean hands, and impossibility. The historical explanation for this rule is that the partial defences are only available in respect of orders that, unlike orders for a sum due, originated in the Chancery Court. However, it might be thought that if an order for a sum due is in substance a kind of specific performance (as I have argued), then in principle it should be subject to the same defences as actual specific performance. Indeed, if the partial defences are *remedial* defences (as I have argued), then in principle they should be available in respect of all remedies, whatever their origin or purpose. However, there is a simple, practical explanation for why they are not available in respect of orders for a sum due (and, as we shall see, in respect of other orders that originated in the Royal Courts). As I explain in the discussion of specific performance (and further in Chapter 9), the partial defences are, in general, reasons for courts to substitute easily performed, supervised, and enforced monetary awards in lieu of less-easily performed, supervised, and enforced non-monetary awards. In short, courts prefer monetary remedies to specific performance for (largely) administrative reasons. These reasons rarely apply to monetary awards, such as orders for a sum due. The concerns that underlie defences such as adequacy of damages, supervision, personal duties, clean hands, and impossibility do not arise in respect of orders for a sum due.

iii. Are Orders for a Sum Due Replicative?

Throughout this book, I treat an order for a sum due as a clear example of a replicative order. This interpretation might be queried on the ground that courts only issue orders for a sum due after the date on which the payment was due. It might be thought once the date for payment has passed it is too late to issue an order that replicates the defendant's substantive duty. Payment on a court-ordered date of 1 July is not the same as payment on a contractually specified date of 1 April.

Ordinary linguistic usage rejects this argument. Lawyers describe late payment as 'payment' and orders for a sum due as orders for a 'sum due' because they assume that paying the relevant sum fulfils an existing duty to pay. The ordinary understanding of why late debtors should pay is also inconsistent with this argument. Late debtors should pay, in that understanding, for the same reason that they should have paid on time, namely, that they promised to pay. If I want to explain to you why you should pay for goods for which payment was due two weeks earlier, my explanation will be the same one that I would have given two weeks earlier: you must pay because you promised to pay.

The question is how to explain this usage and understanding. One possibility is that a contractual duty 'to pay £100 by 1 April' comprises two duties—a duty to pay £100 and a duty to make the payment by 1 April—and that only the first of these duties exists after 1 April. The difficulty with this explanation is that it is supposes that the substantive law is indifferent as to when debtors make overdue payments. In this view, once 1 April has passed, the debtor can pay whenever he or she likes. The more plausible explanation, therefore, is that the debtor's substantive duty to pay by 1 April transforms, once 1 April has passed, into a duty to pay as soon as possible—and that it is this transformed duty that a subsequent order to pay the debt replaces. Suppose that on 2 April, I realise that I have broken a promise to you to repay a loan of £100 by 1 April. Obviously, I should still repay the money and, further, I should do so as soon as possible. Exceptional circumstances aside, the reasons that supported my duty to pay you by 1 April continue to apply after 1 April.[22] This continuity explains why failing to pay on time does not bring a contract to an automatic end. Even in contracts in which the duty to pay on time is an essential condition, a failure to pay on time does not terminate the contract unless the payee chooses to terminate. In short, my duty to pay you on 1 April, once breached, becomes a duty to repay you as soon after 1 April as possible. And if that duty is breached, it is replaced by a similar duty, and so on. When a court then orders me to pay a debt, it replicates this transformed duty.

C. Orders for the Recovery of Land ('Ejectment')

Orders for the recovery of land, traditionally described as 'ejectment', direct defendants who are unlawfully occupying the claimant's land to vacate it: '[T]he Court orders that: the defendant give the claimant the possession of . . . on or before . . .'.[23]

Ejectment orders are similar to orders for a sum due in a number of respects. To begin, like orders for a sum due, ejectment is practically important: ejectment is the second most common private law remedy.[24] Second, the law governing ejectment is simple. As in the case of orders for a sum due, the core of the law consists of a single rule: on proof that the defendant is unlawfully occupying the claimant's land, the court will order the defendant to vacate the land. The rights-threat is established by the defendant's ongoing breach of the claimant's right to exclusive possession. Determining whether an occupation is lawful sometimes raises difficult questions, particularly in the case of residential tenants (whose status is typically

[22] I discuss this idea, which draws on Raz (2004), Ripstein (2007), Weinrib (2008), and Gardner (2011), in more detail in Chapter 7's discussion of the 'continuity thesis'.

[23] *CPR* PD 4, Form N26, Table 1.

[24] See *Civil Justice Statistics Tables: October to December 2016*: (https://www.gov.uk/government/statistics/civil-justice-statistics-quarterly-october-to-december-2016).

governed by complex statutory regimes[25]). However, these are questions of substantive law. From the perspective of remedial law, all that matters is whether the occupation is lawful.

A third similarity is that ejectment receives little attention in general works on private law or remedies. This neglect (together with the neglect of orders for a sum due) has contributed to the common, but mistaken, assumption that there are two basic kinds of private law remedies—specific relief and damages—and, further, to an overemphasis of the latter's importance. Because ejectment originated in the Royal Courts, it is not technically 'specific relief'. However, in substance ejectment is a specific remedy because, like an order for a sum due, an ejectment order directs the defendant to do exactly what the substantive law requires—in this case, to cease an unlawful occupation. In substance, the overwhelming majority of private law remedies are specific remedies.

Fourth, while it is not possible to obtain *quia timet* ejectment orders (because only defendants already in occupation can be 'ejected'), functionally similar orders are available under a different name. Courts will grant *quia timet* injunctions forbidding defendants from trespassing. In addition, courts will grant ejectment orders that extend to land not currently occupied by the defendant.[26] Such orders are *quia timet* in substance as they aim to prevent the unlawful occupation of land not currently occupied by the defendant.

Fifth, like requests for orders for a sum due, requests for ejectment are not subject to the partial defences, such as adequacy of damages, supervision, clean hands, laches, and so on. The explanation is twofold. First, as in the case of orders for a sum due, the concerns that animate the partial defences rarely arise in the case of ejectment. Like orders for a sum due, ejectment is easy to express, supervise, and enforce. Admittedly, ejectment is more difficult to supervise and enforce than a monetary order. If trespassers refuse to leave, the only enforcement option is forcible ejectment (which may lead, in turn, to imprisonment if the defendant resists). From an enforcement perspective, ejectment resembles orders to which the partial defences are applied. But this factor is outweighed by the second reason that the partial defences are unavailable: damages are rarely an adequate substitute for ejectment because it is rarely, if ever, possible for a disposed landowner to purchase substitute performance. Every piece of land is unique (or so English courts have always assumed).[27]

[25] See *Landlord and Tenant Act* 1985.

[26] See e.g. *University of Essex v Djemal* [1980] 1 WLR 1301. The defendant must occupy at least part of the claimant's property.

[27] This assumption may also reflect the importance that the common law traditionally accorded to rights to land. As I discuss below, the common law takes a decidedly different view of rights to chattels. The Canadian Supreme Court rejected the assumption in *Semelhago v Paramadevan* [1996] 2 SCR 415. Though it is no doubt true today that not all land is unique, the decision has led to practical problems: see note 86.

A final similarity to orders for a sum due is that there is a possible technical objection to the classification of ejectment as replicative. Lawyers traditionally understand rights to the exclusive possession of land as rights *in rem*. My rights to my land are binding on the whole world: everyone in the world has a duty to stay off it. However, private law orders are personal: they only bind the defendant. It might be argued, then, that ejectment does not so much replicate the defendant's substantive duty as create a new duty.

A partial response to this objection is that it does not apply to all ejectment orders. Unlike the other orders examined in this work, courts sometimes address ejectment orders to the world: 'The court ordered that all person(s) in occupation of . . . must vacate the premises . . . '.[28] In these cases, ejectment replicates the content of the claimant's *in rem* right.

As for individualized ejectment orders, one suggestion is that such orders replicate *in personam* duties to give up possession that came into existence either at the moment that the defendant entered into wrongful occupation[29] or the moment the order was issued.[30] However, it sounds odd to suppose that my duty not to trespass over your land only comes into existence once I have begun to trespass or only once a court orders me not to trespass. Further, if my duty not to trespass only arises when I begin my trespass, why does the law allow you to waive that duty (while leaving others' duties intact) before I have committed a trespass? The simpler explanation is that an ejectment orders replicates a part of the claimant's substantive right.[31] Part of my right that no one trespass on my land is a right that you not trespass on my land. It is this right that ejectment orders replicate.

D. Orders for the Recovery of Chattels ('Delivery Up')

Orders for the recovery of chattels (goods), traditionally described as 'delivery up', direct defendants who are wrongfully in possession of the claimant's chattels to release them to the claimant. As was true in respect of ejectment, claimants seeking delivery up must prove that the defendant is in unlawful possession of their property. The threat to the claimant's rights is therefore established by proving an ongoing breach. It further follows that *quia timet* delivery up is not possible. However, as was true of ejectment and orders for a sum due, functionally

[28] Form N134 Interim possession order: *CPR* PD 4 Table 3. Where the occupier's identity is known, the order will refer specifically to a named defendant: '[T]he Court orders that: the defendant give the claimant the possession of . . . on or before . . . ': *CPR* PD 4, Form N26, Table 1.

[29] Birks appears to adopt this view: Birks (2000a) 6; (1996) 40; (1997) 11.

[30] Grantham & Rickett (2003) 733 appear to adopt the second alternative: 'the right *in rem* is inert and can be made to bear directly on the particular defendant only through the imposition of a further personal obligation'.

[31] This explanation is consistent with—but does not require full adherence to—Hohfeld's view that *in rem* rights are merely collections of innumerable *in personam* rights: Hohfeld (1917).

equivalent *quia timet* orders are available in principle (though, in practice, it is difficult to prove an intent to take the claimant's chattels, and if such an intent is proven the defendant may be liable criminally). The content of an order for delivery up is also similar to ejectment: delivery up replicates the defendant's substantive duty not to interfere with the claimant's rights to exclusive possession of the claimant's property.

However, the rules governing delivery up differ from those governing ejectment in one important respect. Requests for delivery up are subject to the partial defences discussed in Chapter 9, including, in particular, the defence of adequacy of damages. The consequence is that delivery up is relatively rare in practice. Courts usually assume that damages are an adequate remedy because the claimant can purchase similar chattels in the market. Accordingly, the normal remedy for unlawful possession of the claimant's chattel is an order that gives the defendant the option of paying damages (set at the chattel's value) or returning the chattel. Courts reserve delivery up for cases where the chattel is unique or otherwise has special value to the claimant.[32]

The common law's different approaches to ejectment and delivery up have influenced how common law lawyers describe and think about substantive rights in property. Common law lawyers describe chattels as 'personal property' because the standard remedy for wrongful possession of chattels—damages—is a personal remedy. The dispossessed owner gets money, not the chattel. In contrast, land is 'real property' because the remedy for wrongful possession of land—ejectment—is a 'real' remedy. The claimant regains possession of the actual land. Similar thinking has influenced how common law faculties traditionally teach property law (namely, in separate courses on land and personal property). Most dramatically, the common law's different approaches to ejectment and delivery up have led some writers to suggest that it is not possible to own chattels in the common law.[33] Echoing Holmes' better-known view of contractual rights (discussed below), this view supposes that our only rights with respect to chattels are rights to damages for their loss.

The latter view illustrates the misunderstandings that can arise from conflating remedial rights with substantive rights. The explanation for why courts rarely order delivery up is the same as the explanation (the 'administrative' explanation) for why they rarely order specific performance of contractual duties to deliver goods or specific restitution of goods transferred by mistake. On the one hand, monetary orders are generally simpler to express, supervise, and enforce than nonmonetary

[32] See *Whiteley Ltd v Hilt* [1918] 2 KB 808, 819; Peel & Goudkamp (2014) 566. The authority to award delivery up in the UK is statutory: *Torts (Interference with Goods) Act* 1977 (which was based on the *Common Law Procedure Act* 1854, s 78). As the statute says nothing about when courts should award delivery up, courts continue to apply the relevant pre-statutory principles. And since delivery up originated in the Chancery Court, those principles include the traditional limitations on specific relief, including adequacy of damages.

[33] See e.g. Kiralfy (1949) 424 ('[t]he law of property in chattels . . . may hardly be said to be a law of property at all').

orders. On the other hand, paying money is typically a close substitute for handing over a chattel because it is usually possible to purchase a similar chattel from a third party. (I discuss these reasons in more detail in the discussion below of specific performance.) Of course, close substitutes are not always available, as in case of unique goods. However, as noted above, it is in precisely such cases that courts normally award delivery up (and the same is true with respect to specific performance and specific restitution[34]). Finally, the same considerations explain why courts treat ejectment differently: land is always unique (or at least English courts have always assumed as much).

The common law's approach to delivery up is not immune from criticism. Contemporary common law courts should probably be more receptive to requests for delivery up. The number, sophistication, and funding of contemporary courts means that the practical advantages of monetary remedies are less significant than was previously the case. That said, the common law's preference for monetary remedies is fully intelligible. This preference explains why the common law recognizes ownership in chattels and, at the same time, protects ownership primarily through monetary remedies.

E. Injunctions

Strictly defined, an injunction is a judicial order that directs the defendant to do or not to do something.[35] All the orders examined in this book fit this description. However, it is conventional to confine the label to orders that originated in the Chancery Court or that would have originated there had they been introduced prior to the Judicature Acts. It is also conventional to describe orders for the recovery of chattels and orders to perform positive contractual obligations (both of which originated in the Chancery Court) as, respectively, delivery up and specific performance, rather than as injunctions (even though they satisfy the definition). This chapter adopts these conventions, with the practical consequence that it focuses on injunctions that prohibit torts or breaches of negative contractual obligations.[36] Common examples include injunctions against trespasses, nuisances, and breaches of restrictive covenants.

An injunction is a clear example of an order issued in response to a rights-threat: 'Injunctions are given to prevent wrongs which are threatened'.[37] To obtain

[34] In *Cohen v Roche* [1927] 1 KB 169, 180–1, the court held that delivery up was available in the same circumstances as specific performance of a duty to deliver goods.

[35] See Spry (2014) 332.

[36] The term 'injunction' also refers to a number of orders not discussed in this work, such as orders made in support of equitable rights (e.g. orders for the execution of a trust) and various procedural orders: see Sharpe (2017) [5.190–5.540].

[37] *Leeds Industrial Co-Operative Society Ltd v Slack* [1924] AC 851, 859. See also *Carlton Illustrators v Coleman & Co Ltd* [1911] 1 KB 771, 782: '[A]n injunction is not a remedy for a past breach, but is a means for preventing further breaches'.

an injunction, the claimant must prove either an ongoing wrong or an impending wrong. Following such proof, courts normally grant an injunction, and the content of that injunction normally requires the defendant to comply with the relevant substantive duty. For example, if the claimant establishes that the defendant is committing a nuisance or is about to commit a nuisance, the court normally orders the defendant to cease the relevant activity. Similarly, if the claimant proves that the defendant is in breach of a restrictive covenant or is about to breach a restrictive covenant, the court normally orders the defendant to comply with the covenant. At the same time, courts normally refuse injunctions where, notwithstanding that the defendant committed a wrong, there is little risk of a future wrong—for example, where the wrong was a one-off accident or where the defendant gave an undertaking to the court to cease the relevant activity.[38] There are exceptions, but as I explain below, in these cases the court either grants a substitute for an injunction or the exception is not actually an exception (because the apparent rights-threat is not actually a rights-threat).

i. *Quia Timet* Injunctions

Alongside injunctions against ongoing wrongs, injunctions are also available in cases where, although the defendant has yet to commit a wrong, he or she is likely to do so in the future. To obtain a *quia timet* injunction, the claimant must prove that the threatened wrong is imminent, that it would cause significant harm, and that damages would be an inadequate remedy if the wrong occurred.[39] The courts impose these conditions because of the risk that a *quia timet* injunction may turn out to be unnecessary.

The primary reason that courts issue orders on proof of a rights-threat is to provide the defendant with a new reason to do what the substantive law already requires. The primary question for courts contemplating such orders, therefore, is whether a new reason is needed. In cases where the defendant is engaged in an ongoing rights infringement such a reason is clearly needed. The facts show that the defendant is likely to continue to infringe the relevant right if nothing changes. The ongoing rights-infringement is close to conclusive evidence that the defendant is unwilling to comply with her substantive duty. Such evidence does not exist where the defendant has yet to breach the relevant duty. In these cases, the most that the claimant can establish is that the defendant appears to be willing, in future, to infringe the plaintiff's rights. In short, where the claimant seeks a *quia*

[38] See *Evans Marshall & Co Ltd v Bertola SA* [1973] 1 WLR 349. Although breaching an undertaking can lead to the same consequences as breaching an injunction (e.g. imprisonment), undertakings provide different reasons to do what they require than injunctions: see Chapter 5.

[39] See *Redland Bricks Ltd v Morris* [1970] AC 652, 655.

timet injunction, it is less certain that an alleged rights-threat is actually a threat, and so less certain that an injunction is required. As one judge noted, 'it would be wrong for this court in *quia timet* proceedings to grant relief by way of injunction to compel this defendant to do something which it appears willing to do without the imposition of an order of the court'.[40]

The special requirements for *quia timet* orders reflect this principle. The wrong must be imminent because the more imminent the wrong, the more likely it will occur if the court does nothing. And the magnitude of the threatened harm matters because courts must balance the costs of unnecessary orders against the harm to the claimant that may arise from refusing a necessary order. In cases where the claimant is likely to suffer a significant harm if the court mistakenly assumes that an injunction is not needed, the court should be more willing to issue an injunction—and vice versa.[41] (The same reasoning underlies the '*de minimis*' principle—the principle that courts will not get involved in trivial disputes: see Chapter 9.) Finally, damages must be an inadequate remedy for the same reason. If damages are adequate—for example, if the harm is pecuniary and the defendant is solvent—then the harm that may arise from refusing a necessary order will be relatively minor.[42] If the wrong occurs, the plaintiff can bring an action for damages.[43]

Courts place special weight on the requirements for *quia timet* injunctions in the relatively rare cases where the claimant seeks a positive ('mandatory') *quia timet* injunction. An example is an injunction directing the defendant to reinforce a wall that, absent reinforcement, is likely to fall onto the claimant's property. Mandatory injunctions raise special concerns. Some of these concerns are similar to those raised by other positive, non-monetary orders (e.g. most specific performance orders). Like specific performance, mandatory injunctions are more likely to lead to further litigation than ordinary injunctions because defendants often resist positive orders and, more generally, because it is often difficult to determine whether the defendant has complied with a positive non-monetary order. Mandatory injunctions are also more intrusive than ordinary injunctions. Defendants must

[40] *Bridlington Relay Ltd v Yorkshire Electricity Board* [1965] Ch 436, 445 (Buckley LJ).

[41] As recognized in Lord Brougham LC's reference to 'balancing the magnitude of the evil against the chances of its occurrence': *Earl of Ripon v Hobart* [1834] 3 My & K 169, 176.

[42] As I discuss in more detail in Chapter 9, 'adequate' has a different meaning here than it does in the typical case where it is the basis for refusing specific performance or delivery. In the typical case, damages are adequate because the claimant can purchase a substitute. In the cases involving *quia timet* injunctions, substitute performance is rarely possible. In these cases, courts assess adequacy by asking whether damages provide reasonable compensation for the anticipated harm. The answer to this question turns primarily on whether the anticipated harm is pecuniary or non-pecuniary.

[43] These considerations explain why *quia timet* orders to perform positive contractual obligations are rare: it is difficult to prove an unwillingness to perform positive obligations, and damages are usually an adequate remedy (because the plaintiff can purchase substitute performance). However, such orders are available: *Turner v Bladin* [1951] 82 CLR 463; *Hasham v Zenab* [1960] AC 316; *Zucker v Tyndall Holdings Plc*, [1992] 1 WLR 1127; Spry (2014) 80–1; see also notes 21, 82 and related text.

expend resources to fulfil them; more generally, positive restrictions are more intrusive than negative restrictions.

In addition to these concerns, *quia timet* mandatory injunctions raise a special concern. Ordinary mandatory injunctions typically direct defendants to undo wrongs, for example, to tear down a structure that encroaches on the claimant's land. In contrast, *quia timet* mandatory injunctions direct defendants to perform actions to prevent future wrongs from occurring. For example, in *Redland Bricks Ltd v Morris*[44] the claimant sought a *quia timet* injunction directing the defendant to restore support to the defendant's land. The claimant sought the support to prevent future land slippages, which, if they happened, would constitute a nuisance.[45] Requests of this kind pose a dilemma for courts.[46] On the one hand, an order that is framed in terms of the desired result—for example, an order directing that 'the appellants take all necessary steps to restore the support to the respondent's land within a period of six months'[47]—is too demanding. There is no limit to what 'all necessary steps' might require. The defendant might be required to incur costs that the court would never have ordered directly. On the other hand, if the order directs the defendant to perform a specific action—for instance, 'the appellant must place 20 tons of ½ inch gravel covered with compacted soil . . .'—it is open to the objection that there may be other ways of preventing the wrong. Perhaps 15 tons of ¾ inch gravel is sufficient. The result is that in practice *quia timet* injunctions are usually restricted to cases where there is only one way to prevent the future wrong, and where it is possible to describe the required actions precisely.[48]

ii. Injunctions to Take Care?

In principle, injunctions should be available in response to a threat to any kind of substantive right. However, in practice, the vast majority of injunctions protect claimants from breaches of negative covenants and from intentional torts that involve property, such as nuisance, trespass, and breach of copyright.[49] This pattern

[44] *Redland Bricks Ltd v Morris* [1970] AC 652.

[45] Burrows argues that the order sought in this case was not *quia timet* because the appellant's earthworks had caused previous slippages: Burrows (2004) 513. However, if the distinction between ordinary and *quia timet* orders turns on whether the relevant wrong is ongoing—as I have argued—then the order sought in *Redland Bricks* was *quia timet.*

[46] The dilemma described below does not arise with *quia timet* mandatory injunctions to tear down a structure that, if completed, would constitute a nuisance or other wrong because such orders are in substance negative: they prohibit the relevant structure.

[47] This quote is from the order granted by the trial judge in *Redland Bricks.*

[48] For example, in *Express Newspapers plc v Mitchell* [1982] IRLR 465 the court ordered a union official to remove a notice to strike that, if acted upon, would constitute the tort of interference with contractual relations.

[49] However, courts have issued injunctions against injuring or interfering with the claimant's person: see e.g. *R v R and I* [1961] 1 WLR 1334; *Egan v Egan* [1975] Ch 218.

is unsurprising. The easiest way to establish a rights-threat is by proving an ongoing rights-infringement. For most torts, such proof is impractical because the tortious activity is over before the victim could get before a judge. The actions that constitute the torts of assault, battery, or damage to property typically last no more than a few seconds. In contrast, the actions that constitute property torts are usually ongoing. Nuisances and trespasses are often of potentially indefinite duration. The same is true for breaches of negative covenants. Further, the main hurdle to obtaining a *quia timet* injunction—namely, proof that the wrong is imminent—is usually easier to satisfy in cases involving property wrongs and breaches of negative covenants. In such cases, it is often possible to establish the threat by pointing to physical actions undertaken by the defendant, such as commencing construction of a building, advertising an event, or seeking work with a competitor. By contrast, even if it is sometimes possible in theory to prove an imminent battery or assault, it is almost never possible to get before a judge in time to obtain an injunction.

Still, it might be thought surprising that English courts do not appear to have ever issued injunctions prohibiting the most common and important contemporary tort—the tort of negligence.[50] Why? One possibility is that the common law does not recognize a substantive duty to take care not to injure others.[51] According to this view, the only legal significance of carelessly injuring others is that the injurer becomes liable to pay damages.[52] It follows, in this view, that threatening negligence is not a rights-threat. From this perspective, carelessly harming another is like earning taxable income: it attracts legal consequences (in the form of a liability to pay money), but it is not a wrong.

The suggestion that the common law does not recognize a substantive duty to take care not to carelessly injure others is implausible on its face.[53] Judges regularly say that there is a duty not to carelessly injure others and they regularly describe carelessly injuring others as a wrong.[54] Further, it is difficult to think of any reason that courts would require defendants who have carelessly injured others to pay

[50] '[T]here is no case, so far as I know, where [an injunction] has been granted so as to stop a man being negligent': *Miller v Jackson* [1977] QB 966, 980 (Lord Denning MR). However, it appears that American courts have issued such injunctions: *Shimp v New Jersey Bell Telephone Co* 368 [1976] A 2d 408. See also McBride (2004) 427–9; Goldberg & Zipursky (2002) 1709–15. There does not appear to be a rule prohibiting such an injunction. To the contrary, '[A]n injunction may issue in the protection of any legal right whatever, save where an applicable statutory instrument provides to the contrary': Spry (2014) 342.

[51] See Atiyah & Cane (2013) 67; Hedley (2011) 26. The best-known general statement of this view is Calabresi & Melamed (1972).

[52] 'To say that a person owes a duty of care in a particular situation means (and only means) that the person will be liable for causing damage by negligence in that situation': Atiyah & Cane (2013) 67.

[53] See generally, McBride (2004); Zipursky (1998b); Goldberg & Zipursky (2000); Zipursky & Goldberg (2001).

[54] '[A] motorist owes a duty to take care not to injure other road users or damage their property': *N v Agrawal* [1999] All ER 515 [14] (Stuart-Smith LJ). 'The basis of the claim to which they give statutory authority is negligence causing injury, and that is a wrong which I believe that law of every civilised country treats as an actionable wrong': *Davidson v Hill* [1901] 2 KB 606, 613–15 (Kennedy J).

damages yet at the same time be indifferent as to whether those injuries occurred. Carelessly injuring others is not the same as earning taxable income. The only possible reason for supposing that there is no duty not to carelessly injure others is that the courts have not (at least until now) issued orders requiring compliance with this duty. This explanation conflates substantive and remedial law. The existence of a substantive duty is perfectly consistent with courts refusing to order defendants to comply with that duty so long as the reason for their refusal is remedial.

One possible partial explanation for unavailability of injunctions against negligence is that it is not possible to engage in ongoing negligence because negligence consists not merely in failing to 'take care', but in 'injuring another through failing to take care'.[55] In this understanding, the only way that I could be engaged in ongoing negligence against you is if I were continuously injuring you by continuously failing to take care. In practice, such conditions would be difficult to prove (and if proven would likely amount to an intentional tort, such as battery).

The interpretation of negligence that underlies this explanation is far from self-evident.[56] But even if it is accepted it does not explain why courts do not issue *quia timet* injunctions against negligence. In theory, it should be possible for claimants to prove that they face an imminent risk of injury because the defendant is engaging in, or about to engage in, risky behaviour. Of course, in most cases where it could be proven that a defendant is engaged in careless behaviour it will be difficult to prove that the claimant in particular is likely to be injured by this behaviour. Your habit of texting while driving may be likely to lead to an accident, but it will be difficult for me to prove that I am likely to the victim of such an accident. However, it seems possible to establish such a risk in some cases. For example, it might be possible to prove that my neighbour's careless habit of leaving a ladder unattended at the side of his house is likely to eventually result in the ladder toppling onto my house. Similarly, it might be possible to prove that my colleague's habit of carelessly roller-skating past my cubicle is likely to eventually to cause me an injury. Why have courts not issued injunctions against such kinds of behaviour?

It is possible that the explanation is that no one has yet sought such an injunction. There are normally other, simpler, ways of stopping the kinds of behaviours illustrated by the above examples. Leaving a ladder unattended is likely to be contrary to a municipal by-law or building regulation. Few employers would allow an employee to roller-skate recklessly through their office. However, a further reason is that even if such a case came before the courts, there is almost always an alternative, and more practical, remedy available. Leaving a ladder that is at risk of falling

[55] '[D]amage is the gist of negligence': *Gregg v Scott* [2005] UKHL 2 [217] (Lord Phillips). See also Stapleton (1988).

[56] The alternative interpretation is that the duty in negligence is to take reasonable care to avoid injuring others, and that it is only the actionability of that duty (i.e. the availability of a remedy) that is contingent on proof of an injury: see Smith (2015); McBride & Bagshaw (2015) 123–5; Chapter 8, note 71.

onto my property is a nuisance (because it prevents me from using my property in the normal way), and so could be restrained by an injunction. Similarly, in the roller-skating example, I could obtain an injunction against my employers, based on their duty to provide a safe workplace, directing them to ban roller-skating in the office. In practice, it is difficult to think of examples of 'failing to take care to avoid injuring the claimant' that would not be actionable on other grounds.

Admittedly, the availability of an alternative remedy is not usually a reason for a court to refuse the remedy that the claimant has requested. However, there is an additional reason for courts to limit claimants to an alternative to an injunction against negligence. It is difficult to frame an injunction to 'take care' without unduly restricting the defendant's liberty. There is little point in ordering defendants simply to 'take reasonable care' since defendants presumably believe that they are already taking care. Further, there is a significant risk that such an order would lead to litigation over the meaning of 'reasonable care'. At the same time, orders that prohibit specific actions—for example, 'the defendant is ordered not to leave unattended ladders propped against the north side of his house'—are likely to be unduly intrusive. An unattended ladder is not a risk if it is secured to a house. Nor is an unattended ladder dangerous if it is fixed to the ground, boxed in, or surrounded by a high barrier. As we have seen, similar concerns about over-specificity underlie the courts' hesitation to issues mandatory *quia timet* injunctions. However, the problem is more serious and pervasive where claimants seek injunctions against carelessness. A failure to take care invariably consists in a failure to perform one of a number of possible precautionary actions (e.g. slowing down, giving a warning, providing a barrier, and so forth). It is rarely the case that there is only one set of actions that must be followed to ensure that an activity is engaged in safely. For these reasons, the absence of injunctions against negligence is unsurprising.

iii. Are Injunctions Always Replicative?

As is true generally of orders issued in response to rights-threats, injunctions typically command defendants to do what they already have substantive duties to do. An order to cease a trespass or a nuisance replicates the content of the defendant's substantive duty not to commit trespasses or nuisances. Similarly, an injunction directing the defendant to comply with a non-competition covenant replicates the defendant's substantive contractual duty not to compete. Of course, courts typically frame tort injunctions in narrower and more concrete terms than the terms used to describe substantive tort duties. The substantive duty that is the focus of nuisance law is, roughly, a duty not to interfere unreasonably with another's enjoyment of land. Injunctions against nuisance are much more specific ('the defendant is ordered not to do excavation works on her property other than between 9:00 a.m. and 5:00 p.m. on weekdays'). However, if the enjoined activity is a nuisance, then the defendant has a substantive duty not to engage in that activity. The content of the injunction replicates the content of that duty.

Most of the rights that courts protect with injunctions are correlative to duties that everyone—not just the defendant—owes the claimant. My right to the reasonable enjoyment of my land is conventionally understood as a right that 'no one' disturbs that enjoyment. It is not merely a right that you, in particular, not disturb my enjoyment. It might be argued, then, that injunctions against nuisances, trespasses, and so on, are not replicative because they are always directed at specific, named, defendants. In the discussion of orders for the recovery of land (where the relevant right is also held against the world), I considered a parallel objection. The response to the objection also applies to the present objection. Part of what it means to say that the claimant holds a right 'against the world' is that the claimant also holds rights against the particular individuals who make up the world. When a court orders a specific defendant to quit the defendant's land or to cease a nuisance it is this right that the order is replicating. If such rights did not exist it would make no sense to say—as lawyers, judges, and writers say all the time—that you have a duty not to trespass on my land. Nor would it possible to explain why, if you trespass on my land, you are liable to being ordered to pay me damages. You are liable because you breached a duty owed to me. The existence of individuated rights also explains why I can agree to allow you to walk over my land; if my right was only 'against the world', then any agreement to waive this right would have to be made with the world. In short, the idea that particular individuals owe duties to other particular individuals not to trespass on their land, and so forth, is assumed in the ordinary and conventional understanding of legal rights.[57]

However, there are three exceptions to the principle that injunctions are replicative. First, *quia timet* injunctions sometimes direct defendants to cease activities that, while not wrongful at the moment of the injunction, will, if continued, constitute, cause, or lead to a wrong. For example, a court might order the defendant to cease construction of a building that, once completed, will block the claimant's right to light.[58] Similarly, a court might order the defendant not to dump waste that, in time, will leach onto the defendant's property.[59] Courts also sometimes

[57] The suggestion that you do not owe me a legal duty not to trespass on my land is so at odds with ordinary legal terminology that it may be helpful to mention that its genesis lies in the view that legal rights are by definition rights which are held by one individual against another individual *and* which courts will support through replicative orders: see e.g. Birks (1997a) 11–12. If this broadly Romanist definition is accepted, then you cannot have a right that I not trespass over land until I have actually trespassed or threatened to trespass because a court will not order met not to trespass without proof that I trespassed or threatened to do so. One reason for rejecting this view is precisely that it entails the odd conclusion that your duty not to trespass arises only at the moment that you commit or threaten a trespass. This view also entails the equally odd conclusion that contracting parties have no duties to comply with negative contractual obligations until they have breached them (because courts will only enforce such obligations on proof of a breach).

[58] See *Dicker v Popham, Radford, & Co* [1890] 63 LT 379.

[59] See *Fletcher v Bealey* [1885] 28 ChD 688. The court was willing in principle to grant an injunction against dumping waste but declined to do so because the injury was not sufficiently certain and

issue *quia timet* injunctions that direct defendants to perform positive actions intended to prevent future wrongs. For instance, a court might order the defendant to restore land to ensure that the claimant's house does not slip in future.[60] The orders in these examples are not strictly replicative. Constructing a building that could become, but is not yet, a nuisance is not a tort. Dumping waste on your own land or not supporting your own land are not torts. However, these orders are close cousins of replicative orders. They are responses to rights-threats. And, like replicative orders, they direct defendants to perform actions that, in the court's view, are necessary to ensure that the defendants comply with their substantive duties. They differ from replicative orders only in that the actions they require may not be the only way to comply with the relevant substantive duty. This difference is one reason that such orders are relatively rare.

The second, closely related exception is an injunction to remove or destroy something that, by its very existence, constitutes an ongoing wrong. The typical example is an order to remove a structure that constitutes a nuisance or other ongoing wrong.[61] The fulfillment of such an order guarantees that the ongoing wrong will cease. If the defendant removes a structure that constitutes a nuisance, the nuisance ceases. However, in theory the same result can be achieved without the defendant's assistance. For example, if a hurricane blows down a nuisance-creating structure, the defendant is no longer committing a nuisance. It follows that these orders are not strictly replicative. Yet, as was true of the orders discussed in the previous paragraph, they are close cousins of replicative orders. These orders direct defendants to perform actions that, in the court's view, are necessary to ensure that defendants comply with their substantive duties.

Finally, courts sometimes issue injunctions that direct the defendant to undo a wrong's consequences (as opposed to ceasing the wrong itself), typically by conveying property that is lawfully held, but that was obtained because of a wrong. I argue that the cause of action for such injunctions is an injustice; accordingly, they are discussed in Chapter 8.

iv. Injunctions and Partial Defences

Courts may refuse injunctive relief, notwithstanding that the claimant has established a rights-threat, if the action is subject to a partial defence, such as adequacy

imminent. A third, slightly different, example is an order directing a defendant who had been tortiously harassing the claimant to stay a distance from the claimant's home: *Burris v Azdani* [1995] 1 WLR 1372.

[60] See *Hooper v Rogers* [1975] Ch 43. The court did not actually grant an injunction , but rather held that the trial judge could have ordered an injunction (and, therefore, that he had the authority to award damages in lieu, which was the actual issue).

[61] See e.g. *Kelsen v Imperial Tobacco Co (of Great Britain and Ireland) Ltd* [1957] 2 QB 334.

of damages, supervision, laches, or clean hands. Where courts refuse injunctions on this basis, they normally award damages in lieu.

I discuss the partial defences in detail in Chapter 9. However, three points from that discussion should be mentioned here. The first is that notwithstanding their origins in the Chancery Court, the reason that courts continue to apply the partial defences is that they reflect, even if imperfectly, general remedial-law concerns—concerns that any court contemplating an order should take into account. The explanation for why these defences developed in the Chancery Court and why they remain tied today to historically Equitable remedies is that in practice the concerns that animate them are only an issue in respect of historically Equitable remedies. These concerns, which are largely (though not exclusively) administrative in nature, apply particularly to non-monetary remedies, and so in practice to injunctions, specific performance, and delivery up. From the perspective of remedial law, the main distinguishing feature of the historically Equitable remedies—and the main reason they are subject to special defences—is that they are non-monetary remedies.[62]

Second, it is relatively rare for courts to refuse injunctions because of a partial defence. Courts normally grant injunctions to claimants who establish a threat to a substantive tort right or to a negative contractual right. Thus, they issue injunctions against trespasses, nuisances, copyright infringements, and breaches of negative contractual duties 'as a matter of course'. In contrast, delivery up and (as discussed below) specific performance are relatively rare. In practice, these awards are available only where the defendant failed to deliver or retained unique property. The explanation for this difference is that while damages are typically an adequate remedy for the breach of positive contractual obligations or for the wrongful taking of goods (because the relevant goods or services can be purchased from a third party), they are rarely adequate where an injunction is sought. It is not possible to purchase the equivalent of 'no trespassing by the defendant', 'no breach of a restrictive covenant', and so on from a third party.[63] In addition, injunctions are typically negative orders, and so are comparatively simple to express and supervise. Finally, injunctions do not raise the concern for state-ordered personal duties that arises with some specific performance orders.[64] It is true that positive ('mandatory') injunctions, such as orders to reinforce a wall or tear down a building, sometimes raise similar

[62] There are exceptions. As I explain below, specific performance of a monetary duty, though rare, is possible, and, as we saw above, orders for the recovery of land, which originated in the Royal Courts, are non-monetary. These exceptions are consistent with the above explanation.

[63] The rare exception is where the claimant can take (or have others take) physical steps to prevent the rights-infringement. For example, in *Hooper v Rogers* [1975] Ch 43, the claimant, as co-owner of the relevant land, was able do the work necessary to restore support to his house.

[64] Aside from the exceptional cases where a negative injunction would leave the defendant with no choice but to comply with a positive, personal, contractual duty. The courts properly refuse such injunctions: *Mortimer v Beckett* [1920] 1 Ch 571.

concerns. However, this exception proves the rule, as courts are generally reluctant to issue mandatory injunctions for precisely these reasons.[65]

The third, related, point is that in the relatively rare cases where courts refuse injunctions because of a partial defence they usually do so for substantive-law reasons. I discuss these cases next.

v. Substantive-Law Reasons for Refusing Injunctions

As we saw in Chapter 4 (and as I discuss further in Chapter 9), courts sometimes refuse specific relief, and award damages in lieu, for substantive-law reasons. In these cases, while the courts appear merely to be choosing one form of remedy over another (namely, damages over specific relief), in substance, they are denying the existence of the alleged rights-threat. I argue that the courts refuse specific relief in these cases because, in their view, it is permissible for the defendant to engage in the actions that the claimant wants enjoined. Most of the cases where courts refuse injunctive relief because of a partial defence fit this pattern. These cases fall into two main categories.

The first, and by far the larger category, is comprised of nuisance cases where the court refuses an injunction because the cost of compliance—whether to the defendant, the public, or a combination—is disproportionate to the harm that would arise from non-compliance. For example, in *Miller v Jackson*,[66] the claimants alleged that the defendant cricket club's operation constituted a nuisance because of the risk of cricket balls landing on their residential property. The majority of the court agreed,[67] but they refused the injunction, citing the significant public interest in cricket and (in their view) the relatively small inconvenience that the claimants would suffer.[68] In a similar vein, in the American case of *Boomer v Atlantic Cement Co*,[69] the claimant homeowners alleged that the defendant factory was committing a nuisance by emitting dust and other particles onto their property. Again, the court agreed with the allegation (or at least appeared to agree), but they refused the injunction on the ground that it would lead to closing the factory, which employed over 300 workers. In the court's view, the harm that would have resulted

[65] See *Redland Bricks Ltd v Morris* [1970] AC 652.

[66] *Miller* v *Jackson* [1977] QB 966. See also *Dennis v Ministry of Defence* [2003] EWHC 793; *Bracewell v Appleby* [1975] Ch 408; *Denne v Light* [1857] 8 De GM & G 774; *Behrens v Richards* [1905] 2 Ch 614.

[67] Lord Denning held that the activity was not a nuisance, but then, in an apparent inconsistency, went on to consider whether the court should award an injunction. The usual explanation of Denning's reasoning is that he was merely considering whether, in the case that he was wrong on the first issue, an injunction should be awarded. However, if my interpretation of *Miller* is correct, the two reasons for refusing relief raised by Denning are different ways of saying the same thing. The other judges held that there was a nuisance.

[68] The judges also mentioned that the claimants knew that their property abutted the cricket club when they purchased it. I explain why this factor is relevant in note 73.

[69] 26 NY 2d 219 (1970).

from closing the factory was disproportionate to the relatively minor inconvenience caused by the emissions.[70]

The second category is comprised of trespass cases where the court refuses to award an injunction for a trivial trespass. For example, in *Woollerton and Wilson Ltd v Richard Costain Ltd*[71] the claimant sought an injunction to prevent the defendant's construction crane from passing over its airspace. The court technically agreed to issue an injunction, but then suspended the injunction's operation for the period of the work. In substance, the suspension was equivalent to an outright refusal to issue an injunction. In their decision, the court noted that there was no other practical way for the work to be completed and that the crane's operation would not cause the claimants any harm.

Miller, *Boomer*, and *Woollerton* ('*MBW*') are controversial decisions. But whatever one may think of the courts' reasons (see below), they have little to do with remedial law. The courts' fundamental concern in these cases is the desirability of the *action* requested by the claimant, not the desirability of *ordering* the defendant to perform the action. Broadly speaking, the reason the courts refused injunctive relief was that, in their view, the cost of complying with the asserted right was disproportionate to the harm occasioned by non-compliance.[72] This disproportion was the same regardless of whether the defendants performed the relevant action because the courts ordered them to perform it or because they chose to comply with their (alleged) substantive duty. In other words, the courts' reasons for refusing the injunctions were also reasons for the defendants not to comply with their alleged substantive duties (regardless of whether the court ordered them to comply). The courts' decisions to refuse an injunction was effectively a denial that the claimants' substantive rights were under threat.[73] Consistent with this explanation,

[70] Until relatively recently, the courts' approach to injunctions for nuisance was in a state of flux: Burrows (2004) 517. One line of authority, which includes *Miller*, gave courts a broad discretion to refuse injunctions. The other line, represented by *Shelfer v City of London Electric Lighting Company* [1895] 1 Ch 287, held that refusals should be exceptional. The Supreme Court affirmed the first line in *Lawrence v Fen Tigers Ltd* [2014] UKSC 13. Lord Sumption went so far as to opine that 'There is much to be said for the view that damages are ordinarily an adequate remedy for a nuisance' [279].

[71] [1970] 1 WLR 411.

[72] Thus described, these cases appear to be examples where specific relief is refused because of the 'hardship' defence (see Chapter 9). But while the courts occasionally invoke this defence, it is more common, particularly in nuisance cases, for the courts simply to refer to the *Shelfer* test or, today, to the *Fen Tigers* test: *Shelfer v City of London Electric Lighting Company* [1895] 1 Ch 287; *Lawrence v Fen Tigers Ltd* [2014] UKSC 13.

[73] In addition to weighing the costs and benefits of performance, courts sometimes consider two further questions in cases like *MBW*. The first is whether damages are adequate in the sense that, while it is not possible to purchase a substitute, the harm is of a kind for which money might plausibly compensate (which usually rules out refusing injunctions to prevent physical injuries). This question is relevant because the magnitude of the harm caused by non-performance of the alleged duty depends partly on the extent to which an award of damages can ameliorate the harm. The second question is whether the defendant acted 'reasonably'. In the typical case where this question is raised, the concern is whether the claimant attempted to 'steal a march' on the claimant by knowingly commencing an unlawful activity (e.g. constructing a building that encroached on the claimant's property) in the hope that, by the time the claimant discovered the activity, courts would refuse to order it torn down. This question is relevant because in many cases where courts refuse injunctions for substantive-law reasons, they would have

the damages in *MBW* and similar cases are not set at the cost of substitute performance, but instead at the loss the defendant will suffer from non-performance. These awards are not substitutes for specific relief and their cause of action is not a rights-threat.[74]

Courts and commentators often criticize cases like *MBW* for allowing defendants to infringe claimants' rights for a fee.[75] The above interpretation suggests that this criticism is misplaced or at least misleading. Rather than allowing the infringement of the claimant's substantive rights for a fee, the courts in these cases have effectively concluded that the alleged rights do not exist. However, this interpretation raises two other possible criticisms. The first, which has been largely ignored by courts and commentators (though it is particularly relevant for this chapter), concerns judicial methodology. Throughout this work, I have argued that it is dangerous to draw conclusions about substantive law from decisions about remedies. However, my interpretation of cases like *MBW* draws just such conclusions. In these cases, the courts say they are merely choosing one form of remedy over another, but, in substance, they are denying the substantive right on which the claimant's action rests. Why do courts use remedial law in this way?

One explanation is that courts employ remedial law because it provides an easy legal route to the desired result. It is orthodox law that courts have discretion to refuse an injunction even where the claimant establishes a rights-threat. In Chapter 9, I argue that this discretion exists because the range of factors that courts are rightly required to consider when contemplating an injunction (i.e. the partial defences, such as adequacy of damages, supervision, laches, clean hands, and the like) are both incommensurable and matters of degree. These factors reflect remedial-law principles, and so are not directly relevant to cases like *MBW*. However, the discretion that they justify is not formally limited to cases in which partial defences are pleaded, and as such is available for other purposes. The suggestion, then, is that

granted them if the claimants had requested them earlier. For example, if, at the start of construction of the factory in *Boomer*, the claimants could have proven that, once completed, the factory would emit significant dust, a court likely would have issued an injunction prohibiting further construction (or requiring filters, and so forth). At that point, the cost of complying with the injunction would have been relatively small. Courts rightly penalize defendants who attempt to conceal their wrongdoing (or future wrongdoing) at a time when it is not too late to undo or prevent that wrongdoing. As this example illustrates, there are many situations where courts can rightly prohibit the construction of a building (or analogous structure, products, and the like) notwithstanding that, if the building were already completed, the court would rightly refuse to order it torn down.

[74] Some writers accept the substance of the above argument but insist that the defendant is still engaged in a wrong: Gardner (2011) 42–9. In this view, the defendant's behaviour can be justified yet is still wrongful. The concept of 'justified wrongdoing' is not easy to understand, at least in a legal context. The natural interpretation of what the law means when it says 'X is wrong' is that citizens should not engage in X. However, even if the concept of justified-wrongdoing view is accepted, cases like *MBW* remain difficult to square with the traditional understanding of damages. In that understanding, damages are a response to actions that the defendants should not have done.

[75] See the minority judgment in *Boomer*.

the courts use their authority to refuse injunctions to modify the substantive law because that authority comes with an inherent discretion to refuse relief for any reason that they see fit.

This suggestion is undoubtedly part of the answer. But it does not explain why courts in cases like *MBW* do not pursue the more obvious—and transparent—route of modifying the substantive law. Why do courts not simply hold that the claimants' substantive rights are not under threat? There appear to be two reasons. The first is that it is difficult to incorporate the considerations that courts take into account in deciding cases like *MBW* into substantive rules. Whatever one thinks of the courts' conclusions in these cases, they were the product of a complex weighing of difficult-to-balance factors. In *Miller*, the court weighed the value of village cricket against the value of the claimants' undisturbed enjoyment of their land. A broadly similar balancing of public and private interests underlay the decisions in *Boomer* and *Woollerton*. Courts are rightly hesitant to incorporate balancing tests of this kind into rules that are meant to guide citizens in their day-to-day lives. And courts are particularly hesitant to make this modification when the substantive rules in question are property law rules (as was true in *MBW*). Property law rules must be relatively simple if they are to operate effectively.[76] A rule that requires individuals to engage in complex balancing exercises to determine whether they are trespassing or committing a nuisance is impractical. By employing remedial law to assess the defendant's activities in cases like *MBW*, the courts leave these balancing exercises to judges, not citizens.

The other practical advantage of the current approach is that it provides courts with a simple basis on which to award damages. When courts refuse injunctive relief in cases like *MBW*, they normally award damages in lieu. These awards are uncontroversial. Although many courts and commentators have questioned the practice of refusing injunctions in cases like *MBW*, they have not questioned the practice of awarding damages where the injunction is refused. It is assumed that claimants who are refused injunctions in cases like *MBW* should at least receive damages. But what is the legal basis of such awards? Both the reason for issuing these awards and their magnitude (which is set at the amount of the claimant's loss, not the cost of substitute performance) are inconsistent with interpreting them as substitute specific relief. Nor are they responses to wrongs, at least if the preceding explanation is correct. In Chapter 8, I argue that these awards are responses to injustices. However, it is understandable that courts might prefer to ground them on the more orthodox ground that they are compensation for a wrong, or at least a future wrong. This explanation is obviously not available if the court holds that the reason for refusing the injunction is that the defendant's activity is not wrongful. In short, courts decide cases like *MBW* on ostensibly remedial grounds because this

[76] See H Smith (2012).

allows them to award damages on the orthodox ground that the defendant committed a wrong.

The courts' conflation of remedial and substantive law in cases like *MBW* is understandable, and perhaps even unavoidable. Still, it comes with a cost. Framing the issues in these cases in remedial terms obscures their significance. It also provides fodder for the view that assumes our substantive rights are determined by the remedies claimants can obtain. The reality is that cases like *MBW* are exceptions to the general rule.

The other issue raised by cases like *MBW* is whether it is appropriate to permit individuals to engage in prima facie rights-infringing activities on the basis that (roughly) the benefits of the activity far outweigh their costs. This issue is one of substantive law, so my comments are brief.

An initial observation is that characterizing the underlying issue in cases like *MBW* as one of substantive law makes these cases more, not less, controversial. As I have argued throughout this work, it is perfectly appropriate for courts to consider the costs of expressing, supervising, and enforcing orders when contemplating requests for specific relief. However, the suggestion that substantive rights should be determined through a cost-benefit analysis is more controversial. It is true that contemporary courts appear to support such reasoning in certain contexts.[77] But if it is generalized, this kind of reasoning is inconsistent with the very idea of substantive rights. My right to my land is hardly a right if anyone who values it more than I do may take it.

However, there is an alternative explanation for many (though not all) of the cases in which courts refuse injunctive relief because of disproportion in harm. Courts in civil law systems would deny relief in cases like *Woollerton* on the ground that the claimants were abusing their substantive rights.[78] According to this explanation, the claimants' right to their airspace does not include the right to preclude trivial encroachments where (as in *Woollerton*) there is a valid reason for the encroachment. The common law does not officially recognize the concept of abuse of right. Yet, common law courts frequently manipulate other doctrines—including, in particular, remedial doctrines—to reach results that are difficult to explain on any other basis.[79] *Woollerton* appears to have involved such a manipulation: arguably, the court treated the case as a matter of remedial discretion precisely

[77] Aside from the present context, the most obvious instance is the 'public policy' element of the test for the existence of a duty of care in negligence: see, e.g. *Robinson v Chief Constable of West Yorkshire Police* [2014] EWCA Civ 15. In recent years, English courts have narrowed the range of cases in which this element is relevant (see e.g. *McFarlane v Tayside Health Board* [2000] 2 AC 59), and, even where the courts invoke public policy, the decision can usually be explained on other grounds: see Stevens (2007) 20–57, 306–19).

[78] See Gambaro (1997); Reid (1998).

[79] See Weir (1998) 124; Perillo (1995) 113. In *Woollerton,* the court's discussion of the reasonableness of the parties' behaviour came close to adopting an abuse of rights approach explicitly.

so that they could police an abuse of rights without explicitly saying that there were policing an abuse of rights.[80]

Abuse of rights is a flexible concept, but it probably cannot explain cases like *Miller* and *Boomer*. In these cases, the claimants' injuries were not trivial. Further, the main reason for refusing the injunctions was the public's interest. In private law contexts, an abuse of right is always an abuse of another person's rights. The courts in *Miller* and *Boomer* appeared to be engaged in a straightforward cost-benefit analysis.

However, these cases are distinctive in another respect: each involved disputes over competing private and public interests in the use of land. Today, disputes of this kind are typically resolved through zoning laws or special legislation. And this process invariably takes the public interest explicitly into account. It is normal and appropriate for legislatures that are contemplating legislative solutions to disputes like those in *Miller* and *Boomer* to do exactly what the courts did in these cases. Against this background, it is difficult to resist the conclusion that the courts in *Miller* and *Boomer* viewed the claimant's action as one that required an essentially legislative response—and that they then provided such a response. Just as the legislature would have done, the courts assessed the impugned activity's costs and benefits to the broader public.[81]

Of course, it is not generally appropriate for courts to act like legislatures. Courts are poorly equipped to assess the public interest, no one represents the public in private litigation, and there is no rule that courts can apply to balance the public and private interests. On what basis did Lord Denning determine that the public's interest in cricket trumped the claimants' interests in using their property? It is precisely because such decisions require a balancing of incommensurable values that judges typically, and appropriately, leave them to democratically elected legislatures. These observations explain why cases like *Miller* and *Boomer* are exceptional and often criticized. Still, it should not be surprising to find that courts sometimes take on a legislative role when presented with cases like *Miller* and *Boomer*. Until relatively recently, there were few legal controls on land use aside from those found

[80] Some writers try to explain the concept of abuse of right in economic terms: Summers (1968); Cohen (1991). However, the orthodox understanding is not economic. Briefly, in the orthodox understanding, substantive rights exist to protect our freedom. Asserting substantive rights in order to harm others is therefore inconsistent with the reason for their existence and, as such, qualifies as an abuse of rights: see Weinrib (2012) 112–14.

[81] If this argument is correct, the substantive law of nuisance should reflect similar concerns, at least in cases where the public interest is an issue. An example of such a concern is the rule that 'coming to the nuisance' is not a defence. Under ordinary private law principles, a claimant's voluntary decision to expose themselves to noise, smell, and the like, would bar an action for harm arising from the noise, smell, and so forth. The claimant voluntary assumed the risk (and presumably obtained financial compensation in the form of a reduced purchase price for doing so). However, nuisance law does not allow this defence. The reason, presumably, is that if the courts allowed the defence, feedlots, tanneries, pollution-spewing factories, and the like might still exist in the midst of residential areas (unless the legislature stepped in). More broadly, it is arguable that the basic idea that reasonableness is a function of the 'character' of the neighbourhood cannot be explained using ordinary private law principles.

in the law of nuisance. Today, the vast majority of public interest questions that arise from competing land uses are decided by zoning regulations (or by environmental, health, safety, or other legislation). However, cases sometimes arise that the legislation does not address or does not address adequately. In principle, the courts should leave questions of the public interest to the legislatures. But in practice, this approach often means that the public interest is simply never heard. It is not surprising, then, to find that courts are willing—in exceptional cases—to step into a legislative role.

F. Specific Performance

Specific performance is a judicial order that directs a defendant to comply with a contractual obligation. It is conventional to describe orders to comply with negative contractual obligations as injunctions, not specific performance; however, the same principles govern both orders. Indeed, the same principles govern specific performance and injunctions generally.

Notwithstanding this overlap, it is useful to examine specific performance separately. Throughout this book, I have argued for the importance of distinguishing substantive law from remedial law. It is in discussions of contract rights and remedies that this distinction is most often ignored. And the rules that are typically under examination in such discussions are those governing the availability of specific performance.

i. Cause of Action and Content

The cause of action for an award of specific performance is a right-threat. As in the case of the other orders discussed in this chapter, the standard way that claimants establish such a threat is by showing that the defendant is in breach of an ongoing substantive duty. For example, if the claimant proves that the defendant is in breach of a contractual promise to convey land, the court will normally order the defendant to convey the land.

Quia timet specific performance orders are possible in principle,[82] but rare in practice. In part, they are rare because specific performance is rare generally. In

[82] See *Marks v Lilley* [1959] 1 WLR 749, *Hasham v Zenab* [1960] AC 316, and Spry (2014) 81–2, 393–5. Although not usually described as such, orders to make periodic payments (e.g. under an annuity), which are relatively common, are *quia timet: Ball v Coggs* [1710] 1 Bro Parl Cas 140; *Clifford v Turrell* [1841] 1 Y & CCC 138; *Beswick v Beswick* [1968] AC 58. The defendants in such cases have invariably failed to make a past payment, but the order applies to the future payments (to recover the past payments, an order for a sum due is sufficient). Burrows suggests that a threat to breach that satisfies the requirements for a *quia timet* order also amounts to an actual, albeit 'anticipatory', breach—with the consequence that an order made in response to the threat is not strictly *quia timet:* Burrows (2004) 456.

most cases where it might be possible to establish that, while no breach has yet occurred, the claimant's contractual rights are under threat—for example, where the defendant has taken no steps to build a house notwithstanding an imminent completion date—specific performance is unavailable for other reasons (as I explain below), even if the defendant was already in breach.

Another reason that *quia timet* orders are rare is that in cases where specific performance is prima facie available—say a contractual duty to deliver unique goods—it is difficult in practice to prove an imminent threat. Courts typically award *quia timet* orders where the claimant can point to physical evidence of the defendant's unwillingness to comply, such as a partially completed structure or advertising for an event. Such evidence rarely exists in contract disputes.

Finally, *quia timet* specific performance orders are rare because the consequences of mistakenly refusing to issue such orders is usually relatively minor. As we have seen, the main reason that courts subject *quia timet* orders to special conditions is that they may turn out to be unnecessary: the defendant may perform regardless. Courts contemplating such orders must therefore weigh the harm that would result from unnecessarily awarding specific performance against the harm that would result from mistakenly refusing to order performance. For the kinds of contract breaches that might, in principle, support specific performance—which basically means breaches of duties to transfer unique goods or land—the harm from mistakenly refusing the order is usually relatively minor. If a breach happens, the court can award specific performance and, in addition, can award damages to compensate for any losses caused by the delay. An award of damages provides reasonable compensation for such harm. Of course, if specific performance is impossible (e.g. because the defendant had sold or destroyed the relevant property) then, assuming that the land or goods are unique, the claimant will be unable to purchase a perfect substitute. Still, close substitutes are usually available. In contrast, claimants who are mistakenly refused *quia timet* injunctions against nuisances or trespasses usually cannot purchase anything remotely resembling a substitute form of performance. In short, the normal preconditions for the grant of *quia timet* orders are difficult to satisfy in contract disputes.

Specific performance is a clear example of a replicative ruling. Courts express such rulings literally as orders to complete the contract ('It Is Ordered That the contract dated . . . referred to in the Particulars of Claim be specifically performed.'[83]). And in contrast to injunctions against torts, specific performance orders can in principle replicate the entirety of the claimant's threatened right, since (unlike in the case of most torts) that right is held uniquely against the defendant. The one

However, a threat to breach only qualifies as an anticipatory breach if it is accepted as such by the innocent party, which did not happen in the above cases.

[83] Atkins (2015) Vol 37 (1) [159].

small wrinkle in this picture is that, as was true of orders for a sum due, specific performance orders do not strictly replicate the defendant's original duty. An order issued on 1 February to fulfil a contractual duty to 'convey land on 1 January' does not strictly replicate the 1 January duty. However, the 1 February order replicates the defendant's substantive duty as it was on 1 February. As I explained when discussing orders for a sum due, so long as it remains possible to perform the substance of a time-specific duty, and so long as the other party has not terminated that duty, the duty persists, albeit as a duty to perform as soon as possible.[84]

ii. Restrictions on the Availability of Specific Performance

Courts and commentators often describe specific performance as a 'secondary' or 'exceptional' remedy for breach of contract. It is true that, in absolute terms, specific performance orders are relatively rare. However, it is misleading to describe specific performance as secondary or exceptional. As I explained above, one of the most common private law remedies—an order for a sum due—is in substance, even if not in name, specific performance. Orders for a sum due direct defendants to do what they contractually agreed to do. In addition, the standard remedy for the actual or anticipated breach of a negative contractual obligation is an order to comply with the obligation. For historical reasons, common law lawyers describe these awards as injunctions, but they are injunctions that command the performance of contractual duties. Finally, in most contract litigation it is simply not possible to award specific performance, even if the court were inclined to do so. Specific performance is only possible in respect of contractual duties that remain alive at the time of judgment.[85] Yet by the time a contractual dispute is litigated (and usually much earlier), the claimant has normally terminated the contract for breach. Indeed, even where the innocent party elects to affirm the contract following a breach, the law regularly deems the contract (or at least the breached obligation) terminated. Termination by 'operation of law' is common.[86]

[84] I discuss this idea, which draws on Raz (2004), Ripstein (2007), Weinrib (2008), and Gardner (2011), in the discussion of the 'continuity thesis' in Chapter 7.

[85] 'It is easy to see that a party who has chosen to put an end to a contract by accepting the other party's repudiation cannot afterwards seek specific performance': *Johnson v Agnew* [1979] 1 All ER 883, 894 (Lord Wilberforce).

[86] Admittedly, it is orthodox law that a breach of contract, even a serious breach, does not end the contract: the innocent party has the choice of terminating or affirming the contract: *Photo Production Ltd v Securicor Transport Ltd* [1980] AC 827. However, if the breaching party is clear that they are unwilling to perform in future, and if the duty is one for which specific performance is unavailable, it appears (despite some dicta to the contrary) that in a subsequent action for damages courts will assess the innocent party's losses as if they mitigated on breach: Kramer (2017) 396–99; *Melachrino v Nickoll & Knight* [1920] 1 KB 693; *Coastal (Bermuda) Petroleum Ltd v VTT Vulcab Petroleum (No 2)* [1994] 2 Lloyd's Rep 605; *Asamera Oil Corporation Ltd v Sea Oil & General Corporation et al* [1979] 1 SCR 633. Crucially, reasonable mitigation in such cases includes seeking substitute performance from a third party. As a matter of strict law, the contract remains alive in such cases until the innocent party obtains substitute performance (*Gunton v Richmond-upon-Thames LBC* [1981] Ch 488). However, in practice,

All that said, it is true that specific performance, strictly defined, is not available in many cases where in theory it might be awarded. For example, specific performance is rarely available for the breach of a contractual duty to provide goods or services, even where that duty remains alive. Why? The obvious and normal judicial response to proof of a rights-threat is to order the defendant to comply with the right. Why is this response frequently unavailable when the threatened right is contractual?

Perhaps the best-known answer (which is also representative of most contemporary answers[87]) is the 'efficient breach' theory.[88] According to this theory, the reason that courts typically refuse to order specific performance, even where performance remains possible, is that the law wants to allow, indeed to encourage, individuals to break contractual promises when the cost of performing them is greater than their benefit. Of course, contracting parties typically enter contracts in the belief that what they will receive under the contract is more valuable than what they will give up. This belief is why economists assume that it is generally efficient to perform contracts: each party normally ends up better off, and so the world, as a whole, is better off. However, this assumption may not hold if circumstances change or (what amounts to the same thing) if either of the parties entered the contract because of a mistaken assumption. Suppose that a merchant agrees to buy 100 tons of grain from a farmer for £50 a ton. They agree to the sale because each expects to benefit: the grain normally costs the farmer £25 a ton to produce, while the merchant expects to resell the grain for £75 a ton. On these facts, the contract is economically efficient because each party will be better off following performance.

the contract is terminated from the moment at which the law assumes that a reasonable party would seek substitute performance. The law cannot coherently hold that the innocent party has a right to contractually promised goods or services and, at the same time, hold that the innocent party will be penalized if it fails to obtain those goods or services from someone else. The unavoidable conclusion is that most contractual breaches result in the automatic termination of the contract or at least the automatic termination of the duty that was breached. Some courts have admitted as much. In a case involving an unlawful dismissal, Viscount Kilmuir LC stated that 'the employment is effectively terminated, albeit in breach of contract': *Vine v National Dock Labour Board* [1957] AC 488, 500. The motivation for this exception to the 'no-unilateral-termination-for-breach principle' is undoubtedly the same as the motivation for the exception to the 'no-unilateral-termination-for-an-anticipatory repudiation principle' introduced in *White & Carter* and discussed above. Finally, the rule that claimants may insist on performance in cases where, if they were to bring an action, they would be likely to obtain specific performance appears at first impression an example of reasoning backwards from remedies to rights. However, the rule is merely shorthand for the idea that it is reasonable to insist on performance where the innocent party has a special interest in performance (e.g. because the duty was to deliver unique goods or land). The latter category overlaps with the category of cases for which specific performance is prima facie available. In practice, this rule may penalize innocent parties who incorrectly assume that their contract is one that the court will specifically enforce. In *Semelhago v Paramadevan* [1996] 2 SCR 415, the Canadian Supreme Court held that land is not always unique. This ruling has led to purchasers terminating following a breach by the vendor even where the land appears unique. Purchasers are unwilling to take the risk that a court will refuse specific performance and treat them as if they mitigated on breach.

[87] See note 91.

[88] The literature is voluminous: see e.g. Birmingham (1970); Barton (1972); Schwartz (1979).

However, suppose that shortly after completing the agreement the cost of producing grain rises to £100 a ton. Alternatively, suppose that another merchant, who desperately needs grain to fulfil a contract, offers the farmer £100 a ton for all of her grain. In either of these scenarios, performance of the farmer's promise appears to be inefficient. In each case, the cost of performance (whether measured by of out-of-pocket expenses or lost opportunities) is greater than its value. According to the efficient breach theory, the efficient result is for the farmer to break her promise. It follows, according to the theory, that the reason courts do not order contracting parties to perform their promises is to give contracting parties in the farmer's position the opportunity to breach efficiently. Of course, the farmer remains liable to pay damages. However, assuming that damages are set at the value of performance, this liability is also efficient because it provides the farmer with an incentive to breach when, but only when, the cost of performance is greater than the value. If the cost of performance is greater than its value, then even after paying damages the farmer will end up better off breaching, and vice versa.

Authors often criticize the efficient breach theory for making unrealistic assumptions about how contracting parties react to material incentives.[89] They also criticize the theory for ignoring various factors relevant to assessing the efficiency of specific performance awards. Thus, it is argued that once the possibility of renegotiation, administrative costs, difficult-to-prove losses, and similar factors are taken into account, specific performance turns out to be an efficient remedy.[90] However, the most important objection to the efficient breach theory has nothing to do with its assumptions or scope. The most important objection to the efficient breach theory (and to most contemporary attempts to explain specific performance[91]) is that it cannot explain why the law recognizes a substantive duty to perform contractual promises. According to the efficient breach theory, the law encourages efficient breaches by giving contracting parties the option of performing their contractual promises or paying damages. In Holmes' famous words '[T]he duty to keep a promise at common law means a prediction that you must pay damages if you do not keep it—and nothing else'.[92] Yet, the substantive law is clear that

[89] Elster (1993); Ellickson (1989).

[90] This view is arguably dominant amongst economic analysis of law scholars, see e.g. Schwartz (1979); Posner (2003); Shavell (2006).

[91] The objection applies to any theory that seeks to justify the common law's approach to specific performance on the ground that contracting parties should have the option of choosing not to perform their contractual promises. For example, it has been argued that this option promotes the value of detached relationships: Kimel (2003) 83. Such theories differ from the efficient breach theory only in their understanding of the value that the alleged option promotes. Strictly speaking, the objection does not apply to the suggestion that the typical contractual promise is in fact a promise to perform or pay damages: Markovits & Schwartz (2011). However, this suggestion cannot explain why courts do not describe contractual promises as disjunctive obligations (nor why contracting parties never write their contracts in these terms).

[92] Holmes (1897) 462. Holmes was not defending the efficient breach theory (which was developed much later), but his work clearly inspired its defenders. They saw their task as explaining why the law gave contracting parties the choice to perform or pay damages.

individuals should perform their contractual promises: a contractual duty is a 'duty' because it is obligatory, and the failure to fulfil a contractual duty is a 'wrong' for the same reason. In Lord Diplock's words, 'Each promise that a promisor makes to a promisee by entering into a contract with him creates an obligation to perform it owed by the promisor as obligor to the promisee as oblige.'[93] If the law wished to give contracting parties the liberty to pay money in lieu of performing their contractual promises, the obvious way to grant this liberty would be to recognize it in the substantive law. Rather than proclaiming that it is wrong to breach a contractual promise, the law would tell contracting parties that they are at liberty to pay damages in lieu of specific performance. However, the law says that contracting parties have duties to perform their contractual promises. In short, the efficient breach theory cannot explain the most basic feature of contractual obligations—namely, that the law presents them as obligations.[94]

To explain the common law's approach to specific performance, it is necessary to explain not only why courts regularly hold that damages are an adequate substitute for specific performance, but also why the same courts hold that contracting parties have duties to perform their contractual promises. What I will describe as the 'administrative' theory provides such an explanation. This theory (which I explain further in Chapter 9) rests on two propositions. First, damages are typically a reasonable, even if imperfect, substitute for specific performance because it is usually possible for claimants to purchase substitute performance (goods, services, and so forth) from third parties. Second, damages awards, like monetary awards generally, typically impose fewer costs on the legal system because they are easier to express, supervise, and enforce. In particular, damages awards are less likely to lead to further litigation and are simple to enforce through execution against the defendant's assets. In combination, these propositions suggest that courts prefer damages to specific relief because they are typically a cheaper means (for the court) of achieving the same or nearly the same result.[95] They also suggest that there

[93] *Moschi v Lep Air Services Ltd and another* [1972] 2 All ER 393, 400. See also Saville J in *Law Debenture Trust Corporation v Ural Caspian Oil Corporation Ltd* [1995] Ch 152 ('In the context of contract . . . the contracting parties make promises to each other. It is their primary obligation to perform those promises'); and Windeyer J's in *Coulls v Bagot's Executor and Trustee Co Ltd* [1967] 119 CLR 460, 504 ('It is . . . a faulty analysis of legal obligations to say that the law treats the promisor as having a right to elect either to perform his promise or to pay damages. Rather . . . the promisee has a "legal right to the performance of the contract" '). The existence of the tort of interference with contractual relations presumes the existence of a duty to perform contractual promise. The same is true of the existence of the defence of frustration (since it is never impossible to pay damages).

[94] It is no response to this objection to suggest that the courts' language is merely a smokescreen or a charade because, smokescreen or not, what courts say about substantive duties influences the behavior of contracting parties: Smith (2011c). More generally, the efficient breach theory does not explain why courts would engage in such a charade.

[95] Whether or not it is proper for lawmakers to consider financial considerations when determining individuals' substantive rights, it is clearly appropriate for courts—publicly funded institutions—to consider such factors when determining how they should respond to requests for their assistance: see Chapter 9.

should be exceptions to the general preference for damages in cases where it is not possible to purchase substitute performance and where a specific performance order will be relatively easy to express, supervise, and enforce. The standard cases in which courts award specific performance—cases involving duties to transfer title to land or to deliver unique goods—satisfy these criteria.[96] This explanation also accounts for other exceptions to the general rule. For example, courts generally refuse to order specific performance of building contracts. However, such orders are available in respect of contractual duties to build roads or bridges over land that the defendant purchased from the claimant and that the claimant cannot access if the defendant does not fulfil the duty.[97] In these cases, damages are inadequate because (unlike in the usual case of a breached contract to build) the claimants cannot purchase substitute performance from a third party (since only defendants can build on their own land). Similarly, the main reason that courts readily grant injunctions in support of threatened negative contractual rights is that it is not possible to purchase substitute performance of a negative duty. Only the subjects of non-competition covenants can ensure that they do not compete.

The common law's approach to specific performance is far from perfect. The widespread assumption that specific performance is an exceptional remedy may be mistaken, but it is also self-fulfilling. More generally, the contemporary approach to specific performance undoubtedly reflects the remedy's origins in a time when the costs of supervising and enforcing orders was, in relative terms, more significant than it is today. The practical advantages of monetary remedies depend in large part on how easy it is to access courts. Until relatively recently, England had few permanent courts: today, it has many (though accessing them remains costly). Thus, the advantages of monetary remedies are less significant than they were previously. For these reasons, contemporary courts should probably be more open to awarding specific performance. Still, the administrative theory explains why, even today, courts prefer monetary remedies to specific performance.

iii. Substantive-Law Reasons for Refusing Specific Performance

As we have just seen, the usual reason that courts award damages in lieu of specific performance is that damages are 'adequate' (meaning that it is possible to purchase substitute performance) and, in addition, easier to administer than specific

[96] In rare cases, goods may be 'commercially unique' in the sense that, while not literally unique, they cannot be obtained in the current market: *Sky Petroleum Ltd v VIP Petroleum Ltd* [1974] 1 WLR 576. See also *Uniform Commercial Code*, s 2.716(1). Personal service duties are typically unique, but they also raise other, more significant, remedial concerns, as I explain in Chapter 9.

[97] See e.g. *Wolverhampton and Walsall Railway Company v London and North-Western Railway Company* [1873] LR 16 Eq 433.

performance. This reason is concerned entirely with the form of the requested remedy: it is a 'remedial-law' reason for refusing specific performance. The same observation applies to most of the other reasons for awarding damages instead of specific performance, such as supervision, personal liberty, laches, and clean hands. As I explain in Chapter 9, these are all reasons for preferring monetary over non-monetary remedies.

However, there are exceptions. As was true with respect to injunctions, courts occasionally refuse specific performance (and award damages instead) for substantive-law reasons. For example, in *Patel v Ali*,[98] the court refused specific performance of a contract for the sale of a residential property on the ground that conveying the property would cause the defendant severe hardship. Subsequent to the sale agreement, the defendant's husband was sent to jail, one of her legs amputated, and she bore two additional children—all of which meant that she relied heavily on neighbours and nearby relatives for assistance. A second example is *Tito v Waddell*,[99] where the court refused to order specific performance of the defendant mining company's contractual duty to replant the claimants' land on the ground, inter alia, that '[i]t would be a sheer waste of time and money to do this'.[100] The land was on an island that, subsequent to the mining, had been rendered uninhabitable (or so it was assumed[101]) by bombing during the Second World War.

The courts' concern in these cases is not the form of the requested remedy. As in the tort cases of *Miller*, *Boomer*, and *Woolerton*, discussed earlier, their concern is the desirability of the action that is the object of the alleged substantive duty. The hardship that Mrs Ali would have suffered if she lost her property would have been the same whether she lost it because she complied with an order to convey it or because she fulfilled her (alleged) substantive duty to convey it. Similarly, replanting the claimant's land in *Tito* would have been wasteful (in the court's view) regardless of whether the replanting was done to comply with a court order or to fulfil a substantive duty. The courts' reasons for refusing specific performance in these cases were in substance reasons for denying the validity of the substantive duties that the orders were meant to reflect. These decisions effectively modify the substantive law. In other words, these are cases where Holmes and his followers would be correct to draw inferences about substantive duties from the courts' refusal to award specific performance.

As was true of the cases where courts refuse injunctive relief for substantive reasons, cases like *Patel* and *Tito* can be explained on the basis of a simple

98 [1984] Ch 283. A similar Canadian case is *1110049 Ontario Ltd v Exclusive Diamonds Inc* [1995] 25 OR 417.

99 [1977] Ch 106. See also *Webb v Direct London and Portsmouth Ry Co* [1852] 1 De GM & G 512; *Denne v Light* [1857] 8 De GM & G 774.

100 Ibid 312 (Megarry J).

101 This assumption proved incorrect as some of the claimants eventually returned to the island.

cost-benefit analysis or, equally, on the basis of a concern for abuses of rights. However, another possibility, which strictly speaking does not arise in respect of injunctions, is that the courts are effectively modifying the substantive law governing discharge for frustration. In cases like *Patel* and *Tito,* the reason that the cost of performing the relevant promise was disproportionate to its value is that circumstances changed after the contracts were formed. In principle, contracts may be set aside for changed circumstances if they are 'frustrated'. However, pleas of frustration rarely succeed in practice. Courts are understandably reluctant to set aside validly formed contracts: it is part of the very meaning of a promissory obligation that it remains binding, even if the promisor later regrets the promise. But it is also understandable that courts might want to create occasional exceptions to this practice, particularly if they can place the cost of those exceptions on the party who seeks them through an award of damages. Courts can create this exception—and leave the substantive-law principle unchanged—if they justify the exceptions on remedial grounds.

I explored the merits of this kind of reasoning in the earlier discussion of cases where courts refuse injunctions for substantive-law reasons. I also noted that courts refuse injunctions for substantive-law reasons more often than they refuse specific performance for similar reasons. However, cases like *Patel* and *Tito* are probably not as rare, at least in relative terms, as might appear at first impression. Cases in which the cost or value of performance change dramatically typically involve contractual duties to build or to provide services. Courts typically refuse specific performance in such cases because of concerns over supervision or ordering personal duties (see Chapter 9). These concerns arise regardless of whether the cost or value of performance changed. It follows that courts are able, if they wish, to refuse specific relief in cases like *Tito* without entering into a discussion of possible substantive-law reasons for refusing relief. The court can simply invoke the rule that specific performance is generally unavailable in respect of building or service contracts. However, if there is a substantive-law reason for refusing specific performance (as was the case in *Tito*) it will often affect the measure of damages awarded. Specifically, if the case is one where, although substitute performance is possible, damages are set at the amount of the claimant's consequential losses (as happened in *Tito*[102]), the court's reasons for refusing relief must be substantive. If the only reason for refusing specific performance were remedial, damages would be set at the cost of obtaining substitute performance.

[102] The claimant in *Tito* asked for the 'cost of cure' but was awarded 'diminution in value', which, on the facts, was nominal. In *Patel,* the choice between these measures was not an issue because the defendant's duty was to deliver unique property (land), for which substitute performance was not possible.

iv. The Vendor-Purchaser Constructive Trust

In a contract for the sale or lease of property, if the vendor's duty is one for which an order of specific performance is in principle available, courts deem the vendor to hold the property on trust for the purchaser from the moment of formation.[103] It follows that in contracts for the sale of land the vendor normally holds the property on trust for the purchaser. The 'vendor-purchaser rule' is part of the substantive law of trusts. However, the rule merits a brief discussion here because it appears to be a clear example of the law doing exactly what I have argued it should not do, namely, making the existence of a substantive right turn on the availability of a remedy.

The vendor-purchaser rule is often explained as an application of the equitable maxim that 'equity treats as done that which ought to be done'. However, the maxim is hardly an explanation—why assume that something happened which did not happen?—and in any event, the rule is narrower than the maxim suggests it ought to be. All contracts for the sale of property presumably ought to be performed, yet the vendor-purchaser rule only applies to contracts that are specifically enforceable.

The rule requires more discussion than is possible here, but I tentatively suggest that the clue to understanding it is that the vendors (as I will call them) in such cases are not trustees in the normal sense.[104] Unlike normal trustees, defendants who have agreed to convey their land are not bound to hand over any profits that they make from the property prior to conveyance. The purchasers' interest more closely resembles a security interest: if the vendor does not convey the land, the purchaser obtains a right roughly similar to that enjoyed by a mortgagee. Viewed from this perspective, it is understandable that a (so-called) 'trust' only arises in cases where the purchaser could have obtained specific performance. The reason that specific performance is available in such cases is also a reason to give purchasers a security interest. As we have seen, courts only award specific performance of duties to transfer property in cases where close substitutes are unavailable. In cases involving such duties, the only way to protect purchasers' rights to performance is to ensure that they get the very thing that the vendor promised to provide. This protection is illusory if, prior to conveyance, the vendor can freely transfer the property to third party. The vendor-purchaser rule provides a security interest against such transfers. It ensures that the transfer will have no effect, at least in most cases. Thus interpreted, the rule is broadly analogous to the rules governing the dissipation of assets prior to insolvency (which render ineffective various ways of dissipating assets in advance of insolvency) or to freezing orders (which prohibit potential defendants from dealing with assets that might be the subject of litigation).

[103] *Walsh v Lonsdale* [1882] 21 Ch D 9. See also *Re Anstis* [1886] 31 Ch D 596.

[104] See Penner (2014) 109–12; Swadling (2005); Chambers (2005).

G. Substitutionary Damages

'Substitutionary damages' is not a legal term of art. In this book, it refers to awards that are monetary substitutes for specific relief. Courts award substitutionary damages, I argue, in cases where the prima facie appropriate remedy is specific relief, but where, for largely administrative reasons, monetary awards are more convenient or otherwise preferable. Like specific relief, therefore, substitutionary damages are responses to rights-threats. They differ from specific relief primarily in terms of their form: rather than requiring defendants to comply directly with their substantive duties, they require them to perform monetary substitutes for those duties. An example is the award in *Cohen v Roche.*[105] The claimant had brought an action for delivery up of a set of 'ordinary Hepplewhite chairs' purchased from the defendant auctioneer. The court refused delivery up, instead awarding damages set at the price of obtaining similar chairs on the market (and noting that the result would have been the same had the claimant sued for specific performance). This award was substitutionary.

English law is familiar with the idea of awarding damages in lieu of specific relief. Section 50 of the *Senior Courts Act* 1981 (superseding the *Chancery Amendment Act* 1858, s 2, commonly known as '*Lord Cairns' Act*') provides that courts may award damages 'in substitution for an injunction or specific performance' in any case where they have 'jurisdiction to entertain an application for an injunction or specific performance'. However, while most awards of so-called 'equitable damages' are substitutionary as the term is used in this work, the overlap is not perfect. Courts have held that they lack 'jurisdiction' to entertain an application for specific relief because damages are adequate or the duty is personal. In these cases, damages are normally substitutionary notwithstanding that the courts have said that they do not fall under s 50. Further, in many cases where courts invoke s 50 to support damages, the award is not substitutionary. As explained above, courts sometimes deny specific relief for substantive-law reasons and, at the same time, award damages. In these cases, while damages are often portrayed as 'substitutes' for specific relief, they are not responses to rights-threats and, accordingly, are not substitutionary as the term is used here. Damages awards are only substitutionary if the court awards them instead of specific relief and does this for remedial-law reasons. In other words, substitutionary damages awards are only possible in cases where the court accepts that the claimant's rights are indeed under threat, and is attempting to respond to that threat, albeit indirectly.

The classification of these awards as substitutionary reflects both their justification and, with certain qualifications, their content. The cause of action for substitutionary awards is a rights-threat. The normal and prima facie appropriate judicial

[105] [1927] 1 KB 169.

response to rights-threats is to order the defendant to comply with the threatened right. Where the courts issue a monetary award for reasons related to the form of specific relief, that remedy is a substitute for specific relief. In terms of content, in the typical case where courts award substitutionary damages such damages provide a close substitute for specific relief because the sum awarded is equal to the cost of purchasing substitute performance.[106] For example, where courts refuse to order performance of contractual duties to provide goods or services, the damages awarded normally include an amount sufficient to purchase the goods or services from a third party.[107] Similarly, where courts refuse to order delivery up, damages are set at price of obtaining the goods from a third party.[108] Admittedly, it is not always possible to purchase substantive performance. In these cases (which I discuss in more detail below), the closest substitute is a sum set at the monetary value of the performance (as opposed to the cost of obtaining substitute performance). However, these awards are still substitutionary because the reason for issuing them remains a rights-threat.[109] Although substitutionary awards are usually set at the cost of purchasing substitute performance, an award is substitutionary because of the reason a court issued it, not because of its amount.

In Chapter 8, I discuss general theories of damages awards and I consider how such theories account for (or fail to account for) substitutionary damages. Two points from that discussion are worth noting here. First, general theories that suppose that damages awards are always responses to wrongs or at least that suppose damages always seek to undo wrongs cannot account for substitutionary damages. Substitutionary damages are available in lieu of *quia timet* specific relief (where the defendant has yet to commit a wrong). And even where the defendant has committed a wrong, substitutionary damages are a response to the threat of a future rights-infringement, not to the past wrong.

Second, theories that suppose that paying damages is the next best way of fulfilling a wrongdoer's substantive duty cannot explain substitutionary damages. According to this theory (the 'continuity thesis'), when an individual breaches a substantive private law duty, the duty immediately transforms into, or gives rise to, a substantive duty to do the 'next best' thing. Sometimes—for example, in the case of contractual duties to pay money—the next best thing is to perform late. But in respect of nearly all torts and many contractual duties, the next best thing,

[106] The rules governing orders for delivery up illustrate this point nicely, as the standard order in a case where, as normally happens, the court does not award delivery up gives the defendant the option of delivering the chattel or paying damages in the amount of the chattel's value: *Torts (Interference with Goods) Act* 1977, s 3 (2)(b).

[107] Minus the purchase price if the claimant has not paid in advance. In addition to substitutionary damages (which are a response to a rights threat), claimants may also obtain damages for the wrong and damages for consequential losses. I discuss these awards in Chapters 7 and 8.

[108] *Cohen v Roche* [1927] 1 KB 169.

[109] These cases are distinct, therefore, from cases where courts refuse specific relief for substantive-law reasons. In the latter, courts limit damages to the amount of the claimant's consequential losses even where substitute specific performance is possible (as happened in *Tito*).

according to this theory, is to pay damages. It follows, according to the continuity thesis, that an order to pay damages is similar to an order to pay a debt: the order replicates an already existing substantive duty. It further follows from the thesis that the cause of action for damages awards is, in this work's terminology,[110] a rights-threat: courts order wrongdoers to pay damages because they are in breach of an ongoing substantive duty to pay the claimant a sum of money.

It might be thought that the continuity thesis neatly explains substitutionary damages. The thesis supposes that damages awards are responses to rights-threats and, further, that paying damages is a substitute for performing a substantive duty. Indeed, advocates of the continuity thesis sometimes describe damages awards as 'substitutionary' awards.[111] In Chapter 8, I argue for rejecting entirely the continuity thesis explanation of damages awards. But even if the thesis can explain some damages awards, it cannot explain substitutionary damages. The 'substitutions' that substitutionary damages require are determined by the court, at the moment of judgment. Substitutionary damages are substitutes for future substantive duties. They are not (as the continuity thesis' account of damages supposes) substitutes for duties that were infringed in the past.

Substitutionary awards are relatively rare. A damages award is not substitutionary merely because it is set at (or includes) a sum equal to the cost of purchasing substitute performance. The most common reason that courts award the cost of substitute performance is that the defendant incurred, or will incur, this cost because of the claimant's breach. If you fail to deliver contractually promised goods, and if I terminate the contract for your breach, I can normally recover the cost of purchasing substitute goods from someone else. This award is not a response to a rights-threat because my right to the performance of your contractual duty ended when I terminated our contract. It is too late for a court to order specific performance, and so too late to order a substitute form of specific performance. In these circumstances, a cost-of-performance award is a compensatory award: it is compensation for my consequential loss, and its cause of action is accordingly an injustice (or so I argue in Chapter 8).

Substitutionary awards are only possible in circumstances where courts could potentially grant specific relief. Thus, substitutionary awards are not possible if it is no longer possible to perform the relevant obligation (e.g. catering for a wedding that has already taken place). And as explained above, substitutionary awards are not possible in respect of terminated contractual obligations. Nor is it possible to issue such awards in respect of past injuries to the claimant's person or property. In the latter two groups of cases, while the defendant may have infringed the

[110] '[T]his work's terminology' because the continuity thesis is consistent with different accounts of the cause of action for replicative orders.

[111] See especially Stevens (2007) 59–62. Other writers who hold the view discussed above include Weinrib (2012) 81–116, Ripstein (2007), and Gardner (2011).

claimant's rights in the past, the claimant's rights are not under threat at the time of the award (absent other evidence of a threat).

For these reasons, substitutionary awards are relatively rare. But exactly how rare depends on the answers to two final questions.

i. Are Substitutionary Damages Always Set at the Cost of Performance?

The first question is whether damages must be set at (or include a sum for) the cost of purchasing substitute performance in order to qualify as substitutionary. The answer is clearly 'yes' in cases where it is possible to purchase substitute performance. The closest monetary substitute to specific relief is an order to pay for the cost of substitute performance. If such an award is possible and the court declines to issue it, the unavoidable conclusion is that the award is not substitutionary. Thus, even if the court in *Tito* had not said that it thought performance was wasteful, its decision to set damages at a sum drastically lower than the cost of replanting the island is clear evidence that the award was not substitutionary.

However, it does not follow that substitutionary awards are always set at the cost of purchasing substitute performance. In some cases where a rights-threat is established, it is not possible to purchase substitute performance. It is true that, precisely because substitute performance is not possible, courts typically grant specific relief in such cases. But not always. Courts occasionally refuse specific relief for remedial-law reasons notwithstanding that it is impossible to purchase substitute performance. For example, courts will refuse to order the performance of personal duties (such as a duty to give a concert recital) even where no substitute is possible (such that, for instance, the concert must simply be cancelled). In such cases, courts typically award claimants sums equal to loss that they suffered or will suffer as a consequence of the wrong.[112] Assuming that the court accepts that the alleged rights-threat is indeed a rights-threat, and therefore that the defendant has a valid substantive duty to perform, such an award is substitutionary. Although an imperfect response to a rights-threat, compensation is, in the circumstances, the closest possible monetary equivalent to specific relief. Compensation provides the claimant with the monetary value of performance, to the extent that this measure is possible. It remains only to add that an award of compensation is only substitutionary in the relatively rare cases where the just-described conditions are satisfied, that is, where the claimant's substantive rights are under threat, where the court refuses specific relief for a remedial reason, and where it is not possible to obtain substitute performance. As I explain in Chapter 8, in most cases where compensatory

[112] *Ryan v Mutual Tontine Westminster Chambers Association* [1893] 1 Ch 116.

damages are awarded, they are a response to an injustice, not a rights-threat, and accordingly serve an entirely different role.

ii. Substitutionary Damages and Termination of Contract

The second question is whether substitutionary awards are only possible if the claimant has requested specific relief. An affirmative answer might seem to follow from my definition of substitutionary damages as substitutes for specific relief. However, I tentatively suggest that a damages award may be substitutionary notwithstanding that the only remedy sought by the claimant was damages.

Imagine that a builder fails to comply with an obligation in a construction contract, but then immediately and repeatedly promises to remedy the breach. The owner agrees to wait, but nothing happens. The owner eventually tires of waiting and sues the builder for damages. The owner does not request specific performance because her lawyer has told her, correctly, that courts almost never grant specific performance of building contracts. The court awards the owner the cost of repairing the defect. Although the claimant never asked for specific relief, this award appears to be substitutionary. It is true that, in some circumstances, the claimant's decision to bring an action for damages may indicate that the claimant is no longer interested in performance, and so wishes to terminate the contract.[113] However, in my example, the owner's decision to sue for damages indicates nothing more than an awareness that a damages award is the only remedy a court will be willing to grant. In my example, the owner would presumably have allowed the builder to make repairs even after litigation commenced. On these facts, the award is substitutionary because it remains a response to a rights-threat.

[113] The decision to bring an action for damages does not, by itself, terminate a contract: *Garnac Grain Co Inc v HMF Faure and Fairclough* Ltd [1966] 1 QB 650 (affirmed [1983] AC 1130n).

7
Wrongs

It might be thought self-evident that courts issue remedies in response to wrongs. Indeed, it might be thought self-evident that remedies generally are responses to wrongs. A 'remedy', in the ordinary understanding, is a cure for something that is undesirable. A legal wrong is obviously undesirable; indeed, from the law's perspective it might be thought that 'undesirable' and 'legal wrong' are synonymous. Expressing this idea more formally, Blackstone held that the law in general could be understood in terms of a three-part sequence that links remedies directly to wrongs. In this view, the law consists of: (1) 'rights' (that we all enjoy as part of our daily life); (2) 'wrongs' (that arise from the infringement of rights); and (3) 'remedies' (that the law provides for wrongs).[1] For Blackstone, remedies were always remedies for wrongs. And for many lawyers, Blackstone's view, or something like it, seems self-evident: what else could remedies be remedies for, if not for wrongs?

For other lawyers, however, Blackstone's view is far from self-evident. Indeed, the most influential contemporary theory of damages rejects it entirely. According to the 'continuity thesis', the only significance of committing a private wrong is that the substantive duty which the wrongdoer breached transforms, in part or in whole, into a substantive duty to pay damages. In this view (which I discuss in detail below), an order to pay damages is the same, so far as remedial law is concerned, as an order to perform a contractual duty or any other substantive duty: the order directs the defendant to comply with a substantive duty. From the perspective of the continuity thesis, orders to pay damages are (in the terminology adopted in this book) responses to rights-threats. Wrongs, in this view, play no role in remedial law.

In this chapter, I defend a position between these two extremes. I argue that while some remedies are responses to civil wrongs, the overall number of such remedies is relatively small. Specifically, I argue that the commission of a civil wrong (or at least the commission of the torts and contract breaches that are my focus), leaves unaltered the parties' substantive rights and duties. More specifically yet—and against the continuity thesis—I argue that the commission of a wrong does not give rise to a substantive duty to pay damages. The significance of civil wrongs lies solely in the realm of remedial law. But even here—and against Blackstone's view—wrongs play a relatively limited role. The commission of a wrong is just one of three private law causes of actions recognized in the common law, and in practical terms,

[1] Blackstone (1979 reprint) Book I 137, Book III 115–16.

Rights, Wrongs, and Injustices. Stephen A. Smith, Oxford University Press (2019).
DOI: 10.1093/oso/9780199229772.003.0007

it is the least important. To be clear, I do not deny that most private law orders are directed at wrongdoers. Nor do I deny that the defendant's wrongdoing is typically demonstrated by the same facts that justify the claimant's remedy. Indeed, I accept that in many cases the remedy is conditional on proof of a wrong. What I deny is that the addressees of private law orders are always wrongdoers, and, further, that in cases where they are wrongdoers, that the remedy is always a response to that wrong. In most (but not all) such cases, the wrong is at most a condition, not the reason, for awarding the remedy.

I began my defence of this view in Chapter 6. In that chapter, I argued that injunctions, specific performance, orders for a sum due, and orders for the recovery of land or other property are awarded not because the defendant committed a wrong (although the defendant may have committed a wrong), but because the defendant threatened the claimant's rights. I do not discuss restitutionary awards until the next chapter, but we will see in Chapter 8 that it is easy to show that restitutionary awards are not responses to wrongs. Receiving a mistaken payment is not a wrong, and claimants seeking the return of such payments are not required to prove a wrong: they merely need to prove that they made the payment.

If the above orders are put to the side, the only orders discussed in this book that remain to be explained are to pay damages. It might be expected that I would argue that all such awards are responses to wrongs. Indeed, it might be expected that anyone who rejects a substantive duty to pay damages (as I do) would adopt this position. It is orthodox law that to obtain damages, the claimant must prove a wrong; it is also orthodox that damages are available automatically ('as of right') on proof of a wrong.[2] More generally, it is widely assumed that the distinguishing feature of damages awards is precisely that they are responses to wrongs.[3]

Nonetheless, I argue that that assumption is also too sweeping. Part of my explanation for why it is too sweeping is found, again, in Chapter 6; specifically, in the argument that damages awarded in substitution for specific relief ('substitutionary damages') are, like specific relief, responses to rights-threats. To obtain substitutionary damages claimants do need not prove a wrong, and, even where such proof is made, the wrong is merely evidence of a rights-threat. However, the main reason to reject the idea that all damages awards are responses to wrongs is that the core damages award—a compensatory damages award—is a response to an injustice,

[2] Edelman (2018) 2.

[3] The first sentence of the most recent edition of *McGregor on Damages* defines damages as 'an award in money for a wrong': Edelman (2018) 1. The previous edition, though less definitive, offered a broadly similar definition: 'Damages in the vast majority of cases are the pecuniary compensation, obtainable by success in an action, for a wrong which is either a tort or a breach of contract, the compensation being in the form of a lump sum awarded at one time, unconditionally and in sterling': McGregor (2003) 1. More cautiously, Tettenborn states that 'there is no categorical definition of damages in English law, and it is probably idle to try to provide one'; but he goes on to observe that 'Broadly, however, the subject of damages can be regarded as covering any monetary award made by a court or arbitrator in respect of a wrong committed against the claimant by the defendant, in order to compensate the claimant or otherwise vindicate his interests': Tettenborn (2010) 1.

not a wrong. As I argue in Chapter 8, for such awards, proof of a wrong is, at most, a condition of their issuance, not the reason for issuing them.

The remaining damages awards (that is, the awards that are neither substitutionary nor compensatory) are responses to wrongs. These awards, which I describe, unoriginally, as 'wrong-based', include nominal damages, exemplary damages, pain and suffering damages, and a variety of awards that, lacking an agreed label (or agreed individual labels), I describe compendiously as 'vindicatory' damages (and individually as user damages, waiver damages, market-price damages, non-pecuniary damages, and gain-based damages).

My overall conclusion, then, is that relatively few remedies are responses to wrongs. But the qualifier is important. As I have already mentioned, some writers suppose that no damages awards—not even those I label wrong-based—are responses to wrongs. The qualifier is also important for a second reason. Courts and commentators often regard nominal damages, exemplary damages, pain and suffering awards, and the various vindicatory awards as anomalies, if not outright mistakes. Against this approach, I argue that these remedies share a common, important, foundation: they are all responses to wrongs *qua* wrongs. Indeed, I devote most of this chapter to proving that each of these awards is basically a variant on a single model. In short, I argue that, in at least one respect, civil wrongs are more significant than is usually assumed.

This book's discussion of damages awards is spread over three chapters: Chapter 6 examined substitutionary damages; the present chapter discusses wrong-based damages; and Chapter 8 examines compensatory damages. However, my characterization of each of these awards presumes a general view about the nature of damages law. Specifically, it presumes that there is no substantive duty to pay damages. I begin by defending that view. Following that defence, I explain the general idea of a wrong-based remedy, and then identify the main categories of wrong-based damages.

A. Damages Law: Substantive or Remedial?

For anyone writing a book on remedies, the first question that needs to be asked about the law of damages is how much of this law, if any, is remedial. The answer to this question is determined, in turn, by the answer to another question: Do damages awards confirm substantive duties to pay damages (the 'duty-confirming view'), or do they create new duties to pay damages (the 'duty-creating view')?[4]

[4] The duty-confirming view is held by, inter alia, Weinrib (1995) 135; Birks (1997b) (2000); Coleman (1992) 374; Stevens (2007) 60; Ripstein (2009) 304; and Gardner (2011) 311. The duty-creating view is defended in Zipursky (1998a) (2002) (2003) 718–21; Goldberg (2005) (2006); Goldberg & Zipursky (2010); Oman (2011a); and Smith (2012) (2014).

If damages awards confirm substantive duties, then little of damages law is remedial law. Remedial law is the law governing judicial remedies. If the duty-confirming view is correct, the remedial part of the law of damages amounts to one rule: if the defendant has not fulfilled a substantive duty to pay damages, the court will order the defendant to fulfil the duty. In this view, the rest of damages law—the rules that determine the magnitude of damages awards—is substantive law. A book on remedies that adopts the duty-confirming view still needs to explain why courts order defendants to comply with unfulfilled duties to pay damages. However, as we saw in the previous chapter, the answer to that question (which arises in respect of all replicative remedies) is straightforward: courts issue replicative orders to motivate recalcitrant defendants to perform their substantive duties.

In contrast, if damages awards create new duties, then to explain why, and in what amounts, courts issue damages orders, it is necessary to explain the entirety of the law of damages. In the duty-creating view, the law of damages consists of a set of rules that determine when, and in what measure, courts must award damages. This view accepts that damages law may incorporate parts of substantive law—for example, courts might require proof that the defendant breached or threatened to breach a substantive duty before awarding damages—but the rule requiring such proof, as well as the rules governing the assessment of damages belongs to remedial law. Further, and critically, the explanation of the rules governing damages will differ depending on whether the duty-confirming or duty-creating view is correct. As I explained in Chapter 5 (and explore in more detail below), the normal reason that the law employs orders rather than substantive rules to impose a duty is that the duty's subject matter is not appropriate for a rule. It follows that the reasons that might explain court-ordered duties are different from those that might explain rule-based duties.

The question of whether damages awards confirm or create duties is fundamentally a question of positive law: Does the positive law recognize a substantive duty to pay damages? I argue that it does not. However, before making that argument I will spend a few moments examining the best-known and most influential theoretical argument for the duty-confirming view—the 'continuity thesis'. The appeal of the continuity thesis helps to explain the appeal of the duty-confirming view. Although I argue that both the broader duty-confirming view and the continuity-thesis version of that view are vulnerable to fatal objections, the continuity thesis presents a prima facie compelling prescriptive theory of damages. And while I conclude that the continuity thesis fails to explain damages awards, it does explain, at least in part, a number of other orders discussed in this book, in particular, a number of the orders examined in the previous chapter.

i. The Continuity Thesis

According to the continuity thesis, when we breach a substantive duty, the duty (or the reasons underlying the duty) continues in force, albeit partly or wholly in the form of (or giving rise to) a duty to pay damages.[5] Simplifying slightly,[6] the continuity thesis argues that wrongdoers have substantive duties to pay damages because the best way (or at least a part of the best way) for them to comply with their original substantive duties, post-breach, is to pay damages. In short, wrongdoers should pay damages for the same reason that they should have performed their original duties. If the reason you should deliver goods to me is that you promised to deliver them, then the reason you should pay me damages if you fail to deliver the goods is, again, that you promised to deliver the goods. Paying damages is the best way of fulfilling the promise, post breach. It follows, in this view, that the law of damages has no more to do with remedial law than does the substantive law of tort: it is comprised of rules that inform citizens how they should act in their day-to-day lives, specifically, what they should do in their day-to-day lives if they have failed to comply with a substantive duty.

The common-sense idea underlying the continuity thesis is that we should do our best to comply with our duties even when perfect compliance is no longer possible. Imagine that you have promised to come to my house at 7:00 p.m. to babysit my children, but you are late because of a traffic jam. It is now 7:05 p.m. and you are still ten minutes away. What should you do? The obvious answer is that you should come to my house as soon as possible. And you should do this for the same reason that you should have come at 7:00 p.m., namely, you promised to babysit. Your failure to show up at 7:00 p.m. does not release you from your promise; rather,

[5] The writers most closely associated with the thesis are Weinrib (1995) 135, (2008) 12; Raz (2004) 191; Ripstein (2009) 304; and Gardner (2011) 30–2.

[6] The label 'continuity thesis' was introduced by John Gardner ((2011) 30–2), but it is used here in a wider sense than in Gardner's work. For Gardner (who draws on earlier work by Raz (2004)), when a duty is breached, it is the reasons that gave rise to the duty, not the duty itself, that continue to apply. These continuing reasons then give rise to a new, post-breach duty. In Raz's words:

> [W]hen we fail to conform fully to a reason we have reason to come as close to full compliance as we can, call it reason to do the next best act. It is the very same reason which we did not conform to which is, or becomes, reason for the next best thing. . . . So if I have reason not to damage your property, and I do damage your fence, I have reason to compensate you, that is to mitigate the consequences of failure, and this reason is the very same reason I had initially (the reason not to trespass or not to disturb your peace). There is no need for an independent principle of compensation to establish the case for it.' Raz (2004) 191.

However, as used here, the label also applies to theories that suppose the duty continues after the breach, albeit in a new form. In Weinrib's words, 'Like Descartes' famous piece of wax that remains the same piece despite its different qualities when heated and cooled, the same duty is continuously correlative to the same right before and after the tort': Weinrib (2008) 13. Or, more succinctly, 'the right to what I had survives any wrongs committed against it': Ripstein (2009) 304. The differences between the 'duty' and 'reasons' versions of the continuity thesis are unimportant for this Chapter's purposes. For convenience—and acknowledging that the terminology is not entirely neutral—I will generally describe the thesis as supposing that it is the original duty that persists.

it simply means that the best way to fulfil that promise has changed. Your original promissory duty is now a duty to show up as soon after 7:00 p.m. as possible. As we saw in the previous chapter, the feature of promissory duties explains why orders to perform contractual promises are replicative even when (as is normal) the date for performance has passed. The order replicates the defendant's substantive duty to perform as soon as possible. Just as 'later-than-promised' babysitting is still babysitting, late payment of a contractual debt is still payment.

As this example illustrates, it seems clear that duties can survive their breach and, further, that courts will order the performance of such duties. As we saw in Chapter 6, these ideas are critical for understanding specific performance orders, orders for a sum due, and orders for the recovery of land or chattels. They explain, inter alia, why an order for a sum due is replicative notwithstanding that by the time such an order is issued the original date for performance has passed.

However, the distinctive contribution of the continuity thesis to understanding remedies is the suggestion that these ideas also explain orders to pay damages. According to the thesis, paying damages in my babysitting example is similar to showing up as soon as possible: it is the best way (or part of the best way) for individuals to comply with their substantive duties when perfect compliance is no longer possible. Thus, the thesis argues that the best way for you to comply with your promise to babysit once the original time for performance has passed is not just for you to show up as soon as possible, but, in addition, to do something else for me, such as offering to babysit another time or, if our arrangement is legally binding, paying me a sum of money. Furthermore, the thesis argues that if late performance is no longer possible (for instance, if the traffic jam continues all evening), then the best way to comply with the promise is simply to pay me a sum of money. In short, the continuity thesis supposes that the best way to give effect to your promissory duty once the time for performance has passed is either to perform late and to pay damages (in cases where late performance in kind remains possible) or simply to pay damages (in cases where performance in kind is no longer possible). Finally, and crucially, the thesis assumes that the same argument grounds substantive duties to pay damages following a tort.[7] According to the continuity thesis, the best way for me to comply with my substantive duty not to carelessly cut off your arm in the case where I have done just that is for me to pay you a sum of money.[8] Like delivering late, paying damages is the best way,

[7] In recent work, John Gardner has acknowledged that the thesis does not explain nominal damages, loss of amenity damages, damages for pain and suffering, and other forms of non-compensatory damages: Gardner (2018) 153–5. Gardner's explanation of these awards as, roughly, a kind of mandated apology resembles, in broad outline, the wrong-based explanation defended here (though Gardner appears to believe that there are substantive duties to pay such damages). In contrast, Ernest Weinrib appears to believe that the thesis (or at least his version of it) explains all the awards that I describe as wrong-based, with the exception of some exemplary awards: Weinrib (2012) 95, 81–185. My comments apply equally to Gardner's narrow version and Weinrib's broad version of the thesis.

[8] 'Suppose that the defendant has tortiously destroyed an object belonging to the claimant. Prior to the tortious act, the defendant was under a duty of care with respect to the object. The defendant's

in the circumstances, for me to comply with my substantive duty not to injure you. By paying damages, and in particular by paying compensatory damages, the defendant can make the wrong 'as if it had never happened'.[9]

From a normative perspective, the continuity thesis's explanation of substantive duties to pay damages is attractively simple. The only values or principles that it invokes are already present in the substantive law. The thesis accepts that it is sometimes difficult to determine how much money wrongdoers should pay their victims. However, it regards such issue as essentially technical: the only question facing wrongdoers is what sum of money is the next-best way of performing the original duty. And the only values that matter in answering this question are the same values that explain the duty that was breached.

The continuity thesis also provides, or at least fits easily with, an appealingly simple explanation of orders to pay damages. The thesis supposes that courts order wrongdoers to pay damages for the same reason that they order debtors to pay their debts: because the defendant failed to fulfil a substantive duty to pay a sum of money. In this book's scheme of causes of action, the continuity thesis supposes that the cause of action for damages awards is a right-threat.[10] If the thesis is correct that there is a substantive duty to pay damages, then the only reason to order defendants to pay damages is that they are unwilling to comply with that duty.

A final observation is that the wrongfulness of the wrongdoer's wrong is irrelevant to the continuity thesis' explanation of substantive duties to pay damages. According to the thesis, the legal question facing wrongdoers after they have committed a wrong is the same question that they faced before the wrong: What is the best way to comply with my substantive duty? The fact that they previously failed to comply with this duty changes the context, but normatively their situation is unchanged. A wrong is no different from any other action or change of circumstance that affects a substantive duty's content. If I have agreed to look after your garden while you are away, I have a duty to ensure that your plants get additional water if they are parched. This duty exists regardless of whether your plants are parched because of unusually hot weather or because I neglected to water them. The continuity thesis regards wrongs in a similar way; they may be part of the causal explanation for why the wrongdoer's duty takes the particular form that it takes (namely, to pay damages), but its wrongfulness is irrelevant. In Arthur Ripstein's words, a

breach of this duty destroyed the object as a physical entity, but it did not destroy the claimant's right as a normative entitlement. Even after the object's destruction, the claimant is linked to the defendant through a right that pertains to the object as an undamaged thing, so that the right now takes the form of an entitlement to the cost of replacing it.': Weinrib (2008) 12.

---

[9] Ripstein (2007) 1. The quoted words are also the article's title.

[10] 'In the scheme defended in this book' because the thesis' defenders have not addressed this question.

wrong 'is a datable event in the history of the world, but one that is entirely without normative significance'.[11]

ii. Conceptual Objections

The primary objection to both the continuity thesis and the broader duty-confirming view of damages is that the common law does not recognize a substantive duty to pay damages. I explain this objection below. However, I first want to consider two objections that are specific to the continuity thesis. Although neither objection is a reason to reject duty-confirming views across the board, each is a reason to reject the most influential defence of such views.

The first objection is conceptual: the duties that the continuity thesis supposes are transformed into duties to pay damages ceased to exist before they could be transformed. As we have seen, the continuity thesis easily explains orders to perform already-breached contractual duties. My duty to pay you a contractually promised sum of money survives my failure to pay the sum on time. However, the reason that the continuity thesis easily explains such orders is that there is an obvious and straightforward sense in which it is possible for me to comply with my duty to pay you a sum of money notwithstanding that the payment may be late. Paying late is still paying. Cases in which the remedy for a contractual breach is damages are different. In such cases, it is typically impossible for the defendant to perform its duty, even in a second-best version of performance. To be sure, it usually remains physically possible, post-breach, for the defendant to perform the actions that were the object of the breached duty. For example, if I am ordered to pay damages because I failed to build your house according to the contractual specifications or because I failed to deliver promised goods, it remains physically possible for me to rebuild the house or deliver the goods at the time of the order. But it will rarely be legally possible for me to fulfil my duty.[12] The duty, and indeed the entire contract, will have been terminated, either by operation of law or by the claimant's choice. Termination by operation of law typically occurs because performance has become futile.[13] For example, a breached duty to provide food for a wedding is terminated—and so unfulfillable—once the wedding has happened. The latter

[11] Ripstein (2016) 248. See also Gardner (2011) 43 ('The continuity thesis . . . is concerned with the continuing pull of reasons to be satisfied, even when their prior nonsatisfaction or undersatisfaction was amply justified').

[12] The exception is cases where courts award substitutionary damages. As I explained in Chapter 6, such awards are substitutes for still-valid duties. Still, the continuity thesis cannot explain substitutionary damages because it is the court (not the substantive law) that transforms the defendant's duty into a duty to pay damages. Until a court awards substitutionary damages, the defendant's duty is to perform its original substantive duty.

[13] However, the most common instance of termination by operation of law occurs in an ordinary sale of goods case where the defendant has failed to deliver the required goods. I discuss this and other examples of termination by operation of law in Chapter 6, note 92.

cases, where termination arises by the claimant's choice, is common, because the claimant will have lost confidence in the wrongdoer's ability or willingness to perform, and accordingly wants to engage someone else to provide the relevant goods or services. These cases are particularly difficult for the continuity thesis to explain because it is the claimant, not the defendant, who terminates the contractual duty. If the claimant chooses to terminate the defendant's duty, it is not clear how that duty can then transform into a duty to pay damages.

Might it be argued that to say that a contract is 'terminated' is just to say that the wrongdoer's duty is transformed into a duty to pay damages? Certainly, this is not how judges and lawyers describe termination. And it is unclear on what ground claimants could unilaterally alter the content of the defendant's duty. Most importantly, contracts can be terminated for reasons other than that they were breached. Contracts frequently contain clauses permitting either or both parties to terminate the contract if specified non-wrongful events occur. In such cases, the terminated duties do not transform into duties to pay damages: they simply cease to exist. The termination of a contract is exactly what the label suggests: the end of the contract. It is unclear how one of the original duties in such a contract could transform into a duty to pay damages. There is no duty left to transform.

The termination of a contract following a breach does not, of course, make the breach disappear. The wrongdoer's wrong remains a wrong. Further, that wrong might give rise to a substantive duty to pay damages or (as I argue) a liability to being ordered to pay damages. But if it gives rise to a substantive duty, that duty is not the duty that the continuity thesis purports to explain. As we have seen, the continuity thesis grounds the substantive duty to pay damages in the persistence of the original substantive duty, not the fact that the wrongdoer committed a wrong.

It might be thought that the continuity thesis can at least explain contract claims for losses from delayed performance. Imagine that you seek damages for losses caused by my delivering goods two weeks late. In such a case, our contract was never terminated. Might we not say, then, that paying damages (in addition to delivering late) is the best way for me to comply, as fully as possible, with my duty to deliver the goods on time? We could certainly say this if I had explicitly or implicitly promised to compensate you for any loss you suffer as a result of my breach. Some contracts include just such clauses. But if our contract lacks such a clause, the only thing that I promised to do is what I promised to do, namely, to deliver goods by a certain date. It is difficult to see how my duty to perform that promise can transform into a duty to pay damages. My promissory duty is circumscribed by the content of my promise. I could have agreed to insure you against losses, but (let us assume) I did not agree. What I agreed to do was to deliver goods on a certain date. I failed in that duty, and the failure had economic consequences for you. But the duty remains a duty to do what I promised.

Unlike contractual duties, tort duties persist indefinitely. My duty not to carelessly injure you exists for so long as you live, and regardless of whether

I have carelessly injured you in the past. However, the duty clearly disappears on your death, and here we see a parallel to terminated contracts. Imagine that I have breached my duty not to damage (or otherwise interfere with) your property by eating the plums growing in your yard. Clearly, I no longer have a duty not to damage your plums. I have a duty not to damage property of yours that still exists, but as the plums no longer exist I can no longer have a duty with respect to them. Could we say, however, that my duty not to damage your plums transformed, at the moment I ate the plums, into a duty to pay you damages? It seems not. If such a transformation occurred, then it should also occur in cases where the plums no longer exist because you or someone else ate them. In the latter cases, I certainly don't have a duty to pay you damages. To be sure, there are lots of reasons that we might think my legal position should be different depending on whether the plums were eaten by me or by you. If I ate the plums, we might conclude that my wrong should attract a sanction and, further, that I should be responsible for the consequences of my wrongdoing. But as we have seen, the continuity thesis cannot adopt this explanation because it supposes that duties to pay damages arise not from wrongs, but from persisting duties. Yet as in the case of terminated contracts, it is not clear how a duty in relation to a particular object can persist once the object no longer exists.

Of course, the commission of a tort often leaves the tort's subject matter intact. A battery does not eliminate or destroy the battered person's body. In such cases, the content of the wrongdoer's substantive duty persists in roughly the same form as it existed prior to the tort. My duty not to batter you persists notwithstanding that I battered you last week. However, the above objection generalizes to these cases also. According to the continuity thesis, if I breach my duty not to batter you, the duty transforms, at the moment of breach, into a duty to pay you a sum of money. But notice that what is allegedly transformed by the breach is not merely the content of my duty. Its exigibility is also transformed. Everyone in the world has a duty not to batter you. Yet the thesis presumes that I alone incur a duty to pay you damages. In other words, the thesis must suppose that the duty has transformed from an *in rem* duty to an *in personam* duty. How does this transformation happen? If the duty that is allegedly transformed is a duty that everyone owes to you, why is the transformed duty to pay damages not also owed by everyone to you? The obvious, and I think the only possible, answer is that the duty to pay damages falls on me because I am the person who breached the duty. But it is not clear why this fact should matter under the continuity thesis. If the duty not to injure applies to everyone, whatever explanation is given for that duty must also apply to everyone. And it would seem to follow, at least under the continuity thesis, that whatever explanation is given for the transformed duty would also apply to everyone. Of course, the explanation does not apply to everyone if it is based on the fact that I alone am responsible for your injury. However, as we have seen, the continuity thesis's focus is not responsibility for harm: its focus is how to comply with our duties when perfect compliance is no longer possible. According to the thesis, the task for me after I have injured you is to determine the best way possible, given the present circumstances of the injury, for me to comply with my duty not to injure you. The fact that I am responsible for the changed circumstances is strictly irrelevant. In short, because the wrongdoer's wrong is normatively irrelevant in the continuity thesis, the thesis cannot explain why it is the wrongdoer alone who has a duty to pay damages following a tort.

In this example, as in all the above examples, the fact that I breached a duty may be (and in my view is) a good reason to hold me responsible for the ensuing harm. It is also a good reason to impose a duty on me to pay for that harm, whether by a substantive rule or, as I argue in Chapter 8, by a court order. However, it is not a reason for supposing that the duty that I breached continues to apply in cases where performance is physically impossible or where the duty has been terminated. Nor is it a reason in cases where the duty that was breached was owed to the victim by everyone in the world.

The above objection to the continuity thesis is conceptual in the sense that it relies on claims about the basic nature of legal duties. If these claims are accurate, the objection should be reflected in lawyers, judges, commentators, and ordinary citizens' descriptions and understandings of the legal effects of breaching a substantive duty. This is exactly what we find. The position defended above is an abstract version of the common sense understanding of breaches. In cases where it remains physically and legally possible to perform a breached duty, lawyers describe such performance as 'performance', or at least as late performance. For example, lawyers describe the late payment of a debt as 'late payment'. But lawyers use different language to describe the wrongdoer's situation in the cases that I discussed above. If I cut off your finger, lawyers do not say that it remains possible for me to perform my duty not to cut off your finger, albeit late or albeit in any other version. Nor do lawyers describe my paying damages in such a case as a modified or imperfect way of me performing my duty not to cut off your finger. The same pattern is seen in contract cases. If, following my failure to provide you with a contractually promised service, you terminate our contract, lawyers would not say that my duty to provide the service remains alive. And if I am required to pay damages because of the breach, lawyers would not describe that payment as a modified or substitute form of performance. To be sure, lawyers describe damages, or at least compensatory damages, as aiming to place innocent parties in the same financial position that they would have been in had the breach not happened. That aim is consistent with the continuity thesis (and also with the injustice-based explanation that I defend in Chapter 8). However, lawyers do not describe such a payment as a modified way of fulfilling the defendant's original duty.

iii. Doctrinal Objections

The second objection is doctrinal: the continuity thesis is inconsistent with the rules governing the assessment of compensatory damages. The main inconsistency arises in respect of the various rules that limit defendants' liability for consequential losses, such as mitigation, contributory negligence, collateral benefits, exoneration of liability clauses (limitation and exclusion clauses), and 'remoteness' ('proximate cause') generally. These limitations are inconsistent with the continuity thesis. If paying damages is meant to make the world as if the defendant had performed its original duty, the fact that the claimant was careless or could have avoided the loss or, more generally, the loss was not reasonably foreseeable, seems irrelevant. We do not have duties to take care not to harm ourselves or duties to avoid suffering losses. Nor does the unlikeliness of a particular consequence make it any less a change from the world that would have existed had the original duty been performed.[14]

It is true, as I argue in Chapter 8, that it may well be unfair to hold defendants liable for these kinds of losses. Courts and commentators typically explain the rules that limit liability for consequential losses on just this basis: '[T]he second inquiry [remoteness] concerns the extent of the loss for which the defendant ought fairly or reasonably or justly to be held liable (the epithets are interchangeable).'[15] Legislation employs similar concepts: '[Damages] shall be reduced to such extent as the court thinks just and equitable having regard to the claimant's share in the responsibility for the damage'.[16] However, this explanation is not available to the continuity thesis. To be sure, the thesis does not suppose that the courts should issue unfair, unjust, or unreasonable awards. But it also does not view the courts' task as working out what is a fair, just, or reasonable allocation of responsibility. According to the continuity thesis, the courts' task is determining the best way, in the circumstances, for defendants to fulfil their original duties. And 'best' means fulfilling the original duty as closely as possible. If the original duty was fair, then the sum of damages that provides the same outcome will also be fair. The continuity thesis

[14] Relatedly, the thesis cannot explain why the remoteness rules are different in contract and tort. There are three main differences. First, the foreseeability of a loss is assessed in contract as of date of contract formation, while in tort it is as of the date of breach. Second, it is generally assumed that the degree of likelihood required of a loss is higher for contract claims than for tort claims. Finally, in contract claims, the courts take into account any assumed or implicit understandings that a reasonable party would have concerning the scope of the parties' contractual duties or their potential liabilities: Burrows (2004) 73–155. Yet, according to the continuity thesis, the question facing wrongdoers is identical in contract and tort cases: what is the best way, in the circumstances, to fulfil the original duty? To answer this question following a breach of contract, it is necessary to determine the contractual duty's content (which is established at the time of formation). Beyond this, it does not matter what happened at formation. Nor can the thesis explain why the test of remoteness is more difficult to satisfy in contract.

[15] *Kuwait Airways Corp v Iraqi Airways Co (No 3)* [2002] 3 All ER 209, 228 (Lord Nicholls).

[16] *Law Reform (Contributory Negligence) Act* 1954, s 1.

does not require courts to ask what is fair, just, or reasonable, or to consider any other values or normative principles. For the thesis, the only question that arises with respect to the assessment of damages is technical: What sum of money will make the world as if the wrong had never happened?

A similar difficulty for the thesis is raised by the rule that compensation is limited to the 'diminution in value' caused by a breach rather than the 'cost of cure' if the latter sum is unreasonable. In *Ruxley Electronics and Construction Ltd v Forsyth*,[17] the claimant contracted for a swimming pool with a depth at one end of 7 foot 6 inches. The completed pool was only 6 foot 9 inches deep. The court held that the difference in depth made no difference to any use to which the pool might be put and that it had no effect on the property's value. However, the cost of rebuilding the pool—£21,460—was nearly a third of the contract price. The claimant sought damages pegged at the cost of cure, but the court refused on the ground that it was 'out of all proportion' to the cure's value. They held that the cost of cure should only be awarded if the defendant intended to do the work, and if it was reasonable to do the work—and the latter requirement was not satisfied. This result is difficult to reconcile with the continuity thesis. Short of actual performance,[18] the next-best way of performing an unperformed contractual duty is to pay a sum of money equal to the cost of obtaining performance from a third party. To be sure, it might be thought unreasonable to hold defendants liable for repairs that the claimant had no plausible reason to undertake (particularly if, as appears to be the case in *Ruxley*, the breach was unintentional). But, again, the reasonableness of holding the defendant liable is irrelevant under the continuity thesis.

Finally—though more tentatively—the continuity thesis has difficulty explaining the scope of damages awards.[19] To begin, the thesis has difficulty explaining awards that go beyond replacement costs for a thing or service that was destroyed, damaged, lost, wrongly retained, or not provided as promised. In other words, it has difficulty explaining compensation for lost profits or incidental out-of-pocket expenses ('compensatory damages'). Duties to pay compensatory damages require defendants to do qualitatively different things than their original substantive duties required them to do. If I contractually promise to deliver a machine to your factory, my contractual duty is to deliver the machine. It is not a duty to ensure that you obtain whatever profits you reasonably expected to obtain as a consequence

[17] [1996] AC 344.

[18] Actual performance is the best way of fulfilling an unfulfilled substantive duty. However, the continuity thesis can adopt Chapter 6's explanation (the 'administrative' explanation) of the courts' preference for monetary remedies.

[19] As I mentioned in note 12, substitutionary damages pose a further problem for the continuity thesis, at least if the thesis is meant to explain all damages awards. Where a substitutionary award is granted, the defendant's duty transforms into a monetary duty. However, it is the court that effects this transformation, and it does this at the moment of judgment. Until judgment, the defendant remains bound by the original substantive duty.

of the delivery. Similarly, my duty to refrain from carelessly destroying your car is not a duty to ensure that you obtain whatever financial benefits you could reasonably expect to obtain from the car. It is simply a duty not to destroy the car. In each case, it would appear that the next-best way of complying with the original duty, post-breach, is to provide funds to obtain a replacement for the machine or the car. This observation is consistent with believing that it would be unfair if wrongdoers were not required to compensate their victims for the harmful consequences of their wrongs. I defend compensatory damages on exactly this basis in Chapter 8. The point is merely, but importantly, that paying compensation for consequential losses is not a substitute form of performance. The consequences of a breach of duty are distinct from the breach.

In his defence of the continuity thesis, Arthur Ripstein justifies compensatory damages on the ground that our substantive rights are rights to our means, and the latter include rights to whatever means we could have realized through those means: 'If you have something as your means, you thereby also have whatever further means follow from having them.'[20] This explanation is puzzling. Even if it is accepted that our rights are rights to our means, it is not clear how we can 'have' means that we expect to realize in future. My right to my car is simply a right to my car, not a right to whatever things I can obtain in future from using the car. Admittedly, once I use my car to obtain further means, I own those further means in the same way that I own my car. But if I were seeking damages for consequential losses flowing from the loss of my car, by definition I would not yet have obtained the further means. More broadly, the idea that individuals own or have a right to future means is inconsistent with the principle that claimants can only recover damages for harm to their future prospects where such harm is consequent to an injury to their person or (presently owned) property. If it were true that individuals 'have' the fruits of their means in the same way that they 'have' their means, then interfering with the former should be a legal wrong. Yet, it is basic common law that, exceptional circumstances aside, losses of this kind (so-called 'pure economic loss') are not recoverable. The standard explanation for this principle, which Ripstein accepts,[21] is that damages are only available on proof of a rights infringement, and we have no rights to make profits. The explanation is inconsistent with the view that paying compensatory damages fulfils the defendant's original duty. There is no original duty not to interfere with the realization of expected profits.

In addition to the difficulty of explaining compensation for consequential losses, the continuity thesis also has difficulty explaining the long-standing rule that only parties to a contract may recover damages for breach, and then only with respect to losses that they suffer themselves. Suppose that you enter into a

[20] Ripstein (2007) 1974.

[21] Ibid; see also Weinrib (2008) 134.

contract with me, in which you agree to paint my sister's house. You then fail to paint the house. It is possible that, in some common law jurisdictions, our contract might fit within an exception to the privity rule such that my sister could recover damages from you or even that I could recover substantial damages. But in most jurisdictions, the traditional privity rule would apply, with the result that, exceptional circumstances aside, I would only recover nominal damages if I sued you (and my sister would receive nothing). My damages would be nominal because I would be unable to show that I suffered a loss. This result is difficult for the continuity thesis to explain. Even assuming that there is good reason not to order specific performance in such a case, the obvious way to give effect to your original duty would be for you to pay me (or my sister) a sum equal to the cost of hiring someone else to paint the house. The payment of nominal damages is hardly a substitute for painting a house.

It is no response to this objection that your contractual promise was made to me rather than to my sister. According to the continuity thesis, the question for those who break their contracts is not 'who did I wrong,' but 'how can I best comply with my original duty in the present circumstances?' The answer to this question does not depend on who owns the house. Suppose that the contract had been to paint two houses, one owned by my sister and one by me. If the best way to comply with your duty to paint my house is to pay me the cost of hiring another painter, then surely the best way to comply with your duty to paint my sister's house should be to make a similar payment. However, the law responds to the breaches of these duties in radically different ways.

B. The Positive Law: No Substantive Duty to Pay Damages

The above conceptual and doctrinal objections apply specifically to the continuity-thesis version of the duty-confirming view of damages. However, the most important objection to the continuity thesis applies to all versions of the duty-confirming view. The objection is that the common law does not recognize a substantive duty to pay damages.[22]

[22] Although some of the arguments that follow apply equally in civil law jurisdictions, prima facie the position in civil law jurisdictions appears to be different. The best-known civilian codal article—Article 1240 of the *French Civil Code* 2016 (formerly Article 1382)—explicitly recognizes a substantive duty to pay damages: 'Any human deed whatsoever which causes harm to another creates an obligation in the person by whose fault it was caused to repair it' (translation). Explaining this difference (assuming it is genuine), would require another book. However, I tentatively suggest that the explanation turns on the different ways that the law was traditionally developed in common law and civil law regimes (i.e. by differences between law that is created in the context of judges addressing complaints and law created by jurists reflecting on rules for conduct).

i. Language: Liabilities, Not Duties

The first clue that the common law does not recognize a substantive duty to pay damages is found in the terminology that courts, commentators, and lawyers employ to describe individuals who have committed civil wrongs. Although there are well-known exceptions, courts typically describe wrongdoers not as having duties to pay damages, but as being 'liable to pay damages'.[23] Even writers who defend the duty-confirming view refer to liabilities, not duties, to pay damages. Throughout *The Idea of Private Law*, Ernest Weinrib refers to tort law as a regime of civil 'liability'. Chapters 6 and 7 are entitled, respectively, 'Negligence Liability' and 'Strict Liability'.[24] Legislative language is similar. The only rights to damages contemplated in the *Sale of Goods Act* 1979 are rights to bring actions for damages. Section 50 (1) states that a disappointed buyer 'may maintain an action against the seller for damages'. Textbooks adopt the same language. The leading English treatise on damages describes damages as 'an award', that is, as a judicial remedy.[25]

A liability is different from a duty.[26] Duties describe things that we must do; liabilities describe things that may be done to us. To say that we have legal duties to do X means that, from the law's perspective, we must do X. In contrast, to say that we have liabilities to X, means that X may be done or imposed upon us by another person or institution. Lawyers say that criminals are liable to be punished—not that they have duties to punish themselves—because punishment is imposed by courts. Thus, to describe wrongdoers as liable to pay damages suggests that they do not have duties to make these payments, but only that they are liable to be ordered to pay them.

It is possible to be liable to incur a substantive duty. For example, a vendor who offers goods to a purchaser is liable to incur a duty to sell the goods if the

[23] *Blundy, Clark & Co, Ltd v London and Northeastern Rail Co* [1931] All ER Rep 160, 172. A sample of other examples include: *Anns and others v Merton London Borough Council* [1977] UKHL 4, [1978] AC 728, 101 ('in each case he would be liable to pay damages for negligence'); *Murphy v Brentwood District* Council [1991] 1 AC 398 ('the defendant would have been liable to pay damages for the resultant physical injury'); and *Ashley and another v Chief Constable of Sussex Police* [2008] 3 All ER 573, 595 ('the judge will find the defendant liable to pay damages'). Probably the best-known counter-example is from Lord Diplock. 'Every failure to perform a primary obligation is a breach of contract. The secondary obligation on the part of the contract breaker to which it gives rise by implication of the common law is to pay monetary compensation to the other party for the loss sustained by him in consequence of the breach': *Photo Production Ltd v Securicor Transport Ltd* [1980] AC 827, 847. Other counter-examples include *Moschi v Lep Air Services Ltd* [1973] AC 331 350–1 and *Law Debenture Trust Corp plc v Ural Caspian Oil Corp Ltd and others* [1995] 1 All ER 157, 173.

[24] Weinrib (1995). A striking example (given his explicit support for the duty-confirming view) was Birks' decision, in his editorship of *English Private Law*, to place damages law as a sub-category of 'Judicial Remedies', which itself was a sub category of 'Litigation': Birks (2000b) xxiv–xxvi. Other examples include: Weinrib (1995) 119, 121, 125, 133, 136, 142, 143, 171, 172; Birks (2000a) 1, 21, 31, 33, 34, 35, 36; Stevens (2007) 1, 11, 12, 21, 22, 34; Gardner (2011) 16, 42; and Ripstein (2016) 5, 7, 13, 235, 236.

[25] Edelman (2018) 1.

[26] Hohfeld (1913) 44–54.

purchaser accepts the offer. In such cases, the substantive duty is triggered by another individual's (not a court's) exercise of a legal power. Might wrongdoers' liabilities to pay damages be similar? Might it be the case, in other words, that while wrongdoers are not immediately duty-bound to pay damages, they are liable to fall under such duty if—as in the case of contractual offerors—another individual exercises a power to impose the duty? This interpretation seems implausible. The only action that might conceivably qualify as an exercise of the relevant power is the initiation of litigation by the victim (since initiating and carrying through litigation is the only act by an individual that is a necessary pre-requisite to a damages order). Yet the courts have never suggested that a defendant's legal duties change when the claimant initiates an action in damages (or at any other moment prior to judgment). Further, to exercise a legal power, it is necessary to communicate an intention to exercise the power.[27] Few, if any, wrongdoers or their victims understand the initiation of litigation as communicating such an intention: claimants bring actions for damages because they want to obtain a damages award. Indeed, as I explain below, the traditional form of a writ for damages explicitly presumed that the defendant had no duty to pay damages prior to judgment. Further, the duty contemplated by this suggestion would presumably only arise if the claimant has a valid claim for damages But how is the defendant to know that the claim is valid? At least some of the relevant facts will be known only to the claimant. Perhaps, the claimant is lying, exaggerating, or badly informed about either the law or the facts. Finally, if this suggestion is accepted, the continuity thesis' explanation of damages must be abandoned. The continuity thesis holds that the duty to pay damages is continuous with the original duty and, therefore, that it arises immediately following a wrong.

Is it possible that courts do not mean what they are saying? In other words, is it possible that courts mean 'duty' notwithstanding they say 'liability'? This explanation seems unlikely, given that courts do not refer to liabilities when describing actions that clearly are the subject of substantive duties. Courts do not say that individuals are liable to perform their contracts or liable not to trespass: they say that individuals have legal duties to perform their contracts and not to trespass.[28] The language in which courts describe the rules governing the assessment and quantification of damages is also inconsistent with this suggestion. Courts describe these rules as establishing guidelines for how they—the courts—should assess damages: 'The court has to perform the difficult and artificial task of converting into

[27] Raz (1972) 79–89; Raz (1999) 98–104; Essert (2015) 145–8.

[28] *Cooper v Jarman* (1866) LR 3 Eq 98, 102 ('The Administrator has a clear duty to perform [the contract]': Lord Romilly); *Letang v Cooper* [1964] EWCA Civ 5 ('Our whole law of tort today proceeds on the footing that there is a duty owed by every man not to injure his neighbor in a way forbidden by law. Negligence is a breach of such a duty. So is nuisance. So is trespass to the person . . .': Lord Denning).

monetary damages the physical injury and deprivation and pain and to give judgment for what it considers to be a reasonable sum'.[29]

Indeed, the phrase 'assessing damages' presumes that there is someone other than the victim that is doing the assessing. Legislation similarly presumes that it is courts, not victims, who assess damages. The *Damages Act* 1996 is typical:

> 1. - (1) In determining the return to be expected from the investment of a sum awarded as damages for future pecuniary loss in an action for personal injury the court shall, subject to and in accordance with rules of court made for the purposes of this section, take into account such rate of return (if any) as may from time to time be prescribed by an order made by the Lord Chancellor.[30]

ii. Doctrine

The language that courts use to describe and explain damages law is inconsistent with the duty-confirming view of damages. However, the most compelling evidence against this view is found in the positive law of damages.[31] I focus below on two rules and one general feature of this law.[32]

No Damages for Failing to Pay Damages

Damages are unavailable in respect of losses that victims of a tort or contract breach could have avoided had the defendant paid them immediately following the injury.[33] This rule is difficult to explain if wrongdoers have substantive duties

[29] *H West & Son Ltd v Shephard* [1964] AC 326, 364 (Lord Pearce). Similar examples abound: 'the court will not value the right at the ransom price . . . ': *Jaggard v Sawyer* [1995] 2 ALL ER 189, 203 (Bingham MR); 'the assessment of damages is not an exact science and what to one judge or jury will appear a real danger may appear to another judge or jury to be a serious possibility': *Hadley v Baxendale* [1854] 9 Exch 341, 354 (Alderson B); 'The assessment requires the judge to make a value judgment. That value judgment has been increasingly constrained by the desire to achieve consistency between the decisions of different judges': *Heil v Rankin* [2001] QB 272, 294 (Lord Woolf MR).

[30] *Damages Act* 1996, s 1. See also eg *Law Reform (Contributory Negligence) Act* 1954, s 1 ('[damages] shall be reduced to such extent as the court thinks just and equitable having regard to the claimant's share in the responsibility for the damage').

[31] American law is similar: Oman (2011a) 137. In addition to the rules discussed below, the duty-confirming rule is inconsistent with the House of Lord's holding, in *Harding v Wealands* [2006] UKHL 32, that the rules governing the quantification of damages are 'procedural' for the purposes of conflict of law issues (and thus governed by the *lex fori*). (However, Australian and Canadian courts have classified these rules as substantive: Rogerson (2006) 515). The rules governing set-off and assignment distinguish between debts and damages, with some qualifications: Tettenborn (2010) 10

[32] I noted earlier that the duty-confirming view cannot explain substitutionary damages: see note 12. It also cannot explain damages awards in cases where the claimant has a choice of remedies (e.g. compensatory or gain-based damages) or where the court has a discretion with respect to the magnitude of the award. Examples of the latter group include exemplary damages, nominal damages, and damages for pain and suffering. In all these cases, the amount of damages is indeterminate until the court makes a ruling.

[33] 'There is no such thing as a cause of action in damages for late payment of damages': *President of India v Lips Maritime Corpn* [1988] AC 395, 425 (Lord Brandon).

to pay damage. If such a duty existed, then failing to pay damages prior to a court order would be a legal wrong. Compensatory damages are generally available for losses caused by legal wrongs. If you deliver goods late, I can recover damages for losses arising from the delay. Similarly, if you are late paying a contractual debt, I can obtain compensatory damages in respect of losses that I suffered because of the delay.[34] But damages are not available for losses caused by the late payment of damages. This objection cannot be avoided by arguing that the duty to pay damages has no completion date. If a duty to perform a positive action has no completion date, it is not actually a duty. The supposed duty could never be breached.

The interest awards that are now available on monetary awards,[35] including damages awards, are usually equal to any loss suffered by a claimant resulting from the failure to perform a monetary obligation. But not always. For example, claimants who borrow funds at high rates to cover a short fall will incur losses greater than the interest rate. This possibility explains why courts allow claimants suing for overdue contractual debts to recover damages for consequential losses in addition to an interest award. Equivalent awards are not available in the case of non-payment of damages. The most straightforward explanation for this rule is that there is no duty to pay damages prior to a court order.[36]

[34] *Wadsworth v Lydall* [1981] 1 WLR 598; *Sempra Metals Ltd v Commissioner of Inland Revenue* [2008] 1 AC 561 (overturning *London, Chatham and Dover Railway Company v South Eastern Railway* [1893] AC 429].

[35] *Senior Courts Act* 1981, s 35A. It might be thought that the availability of interest awards supports the duty-confirming view on the ground that interest is intended to compensate for the time the claimant has been kept out of the money. But if this were the reason for interest awards, courts would allow claims for damages where the claimant's loss exceeds the interest rate. As explained above, courts allow such claims for non-payment of debts, but not for non-payment of damages. Interest awards serve two roles. Interest *on* damages, which is statutory (and also available for other monetary awards), ensures that the real time value of money is kept constant (see *Westdeutsche Landesbank Girozentrale v Islington London Borough Council* [1996] AC 669, 696, 736; *Sempra Metals Ltd v Inland Revenue* [2007] UKHL, 32–50, 116, 132, 178–179; Virgo (2006) 25–6; Burrows (2011) 21–5). Interest *as* damages, which is common law, is intended to compensate for losses caused by the original breach (see *Sempra*, where Lord Scott wrote, in respect of common law interest, that 'interest losses caused by a breach of contract or by a tortious wrong should be held to be in principle recoverable, but subject to proof of loss, remoteness . . . ' [132]).

[36] According to traditional English law (but not Canadian, Australian, American, or Scottish law), the payment to an insured under a standard insurance policy is damages rather the fulfilment of the insurer's contractual duty. The insurer's primary duty, it is said, is to hold the insured 'harmless', that is, to ensure that the insured does not suffer a loss from fire, theft, flood, etc: *Forney v Dominion Insurance Company Ltd* [1969] 1 Lloyd's Rep 502, 509. It would seem to follow, therefore, that under standard insurance contracts insurers do not have legal duties to make payments until ordered to do so by the courts—and the courts have confirmed as much by refusing to award damages for failing to make timely payments. This conclusion is counter-intuitive, not to mention substantively unjust, but the root of the problem is the fiction that the insurer's primary duty is to prevent loss rather than to pay money. This much-criticized rule presumably arose because of the difficulty, given the insurer's need to investigate the claim, of determining at what point in time the insurer's duty to pay arises. But whatever the explanation, the traditional interpretation is an obvious fiction: aside from the conceptual impossibility of a strict undertaking to ensure the policy holder does not suffer a loss, the parties almost certainly assume that insurers have duties to make payments. The traditional position is described and criticized in Law Commission & Scottish Law Commission (2010) Issues Paper No 6.

No Defence of Tender or Payment

An action for damages cannot be avoided on the ground that the defendant offered to pay the damages prior to judgment.[37] Indeed, even prior payment of damages does not extinguish the claimant's right to an award of damages (other than where the claimant accepts payment as part of a settlement[38]).[39] If you sue me because I threw a rock through your window, it is no defence that my next act was to place £100 in your mailbox, which you then deposited in your bank account. Even if the judge assesses your damages at £100, your suit will succeed (though I may be able to recover my £100 in a counter-claim for restitution). Except where pre-payment is part of a settlement, it is legally irrelevant in a claim for damages.

The pre-payment rule is clearly inconsistent with a substantive duty to pay damages. If such a duty existed, an offer to pay damages in advance, and even more so actual payment in advance, would fulfil the duty. Where a claimant brings an action for a sum due, the defendant's payment of the sum or offer to pay the sum is a full defence.

Historical Note

Not surprisingly, the pre-payment rule and the 'no damages for non-payment of damages rule' (the 'non-payment rule') rarely come up in litigation. Most pre-payments are made as parts of settlements, and it would be unusual to bring an action for damages if the defendant has already paid voluntarily. It will also be rare that the non-payment of damages will result in claimants incurring losses larger than the sum available by way of interest on a monetary award. It is important to stress, then, that the pre-payment and non-payment rules are not mere technicalities. These rules are a direct implication of what was, until the abolition of the writs in the nineteenth century, the most important distinction within the English law of obligations: the distinction between actions to enforce existing rights (e.g. an action for a sum due) and actions to obtain redress for wrongs, that is, actions for damages (e.g. an action for damages for physical injury)—in short, the distinction between rights and wrongs.[40] The *praecipe* writs that initiated claims to

[37] *IM Properties Plc v Cape & Dalgleish* [1998] 3 WLR 457; *RSM Bentley Jennison v Ayton* [2015] EWCA Civ 1120.

[38] Settlement of an actual or potential legal action is different from performance of an unperformed legal duty. I can settle an action to enforce a contractual obligation to deliver goods valued at £1000 in exchange for a payment of £100. See *British Russian Gazette & Trade Outlook Ltd v Associated Newspapers Ltd* [1933] 2 KB 616, 643.

[39] See e.g. *Edmunds v Lloyds Italico & l'Ancora Compagnia di Assicurazione & Riassicurazione S.p.A. and Administration of State Insurance (ADAS)* [1986] 1 WLR 492, 495–x6; Tettenborn (2010).

[40] 'The modern law of obligations, roughly that concerning contract, tort and personal chattels, is the result of a continuing interplay between two simple ideas from which the common law started . . . the demand for a right and the complaint of a wrong. . . . [T]here is an underlying juridical difference: in *praecipe* situations the defendant can put matters right by a definite render, whereas in most *ostensurus quare* [trespass] situations he has done an irreparable wrong for which compensation must be assessed': Milsom (1981) 243–4. See also Baker (2002) 67.

enforce rights demanded that defendants fulfil the asserted right or come to court to explain themselves. Thus, where defendants were sued for a sum due, they could avoid going to court by paying the sum to the 'demandant' (as the claimants in such actions were described). In contrast, the trespass writs that initiated claims for damages left defendants no option: they had to come to court. The defendant could not avoid court by paying damages because the 'complainant' (as they were called) had no right to damages.[41] There was no demand that the defendant could satisfy because the complainant was not seeking to enforce a right, but, instead, to obtain redress for a wrong. The distinction between actions to enforce rights and actions to obtain redress for wrongs explains why pre-payment of damages is no defence and why failing to pay damages is not a wrong. There was no right to damages prior to a court order. More generally, the distinction explains why common law lawyers refer to liabilities, not duties, to pay damages: the origins of this language lie deep in the common law's DNA.

An Unknowable Duty

In addition to the pre-payment and non-payment rules, the entire set of rules governing the assessment of compensatory damages is inconsistent with the duty-confirming view. The application of these rules turns on facts that wrongdoers cannot reasonably be expected to know and, in some cases, on decisions that have yet to be made. If a substantive duty to pay damages existed, it would be an unknowable duty.

To begin, wrongdoers will often be unaware that they have even committed a wrong. Vendors who sell defective goods may not know that their goods are defective. Similarly, manufacturers will often be unaware that their products have caused an injury. Further, even when wrongdoers are aware that they have committed a wrong, they will rarely know the extent of damage that it caused. By definition, the facts on which such claims are based are in the victim's hands. The extent of a victim's losses depends on the victim's income, business prospects, leisure activities, medical expenses, pain and suffering, insurance, pre-existing medical condition, living arrangements, life expectancy, and so forth. Even a simple claim for the value of goods that were destroyed, damaged, or lost, depends on the goods' characteristics and condition. All of these facts are in the victim's hands (though in some cases even the victim cannot ascertain them). The wrongdoer's liability also depends on the extent to which the victim was contributorily negligent (for

[41] 'Whereas a *praecipe* writ ordered the defendant to accede to a demand or justify himself, a trespass writ brought the defendant directly to court to explain why he had done wrong. Trespass writs were therefore not concerned with the vindication of rights, but with punishment and amends for past transgression. A writ of trespass offered no option, even fictitious, of doing right: as Blackstone put it, while a *praecipe* writ was 'optional', trespass was 'peremptory'. It embodied a complaint rather than a demand. As with the assize and the appeal, trial was by jury. And the outcome of a successful suit was damages, with a fine to the king in serious cases': Baker (2002) 67.

instance, was the victim wearing a seatbelt?) and the extent to which others may be contributorily negligent. Finally, even where wrongdoers could somehow determine the extent of their victims' losses, it is impossible for them to determine how much to pay in cases where the victim has a choice between remedies (for instance, between damages or restitution) or between different tortfeasors (for instance, between employee and employer).

In theory, victims could provide the above information to wrongdoers, but there is no legal duty to do so, and many victims understandably want nothing further to do with those who have injured them. In any event, even if the victims provided such information, wrongdoers—or more strictly potential wrongdoers—cannot be expected to accept without question what the victim says. The victim's description may be false or exaggerated. And there is no reasonable way for wrongdoers to assess victims' claims. Does the victim have to provide receipts? Witnesses? Expert reports? Must the parties engage arbitrators to assess the evidence?[42]

A further reason that a substantive duty to pay damages is unknowable is that courts, and juries where they are used, enjoy considerable discretion when assessing certain categories of damages. These categories include damages for pain and suffering, damages for loss of amenity, damages for loss of reputation, and exemplary damages.[43] Courts also enjoy significant discretion when applying the basic rules governing remoteness of damages. There is no formula for determining which losses are 'reasonably foreseeable',[44] much less which losses it is 'fair, just, and reasonable' to attribute to the defendant. It is impossible, even in theory, to determine in advance of litigation the amounts that wrongdoers might owe under such headings. And while the courts' discretion in these areas is not unfettered, it is a true discretion. Appeal courts will not overturn an award of exemplary damages simply because they would have awarded a different sum.

Aside from cases where a duty's unknowability arises from its dependence on a victim's future choices (e.g. who to sue) or on a future exercise of judicial discretion, it is not strictly impossible to fulfil an unknowable duty. Wrongdoers might correctly determine that they have committed wrongs and then correctly guess or estimate the sum that, if the issue where litigated, a court would require them to pay—and then pay the claimant this sum. But it would be impossible for wrongdoers to know that they have complied with such a duty or, more generally, to be

[42] Even victims may not know this information, which explains why, in their statement of claim, they are only required to specify an amount that they reasonably expect to recover within three financial bands: O'Hare & Browne (2017) 202. Further, courts can award provisional damages in personal injury cases, which are sums based on assumptions that, if proven wrong, leave the claimant free to apply for further damages: *Supreme Court Act* 1981, s 32a.

[43] Courts openly acknowledge that the quantification of, for example, damages for pain and suffering involves a large subjective element: see e.g. *Wise v Kaye* [1962] 1 QB 638, 669; Tettenborn (2010) 81. In the United States, where juries still assess such damages, awards vary enormously: Dobbs & Roberts (2018) 659

[44] In contract cases, English courts are simply told to consider whether a loss was "'not unlikely', a 'real danger', a 'serious possibility'", or something similar: Tettenborn (2010) 133.

guided by it. A rule that imposed substantive duties to pay damages could not fulfil the most basic role of legal rules—and the most basic requirement of the rule of law—namely, to guide behaviour.[45] The only practical role that such a rule could fulfil would be to provide a basis for awarding damages once a court had determined what the duty required. But if that is all that a duty-imposing rule is doing, it is actually a liability-imposing rule

iii. Theory: An Inchoate Duty?

A possible response to the unknowability objection is that the duty to pay damages is an inchoate duty. According to this response, the duty to pay damages exists 'in principle' from the moment of injury, but the duty is not crystallized—and so not in force—until a court has specified its content.[46] On this basis, it might be argued that the pre-payment and non-payment rules are merely responses to the practical difficulties that (as we have seen) would arise if lawmakers attempted to draft a rule specifying how and when wrongdoers should pay damages. In an ideal world, according to this argument, wrongdoers ought to pay damages immediately following their wrongdoing. But in the real world, it is practically impossible for wrongdoers to know when and how to fulfil such a duty without a court's assistance. Thus, the duty must remain inchoate until fixed by a court. In principle, however, the reasons for the duty are reasons for wrongdoers to pay damages at the moment of injury.

One difficulty with this response is that it is not clear that an inchoate substantive duty is a duty at all. Duties should be able to guide those subject to them. By definition, inchoate duties cannot provide guidance. A substantive duty that is inchoate until confirmed by a court seems indistinguishable from a duty that is simply created by a court. Another way of making this point is that a duty that is inchoate until confirmed by a court lacks the generality that is a hallmark of substantive duties. As Lon Fuller demonstrated with his parable of the ruler who, by framing his laws as directions to specific individuals to do specific things, failed to make law at all,[47] a 'substantive rule' that merely stipulates that individuals must do what legal officials tell them to do on a case-by-case basis is arguably not a substantive rule at all. In other words, an inchoate duty-imposing rule is actually just a liability-imposing rule.

[45] 'This is the basic intuition from which the rule of law derives: the law must be capable of guiding the behavior of its subjects': Raz (1977) 214.

[46] Though not presented as such, Arthur Ripstein's Kantian explanation of the role of adjudication in solving problems of indeterminacy might be invoked to support an inchoate duty to pay damages: Ripstein (2009) 168–76.

[47] Fuller (1969) 33–9; see also Hart (1961) 20–1.

The inchoate duty interpretation also appears to be inconsistent with the continuity thesis. The continuity thesis supposes that the substantive duty to pay damages is a continuation, in a new form, of the wrongdoer's original substantive duty. In this view, it is part of the very meaning of duties to keep promises, duties not to lie, duties not to carelessly injure others, and so forth, that they immediately transform, when breached, into duties to do the next-best thing. The original duties remain in force, albeit in a new form, until they are fulfilled. Yet, if this were the case, it should be possible to specify the post-breach duty in a rule. There might be special considerations that the law should take into account when it comes time to enforce substantive duties (e.g. supervision costs), but such considerations should not, and elsewhere in the law do not, enter when lawmakers contemplate duty-imposing rules.

Finally, but most importantly, the inchoate duty argument does not fit the positive law. To begin, the argument cannot explain the pre-payment rule. If it were true that in principle damages ought to be paid prior to an award, then proof of a payment or offer to pay equal to or greater than the court's award should be a good defence against such an award.[48] Yet it is not a good defence. In addition, the inchoate duty argument is inconsistent with the form of damages award. If damages awards were intended to fix inchoate duties, they would not be expressed as orders: they would be expressed as declarations. Declarations are the normal and appropriate way for courts to specify uncertain duties. They are the individualized counterparts to legal rules: in the same way that legal rules tell citizens generally how they ought to behave, declarations tell specific individuals how they ought to behave.[49] Indeed, the connection is even closer, because a legal rule does not strictly 'tell' citizens how to behave but rather affirms the existence of a legal duty. As we saw in Chapter 5, duty-imposing legal rules are essentially statements about the existence of legal duties ('everyone has a duty to perform their contractual promises').[50] Austin's command theory of law failed because it is part of the essence of legal rules that, unlike mere commands, they affirm duties.[51] Judicial declarations carry the same meaning; the only difference is that rather than affirming duties that bind everyone, they affirm duties that bind particular individuals. Yet damages

[48] A related point is that historians have never explained the historical distinction between claims to enforce rights and claims to obtain redress for wrongs (on which the pre-payment rule is based) on the basis that the latter were claims to enforce unliquidated rights: see Baker (2002) 67; Milsom (1981) 243–4. Nor, for that matter, do courts today characterize the rules on damages as one might expect if the inchoate duty explanation were correct. Courts do not portray the task of assessing damages as a matter of determining how, ideally, the defendant should have acted from the moment of injury. They portray the task as a matter of determining what judges (or juries) should do.

[49] Dobbs & Roberts (2018) 7 ('Declaratory remedies furnish an authoritative and reliable statement of the parties' rights.'); Woolf (2011) 1 ('A declaratory judgment is a formal statement by a court pronouncing upon the existence or non-existence of a legal state of affairs').

[50] This language is often explicit in civilian codes. See e.g. *Civil Code of Québec*, art 1458 ('Every person has a duty to honour his contractual undertakings.').

[51] Hart (1961) 82–91.

rulings are framed as commands, that is, as orders. It would be extremely odd, and inappropriate, for courts to employ orders (or, in earlier times, 'judgments'[52]) to specify inchoate duties.[53] Ordering individuals to comply with duties without first giving them the opportunity to comply with those duties is inconsistent with the very idea of a duty.[54] Courts only issue injunctions, specific performance orders, orders for a sum due, and other incontrovertibly duty-confirming orders on proof that the defendant is unwilling to comply with the substantive duty that the order replicates. And courts are particularly hesitant to order defendants to comply with duties that they have yet to breach. As we saw in Chapter 6, courts rightly demand clear proof that the defendant is likely to breach the relevant duty in the immediate future. Yet the inchoate duty interpretation supposes that courts routinely order defendants to pay damages without requiring proof that they are unwilling to pay voluntarily.[55]

[52] As I explained in Chapter 3, the 'judgments' that were formerly issued with respect to rulings that originated in the Royal Courts were in the form of impersonal pronouncements that the claimant shall 'recover' a particular sum of money, land, or other property. In practical terms, the main difference between an order and a judgment is that while an order cannot be coercively enforced until after the date of performance, a judgment is in principle enforceable at the moment it is issued. It is therefore even less likely that courts would issue judgments for damages if such rulings were intended to fix inchoate duties. The defendant might have no opportunity to comply with her supposed duties.

[53] This objection to the inchoate duty interpretation cannot be avoided on the ground that, whatever the theoretical appropriateness of using declarations to specify inchoate duties, courts do not use them for the practical reason that it would lead to additional litigation. A declaration states as clearly as a damage award the sum of money that the defendant must pay. In practice, declarations of duties to pay damages could function, as far as enforcement is concerned, exactly as orders to pay damages currently function in English law. The defendant would need to be given a period of time, which could be very short, to do what the declaration required. But once the period expired, if the defendant had not performed, the claimant could immediately seek permission to engage bailiffs to execute the ruling.

[54] There are also practical reasons to announce legal duties in advance of ordering them or authorizing their execution. To the extent that paying damages is presented as a legal duty, citizens who are disposed to view their legal duties in the way the law wants them viewed—namely, as obligatory—will approach payment differently than they would if they were merely ordered to pay. For law-respecting citizens, settlements made in advance of litigation will not be regarded as akin to plea-bargaining deals, but rather as attempts to determine, so far as practical, their obligations. Similarly, post-litigation payments will be regarded as fulfilling an obligation, not merely as something that one has been forced to do. For these citizens, there will be a stigma attached to attempts to avoid payment (for instance, by hiding assets) that would not exist if the only reason for making the payment were that the law commanded such payment. Thus, if the law in fact regarded paying damages as an obligation, it would be in its interest to say this explicitly.

[55] In practice, common law courts make declarations relatively rarely, and they make declarations that create new duties even more rarely. Does this disprove the above arguments? It does not, though the argument raises issues that I can only flag here. The practical limitations of rules described above show that there are certain kinds of behaviours that are not easy to specify in rules. But it does not show that those same behaviours are even in principle an appropriate subject matter for legal rules or for any other kind of legal intervention. It is likely that there are duties whose content cannot be described in a rule. However, whether such duties are the kind of duties that the law ought to be concerned with is another question. It may well be that the category of duties that are not appropriately the law's concern includes duties whose content cannot be expressed in rules. It may not be coincidental, in other words, that the core example of private law duties, such as duties not to injure, steal, trespass, assault, and so on, are all easily expressed in rules.

C. The Duty-Creating View of Damages

If duties to pay damages only arise once courts order defendants to pay damages (as I have argued), then the entirety of damages law is part of remedial law. The question is how to explain these duties and the rules that govern them. Having rejected the continuity thesis' account of substantive duties to pay damages, it would be convenient if I could offer in its place a similarly simple, yet equally comprehensive, theory of court-ordered duties to pay damages. But such a theory is not possible. Although all orders to pay damages create new duties, they do this for different reasons and in different ways. It is because of these differences that discussions of damages law are so often at cross-purposes. For many writers, it goes without saying that the overriding goal of damages law is to ensure that victims obtain compensation for their loss.[56] Others reject the language of compensation entirely.[57] Each approach glimpses a part of the truth.

I argue that courts award damages for three main reasons. The first reason—to provide an administratively convenient substitute for non-monetary orders—was discussed in the previous chapter. The second reason—to provide compensation for losses—is examined in Chapter 8. The third reason—to provide redress for a wrong—is the focus of the remainder of the present chapter.

D. Wrongs-Based Damages: Introduction

As understood here, 'wrong-based damages' are roughly the private law equivalent of criminal punishment.[58] To be clear, I am not suggesting that wrong-based damages are a form of criminal punishment or that they have the same aim as criminal punishment. The suggestion is only—though importantly—that wrong-based damages are structurally similar to criminal punishment. Specifically, wrong-based damages and criminal punishment share four structural similarities. I explain these similarities below, using nominal damages as an illustrative example. Nominal damages are relatively rare and, even when they are awarded, they usually have limited practical significance. However, I refer to them merely to establish that wrong-based damages exist at all, and to illustrate their characteristic features. Afterwards, I explain why various other damages awards are similar to nominal damages.

[56] Wright (1942) 238; Williams & Hepple (1976) 26.

[57] See e.g. Weinrib (2012); Stevens (2007) 1, 59–62, 320–1.

[58] Though it is framed using different terminology and presented at a more abstract level, the account that follows is broadly consistent with a range of approaches to explaining damages law that, explicitly or not, assume there is no substantive duty to pay damages. Examples include civil recourse theories (eg Zipursky (1998a); Goldberg (2005); Goldberg & Zipursky (2010)); communicative theories (eg Hershowitz (2014) 86); and deterrence theories (eg Landes & Posner (1987)).

The first similarity between both wrong-based damages and criminal punishment is that both are responses to wrongs *qua* wrongs. They differ in this respect only in the nature of the wrongs to which they respond. Criminal punishment responds to wrongs to the public; wrong-based damages respond to wrongs to particular individuals.[59] This feature of wrong-based damages is manifest in the cause of action for nominal damages, which is simply proof of a wrong to an individual. If I trespass over your land or fail to deliver promised goods, you can obtain nominal damages even if my wrong caused you no harm. Indeed, courts typically define nominal damages as damages that will be awarded merely on proof that 'your legal right has been infringed'.[60]

Second, both wrong-based damages and criminal punishment direct defendants to do things (or direct that things be done to them) that do not amount merely to requiring them to do things that they already had legal duties to do. Paying a fine or enduring incarceration is not a transformed version of a substantive criminal law duty. Spending ten years in prison is not the 'next best way' of not killing someone. Likewise, paying nominal damages is not the next best way of not trespassing or not breaking a contractual promise. More generally, just as it is difficult to imagine that criminal wrongdoers could have a substantive duty to punish themselves, it is difficult to imagine that private wrongdoers could have a substantive duty to pay nominal damages. Aside from the fact that courts have a discretion in setting the magnitude of nominal damages (see below), they explicitly say that they are trying to send a message through such awards ('to mark the fact that there has been a breach of contract'[61]).

Third, the content of both criminal law and private law's responses to wrongdoing is determined by choice and convention. Contemporary criminal courts normally punish by ordering incarceration or a fine, but no one supposes that these are the only possible methods. Nor does anyone suppose that sentencing a thief to two years in prison or fining a polluter £10,000 is the uniquely appropriate measure of punishment for these crimes. Nominal damages are similar. Ordering the payment of a small sum of money is clearly not the only way to mark a wrong. It is equally clear that it is not possible to explain why the usual sum awarded by way of nominal damages is, today, £5. Why not £4? Within private law, wrong-based private remedies are unique in this regard. As we saw in the previous chapter, the content of an order issued in response to a rights-threat follows automatically from the reason for issuing the order: an order issued in

[59] Of course, crimes are typically committed against particular individuals: the crime of murder involves killing a particular person. However, crimes are understood as crimes against the public generally. This understanding explains why crimes are prosecuted by public prosecutors, fines are paid to the state, and incarceration occurs in public prisons.

[60] *The Mediana* [1900] AC 113, 116; see also *Ashley and Another v Chief Constable of Sussex Police* [2008] UKHL 25 [60].

[61] *Mappouras v Waldrons* [2002] EWCA Civ 842 [15].

response to a rights-threat directs the defendant to comply with the threatened right (or to comply with a close monetary substitute for that right). If the defendant is threatening to trespass on the claimant's land, the standard judicial response is an injunction prohibiting the trespass. And as we will see in the next chapter, the same pattern applies to orders issued in response to injustices. Injustice-responding orders invariably direct the defendant to correct the injustice. For example, if the injustice is a mistaken payment, the court will order the defendant to return the payment. But in the case of wrongs (civil or criminal), there is no logical or natural or inevitable response. As Peter Birks famously remarked, the courts would not be acting inconsistently if their response to wrongs were to 'allow the claimant to punch the defendant or cut off his ears'.[62] Of course, the law's response to wrongdoing should be humane, proportional to the wrong, administratively practical, and respect the rule of law. External considerations of these kinds explain why thieves are no longer drawn and quartered, why there are sentencing guidelines, and why the magnitude of punishment is a function of a crime's seriousness. They also explain, as we will see, why wrong-based remedies are monetary, quantified according to the wrong's seriousness, and pegged to predictable standards (e.g. the market price) where feasible and proportionate. Yet, at the end of the day, it is not possible to explain why sentencing a thief to two years in prison or ordering a trespasser to pay £5 is the uniquely appropriate response to their wrongs.

Finally, and critically, the justifications for wrong-based damages and criminal punishment are structurally similar. There is no universally accepted justification for criminal punishment. However, the most plausible and influential justifications all have private law equivalents.[63] In the traditional and probably still dominant view, criminal punishment is an instance of retributive justice. Briefly, this view supposes that criminal punishment aims to restore a moral (or 'normative') balance that the criminal's wrong has upset. By exercising a liberty—breaking the law—from which others have refrained, the criminal gains an unjust normative advantage. Criminal punishment removes from the criminal a proportionate liberty, restoring the balance of advantages and, at the same time, affirming that the law applies equally to everyone.[64] Thus understood, the main difference between criminal punishment and wrong-based damages is that while the former aims to restore a balance between wrongdoers and society, the latter aims to restore a balance

[62] Birks (1997b) 31.

[63] Aside from the retributivist justification discussed above, the best-known theories of punishment are deterrence theories (eg Bentham (1970, reprint) and communicative theories (e.g. von Hirsch, (1993); Duff, (2001)). There are private law equivalents for both: see, respectively, Landes & Posner (1978), Hershowitz (2014). My argument does not depend on accepting a retributivist theory of punishment.

[64] For a fuller exposition, see e.g. Finnis (1980) 262–4. See also, Kant (reprinted 1996) 333; Moore (1997).

between wrongdoers and their victims.[65] Private law defendants pay damages to the claimant because the relevant wrong, in private law, is a wrong to the claimant.

In principle, private law might pursue this aim in different ways. For example, we might imagine courts issuing pronouncements that condemn wrongdoers' actions and affirm victims' rights. Alternatively, courts might order wrongdoers to apologize to their victims. But as criminal punishment illustrates, for the law's condemnation to be taken seriously it is important that it be conveyed at least in part in a tangible form.[66] And it is important that this form reflect, however abstractly, the nature of the wrong. In practical terms, a mere announcement is just words. By requiring that wrongdoers do or provide something for their victims, the law expresses concretely that the defendant wronged the claimant and, at the same time, that the affirmed right was held by the claimant against the defendant. In criminal law, where the wrong is against the public, this message is often conveyed by directing the wrongdoer to pay a fine to the state.

In private law, damages can serve a similar role, or at least they can serve this role if, like criminal punishment, they are imposed by judicial orders, rather than substantive rules. In Chapter 5, I explained that the law imposes criminal punishment by orders because only in this way is it clear that the required action is punishment for a wrong. If the legislature attempted to impose substantive duties to pay fines,

[65] It is tempting to describe wrong-based damages as an instance of 'corrective justice'. In *The Idea of Private Law*, Ernest Weinrib, who re-introduced corrective justice to contemporary private law theory, described the concept in terms similar to those that I use in my account of wrong-based damages: 'A controversy in corrective justice involves an allegation that the defendant has disturbed the equality pertaining to transactions': (2012) 63. A wrongdoer, Weinrib explains, obtains a 'normative' gain at the victim's expense, which damages are meant to eliminate: 'the same sum represent[s] the injury to the claimant's right and the violation of the defendant's duty' (143). Consistent with my account of wrong-based damages, Weinrib further explains that it is judges who bring about the correction that corrective justice requires:

> The agent of this rectification is the judge. . . . Aristotle compares the judge to a geometer. We are to imagine a line divided into unequal segments. The judge is like one who re-establishes the midpoint of the line . . . By splitting the line into two equal parts, the judge vindicates quantitative equality. (65)

Nonetheless, the temptation should be resisted. Elsewhere in *The Idea of Private Law*, and more explicitly in later work (2008), Weinrib clearly assumes that there are substantive duties to pay damages, and he explains these duties as transformed versions of the substantive duty that was breached. It remains somewhat unclear, at least to me (Smith (2014)), how this explanation fits with the idea that damages restore the parties' prior equality, but it is clear that for Weinrib corrective justice is something more than the private law analogue of retributive justice. More generally, the term 'corrective justice' is often understood today to refer to any non-utilitarian (or 'rights-based') theory of private law.

[66] Hershowitz (2014) makes this point in a discussion of *Alcorn v Mitchell* [1872] 63 Ill. 553. In *Alcorn*, the court ordered the defendant, who had spat on the plaintiff, to pay the plaintiff what was a huge sum for the time ($1,000). The court explicitly described the damages as 'vindictive' (554). Hershowitz writes, 'When the jury found Alcorn liable for battery, it marked his conduct as a wrong . . . And when it awarded substantial damages, it said something about how serious that wrong was. . . . By attaching substantial damages to its verdict, the jury made its message unmistakable: Alcorn's conduct was wrong, and seriously so. That message still comes through loud and clear today, in no small part because the damages were so generous. Damages can do many things beyond express the jury's judgment about the gravity of a wrong. But they can do that too, and in *Alcorn*, there is no question that they did. Indeed, they did it far more effectively than any words the jury might have used to capture its judgment' (13–14).

citizens would interpret the relevant sums as prices or taxes. A parallel observation applies to wrong-based damages. A substantive duty to pay damages would be no different from a substantive duty to pay a contractual debt. Rule-based duties are all variations of 'anyone who is in such and such factual circumstances has a duty to do X'. A rule that required trespassers to pay their victims sums of money would be identical in form to the rule that requires contracting parties to perform their contractual obligations: 'anyone who enters onto another's land (anyone who enters into an agreement) is under a duty to do X'.[67] The wrongness of the duty-precipitating event is irrelevant in such formulations. For the payment of money to be redress for a wrong, it must be clear that the payment is a response to the wrong. This message would not be clear if the payment were made pursuant to a substantive duty.

Of course, an order, standing alone, is also neutral in its purpose. However, if there is no substantive duty to do what the order requires, and if the cause of action for the order is proof of a wrong, it follows automatically that the order is a response to a wrong. More generally, where the law imposes damages through an order, then, as in the parallel case of criminal punishment, it necessarily carries a different message than an order for a sum due. Just as in the case of criminal punishments, nominal and other wrong-based damages awards are imposed by orders to make clear that the payment is redress for a wrong. A criminal fine is imposed not because the defendant failed to pay an already-imposed fine, but because the defendant committed a criminal wrong. The court-ordered fine is the law's response to the criminal wrong. Court-ordered wrong-based damages are the law's response to private wrongs.

E. Wrongs-Based Damages: A Provisional Catalogue

It follows from the classification of damages awards as either substitutionary, wrong-based, or compensatory, that a quick method for determining if an award is wrong-based is to ask whether it could plausibly be interpreted as either substitutionary or compensatory. If the answer is no, then the award is wrong-based. Thus, nominal damages are wrong-based because they cannot plausibly be explained as a close-substitute for specific relief or as compensation for the claimant's loss.

[67] The purpose of a substantive rule to the effect that 'anyone who commits a wrong has a duty to pay damages' would be clear, but the rule would fail in its basic task of providing guidance because the amount of damages payable for a wrong varies according to the wrong. The rule could be rewritten as a series of the wrong-specific rules (e.g. 'anyone who enters onto another's land/defames another/injures another commits a wrong and, for that reason, must pay X sum to the owner'). But we never see legal rules in this form because the purpose-defining middle section ('commits a wrong and, for that reason') is superfluous.

However, it is also possible to identify wrong-based damages by their characteristic features. Each of these features follows from wrong-based awards' structural similarities to criminal punishment. The first and most obvious feature is that the cause of action for a wrong-based award is proof of a wrong. Second, wrong-based damages are 'creative': they impose new duties on defendants, different from the duties already required by the substantive law. Third, the sums awarded as wrong-based damages are ultimately a matter of choice or convention. Fourth and finally, while the sums awarded as wrong-based damages are ultimately a matter of choice and convention, in relative terms they should reflect the wrong's seriousness. Courts should award larger sums for more serious wrongs.

What makes a wrong more serious? There is no formula for answering this question. However, broadly speaking, three factors are relevant. Each reflects the ordinary understanding of wrongs or, more strictly, of wrongfulness. The first factor is the nature and extent of the rights-infringement. Some rights are more important than other rights, and thus infringing them is a more serious wrong. Infringing a right to physical integrity is generally more serious than infringing a property right, and infringing a property right to land is generally more serious than infringing a property right in chattels. For similar reasons, repeated, sustained, or extensive infringements are more wrongful than single interferences. Falsely imprisoning someone for ten hours is a more serious wrong than falsely imprisoning someone for ten minutes.

The second factor is the defendant's conduct when committing the wrong, including, in particular, the defendant's awareness of, and motivations for, the relevant actions. Deliberate wrongs are typically more wrongful than accidental wrongs. And deliberate wrongs motivated by financial considerations (e.g. defaming someone to sell more newspapers) are typically worse than wrongs done out of anger.

The third and final factor is the wrong's consequences. The more significant a wrong's negative consequences, the more serious the wrong. It is a more serious wrong to smash a pianist's fingers than a singer's fingers. Of course, it may just be bad luck that the person whose fingers I smashed is a pianist. Or it may be bad luck that I smashed her fingers at all—perhaps I was just trying to give her a bad scare and she moved her fingers at the last moment. But assessments of wrongfulness always depend on consequences that are at least partly a matter of luck.[68] We condemn careless drivers who cause injuries more severely than we condemn those who are lucky enough not to cause an injury. A completed murder is more serious than a mere attempt, even if the attempt failed through chance. In any event, unless we are to disregard an action's consequences entirely, it is impossible to eliminate

[68] '[T]he risk of bad luck is inherent in the basic form of responsibility in any society': Honoré (1999) 14. See also Williams (1981); Nagel (1979); Ripstein (1999) 269–70; Gardner (2001) 127; Cane (2002) 66.

luck from assessments of wrongfulness. Every consequence, even the apparently most predictable consequence, is at least partly a matter of luck. If I stick out my foot to trip you, it is likely that you will fall—but it is not certain. You may be lucky, and regain your balance. However, if you fall, I will have committed a worse wrong than if you did not fall.

In the following sections, I discuss ten categories of wrong-based damages awards. There are probably other examples, but for my purposes, it is sufficient to idenfity a non-trivial number of wrong-based awards. It should also be kept in mind that some of the categories are poorly defined. What one court might describe as 'aggravated damages' another might describe as 'exemplary damages' and yet a third as 'damages for pain and suffering'. The fluidity of these categories is neither significant nor surprising if, as I contend, these awards are all variations on a single theme. Finally, I mentioned above that some writers argue that, contrary to my interpretation, these awards are actually compensatory or restitutionary. I do not address such arguments individually, but in cases where they have been put forward I explain why the award is neither compensatory nor restitutionary.

i. Nominal Damages

As I have already suggested, an award of nominal damages is a clear example of a wrong-based remedy. The only fact that claimants must prove to obtain nominal damages is that one of their substantive rights was infringed by the defendant. Consistent with this interpretation (and with the absence of a feasible conventional benchmark, such as the market price), the actual sums awarded as nominal damages vary. In England today, the norm is £5, but it was previously £2, and at all times courts have departed from the norm.[69] If courts awarded significant sums under this heading, concerns for the rule of law and proportionality would likely lead them to develop guidelines stipulating appropriate sums. But precisely because nominal damages are nominal, these concerns are not significant. And the reason that nominal damages are nominal is that the wrongs to which they respond may be trivial. A trespass to land is frequently momentary, innocent (unintended and not careless), and causes no harm.

It seems clear that nominal damages awards are neither substitutes for specific relief nor compensation for the claimant's losses. The courts agree. They explicitly describe such awards as symbolic: 'battery or trespass to the person is actionable without proof that the victim has suffered anything other than the infringement

[69] Edelman (2018) 409–10; Pearce & Halson (2008) 76. Courts occasionally award substantial sums under this heading. The trial court in *New South Wales v Stevens* [2012] NSWA 415 awarded £10,000 as nominal damages. On appeal, the sum was reduced to £100.

of his right to bodily integrity: the law vindicates that right by awarding nominal damages'.[70]

Nominal damages are only available for certain wrongs, primarily various forms of trespass to persons and property, and for breaches of contract. One possible explanations for this limitation is that it is not possible to commit the excluded torts—for example, the tort of negligence—except where the defendant's action causes a loss and, therefore, where the wrong gives rise to a liability to substantial compensatory damages. However, an alternative, and preferable, explanation is that while the wrong in these cases may be committed without causing a loss, where this happens the wrong is too trivial to merit an award of even nominal damages.[71] According to this view, although we are always legally bound to exercise reasonable care not to injure others, courts will only respond to transgressions of this duty when it leads to an injury.

ii. Exemplary Damages

A second clear example of a wrong-based remedy is exemplary ('punitive') damages. Although courts occasionally award exemplary damages to compensate for non-compensable or difficult-to-prove losses,[72] they are normally awarded for the same reason as nominal damages: because the defendant committed a private wrong. The primary difference between nominal and exemplary damages is that the latter are employed in cases where, because of the defendant's egregious conduct, the wrong is more serious.[73] For example, in *Broome v Cassell & Co Ltd*,[74] the court awarded exemplary damages against a defendant who published a known libel in the expectation that it would profit from the publication even if it were required to pay compensatory damages. Similarly, in *McMillan v Singh*,[75] the

[70] *Ashley and another v Chief Constable of Sussex Police* [2008] UKHL 25 [60] (Earlsferry LJ). See also *Kuddus v Chief Constable of Leicestershire Constabulary* [2001] UKHL 29, [63]–[65]; Burrows (2004) 589; Tettenborn (2010) 26.

[71] See Chapter 8, note 71; Smith (2015); McBride & Bagshaw (2015) 123–5.

[72] Particularly in the US, where exemplary damages are frequently awarded as compensation for legal costs: see Dobbs (1989) 888–9. The availability of exemplary damages in cases where the defendant has been criminally punished shows that they serve a different role than criminal punishment: *Borders v Commissioner of Police of the Metropolis* [2005] EWCA Civ 197. Courts sometimes justify exemplary damages partly or wholly on deterrence grounds: *Broome v Cassell & Co Ltd* [1972] AC 1027, 1073. This justification does not reduce exemplary damages to covert criminal punishment, since, as I noted earlier, wrong-based damages in general can be explained on deterrence grounds (though this is not my own explanation).

[73] See e.g. *Kuddus v Chief Constable of Leicestershire Constabulary* [2002] 2 AC 122 [89]; *A v Bottrill* [2003] 1 AC 449. Egregious behaviour can amplify wrongdoing in two ways. The first, which is the usual focus of exemplary damages, is by amplifying the wrongfulness of the defendant's conduct. The second, which is typically addressed in England by an award of aggravated damages, is by amplifying the negative consequences of the defendant's conduct, in particular the intangible consequences. I discuss aggravated damages below.

[74] [1972] AC 1027.

[75] [1984] 17 HLR 120.

court awarded exemplary damages against a landlord who ejected a tenant and his belongings so that he could rent the room to a higher paying tenant. A final example is *Whiten v Pilot Insurance Co*,[76] where the Supreme Court of Canada awarded exemplary damages against an insurer who tried to escape a valid claim under the parties' contract by stalling and browbeating the claimant. As is typical where courts award exemplary damages, the defendants in these cases treated the claimants as, in effect, property. The court responded by awarding damages far in excess of the claimant's loss.

There is no formula for determining the magnitude of exemplary awards: courts and, where they are used, juries enjoy considerable discretion.[77] The only clear principle is that the sum should reflect the egregiousness of the defendant's behaviour.[78] The more egregious the behaviour, the larger the award.

In England, exemplary damages have historically been restricted to a small number of torts.[79] In principle, this limitation (which other jurisdictions have dropped[80]) is difficult to justify, although in practice most cases where exemplary awards are appropriate fall within the historical categories. In addition, where a meritorious case falls outside the historical categories, English courts can often substitute a functionally similar award of aggravated damages (see the discussion below on pain and suffering awards).

iii. Vindicatory Damages: An Introduction

The above interpretation of nominal and exemplary damages is hardly radical. Although courts and commentators may not use the label 'wrong-based', they typically explain these awards in substantively similar terms. In *A v Bottrill*, the Privy Council described exemplary damages as 'an emphatic vindication of the [claimant's] rights'.[81] Courts use similar language, as we saw, to

[76] 2002 SCC 18. In *Whiten*, the action was in contract, which would not support an exemplary award in England: see note 79 and related text.

[77] *Rookes v Barnard* [1964] AC 1129, 1227; *Gray v Motor Accident Commission* [1998] 196 CLR 1, 9 [20].

[78] Courts also take into account the defendant's wealth: *John v MGN Ltd* [1997] QB 586 (CA) 625. Although the defendant's wealth is unrelated to the egregiousness of his behaviour, it is relevant when determining the appropriate response to his wrongdoing. If damages are meant to restore something like a 'moral balance' between the parties, the defendant must suffer a proportionate loss of liberty (which, in money terms, must be larger for wealthier defendants). Consistent with this interpretation, courts consider the defendant's wealth when setting criminal law fines: s 164 *Criminal Justice Act* 2003.

[79] Specifically: torts by public officials; torts committed for profit; and torts for which there is statutory authority to award exemplary damages: *Rookes v Barnard* [1964] AC 1129, 1221.

[80] *Uren v John Fairfax & Sons Pty Ltd* [1966] 117 CLR 118 (Australia); *Vorvis v Insurance Corp of British Columbia* [1989] 1 SCR 1085 (Canada); *Taylor v Beere* [1982] 1 NZLR 81 (New Zealand). The limitation has been widely criticized: Law Commission Report No 247 (1997) Pt V.

[81] *A v Bottrill* [2003] 1 AC 449 [29]; see also Stevens (2007) 85–8; Goldberg (2006) 460–1.

describe nominal damages ('the law vindicates that right by awarding nominal damages'.[82]).

However, my classification of the other awards discussed in this section as wrong-based is controversial. Although some courts and commentators share my interpretation (though, again, they typically express themselves in different language),[83] the more common view is that most of these awards are compensatory or restitutionary,[84] and, further, that where they are not compensatory or restitutionary they are mistakes.

Courts and commentators describe the awards discussed in this section using a variety of labels. The label adopted here—'vindicatory damages'—should be used with care. The replicative remedies discussed in Chapter 6 could easily be described as vindicatory: they vindicate rights by ordering defendants to comply with them. Indeed, all remedies are vindicatory in some sense. A restitutionary order vindicates the claimant's right to obtain that order. However, the label is usually associated with damages awards that are neither compensatory nor substitutive.[85] In the scheme defended here, such awards are necessarily wrong-based.

The various sub-categories of vindicatory damages are similar to nominal damages—and different from both exemplary damages and (as we shall see) damages for pain and suffering—in that their magnitude is determined primarily by the importance of the infringed right. Like the cause of action for nominal damages, the cause of action for vindicatory damages is simply proof of a rights-infringement; however, the sums awarded under this heading are substantial because of the right's significance.

As is true generally of wrong-based damages, the actual sums awarded as vindicatory damages are ultimately a matter of choice. However, in many cases that choice has been curtailed by conventions. These conventions reflect the importance, mentioned earlier, of external factors such as the rule of law and proportionality. They also reflect the availability of obvious, proportionate, and practically feasible benchmarks (such as the 'market price'). Similar benchmarks are not available for nominal or exemplary damages.

[82] *Ashley and another v Chief Constable of Sussex* Police [2008] UKHL 25 [60] (Earlsferry LJ).

[83] See e.g. *Marathon Asset Management LLP v Seddon* [2017] EWHC 300, [202], where Leggatt J said that a gain-based award could be considered compensatory only if compensation were defined merely to mean 'redress for wrongdoing'.

[84] See e.g. Chadwick LJ in *WWF World Life Fund for Nature v World Wrestling Federation Entertainment Inc* [2008] 1 WLR 445 [25]–[56]; Clarke LJ in *One Step (Support) Ltd v Morris-Garner* [2018] 2 WLR 1353

[85] Judicial usage is broadly consistent with the meaning adopted here, although the courts have only applied the concept to a narrow range of cases: see *Attorney-General of Trinidad and Tobago v Ramanoop* [2006] 1 AC 328; *Lumba v Secretary of State for the Home Department* [2012] 1 AC 245. On vindicatory damages generally, see Varuhas (2014); Pearce & Halson (2008) 73; Witzleb & Carroll (2009) 28–31; McBride & Bagshaw (2015) 839–50; Barker (2013) 59. This section draws on these works and on Stevens (2007) 59–92; Goldberg (2006) 435; and Hershowitz (2014).

iv. User Damages

If I use your land or other property without permission, you can obtain an order that I pay you the market rental rate for the property. For example, if I unlawfully occupy your apartments, you can obtain damages equal to the apartments' rental rate for the occupied period. [86] 'User damages' are not compensatory as they are available where the wrongful use caused no loss.[87] Nor are user damages restitutionary: again, the claimant need not suffer a loss; further, the defendant need not have made a gain. The only thing that claimants need to prove is that the defendant used their property without permission. In other words, the only thing they need to prove is a wrong.

User damages are set at the market rental rate because it provides a predictable, proportionate, and easily-administered measure of the defendant's wrongdoing. More generally, awarding the market rate is an obvious and natural way to represent the infringement in a market economy. If the infringement is done in an egregious fashion or if it leads to pecuniary or non-pecuniary harms, other responses are available. But a market value award is a prima facie appropriate way to mark the mere breach of a property right. The market rate is not a measure of the claimant's loss because it is available regardless of whether the defendant's actions prevented the claimant from renting the property to someone else.

It is not possible to combine user damages with compensatory damages. In principle, there should be no objection to such combinations; for example, exemplary damages may be combined with compensatory damages. However, the combination of user damages and compensatory damages will typically impose disproportionate burdens on defendants. If claimants seek damages in excess of the market rental rate they must show that they suffered compensable harms that exceed that rate.

v. Waiver Damages

If you breach a negative duty owed to me, I may be able to obtain damages set at the sum that a reasonable person would have accepted to waive that duty. For example, in *Wrotham Park Estate Co Ltd v Parkside Homes Ltd*,[88] the defendant breached a

[86] *Inverugie Investments Ltd v Hackett* [1995] 3 All ER 84. The same principle has been applied where the defendant's wrongful act prevented the claimant from using its property. In *The SS Valeria* [1922] 2 AC 242, the Court of Appeal awarded the market rental rate in respect of a vessel that was disabled due to the defendant's negligence; the court refused to make a deduction for the likelihood that the vessel would not have been rented the full period.

[87] *Inverugie Investments Ltd v Hackett* [1995] 3 All ER 84; *Strand Electric Engineering Co Ltd v Brisford Entertainment Ltd* [1952] 2 QB 246; *Rodocanachi Sons & Co v Milburn Bros* [1887] 18 QBD 67; *Whitwham v Westminister Brymbo Coal & Coke Co* [1896] 2 Ch 538; *Penarth Dock Engineering Co Ltd v Pounds* [1963] 1 Lloyd's Rep 359.

[88] [1974] 1 WLR 798; affirmed in *One Step (Support) Ltd v Morris-Garner* [2018] 2 WLR 1353 [30].

covenant that limited development on a property purchased from the claimant. The court ordered the defendant to pay a sum set at the amount that a reasonable person in the claimant's position would have charged to waive the covenant.[89]

Waiver damages are closely related to user damages. Like user damages, they are available merely on proof of a wrong; the claimant need not have suffered a loss. Although waiver damages are sometimes described as 'negotiated damages', they are available regardless of whether, and if so at what price, the claimant would have negotiated a waiver. The sum awarded—the 'reasonable waiver fee'—is a variant of the market rate amount that is awarded in user damages cases. Although there is no market for restrictive covenants, there are markets for the rights that are their subject matter. Prior to obtaining the covenant, the claimant in *Wrotham Park* could have sold the right to do what the defendant eventually did on its land. The sum awarded in *Wrotham Park* corresponds roughly to the sum that this right would have obtained on the market. The primary difference between user and waiver damages is that the former are awarded for temporary property-rights infringements and the latter for permanent property-rights infringements.

vi. Market-Price Damages

Similar remedies are available where the defendant breached a contractual promise to provide goods.[90] A vendor who fails to deliver promised goods is liable to pay damages set at the goods' market price.[91] Likewise, a vendor who delivers defective goods is liable to pay damages set at the difference in market value between the goods as delivered and the goods as promised.[92] Recently, this principle was extended to a contract for services: the claimant, who had hired the use of a Formula One racing car for a minimum of 6,000 kilometres but was only allowed to use the car for 2,000 kilometres, was awarded the market value of a 6,000-kilometre rental without having to prove that he suffered any loss or intangible harm.[93] Tort cases are more varied, but many display the same pattern.[94] A defendant who converts or

[89] A similar award was issued in *Experience Hendrix LLC v PPX Enterprises Inc* [2003] EWCA Civ 323, where the defendant breached a contractual promise limiting the ways in which it could use recordings that it had obtained from the claimant.

[90] See generally Stevens (2009) 177; Edelman (2018) 775. Courts sometimes take the same approach to contracts for services or money. In the Canadian case of *Smith v Landstar Properties Inc*, 2011 BCCA 44, the court awarded the difference between the market rate for a secured loan (which the claimant had been promised) and an unsecured loan (which he received), even though the breach caused no loss.

[91] *Sale of Goods Act* 1979, s 51(3); *Williams Bros v Ed T Agius Ltd* [1914] AC 510.

[92] *Slater v Hoyle & Smith* Ltd [1920] 2 KB 11.

[93] *Van der Garde v Force India Formula One Team Ltd* [2010] EWHC 2373.

[94] McBride & Bagshaw (2015) 839–50. Tort awards for damage or loss of property are rarely limited to the actual loss if that loss is less than the market value: Tettenborn (2010) 288–90.

damages the claimant's goods is liable to pay damages set at, respectively, the goods' market value or the difference in market value.[95]

Where a defendant has destroyed, converted, or not provided goods, the claimant typically suffers a consequential loss at least equal to the goods' market value. But this is not always the case. For example, a vendor may be able to use or sell defective goods at no loss. In the cases cited in the footnotes to this section, the claimants' losses were less than the market value. As these cases illustrate, market-price damages are available regardless of whether the claimant suffers a loss. As with user damages and negotiated damages, market price damages are available simply on proof that the claimant's rights were infringed.

vii. Gain-Based Damages

As understood here, an award of damages is gain-based if its magnitude is determined by the pecuniary gain that the defendant made from its breach. Clear examples of gain-based damages awards for torts or contract breaches are rare.[96] Although user damages and waiver damages are sometimes described as gain-based, they are available, as we have just seen, where the defendant made no gain from its wrong. Until recently, the only wrongs for which gain-based awards were clearly available involved the use or sale of another's property.[97] For example, in the famous American case of *Edwards v Lee's Administrators*,[98] the defendant profited by charging tourists to visit the Great Onyx cave in Kentucky. Although the defendant owned the land on which the entrance was situated, part of the cave that was shown extended under the claimant's land. The claimant sued, and the court ordered the defendant to hand over the portion of his profits that could be attributed to the use of the defendant's land. In 2001, a similar remedy was awarded for the first time for profits gained through a breach of contract. In *Attorney General v Blake*,[99] the defendant, a double agent who had fled to Russia, was ordered to hand over the profits from a book that he wrote in contravention of a contractual non-disclosure covenant.

Neither of these awards were compensatory. In *Lee*, the defendant's actions had no effect on the claimant's use of his land (the defendant could not show his part

[95] *Kuwait Airways Corp v Iraqi Airways Co* [2002] 2 AC 883; *The Charlotte* [1908] P 206; *The Sanix Ace* [1987] 1 Lloyd's Rep 465; Tettenborn (2010) 29.

[96] Though outside this book's scope, a gain-based 'account of profits' award is available for an equitable wrong (e.g. breach of fiduciary duty) and for a variety of intellectual property torts, such as breach of copyright or passing off, that trace their roots to Equity: see Burrows (2004) 384.

[97] *Kuwait Airways Corp v Iraqi Airways Co (Nos 4 & 5)* [2002] 2 AC 883, 1093; *Oughton v Seppings* (1830) 109 ER 776; *Powell v Aiken* (1858) 70 ER 144; *Chesworth v Farrar* [1967] 1 QB 407; Burrows (2004) 375–95; Edelman (2018) 487–94.

[98] [1936] 96 SW 2d 1028.

[99] [2001] 1 AC 268; followed in *Esso Petroleum Co Ltd v Niad Ltd* [2001] EWHC Ch 458.

of the cave to tourists as there was no entrance on his land); in *Blake*, the government suffered no loss because of the defendant's publication (the information was already in the public realm). Nor can either award be interpreted as a disguised restitutionary remedy, or at least they cannot be interpreted in this way if (as I assume throughout this chapter) restitutionary means returning something, or its value, to the claimant. The profits earned by the defendants in *Lee* and *Blake* were not earned from the claimants; nor did the claimants have a right to them prior to the court order.

It might be thought that these awards are responses to injustices, not wrongs, in that they are responses to the defendant having made a profit that, in fairness, belongs to the claimant. Certainly, the defendant has no right to a wrongfully earned profit. But it is not clear in what sense it can be said that the ill-gotten profit belongs to the claimant or even that it should belong to the claimant. The profit that the defendant made in *Blake* would not have gone to the government if he had kept his contractual promise. Had the defendant kept his promise the book would never have been published. The same is true of the cases where the defendants profited through the use or sale of the claimant's property. If the defendants in these cases had complied with their substantive duties, no one would have made the profits they made. Of course, in some cases involving the wrongful use or sale of another's property the defendant's wrongdoing will prevent the claimant from making a similar profit. Your wrongful use of my property, for instance your wrongful use of my truck, might prevent me from using that property in a similar way and thereby earning a similar profit. However, in such cases, I can obtain compensatory damages for the losses I suffer (in the form of foregone profits) because of your wrong. In the cases where courts award gain-based damages, such losses cannot be proven. And in many cases, it is not possible for the claimant to have made an equivalent profit. In *Lee*, there was no way of accessing the cave from the claimant's land

Like the previous examples, gain-based awards therefore appear to be responses to the defendant's wrongdoing. As in *Lee* and *Blake,* they are awarded in respect of deliberate wrongdoing, and they are awarded for wrongs that, under English law, do not support exemplary or aggravated damages. Although the sums awarded under this heading may be significant, by definition they do not exceed the defendant's gain. A gain-based award is thus a predictable and proportionate response to the defendant's wrong. And like the market-price, the defendant's gain is an obvious and natural mark of the relevant wrong: it represents the very thing that the defendant obtained through her wrongdoing. [100]

[100] Further, gain-based awards are plausibly interpreted, in most cases, as a variant of a market-price award in that the defendant's gain is normally equal to the price that, were it possible for the defendant to sell the right that it was infringing, the defendant could have obtained for the infringed right. For example, in *Blake* the right to publish the defendant's memoir, if alienable, would presumably have fetched a price roughly equal to the profits that sales of the memoir could have been expected to generate.

viii. Non-Pecuniary Damages for Wrongs to the Person

Unsurprisingly, the courts' responses to wrongs to the person are more complex than their responses to wrongs to property. However, it is clear that courts frequently award substantial damages in cases where the claimant suffered no loss or only a minor loss.[101] The main difference between these awards and the awards discussed above is that the courts do not have the option, in these cases, of using a market-price measure of damages. There is no market for 'not being battered' or for other non-infringements of personal rights. The consequence is that courts enjoy considerable discretion when assessing wrong-based responses to wrongs to the person.

Courts have long awarded substantial damages for the tort of wrongful imprisonment without requiring proof that the claimant suffered a pecuniary loss or even pain and suffering.[102] In such cases, damages are available 'to vindicate personal liberty, rather than as compensation for loss per se'.[103] Courts take a similar approach in defamation cases.[104] Justice Windeyer's words are often quoted: '[A] man defamed does not get compensation for his damaged reputation. He gets damage because he was injured in his reputation, that is, simply because he was publicly defamed'.[105] Similar again are actions for what is typically called—though the terminology and indeed the entire concept is still evolving—the 'misuse of private information',[106] where courts have given large sums, sometimes explicitly described as vindicatory, far in excess of any amount that could be considered compensatory.[107] In battery cases, it is more difficult to identify a distinctive wrong-based head of damages, but, again, courts often award claimants substantial damages even when no loss was proven.[108] The same is true of claims for malicious

[101] See Stevens (2007) 62–3.

[102] *R v Governor of Brockhill Prison, ex p Evans (No 2)* [1999] QB 1043 1060; *Huckle v Money* (1762) 2 Wils KB 206, 95 ER 768. The recent decision in *Lumba v Secretary of State for the Home Department* [2011] UKSC 12 places the status of the wrongful imprisonment decisions in doubt.

[103] *Ruddock v Taylor* (2005) 222 CLR 612 [147]. See also *Petticrew v Chief Constable Royal Ulster Constabulary* [1988] NI 192, 204 ('any detention even for a very short period, is not insignificant and deserves something more than mere nominal damages for a technical imprisonment': O'Donnell LJ)); *Iqbal v POA* [2010] QB 732 [83], ('the tort is actionable without proof of damage. It follows in my view that the circumstances in which nominal damages would be appropriate are rare almost to vanishing point': Smith LJ).

[104] *Tripp v Thomas* [1824] 3 B & C 427; *Reynolds v Times Newspapers Ltd* [1998] 3 WLR 862.

[105] *Uren v John Fairfax & Sons* [1966] 117 CLR 118, 150. See also *Neville v London Express Newspapers Ltd* [1919] AC 368, 932 ('every violation of a right imports damage': Viscount Haldane). Vindication is explicitly recognized as a head of damages for defamation, and often grounds substantial awards: see Edelman (2018) 1569–70. In *Metropolitan International Schools Ltd v Designtechnica Corporation* [2010] EWHC 2411, the court awarded £50,000 for vindication in a case where there was no provable pecuniary loss and no possible injury to feelings as the claimant was a company.

[106] See *Google Inc v Vidal-Hall* [2015] EWCA Civ 311.

[107] See e.g. *Mosley v News Group Newspapers Ltd* [2008] EMLR 20, 679.

[108] See e.g. *Hurst v Picture Theatres Ltd* [1915] 1 KB 1; *B v NHS Hospital Trust* [2002] 2 All ER 449; *Pelling v Johnson* [2004] EWHC 492. In *Ashley v Chief Constable of Sussex Police* [2008] 1 AC 962, Lord Scott suggested that a vindicatory award for battery might be awarded to the estate of a man shot dead during a police raid.

prosecution.[109] In all of these cases, the courts refer to the nature of the wrong and to awards in other cases when determining the quantum of damages. But there is no formulae. As with an award of exemplary damages, it is not possible to explain why falsely imprisoning the claimant for a day merits an award of, say, £1000, rather than, say, £500.

ix. Miscellaneous

Some of the clearest examples of wrong-based damages awards do not fall under a general rule. For example, in *Ashby v White*,[110] the defendant wrongfully prevented the claimant from voting. Holt CJ awarded substantial damages, far in excess of any loss that the claimant might possibly have suffered (the claimant's candidate won). '[A]n injury', Holt CJ wrote, 'imports a damage, when a man is thereby hindered of his rights'.[111] Closely related to *Ashby* are two recent cases in which courts awarded similar damages—explicitly described as 'vindicatory'—for the infringement of the claimant's constitutional rights.[112] Though the rights at issue were strictly speaking public law rights, they were similar to those infringed in *Ashby v White* and in the false imprisonment cases. And in both cases, the relevant actions were, with minor exceptions, torts. Wrongs committed by the state are often more serious than ordinary wrongs (which explains the courts' relative willingness to award non-compensatory damages for constitutional wrongs), but insofar as the wrong is done to a specific individual, it is similar to the other wrongs discussed here. English courts have long employed tort law to protect what other courts usually describe as constitutional rights.[113]

With the exception of damages for pain and suffering and market price awards, wrong-based remedies are not generally available for the tort of negligence. However, there are notable exceptions. In *Rees v Darlington Memorial Hospital NHS Trust*,[114] the defendant's negligence led to the birth of an unwanted baby. The court ordered the defendant to pay substantial damages to the claimant mother. Lord Bingham stressed that the award was not compensatory (the court explicitly refused compensation for the cost of bringing up the child), but was instead given to 'afford some measure of recognition of the wrong done'.[115] Similarly, in *Chester v Ashfar*,[116] the court awarded the claimant a 'modest solatium' for the paralysis that

[109] *Quartz Hill Consolidated Gold Mining Co v Eyre* [1883] 11 QBD 674. Exemplary damages are also available in such cases, providing an alternative route to the same end.

[110] [1703] 92 ER 126.

[111] Ibid 137.

[112] *Attorney-General of Trinidad and Tobago v Ramanoop* [2006] 1 AC 328; *Merson v Cartwright* [2006] 3 LRC 264; [2005] UKPC 38.

[113] Famously, *Entick* v *Carrington* [1765] 2 Wils KB 275.

[114] [2004] 1 AC 309.

[115] Ibid 8.

[116] [2005] 1 AC 134

she suffered following an operation. The paralysis was a coincidental consequence of the defendant's negligent act (failing to warn the claimant of the 1–2% risk of paralysis) and, as the court accepted, would normally have been considered too remote to merit compensation. Echoing Lord Bingham's language in *Rees*, Lord Hope wrote, 'The function of the law is to enable rights to be vindicated and to provide remedies when duties have been breached'.[117]

Similar reasoning appears to underlie certain contract awards.[118] In *Ruxley Electronics and Construction Ltd v Forsyth*,[119] discussed earlier, the claimant was awarded £2,500 for the defendant's failure to build a pool to the specified depth, notwithstanding that the difference had no effect on the pool's value or use. Some of the court's observations suggest that this award was intended to compensate for the claimant's loss of enjoyment. However, no evidence of such loss was introduced or assumed. It appears that the award was simply a response to the defendant's wrong.

x. Pain and Suffering

Damages for pain and suffering are difficult to explain if, as most theories of damages assume, damages are meant to undo, eliminate, or otherwise compensate for losses.[120] Pain and suffering is a subjective feeling, not a loss. For the same reason, pain and suffering cannot be undone or eliminated or compensated by money awards except in a metaphorical sense. Money cannot buy happiness. And even if it could, there is no way to determine what sum is sufficient to counterbalance a claimant's pain and suffering. As judges routinely observe, the sums awarded under this heading are 'notional or theoretical compensation to take the place of that which is not possible, namely, actual compensation'.[121] Of course, here, as elsewhere, courts should, and do, try to achieve a measure of consistency. Similar levels of pain and suffering (assuming such assessments can be made at all) should attract similar levels of damages. But in absolute terms the sums are arbitrary: 'there is no reason, in logic or economics, why for a specified period of suffering the award should be £100 rather than £1000 or indeed any other figure'.[122]

[117] Ibid [87].

[118] See Pearce & Halson (2008).

[119] [1996] AC 344.

[120] See e.g. Priest (1987) 1546–7, 1553; Cooter (1989) 39. Ripstein does not specifically discuss damages for pain and suffering, but his view that our rights are rights to our 'means' and that damages are meant to uphold that right does not accommodate them: Ripstein (2007) 29–52, 233–5, 252. Our mental state is a not a 'means'. Weinrib's broadly similar view—namely, that 'to recover in tort, the plaintiff's injury must be something, such as personal integrity or proprietary entitlement, that ranks as the embodiment of a right', and that damages are meant to rectify any injury to such rights—leads to the same conclusion: Weinrib (1995) 134, 135–6.

[121] *Heil v Rankin* [2001] QB 272, 293. See also *British Transport Commission v Gourley* [1956] AC 185, 208; *H West & Son Ltd v Shephard* [1964] AC 326, 346; *Andrews v Grand & Toy Alberta Ltd* [1978] 83 DLR (3d) 452, 475.

[122] Edelman (2018) 1402.

The arbitrariness of pain and suffering awards is no surprise if these awards are responses to the defendant's wrongdoing. There is no 'market rate' (or any other plausible benchmark) for the absence of pain and suffering. The *Guidelines* mentioned earlier are intended to provide a measure of consistency in the awards issued for what might be called the ordinary loss of enjoyment arising from the loss of a limb or similar injury. But they provide no guidance in respect of the amounts available for actual pain and suffering, and they apply only to certain sources of pain and suffering. For example, sexual assaults are not amongst the 'injuries' listed in the *Guidelines*. The sums awarded for pain and suffering are effectively picked out of the air.[123]

The extent of a claimant's pain and suffering is often unrelated to the defendant's moral culpability. A momentary lapse of judgment may lead to massive distress. But as we saw above, moral culpability is only one factor in assessing a wrong's wrongfulness. Wrongs that have significant negative consequences are more serious—more wrongful—than wrongs that have trivial consequences, regardless of the defendant's culpability. And the relevant negative consequences may include consequential pain and suffering. A battery that leads to significant pain and suffering is a more serious wrong than a battery that causes minimal pain and suffering, and this is true even if the wrongdoer intentions were the same in each case. Damages for pain and suffering are a response to this aspect of wrongfulness.

However, while the defendant's culpability is generally irrelevant when assessing damages for pain and suffering, it is indirectly relevant in cases where the wrongdoer's intentions and awareness exacerbate the victim's pain and suffering. An assault or other wrong that is intended to humiliate the victim will frequently have just this effect. In such cases, English courts frequently award additional damages under the heading of 'aggravated damages' rather than 'pain and suffering' (or under the heading of exemplary damages awards).[124] Some writers have argued that aggravated damages are a response to a new tort of, roughly, disrespecting others.[125] But whether the relevant behaviour constitutes its own wrong or magnifies the wrongfulness of another wrong, aggravated damages remain a response to a wrong. Humiliation is not a loss, and damages cannot undo or eliminate a humiliating experience. But wrongs are more wrongful if they are accompanied by humiliation.

Closely related to damages for pain and suffering are so-called 'loss of amenity' awards, which are issued on proof of permanent physical injuries, such

123 '[N]o yardstick exists for measuring in money the compensation to be accorded a given amount of physical pain or mental suffering': Edelman (2018) 1402. See also Peel & Goudkamp (2014) 712.

124 See Murphy (2010) 353. Murphy interprets aggravated damages as compensation for harm to dignitary interests, and so distinct from an award for pain and suffering.

125 Birks (1997a) 1.

as the loss of a limb or an eye, and which are intended to respond not to pain and suffering per se but to victims' inability to pursue activities and generally lead their lives as they would have otherwise. The claimants in these cases typically suffer pecuniary losses as well as pain and suffering. However, it is not necessary to prove either to obtain loss of amenity damages.[126] In the words of Lord Pearce, 'If a claimant has lost a leg, the court approaches the matter on the basis that he has suffered a serious physical deprivation no matter what his condition of temperament or state of mind may be.'[127] Courts have awarded loss of amenity damages to claimants who were rendered permanently unconscious or whose only 'loss' was a reduction in life expectancy.[128] Indeed, some of the highest awards have been granted to claimants for whom, because of their brain-damage, the award cannot make a difference in their subjective life experience.[129] Consistent with the classification of such awards as wrong-based, their magnitude was traditionally left to the discretion of judges and juries.[130] Today, English courts follow guidelines published by the Judicial Studies Board,[131] but no one supposes that it is possible to explain why the loss of an eye merits a minimum of £39,150 rather than, say, £49,150.[132] Indeed, the standardization of the sums awarded for an eye or a limb makes clear that these sums are not meant to reflect claimants' losses or their pain and suffering as those consequences will vary from claimant to claimant. Claimants who have lost their hearing, sight, or taste are awarded the standard sum even if they are unlikely to experience the loss as much as the average person (or even if they experience the 'loss' as a benefit) because of their stoic attitude, general capacities, or their family's assistance.[133] The same principle is applied to awards for loss of amenity arising from the loss of a body part. Claimants can obtain additional damages if they prove that the injury affected them more than the average person (e.g. if it leads to special psychological problems), but proof of consequential loss is not required to obtain the standard amount.[134]

[126] Loss of amenity awards typically include non-earmarked sums for pain and suffering: Peel & Goudkamp (2014) 712.

[127] *West & Son Ltd v Shepherd* [1964] 1 AC 326, 365.

[128] *Wise v Kaye* [1962] 1 QB 638; *West & Son Ltd v Shepherd* [1964] 1 AC 326; *Lim Poh Choo v Camden and Islington AHA* [1980] AC 174.

[129] Tettenborn (2010) 592.

[130] Edelman (2018) 1404–9; Peel & Goudkamp (2014) 712.

[131] Judicial College (Guidelines) (2012).

[132] The Guidelines provide a range, and make clear that the amount awarded within that range should reflect, inter alia, mental distress caused by the injury and other non-pecuniary consequences. However, it is presumed that the minimum will be awarded regardless of consequences.

[133] 'The complete loss of sight may bring, and I think often does, a serenity and calm of life which might lead to a happiness hitherto unknown, but I cannot think that a defendant is entitled to pray that in aid in order to reduce the damages he has to pay to the sufferer': *Wise v Kaye* [1962] 1 QB 638, 651 (Sellers LJ)

[134] Judicial College (Guidelines) 47.

F. The Variety of Wrongs-Based Damages

In the preceding section, I argued that a variety of damages awards are responses to wrongs. But why is there 'a variety'? The common law has a single response to 'unfair losses'—compensatory damages (or so I argue in Chapter 8). Why has it not developed a comparable response to wrongs? There appear to be three main reasons. These have been mentioned already, but it may be helpful to repeat them here as each reflects one of this chapter's themes.

First, wrongs vary in their wrongfulness, and this variance is a function of at least three factors: the importance of the relevant right; the defendant's conduct; and the wrong's consequences, both pecuniary and non-pecuniary. Further, there is no formula for quantifying and aggregating these factors. In short, it is difficult to develop general and predictable standards for assessing wrongfulness.

The second reason is that even if measurable criteria for assessing wrongfulness could be developed, there is no uniquely appropriate way for courts to respond to such assessments. In principle, courts could legitimately respond to wrongs in a variety of ways. Courts should, of course, try to ensure that their responses are predictable and proportionate. Similar wrongs call for similar damages awards, and more serious wrongs call for larger awards. In response to these concerns, courts and legislature have achieved a measure of predictability in some wrong-based awards. Still, the absence of a uniquely appropriate response to wrongs has meant that the common law's already-strong inclination towards localized predictability is particularly evident in this area. In short, because the different measures of wrong-based damages are, in the end, determined by choice and convention, courts have been more accepting of variance between those measures than they might have otherwise been.

Finally, widespread misunderstandings about the role of damages awards have undoubtedly contributed to the messiness of the law governing wrong-based damages. Particularly in their less guarded pronouncements, courts and commentators often suggest that the aim of all damages awards is, or at least should be, compensation for loss.[135] Given such pronouncements, it is hardly surprising that courts and commentators have devoted little effort to rationalizing the awards that do not fit this model.

[135] Famously, '[the measure of damages is] that sum of money which will put the party who has been injured or has suffered, in the same position as he would have been in if he had not sustained the wrong for which he is now getting his compensation or reparation': *Livingstone v Rawyards Coal Co* [1880] 5 App Cas 25, 39 (Lord Blackburn). This proposition accurately describes compensatory (but only compensatory) damages.

G. Compensatory Damages?

As understood here, compensatory damages are awards (or parts of them) that are issued on proof of, and set at the value of, consequential pecuniary losses—essentially out-of-pocket expenses and lost profits or earnings. Compensatory damages are therefore different from the awards discussed above, none of which are triggered by, nor set at the value of, the defendant's loss. However, it might be thought that they should be included in the above list.[136] It is orthodox law that claimants must prove a wrong to obtain compensatory damages. And if the wrongfulness of wrongs is determined partly by their consequences (as I have argued), it might seem to follow that courts should issue damages awards that respond to a wrong's pecuniary consequences. Finally, setting such awards at the amount of the claimant's pecuniary loss appears to be a natural, easily administered, and proportionate response to that loss. Nonetheless, I argue that compensatory damages are not wrong-based. I defend this position in the next chapter.

[136] As I once argued: Smith (2012) (2014).

8
Injustices

The third of the main private law causes of action recognized in the common law is an injustice. As understood here, an injustice is, roughly, an unfair loss or gain that has arisen from a transaction between the claimant and defendant. This chapter focuses on demonstrating that an injustice is the cause of action for orders to make restitution following defective transfers ('restitutionary orders') and orders to pay damages for consequential pecuniary losses ('compensatory orders'). However, there are almost certainly other examples of injustice-responding remedies. I will flag (but only flag) some possible candidates.

My classification of restitutionary and compensatory awards as injustice-responding orders rests primarily on two propositions: (1) restitutionary and compensatory awards are duty-creating (and therefore the law governing them is remedial, not substantive); and, (2) the cause of action for restitutionary and compensatory orders is neither a rights-threat nor a wrong (and therefore these orders do not belong within Chapters 6 or 7). Of course, I also argue that the cause of action for restitutionary and compensatory orders is appropriately characterized as an injustice. However, this argument is relatively brief. If the above propositions are accepted, it is difficult to imagine how one might describe the cause of action for these orders without invoking injustice or a closely related concept.

The idea of 'injustice-responding orders' is novel. Unlike 'wrong-responding orders' and 'rights-threat-responding orders', injustice-responding orders cannot easily be accommodated within the 'for every right a remedy' maxim. The suggestion that restitutionary and compensatory orders are related is even more novel. Against this background, I begin by explaining how my understanding of restitutionary and compensatory orders evolved over the course of writing this book. This explanation outlines the chapter's main themes and, at the same time, my reasons for seeking a new interpretation of restitutionary and compensatory orders. The chapter's main goal is, of course, to persuade readers to accept this interpretation. However, its secondary goal, almost as important, is to persuade readers that the questions that motivated it are important.

A. Tertium Quid

The initial motivation for this chapter was not a particular understanding of the meaning or importance of justice. Nor was it motivated by my argument (in

Rights, Wrongs, and Injustices. Stephen A. Smith, Oxford University Press (2019). © Stephen A. Smith.
DOI: 10.1093/oso/9780199229772.003.0008

Chapter 1) that justice is a special concern of remedial law: that argument applies to the entirety of remedial law. Rather, the initial motivation arose from my attempts to fit restitutionary and, later, compensatory orders into my existing categories of rights-threat-responding and wrong-responding orders.

i. Restitutionary Awards

As Peter Birks repeatedly stressed, the striking feature of restitutionary awards is that they can be obtained without an allegation that the defendant committed or threatened to commit a legal wrong. Birks illustrated this feature with the now-famous case of *Kelly v Solari*.[1] Mr Solari had died, and his wife, as the estate's executor, made a claim under his insurance policy. The insurance company paid out, but then discovered that the policy had lapsed and, therefore, that they had not been obliged to make the payment. The court ordered the widow to repay the money to the insurance company. It did not matter that Mrs Solari was also unaware that the policy had lapsed and was, in all other respects, innocent in the transaction. If the money 'is paid under the impression the truth of a fact which is untrue, it may, generally speaking, be recovered back'.[2]

Mrs Solari's liability to repay the money arose merely from her receipt of it. And, without attempting to provide anything like a theory of 'injustices', it seems clear that this receipt is plausibly described as giving rise to an injustice. Mrs Solari obtained a sum of money that would, had no mistake been made, have remained with the insurance company. The standard legal label for this event is an 'unjust enrichment'.

However, along with Birks and (so far as I could tell) other writers, I initially assumed that unjust enrichments of the kind exemplified by *Solari* gave rise first and foremost to substantive duties to make restitution. In other words, I assumed that the rules governing defective transfers were part of substantive law. In this view, the only role for remedial law is to stipulate that, if a substantive duty to make restitution is not performed, the transferee can obtain an order that it be performed.

I first questioned this assumption following the publication, in 2011, of the American *Restatement (Third) of Restitution and Unjust Enrichment*. Given my interest in the distinction between duties and liabilities, I was struck by the Restatement's practice of consistently describing unjust enrichments as giving rise to liabilities (not duties) to make restitution.[3] My doubts increased when I realised that my reasons for rejecting the existence of substantive duties to

[1] (1841) 9 M & W 54. For a more detailed discussion, upon which I draw, see Birks (2005) 5–9.
[2] (1841) 9 M & W 59.
[3] Smith (2013b).

pay damages (e.g. no damages for failing to pay damages, the unknowability of such a duty) also applied to substantive duties to make restitution. Further (and drawing upon Chapter 5's analysis of the differences between rules and orders), it seemed that the usual normative objection to restitutionary duties—namely, that they impose affirmative legal duties on innocent parties—could be avoided, or at least minimized, if those duties were imposed by orders, not rules. For these and related reasons, I came to the view that the common law does not recognize a substantive duty to make restitution. And, given that restitutionary orders are clearly not responses to wrongs, it followed, I concluded, that there are at least some orders that could not be accommodated within Chapters 7 or 8. However, my initial view was that orders to reverse defective transfers (and other analogous unjust enrichment reversing orders) were unique in this regard.

ii. Compensation for Non-Wrongs

My first clue that this view was too narrow came from reflecting on liabilities in the border areas between unjust enrichment law and tort law. In *Great Northern Railway Co v Swaffield*,[4] the defendants sent a horse for transport on the claimants' railway. The defendant had not arranged for a representative to pick up the horse at the destination station, so the claimants arranged for it to be kept in a nearby stable. When the defendants eventually picked up their horse, they refused to pay for the stable charges. The claimants paid and then sued the defendants for their expenses. The court ordered the defendant to compensate the claimants. Finding that the claimant had no choice but to stable the horse, Kelly CB held that 'a right arises in them [the claimants] to be reimbursed those charges which they have incurred for his benefit'.[5] *Swaffield* and other 'necessitous intervention' cases are similar to defective transfer cases, in that the defendant has not committed or threatened to commit a wrong. But the requirements for a defective transfer (such as a mistake) are missing, and the remedy is compensatory. In *Swaffield*, the claimant's benefit was the horse's entire value.

Another set of awards that seemed not to fit within Chapters 7 or 8 are, today, based in legislation. As I mentioned in Chapter 4, most common law jurisdictions have legislation authorizing courts to issue orders dealing with maintenance and the division of matrimonial property following the breakdown of a relationship. In England, Section 23(1)(c) of the *Matrimonial Causes Act* 1973 (the '1973 *Act*') provides that, following divorce or similar proceedings, courts

4 (1874) LR 9 Exch 132.
5 Ibid 136.

may make 'an order that either party to the marriage shall pay to the other such lump sum or sums as may be so specified'. There is no suggestion in the *Act* or elsewhere that claimants seeking such orders must show that the defendant had a duty, prior to the order, to do what the order requires, much less that the defendant breached this or any other duty owed to the claimant. In Lord Denning's words, '. . . there is no right to maintenance, or to costs, or to a secured provision, or the like, until the court makes an order directing it'.[6] Another example is an order under s 2(1) of the *Civil Liability (Contribution) Act* 1978 (the '1978 Act'). Under this Act, courts may order a defendant co-tortfeasor to pay a sum to the claimant co-tortfeasor to offset the latter's liability for damages. As with the 1973 Act, there is no suggestion in the 1978 Act that claimants seeking such orders must show that the defendant had a duty, prior to the order, to do what the order requires. Rather, s 2(1) merely stipulates that the contribution 'shall be such as may be found by the court'.

The above remedies are often ignored or marginalized by private law scholars. However, the next group on my list of 'remedies in search of a home' were difficult to ignore. In my research for Chapter 6, I noticed that courts sometimes award compensatory damages 'in lieu of specific relief' because of the substantive undesirability of the requested action (typically, its disproportionate cost). In cases like *Dennis v Ministry of Defence*,[7] *Boomer v Atlantic Cement Co*,[8] and *Tito v Waddell (No 2)*,[9] the court's decision to refuse specific relief is in substance a decision to award damages notwithstanding that the court regarded the defendant's alleged wrongdoing as permissible and, therefore, not actually a wrong. As I argued in Chapter 6, the damage awards in these cases are not responses to a rights-threat or a wrong.

Further, and unsurprisingly, such awards did not appear to be limited to cases where the claimant had requested specific relief. A famous, if unusual, example is the American case of *Vincent v Lake Erie Transportation Co.*[10] The defendant moored his ship, without permission, to the claimant's dock to prevent it being destroyed in a violent storm. The court held that, while the defendant acted entirely reasonably (there was no other way to save the ship and crew), he must nonetheless compensate the claimant for damage caused to the dock. Other cases in which the courts award compensatory damages notwithstanding that the defendant neither committed nor threatened to commit a wrong include those where the claim is based on vicarious liability, the rule in *Rylands v Fletcher*, or an innocent misrepresentation.

[6] *Sugden v Sugden* [1957] P 120, 135.
[7] [2003] EWHC 793.
[8] 26 NY 2d 219 (1970).
[9] [1977] Ch 106.
[10] [1910] 109 Minn 456.

iii. Compensation for Wrongs

The conclusion that I drew from the above cases is that a significant number of compensatory damages awards did not belong within either Chapter 6 or 8. However, my initial assumption was that these awards were outliers. I assumed that the vast majority of compensatory orders—which were indisputably directed at wrongdoers—were responses to wrongs. My view changed, however, as I developed the ideas that grew into Chapter 7. As we saw in Chapter 7, the clearest examples of wrong-responding remedies are exemplary damages and nominal damages, and the next clearest examples are a variety of awards that, like exemplary and nominal damages, are not compensatory (e.g. user damages, gain-based damages, and waiver damages). Precisely because these awards are not fixed at the claimant's loss or, as with the substitutionary awards that I discussed in Chapter 6, at the price of obtaining substitute performance, they must be responses to the defendant's wrong *qua* wrong. Further, the varied and sometimes highly discretionary approaches to quantifying these awards was exactly what we should expect if they are wrong-based. In contrast to rights-threats and injustices, there is no natural or logical response to wrongs: as in the case of criminal wrongdoing, the law's response to private wrongdoing is ultimately a matter of choice and convention.

As my research progressed, I came to the view that compensatory damages do not fit this pattern. The most obvious difference is that they are fixed at the magnitude of the claimant's loss. Moreover, the courts have developed a massively detailed set of rules for determining a sum that—if the wrong-based interpretation of compensatory orders is correct—is ultimately arbitrary. In addition, these rules limit compensatory awards in all sorts of ways—remoteness, mitigation, contributory negligence, and so forth—that appear to have nothing to do with the wrongfulness of the defendant's wrong. Finally, the courts and legislatures' descriptions and explanations of the rules for assessing compensatory orders appeared inconsistent with a wrong-based interpretation. Rather than asking whether a compensatory award is an appropriate way to mark, condemn, represent, redress, or otherwise respond to the defendant's wrongdoing, the courts and legislatures ask whether it is fair, just, or reasonable to attribute the claimant's loss to the defendant.

I eventually came to the view, then, that even in cases where defendants had committed wrongs, orders to pay compensatory damages awards were different from the wrong-based awards that I discuss in Chapter 7. But where did they belong? Not in Chapter 6, because there is no substantive duty to pay compensatory damages (and therefore no substantive right that defendants could threaten). I entertained the possibility of a fourth category; however, the similarities to the restitutionary awards in my third, yet unnamed, category were too striking. In each case, the courts' focus is the outcome of a transaction between the parties: 'When tort law holds persons responsible for outcomes, its task is primarily allocative, in the sense that assigning particular consequences to particular persons is a way of determining who will bear which costs'.[11] The same is true of defective transfer cases, except that the outcome being allocated is a gain, not a loss. And, in each case, the law's response to the undesirable outcome is to eliminate it by attributing the relevant outcome—the loss or the gain—to the other party. One significant difference, of course, is that, in the case of most compensatory damages awards, the award is conditional upon proof of a wrong. Still, it seemed to me that when these awards are compared to the wrong-based awards discussed in Chapter 7, the wrong is merely a condition, not the underlying reason, for the award. But what is that reason?

iv. The Concept of an Injustice

The answer, it seemed obvious, is that the reason for these awards must be the 'injustice' (or some closely related concept) of the relevant outcome.[12] Courts and commentators consistently explain restitutionary orders using a cognate concept ('unjust enrichment'), and courts regularly invoke justice when they are explaining the rules governing compensatory orders. The 'overall object of tort law', Lord Bingham wrote, 'is to define cases in which the law may justly hold one party liable to compensate another'.[13] More importantly, the subject matter of justice is the subject matter of the rules governing restitutionary and compensatory damages: the allocation of gains and losses. The adjective 'unjust' is characteristically used to describe states of affairs in which a loss or gain has been unfairly imposed, distributed, or allowed to persist.[14]

[11] Ripstein (2001) 47.

[12] In *Torts and Rights,* Robert Stevens distinguishes tort theories that focus on the 'infringement of rights' from theories (which Stevens criticizes) that focus on the 'infliction of loss': Stevens (2007) 1–3. It might be thought that my account of compensatory damages, which supposes that courts issue such awards in cases where no right was infringed, is, in Stevens' terminology, a loss-based account. However, my explanation of compensatory damages is not a theory of tort law or even a theory of tort damages. I agree with Stevens that the core of tort law is a set of substantive, rights-based, duties (e.g. 'everyone has a duty to take care not to injure others'). Further, I argue that most 'tort remedies' confirm such duties (e.g. injunctions), or are responses to their breach (wrong-based damages). Finally, while my account of compensatory damages assumes that their role is to re-allocate losses, its fundamental focus is injustices, not losses. As Stevens rightly notes, if tort law's aim were merely to 'compensate losses' it should almost certainly be replaced by a universal compensation scheme. Most losses are not caused by a person or anything else that could possibly qualify as a defendant in private law litigation. Rather, they are caused by illness, disease, natural events, self-inflicted accidents, and so forth. However, if (as I argue above) the role of compensatory damages is to correct injustices, then a universal compensation scheme is not an alternative route to the same end. Injustice is a relational concept. Correcting injustices always involves transferring a loss or gain from one person (or persons) to another person (or persons). Compensatory damages correct injustices by re-allocating losses, but the underlying aim is to correct injustices.

[13] *Fairchild v Glenhaven Funeral Services Ltd* [2002] UKHL 22 [9].

[14] See, generally, Gardner (2012) 6–7, upon which I have drawn heavily. See also Hart (1961) 157–8; Rawls (1971) 10 ('The concept of justice I take to be defined, then, by the role of its principles in assigning rights and duties and in defining the appropriate division of social advantages'); Aristotle (reprinted 1976) ('The just, then, is a species of the proportionate': 113P29).

Admittedly, the concept of an injustice is sometimes understood in a broader sense. To say that something is unjust is sometimes understood to mean nothing more than that it is undesirable and that someone, usually the state, should fix it. In this understanding, both rights-threats and wrongs qualify as injustices. However, this usage is unusual.[15] It is more common—and more useful—to describe trespasses, nuisances, and contract breaches simply as wrongs (and to describe threats to do these things as threatened wrongs). If I responded to a punch in the nose by exclaiming 'how unjust!', it might be wondered if the punch had affected my linguistic abilities. We characteristically employ the term injustice to describe actions or states of affairs that are in some sense unfair, typically because a loss or a gain (broadly understood) has been unfairly allocated, distributed, or allowed to persist. Save for the exceptional case where a punch in the nose is the outcome of a decision to allocate that punch to one of a number of potential candidates, the wrongness of punching has nothing to do with allocation. In contrast, we ask whether the tax system is just because we want to know whether it allocates the burden of taxation fairly. Similarly, we ask whether the bankruptcy laws are just because we want to know if they fairly allocate bankrupt individuals' assets. And we ask whether a judicial decision was just because we want to know if the proper parties won and lost. Justice is central to law because adjudication is central to law—and adjudication is always about allocation.[16] In the law, to say that something is unjust is nearly always to say that it is unfair.

Thus understood, injustice remains a broad concept. Is it too broad to do any explanatory work? It seemed clear that the explanations for why the outcomes that trigger restitutionary and compensatory orders are unjust would be very different. The facts that must be proven to obtain restitutionary orders have little in common with those that must be proven to obtain compensatory damages (at least in the standard case where the latter's availability is conditional on a wrong). 'Transferring money by mistake' is very different from 'carelessly causing pecuniary losses'. However, it also seemed that the concept of an injustice is sufficiently explanatory for my purposes. This book's classificatory scheme seeks to characterize, at an abstract level, the facts that claimants must establish to obtain private law orders. As we saw in Chapters 6 and 7, these characterizations employ normative concepts ('rights' in Chapter 6, 'wrongs' in Chapter 7). However, I say little about why we have the rights we have or why certain actions count as infringing those rights. Space considerations aside, my explanation of remedial law's structure is deliberately pitched at a level that, if successful, can accommodate different views of the law's normative foundations.[17]

[15] Though not unknown; see e.g. Finnis (1980) 178–9; Weinrib (2012) 87–98 (each of whom draws on Acquinas's concept of 'commutative justice').

[16] Gardner (2012) 256–9.

[17] See the discussion of methodology in Chapter 1. It might be asked whether the category of 'injustices' can accommodate instrumental theories. Such theories explain restitutionary and compensatory orders on the ground that, ideally, they incentivize efficient behaviour. For example, compensatory

However, if I had tried to explain why we have the rights we have and why certain actions count as infringing those rights, the explanations would be as varied as the explanations for why mistaken payments and carelessly caused injuries give rise to injustices. There is little in common between the facts that must be proven to establish—to mention just four examples—a battery, a breach of contract, a defamatory statement, and the breach of a statutory duty. And the explanations for why these actions are wrongs are similarly diverse.[18] What unifies the concept of a legal wrong is not the tests that the law employs to establish wrongs. Rather, the unifying feature is the characterization of the relevant event as a wrong, that is, as something that ought not to happen. The common feature of punching someone in the nose, breaking a promise, uttering a defamatory statement, and acting contrary to a statute is that they are all actions that, in the law's view, we should not do. But if we ask why we should not do these things, the explanations are different. The same is true of injustices. The concept of a wrong (or of a right) and the concept of an injustice operate at the same level. The main difference between them is that the concept of a wrong is used to identify undesirable behaviour, while the concept of an injustice is used to identify undesirable consequences of behaviours.

For similar reasons, I was not concerned that the concept of an injustice seems too vague, at least as I have defined it, to serve as a judicial standard. My interpretation of restitutionary and compensatory orders does not suppose that courts contemplating such orders ask directly whether the claimant has suffered an injustice. Although the required state of affairs is, I argue, properly described as an injustice, it is the state of affairs, not the injustice, that claimants must prove.[19] And the

damages incentivize potential injurers to take appropriate levels of care to avoid injurers, while restitutionary orders incentivize potential transferors to avoid taking too much care to avoid mistaken transfers, etc: see e.g. Landes & Posner (1987); Cooter & Porat (2019). Such explanations have no concern for justice, at least insofar as 'justice' means something that is intrinsically valuable. They take a similar approach to 'rights' and 'wrongs'. However, these approaches still need to distinguish the kinds of events that support restitutionary and compensatory orders. No explanatory theory can avoid classifying the material it is explaining. And when instrumental explanations draw such classifications, they unavoidably rely on conventional legal concepts. To explain the law, one must describe what one is explaining in terms that those familiar with the law can understand. For example, instrumental explanations of 'contract damages' invariably assume, either explicitly or implicitly, that they are explaining the kinds of damages that are awarded for a 'breach' of contract. Such explanations may query whether it makes sense, in some cases, to describe a breach as a breach (or as a 'wrong'), but they still describe the rules that they are explaining as the rules governing damages for breach of contract. In short, while instrumentalists might treat concepts like 'right', 'wrong', and 'injustice' as mere placeholders, their explanations (like all explanations of the law) cannot avoid relying on such concepts. Of course, an instrumentalist might argue that I have used the wrong concepts or that I have drawn the borders between them in the wrong places. But, if this argument is persuasive, it should be persuasive to instrumentalists and non-instrumentalists alike.

---

[18] '[Asking for a unitary theory of tort law] is a very stupid question': Weir (2006) ix; '[T]here is little unity to the subject [of tort law]': Stevens (2007) 299.

[19] In my classificatory scheme, the concept of an injustice operates in broadly the same way that the concept of an unjust enrichment operates in Peter Birks' scheme—as an organizing concept, not a directly applicable standard. The similarity is not coincidental. Like this book, Birks' work on unjust enrichment law focuses on structural issues. For Birks, as for this book, the label for the third category

rules that identify the relevant states of affairs, as well as those that explain what courts should do when claimants prove those states of affairs, are as determinate as the parallel rules in respect of rights-threats and injustices.[20] Further, my interpretation does not suppose that private law provides remedies for all injustices. There are innumerable injustices that lie outside private law's concerns; for example, unjust tax laws, procedural injustices, unjust punishments, and unjust results in sporting or other competitions. Again, there is a parallel with the causes of action examined in Chapters 7 and 8. As is true of the concept of a wrong and the concept of a rights-threat, the law has a tightly circumscribed conception of what counts, legally, as an injustice and complex tests for identifying such injustices.[21]

is a secondary issue. However, in other respects our views differ significantly. The most obvious difference is that I include compensatory damages in my third category. A second difference is that Birks assumed that the law recognizes substantive duties to make restitution and to pay damages. A third difference is that Birks' argument for the unity of 'unjust enrichment law'—his argument for why his third category is not labelled 'miscellaneous'—focuses, at a relatively finely grained level, on the facts that claimants must prove to demonstrate an unjust enrichment. For Birks, all unjust enrichments arise from events where '[t]he defendant is enriched at the expense of the claimant and there is in addition a reason, not being a manifestation of consent or a wrong, why that enrichment should be given up to the claimant': Birks (2005) 22. This approach is not possible for 'injustices'—or, at least, it is not possible if one wants to explain why an injustice is the cause of action for both restitutionary and compensatory orders. This last difference explains why the concept of an injustice does more explanatory work in my account. For Birks, 'unjust enrichment' was, largely, a placeholder (though not entirely—'But for the need to retain *a trace of normativity*, one might just as well speak of pink enrichment': Birks (2005) 275, emphasis added).

[20] The rules governing injustice-responding orders are, in one respect, more determinate than those governing wrong-responding orders. As we saw in Chapter 7, the quantification of wrong-responding orders is ultimately a matter of choice and convention. In contrast, the content of an injustice-responding order is determined by its cause of action. If the claimant establishes an actionable injustice, the standard and appropriate response is to order the defendant to correct the injustice. Thus, in *Kelly*, the widow had to repay the money that she received; in *Vincent*, the ship owner had to pay for the damage that he caused to the dock; and, in *Swaffield*, the owner of the horse had to reimburse the station for its expenses in looking after the horse. The one caveat is that the courts' preference for monetary over non-monetary remedies (which I examined when discussing substitutionary orders in Chapter 7) also applies in respect of injustice-responding orders. Thus, if the relevant injustice arises from the defendant obtaining or retaining fungible property—for instance, gold bars—the court will normally order the defendant to pay the claimant the property's monetary value, rather than to return the property itself. And, because the means by which courts impose restitution *in specie* is the historically equitable concept of a constructive trust, such restitution is, in principle, not available as a right.

[21] There are statutes that come close to requiring claimants seeking injustice-responding orders to prove directly that they have suffered an injustice. Section 23(1)(c) of the *Matrimonial Causes Act* 1973, which I discussed earlier, gives courts wide discretion to issue orders requiring that 'either party to the [now dissolved] marriage shall pay to the other such lump sum or sums as may be so specified'. The legislation simply directs the court to take into account a wide range of factors and then to decide whether it is appropriate, in the circumstances, to issue an order. Courts enjoy similarly broad discretion with respect to orders for contribution made under s 2(1) of the *Civil Liability (Contribution) Act* 1978 (a 'just and equitable' sum) and orders for the financial provision of dependents under section 2(1) of the *Inheritance (Provision for Family and Dependants) Act* 1975 ('reasonable financial provision').

v. Why Orders?

There remained one further question. As I said, I was convinced (and remain convinced) that the only duties to correct injustices recognized by the common law are those created by court orders. The question was why the law limits itself in this way. If the law believes that individuals like the defendants in *Kelly, Vincent*, and *Swaffield* should make restitution or pay compensation, why does it not pursue this aim by imposing rule-based substantive duties to make restitution and pay compensation. If individuals subject to such duties fail to comply with them, then, as in any other case where substantive duties are ignored, there is a role for court orders (as we saw in Chapter 6). But the law's first response, it might be thought, should be to impose rule-based substantive duties. Why, then, does it limit itself to court-ordered remedial duties? My explanation for why the law does not recognize substantive duties to pay nominal, exemplary, and other wrong-responding damages does not provide an answer because, as we saw in Chapter 7, that explanation is limited to wrong-based remedies.

The answer, which I arrived upon after reflecting on Chapter 5's arguments, is that 'correcting injustices' is not a proper aim for a substantive duty.[22] The common law's substantive duties are duties not to wrong others; in particular, duties not to wrong others by interfering with their person, property, liberty, or contractual promises made to them. Battering, trespassing, breaking contractual promises, carelessly injuring others, causing nuisances, and so forth are all non-consensual interferences of this kind. They are ways of wronging others by infringing their rights to their person, property, and so forth. A substantive duty to correct an injustice, if it existed, would be very different from these duties.[23] Failing to correct an injustice is not a wrong, or at least not a wrong in the sense that battery and so forth are wrongs. If I fail to return money that you paid me by mistake or by fail to compensate you for a loss that I inflicted on you, my failure is not an interference with your person, property, liberty, or a promise that I made to you by. More generally, you cannot point to any right of yours that I am infringing by not making restitution or paying damages. All that I have done is fail to correct an injustice.[24]

[22] Another possible answer is that a substantive duty to correct injustices would be an unknowable duty. As I mentioned above, I had already come to the view (which I defend below) that, similar to a substantive duty to pay compensation, a substantive duty to make restitution would turn on facts that those bound by the duty could not reasonably be expected to obtain. In Chapter 7, I considered a parallel explanation in the case of duties to pay damages (and I also considered the possibility that such a duty was 'inchoate' until fixed by a court order). My conclusion—which was to tentatively support this answer—applies equally to injustice-correcting duties.

[23] This argument is broadly similar to arguments defended in Nadler (2013) and Penner (2018) in respect of duties to make restitution. Although the details of their explanations of restitutionary liabilities differ from mine (particularly in the case of Nadler), both Nadler and Penner argue that a substantive duty to make restitution would be qualitatively different from the kinds of duties traditionally recognized in the common law.

[24] Failing to correct an injustice is not the same as acting unjustly. An example of the latter is a wrongful conviction. We often have duties to act justly, typically (if not invariably) because we occupy

This observation does not deny that correcting injustices is valuable. It is because correcting injustices is valuable that we are praised when we return mistaken payments and when we compensate others whom we have harmed. But the fact that it is valuable (or 'virtuous', 'commendable', 'useful' 'beneficial', and so forth) to do something is rarely a sufficient ground for the common law to recognize a substantive duty to do that thing.[25] If it were sufficient, the common law would recognize a substantive duty to rescue and a great many other duties to assist others. There are exceptions to this principle (even the common law recognizes certain 'good faith' duties), but in general, our substantive duties are duties of non-interference. [26] The question of why substantive duties are limited in this way is the subject of a voluminous literature. Almost everything that has been written about the foundations, structure, or history of private law touches on this question. I did not intend to add to this literature. It was sufficient that the limitation is well established and is defensible, at least in principle, from a variety of philosophical perspectives. There is nothing odd about the common law's decision not to recognize substantive duties to correct injustices.

For my purposes, the difficult question was not why the common law does not recognize substantive duties to correct injustices. Rather, the difficult question was why it recognizes court-ordered ('remedial') legal duties to correct injustices. Although orders (unlike duty-imposing rules) are not propositions about the existence of duties, they indirectly give rise to legal duties. As we saw in Chapter 5, the addressees of court orders have legal duties to obey those orders, and, therefore, have derivative legal duties to perform the actions that orders stipulate. The question, then, was how the courts' powers to create court-ordered duties to correct injustices squares with the above explanation for why the law refuses to impose rule-based (substantive) duties to correct injustices?

an office that requires us to make allocative decisions. Thus, referees, judges, and adjudicators in general have duties to act justly. Indeed, it is difficult to conceive of an adjudicator that does not have such a duty. However, we can easily conceive of adjudicators who do not have the authority to correct injustices (their authority having been limited to resolving other kinds of allocative issues).

[25] The distinction between a valuable action and a substantive duty is sometimes expressed, drawing on Kant, by describing the former as an imperfect duty or a duty of virtue: Kant (reprinted 1996) 89–91. See also Kamm (1985); Penner (2018) 229. I have avoided these terms because, inter alia, Kant classified duties of justices as perfect duties and, further, because 'duties', as I use this term, are always mandatory. However, my conception of correcting injustices is consistent with the idea, associated with Aristotle (and, more recently, with Rawls), that justice is a virtue: Aristotle (reprinted 1996) 186; Rawls (1971) 3 ('Justice is the first virtue of social institutions').

[26] The civil law is more open to recognizing such duties. For example, in addition to recognizing a duty to rescue, the Civil Code of Quebec recognizes a duty (albeit qualified) to correct a potential co-contracting party's misapprehensions. Strikingly, it also stipulates that 'every child, regardless of age, owes respect to his father and mother': Civil Code of Quebec, arts 1401, 597; Kasirer (2001). It is an interesting question whether civil codes' openness to such duties explains why they typically affirm substantive duties to make restitution and to compensate.

The answer, unsurprisingly, is that rules, and in particular the duty-imposing rules that are our present concern, are different from orders. As we saw in Chapter 5, the kinds of reasons capable of justifying rule-based duties are qualitatively different from those capable of justifying court-ordered duties. Rule-based duties are owed to other individuals. The duty created by the rule that 'everyone has a duty to perform their contractual promises' is owed to contractual promisees. It follows that this rule can only be justified if it makes sense to suppose that contractual promisees have legal rights to the performance of contractual promises made to them. It is entirely plausible to suppose that such rights exist. But the situation is different if we are trying to justify a rule-based duty to correct injustices. As we have just seen, it is implausible to suppose that individuals have rights that other individuals correct injustices that they have suffered.

However, court-ordered duties are different. Orders are commands ('it is ordered that the defendant pay the claimant £100'). The only duties to which commands give rise are duties to obey whoever issued them, which, in this case, is a court. This difference explains why courts regularly employ orders to direct defendants to do things that, because they are not plausible subject matters of a substantive right, are not appropriate subject matters for rule-based duties. Orders to pay exemplary damages, nominal damages, and the other forms of wrong-based damages all fall into this category. A wrongdoer's non-payment of exemplary damages is not an interference with the victim's person, property, liberty, or anything else to which the victim might plausibly be said to have a right. Nonetheless, there may be good reasons for wrongdoers to pay wrong-based damages to their victims (which I explored in Chapter 7), reasons that can justify a court ordering such payments.[27]

Court-ordered duties to make restitution or pay compensation may be justified in a similar way. The main difference is that their rationale lies not in the value of condemning, deterring, representing, or otherwise redressing a wrong: their rationale lies in the value of correcting injustices.[28] My own view is that the value of correcting injustices is intrinsic, not instrumental—the fewer injustices in the world, the better—but for the present argument all that matters is that correcting injustices is valuable. The courts order defendants to cure injustices because,

[27] As I explain in Chapter 9, the reverse also holds true. Courts often have good reasons to refuse to order the performance of substantive duties, even when those duties are under threat. Such reasons explain, inter alia, why courts may deny relief to a claimant who has unduly delayed or why they may award damages in lieu of specific performance.

[28] Although I will not pursue the idea here, it is possible to interpret wrong-responding remedies as a particular kind of injustice-correcting remedy. In Chapter 5, I argued that wrong-based remedies are, in structural terms, the private law equivalent of criminal punishment. Of course, criminal punishment is traditionally explained as a form of retributive justice. From this perspective, wrong-based remedies and injustice-correcting remedies differ only in the kind of injustice that they seek to correct. In other words, the former focuses on normative losses and gains, the latter, on factual losses and gains.

notwithstanding that failing to correct an injustice is not a legal wrong, curing injustices is valuable.

This understanding of correcting injustices is reflected in our broader legal and social practices. It explains, for example, why the state sometimes corrects injustices through the actions of third parties. In England, individuals who have suffered personal injuries may obtain social security benefits that they would not have obtained but for those injuries. Insofar as such benefits reduce the amount that the injured party could have recovered in a tort action, the *Social Security (Recovery of Benefits) Act* 1997 provides that the state may recover their value from the tortfeasors. In these cases, the injustice is corrected by payments to and from a state body. If the victims of injustices had rights that those who caused the injustice must correct it, this method would be impermissible.

More importantly, this understanding of correcting injustices explains why common law jurisdictions frequently replace tort compensation with statutory compensation. Many common law jurisdictions have 'workers compensation schemes' or 'motor vehicle compensation schemes', whereby anyone injured at work or in a motor vehicle accident may obtain compensation from the scheme.[29] The most extensive scheme of this kind (though still only applying to personal injury claims) is New Zealand's *Accident Compensation Scheme*, introduced in 1974. Although such schemes are typically funded largely, or wholly, by potential injurers, they are not alternative systems for correcting injustices because, inter alia, the injurers are not held liable, even indirectly, for their victim's losses. These schemes are justified on other grounds, such as efficiency or fairness. Needless to say, compensation schemes would not be tolerated if the state or anyone else had a duty to correct injustices in the same way that it has a duty to, say, not kill innocent citizens. Killing innocent citizens is impermissible, even if it might be valuable in various ways (e.g. reducing demands on the health care system). But trading off the value of correcting injustices for other values is permissible, at least in principle. The same trade-offs are made in non-legal contexts. When my children were younger, my wife and I were the closest equivalent to a court in our household. If, following a sibling dispute, one of our children wanted 'justice', they would come to us. But there were many occasions when injustices went uncorrected because we were away, asleep, too tired, or just because we thought that preparing a good meal was more important than ensuring that justice was done.

Thus understood, the decision to give courts the power to correct injustices is a policy decision. The state could legitimately spend the resources that it devotes to supporting private law compensatory and restitutionary orders on statutory compensation schemes, social security schemes, or on building hospitals. For example,

[29] See e.g. *Workers Compensation Act*, RSO 1990 c. W. 11 (Ontario); Article 51, *New York Insurance Law*.

the state could legitimately decide that courts will cease hearing applications to reverse defective transfers, putting the savings into providing additional family law courts. I am not advocating such changes; I merely note that it is because correcting injustices is valuable, not mandatory, that we can contemplate these changes at all. To avoid misunderstandings, I should also add that this understanding of correcting injustices does not lead to the view that courts should take policy considerations into account when determining what is required to correct an injustice. Once the decision is made to allow courts to issue injustice-correcting orders, policy considerations largely, if not entirely, drop out of the picture.[30] Determining what counts as an injustice and what is required to cure injustices are not policy questions.

Finally, does it matter that the addressees of injustice-correcting orders may be innocent of any wrongdoing? It might be thought that, if you have done nothing wrong, the law should leave you alone. The short response to this objection is that it applies equally to alternative explanations of restitutionary and compensatory orders. The alternative explanations assume that restitutionary and compensatory orders confirm substantive duties.[31] If Mrs Solari's innocence is an objection to ordering her to make restitution, it is equally an objection to imposing upon her a substantive duty to make restitution. Whether the duty is imposed by a ruling or a rule, it is imposed (so this objection goes) on an innocent person. It is true, of course, that the innocent addressee of a judicial order will incur the costs and inconveniences of litigation.[32] But, again, this objection applies to the alternative explanations. If it is not possible to determine in advance of litigation the existence and content of substantive duties to correct injustices (as I argue), then whether I am subject to a substantive duty to correct an injustice or am merely liable to being ordered to do so, I am in the same position regarding the costs and inconveniences of litigation. Under either scenario, I cannot be certain of my duty until a court makes a ruling.[33]

For all of these reasons, then, I eventually came to the view that restitutionary and compensatory orders share a similar cause of action, best described

[30] With the proviso that a decision not to make such orders available in particular circumstances is also a policy decision. In Chapter 9, I explain that remedial defences often serve to conserve scarce judicial resources or forward other ends of the state (e.g. fostering diplomatic relations). When courts refuse a remedy for this reason, they are refusing to do what justice requires for policy reasons.

[31] See e.g. Birks (2000), (2005) 168–9; Weinrib (2012) 87–98; Klimchuk (2009); Saprai (2006); Ripstein (2009) 304; Gardner (2011) 30–2.

[32] In the United States, where litigants normally bear the entirety of their legal costs (regardless of whether they win or lose), this objection is more an objection to the litigation system generally than to injustice-responding orders in particular.

[33] I am also equally free in each case to reach a settlement. Under my interpretation of restitutionary orders, there is no duty to make restitution in advance of litigation; however, if I make restitution in advance, my liability to being ordered to make restitution is extinguished. As I explained in Chapter 8, an offer to pay compensation in advance or even actual payment does not extinguish liability, unless it is part of a settlement. However, if I make an offer or a payment in advance, the court would almost certainly require the other side to pay my legal costs.

as proof of an injustice. The remainder of this chapter elaborates upon these reasons, focusing in particular upon the doctrinal claims that I have yet to defend.

B. Restitutionary Awards

If you have transferred money or other property to me in circumstances where your autonomy was impaired, a court will normally grant you an order directing me to return the money or property to you (or to return a sum equal to the property's value). 'Impairment' is typically established by showing that the transfer was motivated by a mistake, duress, undue influence, fraud, incapacity, ignorance, compulsion, or necessity.[34] Thus, as happened in *Solari v Kelly*, if you transfer money to me because you mistakenly believe that you owe me the money, you can normally obtain a court order directing me to return the money. The cause of action for such orders, I argue, is an injustice.

For convenience, I describe these orders as 'restitutionary', but lawyers typically use this label in a broader sense. The category of restitutionary orders is typically understood to encompass orders to return money paid in anticipation of a contract, orders to return money paid under a contract that subsequently failed, orders to pay for mistaken improvements, orders to pay for requested services, and a variety of other orders that, in broad terms, are thought to reverse unjust enrichments. It is likely that the cause of action for some of these orders is also an injustice, but I do not discuss them here. Like those rules, the rules that I discuss in this section are usually described as part of the law of unjust enrichment. Although I refer occasionally to unjust enrichment law, I more commonly refer either to the law governing defective transfers or to the law governing restitutionary orders. The former is employed when I want to make clear that my focus is a subset of unjust enrichment law, while the latter is employed when I want to make clear that my focus is remedial law.

My argument that restitutionary orders are responses to injustices rests upon two propositions. The first is that the common law does not recognize a substantive duty to make restitution. If such a duty existed, the cause of action for restitutionary orders would be the same as for orders for a sum due and other replicative orders—a rights-threat. The second proposition is that the state of affairs that claimants must prove to obtain a restitutionary order is appropriately described as an injustice. I defend these propositions in turn.

[34] Burrows (2011) 201–317, 403–522. The analysis that follows applies equally if the explanation for restitution is not the impairment of the payor's autonomy, but, instead, the absence of a legal basis for the payment. Burrows (2011) discusses the distinction at 86–116.

i. Duty-Confirming or Duty-Creating?

As was true of damages orders, the first question to ask about restitutionary orders in a book on remedies is whether they confirm substantive duties (the 'duty-confirming view') or create new duties (the 'duty-creating view'). If the duty-confirming view is correct, then almost none of the law that appears to deal with restitutionary orders is in fact about such orders. In other words, almost none of this law is remedial law. Remedial law is comprised of rules governing the availability and content of judicial remedies. If the duty-confirming view is correct, the remedial part of the law of restitution reduces to one rule: if the defendant has not fulfilled a substantive duty to make restitution, the court will order that the duty be fulfilled. The rest of the law of restitution, in this view, is substantive law: it is a set of rules specifying when substantive duties to make restitution arise and their content. A remedies book that adopted this view would still need to explain why courts order defendants to comply with unfulfilled duties to make restitution. But, as we saw in Chapter 6, that question (which arises in respect of all replicative remedies) is easily answered: courts issue such orders to motivate recalcitrant defendants to perform their substantive duties. In other words, they order them in response to rights-threats.

In contrast, if the duty-creating view is correct, then the entirety of the law of restitution is remedial law. In this view, the law of restitution is comprised of rules that specify the circumstances in which courts will make restitutionary orders, as well as their content. Further, and critically, the explanation of the rules that make up the law of restitution will differ depending on whether one adopts the duty-confirming or duty-creating view. As I explained above (and in more detail in Chapter 5), the normal reason that the law employs orders rather than rules to impose duties is that the duty's subject matter is not appropriate for a substantive rule. The kinds of reasons that explain exclusively court-ordered duties differ, therefore, from those that explain rule-based duties.

With rare exceptions, textbooks on remedies do not ask whether restitutionary orders are duty-confirming or duty-creating.[35] The same is true of the literature on restitution and unjust enrichment.[36] It is clear that a number of leading writers assume that restitutionary orders are duty-confirming (notwithstanding that their language often suggests the opposite: see below),[37] yet these writers have said little to defend this assumption. In support of his argument that a substantive duty to make restitution arises at the moment of transfer, Birks noted that the transferee's cause of action is complete following transfer.[38] But this rule is also consistent with

[35] A notable exception is Zakrzewksi (2005) 112–14.

[36] See e.g. Burrows (2011); Virgo (2006).

[37] See e.g. Birks (2000a), (2005) 168–9; Weinrib (2012) 189; Klimchuk (2009); Saprai (2006).

[38] Birks (2005) 169. The (alleged) duty could arise at a different moment. For example, it might be thought that the duty arises only when the recipient becomes aware of the impairment, or only when the transferor demands restitution or initiates a lawsuit. I discuss some of these variations below. The

the duty-creating view. Indeed, the most plausible version of the duty-creating view assumes that the cause of action for restitutionary orders arises at the moment of transfer, since the injustice that such orders are meant to correct arises at the moment of transfer.

The little that has been said in defence of the duty-confirming view is not, of course, a reason to reject it. The reason to reject it, as I explain below, is that it is inconsistent with what courts do, courts' explanations of what they do, and the role of substantive duties in our legal system.

ii. Language

The duty-creating view of restitutionary orders is, in one respect, entirely conventional. Although courts occasionally refer to substantive duties to make restitution,[39] they typically describe individuals who have been unjustly enriched as liable to make restitution: 'the agent is liable to make restitution'.[40] Writers, including those who otherwise endorse the duty-confirming view, frequently use similar language. Birks regularly described mistaken payments and similar events as giving rise to liabilities to make restitution.[41] The recent *Restatement Third: Restitution and Unjust Enrichment* consistently adopts similar language. The *Restatement's* opening section states: 'A person who is unjustly enriched at the expense of another is subject to liability in restitution.'[42]

duty-confirming view also allows for the possibility that the duty's content may change over time. Birks presumably believed in this possibility since, in addition to assuming that the duty arises on transfer, he held that if transferees changed their position in reliance on the transfer, then the content and even the existence of their substantive duty could change: Birks (2005) 208–23. In contrast, scholars who believe that the duty arises only after the recipient has knowledge of the transfer and the impairment presumably believe the duty to be invariant, since such knowledge is generally taken to preclude the change of position defence.

[39] See e.g. *Colonial Bank v Exchange Bank of Yarmouth, Nova Scotia* (1885) 11 App Cas 84, 90–2; *Banque Financiere de la Cité v Parc (Battersea) Ltd* [1999] AC 221, 233. Courts frequently state that the cause of action for a restitutionary order accrues at the moment the defendant is enriched (see e.g. *Prudential Assurance v HMRC* [2018] UKSC 39, [69]). These statements support the duty-creating view because, if a substantive duty arose at the moment of enrichment, it would be more natural to refer to that duty arising as opposed to a cause of action arising.

[40] *Portman Building Society v Hamlyn Taylor Neck* [1998] 4 ALL ER 202, 208 (Millett LJ). See also *Kleinwort Benson Ltd v Lincoln City Council* [1998] 4 All ER 2 513, 549 ('If the retrospective legislation positively requires a transaction to be reopened, the liability to repay will arise': Lord Lloyd).

[41] 'The previous paragraphs have shown that a striking feature of the liability to make restitution of mistaken payments is that the liability is strict': Birks (2005) 8. Ernest Weinrib—another leading defender of the duty-confirming view—uses similar language. On three occasions on the first page of the chapter on 'Unjust Enrichment' in *Corrective Justice* Weinrib describes unjust enrichment as a principle or basis of 'liability': Weinrib (2012) 185.

[42] Other examples include ss 2, 5, 13, 14, 15, 16, and 17. It is clear that the *Restatement* authors understand 'liability' to mean liability to a court order because they alternate between describing unjust enrichments as giving rise to liabilities and describing them as giving rise to 'a claim in restitution': see e.g. ss 6, 7, 8, 9, 10, 11, 12, 18, and 19. See generally Smith (2013b).

The courts and writers who employ this language do not appear to attach particular significance to it. It is possible, therefore, that the liabilities to which they refer are liabilities to fall under a future duty. It is also possible that they simply understand 'liability' to mean 'duty'. However, the more straightforward interpretation is that their language reveals an assumption, albeit perhaps unconscious, that the rules that they are discussing are rules about remedies. As I have stressed throughout this book, a liability is different from a duty. Duties describe things that we must do: liabilities describe things that may be done to us. To describe defendants as liable to make restitution suggests that they do not have duties to make restitution, but, instead, that they are only liable to be ordered by a court to make restitution.

iii. Doctrine

The doctrinal evidence does not point consistently in one direction, but on balance it supports the duty-creating view.

No Damages for Failure to Make Restitution

Claimants who incur losses that they could have avoided had the defendant made restitution prior to judgment cannot obtain compensatory damages for these losses. This rule is difficult to reconcile with the duty-confirming view: if there is a duty to make restitution, failing to comply with that duty must be a legal wrong. The common law's standard response to a legal wrong is to hold the wrongdoer liable to pay damages. The courts' refusal to award damages for failing to make restitution prior to an order to make restitution strongly suggests that this failure is not a wrong, and thus that there is no substantive duty to make restitution.

This rule cannot be explained on the ground that the recipients of defective transfers may be entirely innocent, even passive, beneficiaries. The beneficiary's innocence is a reason to question the alleged duty's existence. As the absence of a duty to rescue demonstrates, the common law is extremely hesitant to impose substantive duties to benefit others. However, if a substantive duty to make restitution exists—as the duty-confirming view asserts—then breaching it must be a legal wrong, and damages should follow.

Nor can the unavailability of damages be explained on the ground that the alleged substantive duty to make restitution has, it appears, no date for performance attached. Again, the absence of a date for performance is a reason for questioning the alleged duty's existence. A duty to perform a positive action that has no due date could never be breached. But, if the law wished to enact such a duty, it would be relatively simple to stipulate that it must be performed within a reasonable time.

When contracts are missing dates for performance, the law implies a term that performance must happen within a 'reasonable' time.[43]

Finally, the rule cannot be explained on the ground that courts may award interest, calculated from the date of enrichment, on restitutionary awards.[44] It is true that interest awards are equal in most cases to whatever damages might have been awarded for failing to make restitution immediately following an enrichment. But in some cases they are less than this amount. As I explained in Chapter 7, when considering the parallel issue in the context of compensatory damages, losses arising from a failure to make timely payment may exceed the interest rate. It is because of this possibility that claimants suing for non-payment of an ordinary debt may recover damages in addition to interest.[45] If there were a substantive duty to make restitution, we would expect claimants suing for restitution to have the same option.

Interest Awards

There are three features of the law of restitution that might be thought to support the duty-confirming view. The first is the just-mentioned availability of interest on restitutionary awards. The availability of interest, assessed as of the date of the defendant's enrichment, might be thought to show that the law presumes that defendants should have made restitution immediately after they were enriched. However, this conclusion follows only if the claimant's losses from the non-performance of the alleged duty are equal to the loss of interest—which, as just explained, is not always the case. The more plausible reason for awarding interest on restitutionary orders, which has been adopted by most courts and commentators, is that the interest represents part of the defendant's enrichment.[46]

Change of Position

Restitutionary remedies may be refused or reduced if the defendant changed position in reliance on the enrichment.[47] This defence is only available for bona fide changes of position, that is, only in cases where the defendant was unaware at the time of the change that the enrichment arose from a defective transfer.[48] It might be

[43] 'Where under the contract of sale the seller is bound to send the goods to the buyer, but no time for sending them is fixed, the seller is bound to send them within a reasonable time.': *Sale of Goods Act* 1979, s 29(3).

[44] By virtue of the *Senior Courts Act* 1981, s 35A.

[45] *Wadsworth v Lydall* [1981] 1 WLR 598; *Sempra Metals Ltd v Commissioner of Inland Revenue* [2007] UKHL 34.

[46] *Westdeutsche Landesbank Girozentrale v Islington London Borough Council* [1996] AC 669, 696, 736; *Sempra Metals Ltd v Commissioner of Inland Revenue* [2007] UKHL 34, 34–50, 116, 132, 178–9; *Prudential Assurance v HMRC* [2018] UKSC 39, [76]–[77]. See also Birks (2005) 53; Burrows (2011) 21–5.

[47] *Lipkin Gorman v Karpnale Ltd* [1999] 2 AC 548.

[48] Burrows (2011) 525, 537–40.

thought that if there is no substantive duty to make restitution, it should not matter when the defendant becomes aware of the impairment. If the duty only arises when an order is issued, why does it matter what happens earlier?

An initial observation is that the duty-confirming view is vulnerable to a parallel objection. If there is a substantive duty to make restitution, why should it matter what the defendant does (short of satisfying the duty) after the duty has arisen? If you owe me £1000 under a contract, it is no defence that you did not believe that you owed me this sum, and, as a result, spent all your money on a holiday.

Substantively, the explanation for this rule is that the defendant's knowledge of the defect plays the same role in the duty-creating view as it plays in the duty-confirming view. The rationale for the change of position defence is that innocent transferees should not be required to return assets that they no longer possess. This rationale does not apply, the argument goes, if the transferee dissipated the assets while aware that the transfer was defective. This rationale is not entirely straightforward because, as I explain below, recipients can never be certain prior to a court ruling that a transfer was defective, or even that the plaintiff was the transferor. However, this issue arises on either view. For the moment, what matters is that to the extent that the conventional explanation is persuasive, it is persuasive whether repayment is required because of a duty or because of a liability to a court order. In either case, what is important is transferees' knowledge that they may be legally required—whether by a duty or an order—to make a repayment. This knowledge precludes transferees from arguing that the benefit was foisted upon them.

Section 5(4) of the *Theft Act* 1968

A third and final feature of English law that appears to support the duty-creating model is s 5(4) of the *Theft Act*, 1968. The section appears to assume the existence of a duty to make restitution:

> Where a person gets property by another's mistake, and is under an obligation to make restoration (in whole or in part) of the property or its proceeds or of the value thereof, then to the extent of that obligation the property or proceeds shall be regarded (as against him) as belonging to the person entitled to restoration, and an intention not to make restoration shall be regarded accordingly as an intention to deprive that person of the property or proceeds.

Section 5(4) is of relatively recent origin, and it applies only to cases involving property obtained by mistake. Further, the section does not strictly impose or apply a duty to make restitution: it merely holds that, if there is such a duty, then failing to comply with the duty is deemed theft. Finally, the substance of the provisions seem prima facie incoherent: s 5(4) supposes that it is possible to steal one's own property (since the provision is only needed in cases where title to the relevant property has passed). The section appears to be based on a misapprehension regarding mistaken payors' property rights in their payments.[49] All that said, s 5(4) assumes that duties to return mistaken payments exist, and it has been applied to cases involving mistaken payments in which title to the transferred property passed.[50] To this extent, s 5(4) supports the duty-confirming view.

iv. The Unknowability Objection

The courts' language and the unavailability of damages for failing to make restitution are strong evidence that the common law does not recognize a substantive duty to make restitution. However, the main objection to the duty-confirming view of restitutionary orders is one that we already encountered when we considered, in the previous chapter, the duty-confirming view of damages. The objection is that a substantive duty to make restitution would be unknowable. The duty would therefore be incapable of fulfilling the most basic role of legal rules—and the most basic requirement of the rule of law—namely, to guide behaviour.

As I mentioned above, defenders of the duty-confirming view generally assume that the duty to make restitution arises at the moment of transfer. It follows that if you mistakenly transfer money into my bank account while I am hiking in the wilderness, far from any form of communication, I have a legal duty, from the moment of the transfer, to return the money to you. Admittedly, it is not impossible for me to comply with this duty. I might somehow guess that you are likely to transfer money to me by mistake while I am away and, as a precaution, send you a cheque that arrives, fortuitously, at the moment you make your transfer. But the need to take such actions to comply with my duty demonstrates its implausibility: the law cannot possibly want me to send you cheques on the chance that you may pay me mistakenly.

Further, and critically, even if it is possible in theory for me to comply with a substantive duty to make restitution, it is impossible for me to know that I have complied and, more generally, to know that I am bound by the duty. The alleged duty is therefore incapable, even in theory, of guiding my behaviour. Suppose that you transfer money into my bank account by mistake. And suppose further that I happen to be viewing my account online at that moment, so that I am instantly aware of the transfer (or, alternatively, assume that the alleged duty arises only when you inform me of the defective transfer, or when you initiate litigation). Even in these circumstances, I cannot be certain that I am under a duty to return the

[49] This interpretation is supported by a comparison to the case of debtors who intentionally refuses to pay their debts. If s 5(4) is aimed at defendants who have intentionally breached a duty to pay money, its principle should apply to defaulting debtors; indeed, the principle of s 5(4) should apply more strongly to defaulting debtors because their obligation was undertaken voluntarily.

[50] *Att-Gen's Reference (No 1 of 1983)* [1985] 1 QB 182.

money to you until I know two additional things: first, I need to know that it was you who made the payment; and, second, I need to know that you made the payment because of a mistake.

I cannot determine either of these facts on my own. Even in the unlikely event that I happen to witness you making the transfer, I cannot be certain that I must make restitution to you because I cannot be certain that you were not a conduit for the ultimate payor. Three-party restitution cases are common.[51] In addition, I cannot be certain that the transfer was defective. To confirm that the payment was made by mistake (or because of a threat, fraud, etc), as opposed to being a gift, I need to know your motivation for the transfer. Yet that information is known only by you. Of course, you could tell me that you were the transferor and that the transfer was made by mistake; but you might not do this, and, in any event, how can I know that you are telling the truth? It cannot be sufficient that your explanation appears to be reasonable (since reasonable-appearing explanations may be unsubstantiated). If you were to ask a court for relief, it would not simply accept your word: the court would require you to present evidence, witnesses, and so on. Why should I accept anything less? And even if you presented such evidence to me, am I then supposed to assess your veracity? If nothing else, I might query my impartiality. Admittedly, when a transfer has been made by mistake, the mistake is usually obvious. But the unknowability objection is conceptual: it is sufficient, for this objection, that there could be circumstances in which it is not possible for individuals bound by the alleged duty to know they are bound. Further, this objection applies regardless of whether the alleged substantive duty arises when the transfer is made, when the claimant requests restitution, when litigation commences, or at any other time.

As I explained when discussing the parallel objection to substantive duties to pay compensatory damages, the unknowability objection is not merely a version of the familiar idea that it is difficult to apply general rules to particular circumstances. The objection is that the relevant facts are in the hands of the duty's beneficiary. Duties not to carelessly injure others, not to trespass, not to assault, to keep contractual promises, and so forth are not vulnerable to this objection. Even if it can be difficult to determine what is required to take 'reasonable care not to injure another', the relevant facts are available to those bound by this duty. A substantive duty to make restitution, if it existed, would be different. To ensure that I comply with such a duty, I would have little choice but to accede to any demand to make restitution. To be sure, if the demand is without basis, I would not have a duty to make restitution. However, I could never be certain of a demand's validity, no matter how diligently I investigate. In short, while it would not strictly be impossible for me to comply with a substantive duty to make restitution, it would be impossible for me to know when the duty arises, its content, and whether I have complied with it. If

[51] Burrows (2011) 69–85.

a substantive duty to make restitution existed, it could not guide those subject to it. Its only role would be to serve as an *ex-post* explanation for why courts issue orders to make restitution. In this role, a substantive duty to make restitution appears indistinguishable from a liability to being ordered by a court to make restitution.

The corollary of the conclusion that transferees could know when they were bound by a substantive duty to make restitution is that transferors could know when they had a correlative right to receive restitution. A substantive duty to make restitution would be subject to the defence of change of position. The duty would therefore be reduced or eliminated where the transferee innocently and detrimentally changes position in reliance on the transfer. Yet, the facts that establish a valid change of position (e.g. innocently spending a mistake payment on a vacation) are in the recipient's hands. Thus, just as transferees cannot be sure of the facts that (if the matter went to trial) transferors must prove, transferors cannot be sure of the facts that transferees might offer as a defence. Uncertainty about whether one is the beneficiary of a duty is normally less serious than uncertainty about whether one is bound by a duty. Still, the law's duty-imposing rules should be able to guide not just those who are bound by them, but also those who benefit from them. Occasional limitations on this ability may be justified, but the duty-confirming view supposes that all restitutionary duties are limited in this way.[52]

v. Restitution as a Response to an Injustice

The second proposition on which the classification of restitutionary orders as injustice-responding rests is that the state of affairs that claimants must prove to obtain a restitutionary order is appropriately described as an injustice. The primary argument in support of this proposition is that the alternatives—namely, that restitutionary orders are responses either to rights-threats or wrongs—are implausible.

As *Kelly v Solari* illustrates, the beneficiary of a defective transfer may be an entirely innocent participant in the transfer. It is true that had Mrs Solari agreed to return the payment to the insurance company, then, even if she was innocent at the moment she received the payment, she would no longer be innocent as a result of her failure to perform her promise. [53] However, as is true of the typical defective

[52] The unknowability objection cannot be avoided by arguing that the substantive duty to make restitution is an inchoate duty, which is then fixed by a judicial order. In Chapter 7, I discussed a parallel response to the objection that substantive duties to pay damages are unknowable. The reasons that I gave for rejecting that argument in respect of unknowable compensatory duties apply equally to unknowable restitutionary duties.

[53] The breach of such a promise would not normally qualify as a breach of contract because the promise was not given in exchange for consideration. However, it would be a small step to add promises to return benefits obtained under defective transfers to the list of non-contractual, promissory duties recognized by the common law. Examples of the latter include gratuitous promises to provide bailments or (in select cases) other services, to keep open offers to enter unilateral contracts, to auction goods

transfer case, there was no evidence of such a promise.[54] Mrs Solari's liability arose entirely from the payment. Receiving a payment is neither a wrong nor a threat to commit a wrong.

If restitutionary orders are not responses to either rights-threats or to wrongs, it is difficult to imagine any way of explaining them that does not invoke justice, fairness, or a closely related concept. It is sometimes suggested that the beneficiaries of defective transfers must return what they have received because it would be 'inequitable' or 'unconscionable' for them not to do so.[55] However, this explanation is perfectly consistent with the explanation defended here. The explanation defended here explains why it would be inequitable or unconscionable to retain the benefit of a defective transfer—namely, that the outcome of that transfer is unjust. Indeed, if my account is correct, it is not in the least surprising that writers often invoke 'equity', 'unconscionability', and similar concepts when explaining restitutionary orders. These concepts are characteristically invoked to describe events or transactions that are undesirable notwithstanding that neither party committed a wrong or a rights-threat, as traditionally understood. In this limited sense, restitutionary orders are equitable: they are responses to something other than a wrong or a threatened right.

without reserve, and to provide irrevocable credits: see Peel (2015) 173–84. On some views, liability for promissory estoppel, misrepresentation, and a variety of other torts also fit in this category: see e.g. Stevens (2007) 9–14, 33; Beever (2007) 284–315.

[54] Ernest Weinrib argues that the law 'imputes' that Mrs Solari has 'accepted' her beneficial transfers on the basis that it was non-donative: Weinrib (2012) 204–7. However, as Weinrib's explicit rejection of the 'implied contract' theory of unjust enrichment makes clear, he is not arguing that Mrs Solari agreed to return her benefits. The significance of the imputation, it appears, is to refute the suggestion that transferees are 'passive' participants in the relevant transaction. However, the question remains as to the basis of the duty to make restitution. Weinrib writes, 'The plaintiff cannot retain gratis what was neither given gratis nor accepted [by imputation] as given gratis' (204). But why? If I have understood correctly (and I am not certain that I have), Weinrib's only normative argument is that it would be 'unfair' for the transferee to retain the benefit: (207). I agree. The only proviso is that, unlike Weinrib, I argue that duties to make restitution are created by court orders, not substantive rules. Weinrib does not address this issue, but I note that whether or not he grounds his substantive duties in fairness, the explanation of these duties will be different from the explanation Weinrib offers for our other substantive duties. Consistent with his Kantian roots, Weinrib views our substantive rights basically as rights that others not use or interfere unreasonably with the means by which we pursue our ends—which, in practice, means our persons, property, and contractual rights: 'Among these rights [our substantive rights] are the right to the integrity of one's body as the organ of purposive activity, the right to property in things appropriately connected to an external manifestation of the proprietor's volition, and the right to contractual performance in accordance with the mutually consensual exercises of the parties' purposiveness' (353). It is not clear where substantive duties to reverse unjust enrichments fit in this picture. Mrs Solari's retention of the benefit she received from the insurance company was not an interference with the insurance company's person, property, contractual rights, or, it appears, with anything else to which they might conceivably be said to have a right.

[55] In a series of Australian decisions beginning with *Pavey & Matthews Property v Paul* (1987) 162 CLR 221, Gummow J has argued that the availability of restitution is triggered by 'unconscionable conduct'. The court's reasoning in the seminal case of *Moses v MacFerlan* [1760] 2 Burr 1005 is replete with references to the 'ties of natural justice' 'founded in the equity of the plaintiff's case', and money which '*ex aequo et bono*' the defendant ought to refund, money retained against 'conscience'.

A second suggestion that is sometimes made is that restitutionary orders are responses to property rights, or, perhaps, more strictly to defective property rights.[56] According to this view, in an ideal world a mistaken or otherwise defective transfer would not transfer title to the transferred property. Title would remain with the transferor, who could then bring a simple claim for conversion if the property was not returned.[57] However, for a variety of practical reasons (including, in particular, the need to protect third parties who rely on the transfer's appearance of validity), the law holds that title passes under a defective transfer. The role of restitutionary orders, in this explanation, is to provide an *ex-post* means by which the law can ensure that title ends up in the hands of the party who, in an ideal world, should never have lost it. More broadly, 'these claims [to reverse defective transfers] arise as a means of protecting and effectuating the plaintiff's interest in exclusively determining the disposition of his assets'.[58] In other words, defective transfers are defective precisely because they transfer title in situations where, in retrospect, the transferor would have preferred that title not pass.

As James Penner has pointed out, the main difficulty with this explanation is that there could never be rules of transfer, no matter how perfect, that prevented all mistaken transfers: 'The rules of title transfer, being facilitative, make it the case that they can be used for good purposes or ill . . . It is not the law, but the claimant, who is mistaken, and it is simply not the role of the law, even a perfect law, to make it the case that people cannot effectively make mistakes, for that would *undermine*, not *enhance*, their autonomy'.[59] Further, if restitutionary orders were responding to imperfect property rights, we would expect them to respond by perfecting those rights, that is, by granting or declaring that the claimant has a property right in the relevant property. Yet the typical restitutionary orders are no more proprietary than orders to pay damages or debts: they merely direct the defendant to pay a sum of money to the claimant.[60] If the claimant is insolvent, the defendant must line up with the other creditors. Finally, the subject matter of a defective transfer may not be property.[61] In a typical mistaken payment case, what is transferred is not a property right, but a personal claim against a bank. We do not 'own' the money in our bank accounts; we merely have a right, the same as an ordinary debtor's right, to be paid this money by the bank. In short, while property-based explanations of defective transfers can explain why defective transfers are defective, they fail to identify the problem to which restitutionary orders are responding.

[56] I defended this view in Smith (2013). Others who have defended versions of this view include Stoljar (1989) 5–9; Watts (1995) 49–70; Dietrich (1998) 208–13; Jaffey (2000) 275–9; Webb (2009); McFarlane (2012).

[57] Burrows (2011) 14–15.

[58] Webb (2009) 335.

[59] Penner (2018) 240.

[60] Burrows (2011) 14–15.

[61] See Wilmot-Smith (2016) 1131.

The only other attempt to explain restitutionary orders of which I am aware interprets them as a kind of insurance for potential transfers. According to what I will describe as 'instrumental' theories, the availability of restitutionary orders facilitates the practice of making transfers by allowing transferors to undo transfers that, in retrospect, diverge from their intentions. Absent restitutionary orders, this argument goes, potential transferors would either avoid potentially beneficial transfers or devote excessive resources to making sure that they do make a defective transfer. Most advocates of instrumental theories assume that transfers are beneficial for economic reasons,[62] but non-economic instrumental theories are also possible.[63]

Instrumental theories are not in competition with this chapter's account of restitutionary orders.[64] It is true that instrumental theories are not concerned with 'injustices', at least insofar as 'justice' means something that is intrinsically valuable (instrumental theories regard concepts such as 'rights' and 'wrongs' in the same way). However, instrumental theories still need to identify the events that give rise to restitutionary orders. And to do this, instrumental theories, like other explanatory theories, invariably utilize legal concepts. This move is inevitable because if you are trying to explain the law (or anything else) you need to identify what it is that you are explaining in terms that those familiar with the concept can understand. If one attempted to explain contract law without using the word 'contract', the resulting explanation would not be an explanation of contract law. This requirement explains why instrumental theories of contract law are invariably described as just that—instrumental theories of 'contract law'. In short, while instrumentalists might treat concepts like 'right', 'wrong', and 'injustice' as mere placeholders, their explanations (like all explanations of the law) cannot avoid relying on these or similar concepts to describe what they are explaining.

In the case of restitutionary orders, instrumental theories typically describe them as responses to defective transfers or something closely analogous (e.g. 'impaired' transfers). If asked to generalize this description, instrumental theories invoke concepts such as 'unjust enrichment'. And if asked to generalize further, instrumental theorists might well agree that a defective transfer is just one example of the broader category of 'injustices'. Of course, there is no guarantee that particular instrumental theorists would agree to this classification. However, if they agree that a defective transfer need not involve either a wrong or a rights-threat, then they would, presumably, agree that restitutionary orders belong in a separate category. Instrumental theories have explanations for why there should be remedies for wrongs and rights-threats. But, if my arguments are correct, those explanations will not work for defective transfers (or consequential losses). Thus, another

[62] Levmore (1985); Cooter & Porat (2019).
[63] McBride (2019) 197.
[64] See also note 17.

label is required. Of course, an instrumentalist might argue that I have used the wrong concepts or drawn the borders between them in the wrong places. But, if this chapter's classificatory argument is persuasive, it should be persuasive to instrumentalists and non-instrumentalists alike.

As I mentioned above, if restitutionary orders are not responses to either rights-threats or to wrongs, it is difficult to imagine any way of identifying the events to which they are responding that does not invoke justice, fairness, or a closely related concept. Substantively, claimants seeking restitutionary orders must show that the defendant obtained a benefit under a transfer in which the claimant's autonomy was impaired because of a mistake, fraud, duress, compulsion, necessity, or something similar.[65] The natural explanation for why you should not be able to keep something as, in effect, a gift that was not intended as a gift is that it is unfair to keep it. This explanation is, of course, entirely orthodox. Lawyers standardly describe the outcome of a defective transfer as an 'unjust enrichment'. As the term is ordinarily understood, an unjust enrichment is the same as, or is at least included within, what I have described as an injustice. To say that something is an unjust enrichment is just another way of saying that it is an injustice, and both are just ways of saying that a gain or loss (in this case, a gain) has ended up in the wrong hands.

C. Compensatory Damages

As understood here, compensatory damages are awarded on proof of, and set at the value of, pecuniary losses that the claimant suffered as a consequence of the defendant's actions. These actions are typically described as torts or contract breaches (though I will argue that sometimes they are not wrongs, strictly understood). Consequential losses normally consist in actual or anticipated out-of-pocket expenses and foregone profits or earnings. Common examples include damages for medical expenses and loss of earnings arising from a physical injury and damages for loss of profits arising from a broken contract. Importantly, damages for pain and suffering, mental distress, loss of reputation, or other intangible harms are not compensatory, as this term is used here. Although pain, distress, and so forth may be a consequence of the defendant's wrong, they are not losses, and (for the same reason) they cannot be eliminated by monetary awards. I discussed damages award for intangible harms in Chapter 7, where I argued that they are responses to wrongs.[66]

[65] Burrows (2011) 201–522.

[66] The classification of damages awards (or parts of awards) as compensatory, wrong-based, or substitutionary often turns on complex technical distinctions. For an excellent analysis of a wide range of tort awards (albeit adopting different terminology and explanations of the relevant awards), see Stevens (2007), especially 20–92, 129–72.

Compensatory awards, I argue, are different: like restitutionary awards, they are responses to injustices, not wrongs. Indeed, I argue that compensatory awards are, in certain respects, the mirror image of restitutionary orders. In each case, if the claimant is successful the court responds to an unjust outcome by ordering the party who benefited from the injustice to correct it. The main difference between restitutionary and compensatory awards is that, while the former are responses to unjust gains, the latter are responses to unjust losses.

It is true that courts and commentators traditionally describe, or at least classify, compensatory damages and indeed damage awards generally as responses to wrongs. It is also true that, in most (but not all) cases in which compensatory awards are issued, the defendant has committed a wrong, and, further, the claimant has to prove this wrong to obtain the award. However, I argue that the wrong in these cases is merely a condition of the award, not the reason for issuing it. If the wrong were the reason, the rules for assessing compensatory damages and the rules that establish when compensatory awards are available would be different. As in the case of restitutionary awards, the law's fundamental concern is not the wrongfulness of the defendant's behaviour: its fundamental concern is the fairness of the outcome of the relevant transaction. The wrong is merely a reason (and not the only possible reason) for holding the defendant responsible for this outcome.

This explanation of compensatory damages is assumed, at least in broad outline, by many courts and commentators. The 'overall object of tort law', Lord Bingham wrote, 'is to define cases in which the law may justly hold one party liable to compensate another'.[67] This proposition is too broad (it ignores tort law's substantive duties), but it otherwise lines up neatly with this chapter's view of the 'overall object' of compensatory damages. The same is true of Baron Parke's oft-quoted statement that damages should restore the claimant to 'the same position as he would have been in if he had not sustained the wrong for which he is now getting his compensation or reparation'.[68] Read literally, the proposition is again too broad (it ignores wrong-based and substitutionary damages), and, as we will see, compensatory damages are sometimes available for non-wrongs; however, the general idea of restoring claimants to the positions they were in prior to their injury fits neatly with the injustice-based interpretation of compensatory damages. The appropriate response to an injustice is to cure the injustice, and in the case of unfair losses, this aim is achieved by returning claimants to the positions that they were in before they incurred the losses.

As in the case of restitutionary awards, the main challenge to the injustice-based theory of compensatory damages is posed by alternative theories. If these alternatives are unpersuasive, the explanatory space that remains is difficult to fill without

[67] *Fairchild v Glenhaven Funeral Services Ltd* [2002] UKHL 22, [9].

[68] *Robinson v Harman* [1848] 1 Exch 850, 855. See also *Livingstone v Rawyards Coal Co* (1880) 5 App Cas 25, 39 ('[the measure of damages is] that sum of money which will put the party who has been injured, or had suffered, in the same position that he would have been in if had not sustained the wrong': Lord Blackburn).

invoking justice, fairness, or a similar concept. For this reason, my defence of the injustice-based theory consists in large part of arguments for rejecting these alternatives. However, my defence is not entirely negative. Most of the reasons for rejecting the alternative theories are, at the same time, reasons for adopting an injustice-based account, or something closely similar. Further, there are independent reasons for supposing that an injustice-based theory is the best option for filling the explanatory hole that remains once the leading alternatives are rejected. I discuss these reasons at the end.

I begin with the alternative theories, focusing on the two most influential candidates. The first views compensatory awards as responses to rights-threats; the second views them as responses to *wrongs*.

i. Rights-Based Theories

The idea that compensatory damages are responses to rights-threats was discussed—and rejected—in the previous chapter's introduction to damages awards. To reiterate briefly, the most influential defence of this idea—the 'continuity thesis'—supposes that the commission of a wrong gives rise to a substantive duty to do the 'next-best thing', which, in practice, means a substantive duty to pay damages. If such duties exist, then failing to pay damages subsequent to a wrong's commission is equivalent to an ongoing failure to pay a debt or to perform any other substantive duty. The ongoing failure would qualify as a rights-threat (the threatened right being the right to damages), which, in turn, would support an order directing the recalcitrant defendant to pay damages. In this view, an order to pay damages is analogous to an order for a sum due or to any other replicative order.

We further saw that the main reason for rejecting the continuity thesis and, more generally, for rejecting any theory that regards compensatory awards as replicative is that the common law does not recognize a substantive duty to pay compensatory damages or, indeed, a substantive duty to pay damages of any kind. An order to pay compensatory damages cannot be a response to a rights-threat because the allegedly threatened substantive right—a right to the payment of compensatory damages—does not exist.

ii. Wrong-Based Theories

The other main alternative to an injustice-based explanation of compensatory awards is a wrong-based explanation.[69] According to this view, compensatory

[69] The most important wrong-based explanation of damages is the civil recourse theory developed by John Goldberg & Benjamin Zipursky: Goldberg & Zipursky (1998a), (2010); Goldberg (2005), (2006);

damages are responses to wrongs in the same way that exemplary damages, nominal damages, and the other damages awards that I discussed in Chapter 7 are responses to wrong. In the wrong-based view, compensatory awards belong with these awards.

Of course, the extent of a wrong's consequences are often unrelated to the defendant's moral culpability. A person who was intentionally punched may suffer fewer consequential losses than someone who was carelessly bumped in a crowd. But, as we saw in Chapter 7, the wrongfulness of a wrong is determined not just by the wrongdoer's conduct and mental state but also by its consequences. A punch that causes serious harm is a more serious wrong than a similar punch that, fortuitously, causes little harm. It would seem to follow, then, that if courts are willing to issue wrong-responding damages awards (as I argue), they should also issue damages awards that respond to a wrong's consequences. Finally, setting such awards at the market value of the claimant's pecuniary loss appears to be a natural, easily administered, and proportionate response to that loss. As we saw in Chapter 7, courts adopt a market-price measure when setting wrong-based user damages, waiver damages, and market-price damages.

Courts and commentators frequently assume that compensatory damages are responses to wrongs. The first sentence of the most recent edition of *McGregor on Damages* defines damages as 'an award in money for a civil wrong'.[70] This sentence neatly summarizes the two propositions on which wrong-based theories rest. The first, encapsulated in the description of damages as 'an award', is that the law of damages (including the law of compensatory damages) is remedial law: it is law about the availability and content of a judicial remedy (as opposed to law about a substantive duty). As I explained a moment ago, I fully endorse this proposition. A large part of Chapter 7 is devoted to demonstrating that the common law does not recognize a substantive duty to pay damages, and, accordingly, that the law of damages is a set of rules about 'awards'.

The second proposition, encapsulated in the description of damages as awards 'for a wrong', is that damages awards are response to wrongs. It is this second proposition that I reject, primarily because it is inconsistent with (1) the rules for assessing compensatory awards and (2) the rules for determining when compensatory awards are available. Not coincidentally, these reasons are also reasons for adopting an injustice-based theory.

Zipursky (1998), (2002), (2003). Though broadly consistent with the civil recourse theory, this chapter's model of a wrong-based theory abstracts from various details of civil recourse theory (in particular, its Lockean-inspired argument for why courts provide remedies for wrongs) and, more generally, draws on the interpretation of wrong-based remedies set out in Chapter 7. Goldberg & Zipursky limit their explanation to tort damages (though others have expanded it to contract damages: Oman (2011)). But, within that category, they apply it to all damages (i.e. not just compensatory damages). I defended a wrong-based explanation of tort and contracts damages in Smith (2012), (2014).

[70] Edelman (2018) 1.

The model of a 'wrong-based theory' that I assume in the discussion that follows is based on the wrong-based theory that I developed in Chapter 7, and that I used to explain exemplary damages, nominal damages, damages for pain and suffering, and the various examples of vindicatory damages. This model is broadly consistent with the leading versions of wrong-based theories (e.g. civil recourse theories and deterrence theories). However, it is framed more abstractly than those theories. Specifically, it is meant to allow for different explanations of why the law provides for wrong-responding remedies. This model's understanding of what it means for a remedy to 'respond' to a wrong is, however, strict. It is not sufficient that proof of a wrong supports the claimant's action or even that it is a necessary condition for success in that action: the award must be a response to the wrong *qua* wrong.[71] It may be useful to keep in mind nominal and exemplary damages awards as core examples of wrong-based awards.

iii. The Assessment of Compensatory Damages

Most of the rules governing the assessment of compensatory damages serve to limit the potential scope of liability for consequential losses. These 'limitation' rules shield defendants from liability in respect of losses that were factual ('but-for') consequences of their actions. Limitation rules are generally discussed under the broad heading of 'remoteness' (or 'proximate cause'—the labels are interchangeable), but it includes rules that are often discussed separately, such as mitigation, contributory negligence, collateral benefits, and exoneration of liability clauses (limitation clauses, exclusion clauses). These rules are difficult to explain if one adopts a wrong-based theory. As I mentioned above, the basic argument for awarding compensation as a response to a wrong is that the wrongfulness of a wrong is determined partly by the wrong's consequences, and, further, that the market value of those consequences is a convenient, natural, and proportionate way of marking the wrong. This argument supports liability only for losses that are a factual consequence of

[71] A potential objection to this argument is that for certain torts—negligence is the main example—proof of a wrong is, by definition, a necessary and sufficient condition for an award of compensatory damages since (this objection goes) these torts cannot be committed unless the claimant has suffered an injury. Thus, a claimant who establishes the wrong of negligence has also satisfied the cause of action for compensatory damages. There are two responses to this objection. First, while proof of damage is part of the cause of action in negligence, it is not clear that it as an element of the wrong of negligence. In other words, proof of damage arguably goes to the actionability, not the wrong, of negligence: see Smith (2015); McBride & Bagshaw (2015) 123–5 (who note, inter alia, that in *Donaghue v Stevenson* Lord Atkin did *not* say that 'You must avoid injuring your neighbor by failing to take reasonable care to avoid acts or omissions that reasonably foreseeably would have that effect'. Rather, what he said was, 'You must take reasonable care to avoid acts or omissions which you can reasonably foresee would be likely to injure your neighbor.'). Second, even if damage is an element of the wrong of negligence, this merely shows that in some cases the requirements for a wrong are the same as for injustice. It does not show that compensatory damages are a response to the wrong.

the defendant's wrongdoing. However, it provides no reason to reduce this liability in the ways provided by the limitation rules. My wrong is no less wrongful because the victim was careless, the victim could have avoided some of the loss, a third party also committed a wrong, the victim agreed (explicitly or implicitly) to limit or exclude my potential liability, or the loss was not reasonably foreseeable (though the later may be relevant when assessing the wrongfulness of my conduct). If a wrong's wrongfulness is determined partly by its harmful consequences, all harmful consequences should count.

To be sure, there are compelling arguments for why it would be unfair to hold wrongdoers responsible for losses that are excluded by the limitation rules. If your carelessness was a factual cause of the injury that you suffered, then, even if my carelessness was also a factual cause, it seems unfair to hold me fully responsible for its consequences. Similarly, if you could have avoided a loss by taking reasonable steps to mitigate an injury's consequences or if we had an understanding, explicit or implicit, that I would not be liable for a loss then it seems unfair to hold me liable for that loss. Indeed, it is difficult to think of any other justification for the limitation rules. Consistent with this conclusion, courts and commentators invariably describe and explain the limitation rules in just this way, and legislatures incorporate similar ideas directly into statutory limitation rules. Specifically, they describe the court's task as one of determining whether it is 'fair', 'just', or 'reasonable' to attribute the claimant's losses to the defendant:

> '[T]he second inquiry [remoteness] concerns the extent of the loss for which the defendant ought fairly or reasonably or justly to be held liable (the epithets are interchangeable).'[72]
>
> 'The rationale of the principle that a *novus actus interveniens* breaks the chain of causation is fairness.'[73]
>
> '[M]itigation is a doctrine based on fairness and common sense, which seeks to do justice between the parties'.[74]
>
> 'The common law has treated this matter [the distinction between offsetting and non-offsetting benefits] as one depending on justice, reasonableness and

[72] *Kuwait Airways Corp v Iraqi Airways Co (No 3)* [2002] 3 All ER 209, 228. See also *Overseas Tankship (UK) Ltd v Morts Dock & Engineering (The Wagon Mound, No 1)* [1961] AC 388, 422 ('It does not seem consonant with current ideas of justice or morality that for an act of negligence, however slight or venial, which results in some trivial foreseeable damages the actor should be liable for all consequences however unforeseeable and however significant, so long as they can be said to be "direct"': Viscount Simonds); *Hadley v Baxendale* [1854] 9 Exch 341, 354 ('[T]he damages which the other party ought to receive in respect of such breach of contract, should be such as may fairly and reasonably be considered, either arising naturally, ie according to the usual course of things or such as may reasonably be supposed to have been in the contemplation of the parties': Baron Alderson); *Chubb Fire Ltd v Vicar of Spalding* [2010] EWCA Civ 981, [64] ('The courts have to make a "value judgment" when dealing with issues such as "remoteness of damage" or "causation" . . . the ultimate question is: what is the extent of the loss for which a Defendant ought fairly, or reasonably or justly to be held liable': Lord Justice Aikens).

[73] *Corr v IBC Vehicles Ltd* [2008] 1 AC 884 [15].

[74] *Southcott Estates Inc v Toronto Catholic District School Board* 2012 SCC 51 [25].

public policy.... It would be revolting to the ordinary man's sense of justice, and therefore contrary to public policy, that the sufferer should have his damages reduced so that he would gain nothing from the benevolence of his friends or relations or of the public at large, and that the only gainer would be the wrongdoer.'[75]

'[D]amages... shall be reduced to such extent as the court thinks just and equitable having regard to the claimant's share in the responsibility for the damage.'[76]

'[T]he amount of contribution [to a tortfeasor's liability] available from any person shall be such as may be found by the court to be just and equitable.'[77]

'[In respect of certain torts and contract breaches, liability cannot be limited by contract or a notice except insofar as the term or notice 'satisfies the requirement of reasonableness.'[78]

These quotations, and the broader theme they reflect, are difficult to explain if one adopts a wrong-based theory of compensatory damages. Once a court has determined that it is fair to hold the defendant responsible for the relevant loss, there is no room left for a wrong-based response in respect of the relevant loss. The court has already determined that the defendant is liable for the loss. That conclusion fully determines the remedy (in respect of this loss).[79]

Of course, wrong-based theories do not suppose that courts should issue awards that are unfair, unjust, or unreasonable. However, if courts are seeking to respond to the defendant's wrongdoing, the question is not whether it is fair to hold the defendant responsible for the relevant loss. The court's task is to determine the appropriate response to the defendant's wrongdoing.[80] And, insofar as the court is considering the significance of the claimant's losses, the only thing that matters is whether the relevant loss was a consequence of the wrongdoing. That question

[75] *Parry v Cleaver* [1969] 1 All 555, 557–8.

[76] *Law Reform (Contributory Negligence) Act* 1945, s 1(1).

[77] *Civil Liability (Contribution) Act* 1978, s 2(1).

[78] *Unfair Contract Terms Act* 1977, ss 2(2), 3(2), 6(1A), 7(4), and 8(3).

[79] It might be thought that a counter-example is the rule that, at least in respect of certain torts, where the wrong is deliberate, defendants will be held liable for all the consequences of their wrongdoing (not just foreseeable consequences): *Doyle v Olby (Ironmongers) Ltd* [1969] 2 QB 158 (deceit); *Quinn v Leathem* [1901] AC 495 (conspiracy); *Kuwait Airways Corpn v Iraqi Airways Co (Nos 4 & 5)* [2002] AC 883 (conversion, but with suggestions that the rule should apply generally). As we saw in Chapter 7, in principle deliberate wrongs should attract larger wrong-based remedies. But there is no reason to tie this increase to the amount of unforeseeable consequential losses. In any event, exemplary and aggravated damages already serve this role (and neither set the amount by reference to losses). However, if the question for the courts is whether it is fair to hold the defendant responsible for a particular loss, the fact that the wrong was deliberate is a reason to answer in the affirmative. This conclusion is the flip-side of Viscount Simonds' conclusion in the *Wagon Mound* that it would be unfair to hold a defendant who had only committed a trivial fault liable for massive losses (see note 73).

[80] Exemplary damages are justified, Lord Devlin wrote, where they are needed 'to punish [the defendant] for his outrageous conduct, to mark their disapproval of such conduct, and to deter him from repeating it': *Rookes v Barnard* [1964] AC 1129, 1228. '[B]attery or trespass to the person is actionable without proof that the victim has suffered anything other than the infringement of his right to bodily integrity: the law vindicates that right by awarding nominal damages': *Ashley and another v Chief Constable of Sussex Police* [2008] UKHL 25 [60] (Earlsferry LJ). See also *Kuddus v Chief Constable of Leicestershire Constabulary* [2001] UKHL 29, [63]–[65].

answered, the remaining question is how to represent this aspect of the defendant's wrongdoing in monetary terms. And the answer to this question, as I noted above, is straightforward: the sum awarded should be set at the value of the losses. The limitation rules are inconsistent with this approach.

The courts' focus on fairness in assessing compensatory damages also explains why courts sometimes ignore the beneficial consequences of wrongful acts.[81] For example, insurance or pension payments that would not have been received if the claimant had not been injured are normally not taken into account.[82] The standard explanation for this rule is that it would not be fair to deprive claimants of benefits that they had paid for: 'it would be unjust and unreasonable to hold that the money which [the claimant] prudently spent on premiums and the benefit of it should ensure to the benefit of the defendant'.[83] This explanation is perfectly reasonable (and it is difficult to imagine how any other explanation could account for the proviso that third-party insurance payments are deducted if the claimant did not pay the premiums[84]). But it has nothing to do with the wrongfulness of the defendant's action. In terms of wrongfulness, a payment that would not have been received if the wrong had not occurred reduces the wrong's harmful consequences, and so reduces its wrongfulness. If compensatory awards are responses to wrongs, this reduction should be reflected in a reduced award.[85]

iv. The Availability of Compensatory Damages

If the focus of the assessment of damages rules is responsibility, not wrongdoing, then we would expect to find cases where compensatory damages are awarded notwithstanding that no wrong was committed. The fact that a defendant's action was a wrong may be a good reason to hold the defendant responsible for the

[81] Burrows (2004) 169–74. Not surprisingly, courts also sometimes ignore, in a similar fashion, negative consequences attendant to a defective transfer. For example, if, as a result of you mistakenly paying me £1,000, my uncle decides not to give me a gift of £1,000 that he would otherwise have given me, I remain liable to return your £1,000 to you.

[82] *Bradburn v Great Western Railway Co* (1874) LR 10 Exch 1; *Parry v Cleaver* [197] AC 1.

[83] *Parry v Cleaver* [1967] AC 1, 14 (Lord Reid).

[84] *Hussain v Hew Taplow Paper Mills Ltd* [1988] 1 AC 514.

[85] A final observation is that the sheer quantity of law devoted to assessing compensatory damages is surprising if compensatory damages are wrong-based. Approximately three quarters of the nearly 2,000 pages in the latest edition of McGregor on Damages focuses on the rules governing the assessment of compensatory damages: Edelman (2018). The magnitude and detail of this law is surprising if compensatory awards are wrong-based. As we saw in Chapter 7, there is no natural, logical, or inevitable response to a wrong. In private law as in criminal law, the courts' response to wrongs is ultimately a matter of choice and convention. At the end of the day, damages can never do more than to represent a wrong. Thus, if compensatory damages are wrong-based, the courts appear to be devoting incredible effort to establishing a sum that, at the end of the day, is arbitrary. However, the magnitude and detail of this law is unsurprising if the courts' task is to determine which of the claimant's losses the defendant may be fairly be held responsible. Ascriptions of responsibility, as I explain below, turn on a multitude of complex factors.

consequences of its actions, but (as I explain in more detail below) it is not the only reason. To give just one example, it might be thought (as the law indeed thinks) that, if you engage in a dangerous activity, you should be liable for any harm you cause, even if the activity is lawful.

Such cases are indeed common. Perhaps the clearest examples, albeit not strictly compensatory *damages* awards, are awards that compensate claimants who have intervened in a state of necessity to save or maintain another's property or life ('necessitous interveners').[86] For example, claimants who incur a loss while saving a ship or its cargo may obtain compensation from the owner.[87] Similarly, claimants who have paid for a burial may obtain compensation from the person who had this duty.[88] In the United States, courts have generalized this rule to cover any case where the relevant duty was imposed in the public interest.[89] A third example is compensatory awards for so-called 'agents of necessity', such as individuals who accept bills of exchange to preserve the drawer's 'honour'.[90] This category has been extended to the preservation of a defendant's animals and, in another case, to the preservation of material property.[91] In the United States, similar cases have given rise to a general principle covering the preservation of any property.[92] Another example is compensatory awards for claimants who provide the 'necessaries of life' to the defendant or to someone for whom the defendant is legally responsible.[93] Some courts have extended this principle to cover claimants who provide medical services[94] and to caregivers.[95] A final example is a claim brought under the law of 'general average' by a party to a contract for the carriage of goods by sea whose goods were jettisoned for safety reasons. Such parties may claim compensation from other parties who were transporting goods on the same ship, so that they all share equally in the loss.[96]

The above awards are not conventionally described as compensatory 'damages', presumably because it is not possible, even in theory, to classify the defendant as

[86] See e.g. McCamus (1979).

[87] The leading case of *Falcke v Scottish Insurance Co* (1886) 34 Ch D, 234 argues for keeping this category small, but its authority in this regard is doubtful (see Kortmann (2005) 113). In England, the principle has been extended to aircraft. The sums awarded to salvors often include a non-compensatory 'reward' for the purpose of encouraging future salvors.

[88] *Jenkins v Tucker* (1788) 1 Hy Bl 90.

[89] '[W]hen an obligation is imposed by law upon one to do an act because of an interest in the public to have it done, and that one fails to do it, he who does do it, expecting compensation, may recover therefore of him on whom the obligation is imposed': *Mathie v Hancock* 78 Vt. 414, 63 A. 143 (1906) (Rowell CJ). In England, a similar principle was proposed in *Urmston v Newcomen* (1788) 126 ER 55.

[90] *Howtayne v Bourne* (1841) 7 M & W 595.

[91] *Great Northern Railway Co v Swaffield* (1874) LR 9 Exch 132; *Prager v Blatspiel, Stamp and Heacock Ltd* [1924] 1 KB 566.

[92] The *Restatement (Third) of Restitution and Unjust Enrichment* description of the awards in such cases as 'restitutionary' seems inapt, as s 21 limits the award to the cost of providing the service.

[93] *Williams v Wentworth* 5 Beav. 325 (1842).

[94] *Matheson v Smiley [1932]* 2 DLR 785 (Canada).

[95] *Skibinski v Community Living British Columbia*, 2012 BCCA 17 (Canada).

[96] Rose (2005).

a wrongdoer. But they indirectly support my interpretation of damages awards. Their existence forecloses the argument that compensation in the common law necessarily means compensation for a wrong. Further, these awards are difficult to explain without adopting an injustice-based interpretation or something similar. As Sir Francis Jeune stated in one salvage case, 'admiralty imposes on the owner of property saved an obligation to pay the person who saves it simply because in the view of that system of law it is just he should . . . '[97]

In any event, claimants can obtain compensatory *damages* awards notwithstanding that the defendant did not commit a wrong. I discuss seven situations where such awards are made (though there are almost certainly others). It is admittedly possible that these awards are anomalies. It is possible, in other words, that they tell us nothing about compensatory awards in those cases—by far the majority—where the defendant has committed a wrong. However, this conclusion seems unlikely. The law does not distinguish between damages for non-wrongs and ordinary damages. The courts describe both simply as 'damages'. More importantly, the assessment process is the same in each case. To take just one example that I discuss below, damages for injuries caused by the escape of water collected on your land are the same whether you are liable because the escape was your fault or because, under the doctrine of *Rylands v Fletcher*, landowners are strictly liable for the escape of water collected on their land. If the claimant's cause of action differed depending on whether the defendant committed a wrong, we would expect that the courts' response would also differ. Yet, the law treats both categories identically.

I do not dispute that the awards examined below are discussed in books on 'torts', and that 'tort' is just another word for 'wrong'. However, courts rarely describe the actions that trigger liability in these cases as wrongs or even as torts.[98] Instead, they typically describe them as giving rise only to a liability to pay damages for consequential losses.[99] In any event, regardless of how courts and commentators appear to classify the defendants' actions in these cases, they are not wrongs, or at least not wrongs in any meaningful sense of the word. In particular, they are not wrongs in any sense that could merit a wrong-based response. To describe an action as 'wrong' is generally understood to mean that it is undesirable, that the action is something that we should not do. For example, to say that assaulting another is wrong is generally understood to mean that we should not assault others. And this meaning applies even if the assault arises from an innocent mistake: a

[97] *The Cargo ex Port Victor* [1901] P 243, 249.

[98] Courts sometimes say explicitly that damages are dependent on a breach of duty, but these comments are invariably found in cases where the alleged breach, if proven, is clearly a wrong: see e.g. *Bourhill v Young* [1943] AC 92, 106 ('Damage due to the legitimate exercise of a right is not actionable . . . The damage must be attributable to the breach by the defendant': Lord Wright).

[99] 'We think that the true rule of law is that the person who, for his own purposes, brings on his land, and collects and keeps there anything likely to do mischief if it escapes, must keep it in at his peril, and, if he does not do so, he is prima facie answerable for all the damage which is the natural consequence of its escape': *Rylands v Fletcher* [1861-73] All ER Rep 1, 5 (Lord Blackburn).

mistaken assault is still undesirable. It is this meaning—the 'guidance' meaning of wrong[100]—that was assumed in Chapter 7's explanation of wrong-based awards. The wrongs to which wrong-based damages are a response are undesirable actions. The actions that I discuss below are not wrongs in this sense. These actions are permissible, if not positively desirable. To be sure, if you commit any of the actions discussed below you will be liable to being ordered to pay damages. But this liability does not show that the actions are wrongful in the guidance sense or in any other sense. Earning income makes me liable to pay taxes, but earning income is not a wrong. Similarly, if you agree, as part of an agreement to rent my house, to pay me for the cost of alternative accommodation, your liability to pay this sum does not mean your use of my house is a wrong.

The law is allowed to define its terms as it likes. But if it defines the actions discussed below as wrongs it will be using the term in a different sense than that in which it is normally used and understood, both within and outside the law. The only sense in which these actions are wrongs is that they ground a claim for damages. If that is all that it means to say that these actions are wrongs, this label is consistent with an injustice-based explanation of compensatory damages.

In the discussion below, I use the term 'wrong' in the guidance sense. Thus, I describe the actions discussed below as 'non-wrongs'. However, my arguments would be the same if I described these actions as 'non-wrongs, or at least as not wrongs in any sense that merits a wrong-based response'.

Vicarious Liability

Under the doctrine of vicarious liability, employers may be liable to pay compensatory damages in respect of torts committed by their employees, notwithstanding that they are innocent of any wrongdoing. It is true that the claimant must prove a wrong by the employee to establish vicarious liability, but as it is the employer who must pay the damages, the award cannot be interpreted as a response to that wrong. The defendant employer may be entirely innocent.

Rylands v Fletcher

Under the rule in *Rylands v Fletcher*,[101] landowners are liable to pay compensation for injuries caused by the escape of something that they brought onto their land. This liability arises regardless of how much care the landowner took to avoid the escape.

Merely bringing things onto your land that may escape cannot itself be a wrong.[102] If it were, a great deal of modern agricultural activity would be unlawful (not to mention the ordinary ownership of pets). More generally, the court in *Rylands* did not want to discourage landowners from building dams: they merely

[100] See McBride (2019) 37

[101] [1868] LR 3 HL 330.

[102] See McBride & Bagshaw (2015) 486–9; Zipursky & Goldberg (2016) 743.

wanted to hold them liable for any damage that they caused through this activity. If the courts thought that building dams was wrongful, the obvious thing for them to do would be to agree to issue injunctions prohibiting their construction. Instead, they merely hold individuals who engage in this activity liable for any injuries that they cause, however innocently. It is not coincidental that lawyers describe *Rylands* as giving rise to a 'strict liability' as opposed to a 'strict duty'. The landowners' duty is merely to take reasonable care when constructing dams: it is only their liability that is strict.

It is also not coincidental that lawyers typically do not treat batteries, trespasses, wrongful imprisonments, and other 'intentional torts' as analogous to *Rylands* liability, even though the liability in such cases is also strict. If I touch you because I reasonably, but mistakenly, believe you have consented to me touching you, I commit a battery. But unlike *Ryland's* liability, in the battery cases, it is not just the liability but also (and more fundamentally) the duty that is strict. A battery is undesirable—something that is wrong in the guidance sense—whether or not it is done because of an innocent mistake. You should not touch others without their consent, regardless of whether you believe that they have consented. A non-consensual touching is a wrong even if the wrongdoer is blameless. In contrast, the activities at issue in *Ryland* are permissible, indeed desirable. The distinctive feature of *Rylands* liability is not that it holds morally blameless defendants liable: it is that it holds defendants liable for the consequences of non-wrongful actions.

Consistent with the above interpretation, in the United States *Rylands* liability has been generalized to strict liability for 'abnormally dangerous activities'.[103] English courts have not taken this step, but a variety of common law and statutory rules have led to a broadly similar result. English law recognizes strict liability for injuries caused by dangerous animals (or specific animals known to have dangerous characteristics), nuclear facilities, escape of water from mains, cattle, and, with certain qualifications, fire.[104] English law also recognizes liabilities that are strict in the *Rylands* sense, but which do not involve dangerous activities. Vicarious liability, discussed above, is one example. Another long-standing example is the strict liability (with certain qualifications) of innkeepers for any loss of property suffered by guests.[105]

[103] American courts interpret this category narrowly; most of the cases involve bursting reservoirs, blasting, and dangerous animals: Goldberg (2016).

[104] See McBride & Bagshaw (2015) 499–502. Although 'abnormally dangerous activities' is not a legal category in England, English authors have used it to explain *Rylands* and related liabilities: 'The true situation seems to be that he who maintains for his own advantage a peculiarly dangerous thing in proximity to others, necessarily imposes upon those others a risk of injury . . . greater than is to be reasonably expected in the ordinary circumstances of social life, and it is therefore just and expedient that he himself should bear the risk of making good any damage to others which results from the maintenance of the object. This is certainly a liability, but it is a confusion of ideas to [say that it arises from the breach of] a duty': Allen (1931) 193–4.

[105] This liability is now enshrined in the *Hotel Proprietors Act* 1956, s 2.

Necessity

Individuals who have damaged others' property in order to avoid life-threatening injuries to themselves or to others (or, possibly, to avoid more serious injuries to their own property) are liable to be ordered to compensate those they have harmed.[106] A famous example is the already-mentioned American case of *Vincent v Lake Erie Transportation Co.*[107] The defendant tied his ship, without permission, to the claimant's dock to prevent it from being destroyed (presumably with the crew still aboard) in a storm. The court held that the defendant acted perfectly reasonably, but that he must nonetheless compensate the claimant for damage caused to the dock.

Using another's property without their permission is, of course, normally a wrong in the ordinary ('guidance') sense of the term. As I noted a moment ago, even accidental trespasses are normally undesirable. This observation seems to underlie John Gardner's suggestion that the defendant in *Vincent* was liable because he committed a wrong, albeit a 'justified' wrong.[108] But it is not clear in what sense an action that is justified can, at the same time, qualify as a wrong. Certainly, it is not a wrong in the guidance sense.[109] Nor does the fact that an action like using another's dock without permission is normally a wrong in the guidance sense explain why it remains a wrong in cases, like *Vincent*, where it is not a wrong in the guidance sense. The most straightforward explanation of *Vincent* is that the defendant was responsible for the damage to the dock notwithstanding that he did nothing wrong.

Non-Substitutionary Damages in Lieu of Specific Relief

In Chapter 6, I explained that the usual reason that courts award damages in lieu of specific relief is, broadly speaking, administrative. Particularly in contract cases, the normal reason that courts award damages in cases where specific performance is possible and desired is that monetary awards are simpler to express, supervise, and enforce. However, we also saw that courts sometimes refuse specific relief (and award damages instead) for reasons based on the substantive undesirability of the requested action. In these cases, while the courts appear merely to be choosing one form of remedy over another (namely, damages over specific relief), in substance,

[106] I discussed necessity cases, and also the cases in the next two categories, in Chapter 6 (under the heading 'Substantive-Law Reasons for Refusing Injunctions').

[107] [1910] 109 Minn 456.

[108] Gardner (2011) 43.

[109] Gardner's view, it appears, is that if you intentionally use others' property without their permission then you have necessarily committed a wrong and, accordingly, should pay damages for any injury you caused. But what if you use another's property to save that person's life? Imagine that you are having a heart attack while locked in your car. I break into the car without your permission (because you are unconscious) and save your life. It appears that, on Gardner's view, I should be liable for the damage that I caused to your car (and probably also liable for battery, as I touched you without your permission). There do not appear to be any cases on point, but it is doubtful that a court would agree.

they are denying the existence of the alleged rights-threats. They refuse specific relief not for administrative reasons, but because they regard the actions (or omissions) that the claimant wants enjoined as permissible, if not positively desirable. It follows that the damages awards in such cases are compensation for non-wrongs. Three cases illustrate this category.

In *Dennis v Ministry of Defence*,[110] the Ministry, as part of its pilot training, regularly flew Harrier jets over the claimant's property. The court held that the flying constituted a nuisance, but it refused to order the defendant to cease the flights, citing the cost of moving the airfield and the importance of training pilots. Instead, they awarded the claimant £955,000 in damages.

In the second example, the American case of *Boomer v Atlantic Cement Co*,[111] the claimants lived near the defendant's cement factory. The claimants alleged that pollution from the factory constituted a nuisance, and they sought an injunction prohibiting the factory from creating further pollution. Noting that the requested injunction would effectively shut down the factory, leading to the loss of hundreds of jobs, the court refused the claimant's request. Instead, they awarded compensation for the injuries that the claimants would suffer from the factory's continued operation.

In the third example, *Tito v Waddell (No 2)*,[112] the defendant mining company had a contract with the inhabitants of a South Seas island that permitted them to mine on the island. The contract included a clause requiring the company to replant the island after they completed their mining. However, subsequent to the defendant's mining, the island become uninhabitable (and the islanders moved to another island) following damage from bombing during the Second World War. The company did not replant the island and the claimants brought an action for, inter alia, specific performance of the replanting clause. Holding that replanting an uninhabitable island would be massively wasteful, the court refused specific performance (and also refused to award 'substitutionary' damages, that is, damages set at the cost of purchasing substitute performance), awarding compensatory damages instead.[113]

Dennis, Boomer, and *Tito* are controversial, but they are far from isolated decisions. Injunctions against nuisance, in particular, are regularly refused for broadly similar reasons.[114] And whatever one thinks of the outcomes in these cases, it is clear that the court's concern is not the desirability of *ordering* the defendant to

[110] [2003] EWHC 793.

[111] 26 NY 2d 219 (1970).

[112] [1977] Ch 106.

[113] The actual sum awarded was nominal or almost nominal because the court assumed that the islanders had not suffered any loss because of the failure to replant. This assumption seems to have been misplaced as it turns out that the island was not rendered permanently uninhabitable: many years later some of the islanders were able to return to their homeland.

[114] See e.g. *Dennis v Ministry of Defence* [2003] EWHC 793; *Bracewell v Appleby* [1975] Ch 408; *Denne v Light* (1857) 8 De GM & G 774; *Behrens v Richards* [1905] 2 Ch 614.

perform the relevant action. The court's concern is the desirability of the action itself, regardless of why it is performed. The reason that the courts denied specific relief in these cases was, roughly, that the cost of performing the requested action (including, where relevant, the cost to the public) was, in the court's view, vastly disproportionate to its benefit. Replanting an uninhabitable island is a massive waste of resources. This disproportion is the same whether the defendant performs the action because of a court order or because of a rule-based substantive duty. Stated differently, the courts' reasons for denying specific relief in such cases presume that, as in *Vincent,* the defendant acted, or is at least now acting, reasonably. If the court thought that the defendant ought do what the claimant wanted it to do, the obvious way to bring about this result would be to order specific relief or, at a minimum, substitutionary damages.[115] Courts are perfectly willing to issue injunctions against actions that they regard as undesirable. But the courts in these cases refused specific relief, and awarded compensation instead. The natural interpretation of these awards is that, like the award in *Vincent*, they require the defendants to compensate the claimants for the pecuniary consequences of actions that the courts regard as permissible.

Damages in Lieu of *Quia Timet* Injunctions

Closely related to the previous example is a compensatory award issued in lieu of a *quia timet* (preventative) injunction. In *Leeds Industrial Co-operative Society v Slack*,[116] the court refused to issue an injunction to cease building works that, when completed, would allegedly have infringed the claimant's right to light. Instead, the court awarded compensation for the harm that the completed works would cause. By definition, the defendant in such cases has not committed a wrong. In theory, such an award might be justified on the ground that it is compensation for the wrong that the defendant will commit in the future. But, if the court in *Leeds* believed that the defendant would be committing a wrong once the building was completed—if they believed, in other words, that the defendant ought to cease construction—the obvious way to ensure this result would be to grant the injunction. And, if the court thought that the application for a *quia timet* order was premature (since it was possible that the works would not be completed in the anticipated manner), they could have done what they normally do in such cases—namely, to refuse relief but leave the claimant free to request an injunction in future. By refusing the injunction and granting damages in lieu, the court effectively

[115] Courts never award substitutionary damages in lieu of injunctions (because it is not possible to purchase substitute performance of an injunction). However, they award substitutionary damages in lieu of specific performance, and presumably would have awarded them in *Tito* if they thought the defendant should have performed the requested action. The fact that the court limited the claimants to compensatory damages supports the conclusion that they refused specific relief for substantive-law reasons.

[116] [1924] AC 851.

gave the defendant permission to continue its activity indefinitely. The inescapable conclusion is that the court thought that it was permissible for the defendant to complete the works. As in *Dennis, Boomer*, and *Tito*, the natural interpretation of *Leeds* is that the court awarded compensatory damages for a non-wrong.

Innocent Misrepresentations

Section 2(2) of the *Misrepresentation Act* 1967 provides that, as an alternative to rescinding a contract for a non-fraudulent misrepresentation, a court may 'award damages in lieu of rescission'. This provision applies to wholly innocent misrepresentations, and therefore allows for compensatory damages in cases where the defendant has not committed a wrong. Indeed, the legislation is explicit that the basis for awarding damages in such cases is fairness-based. The provision directs the court to award damages if 'it would be equitable to do so', and further directs them to consider the losses that the parties would suffer under either option.

Wrongs to Third Parties

Finally, claimants are sometimes able to recover damages for losses that they have suffered because of a wrong committed against a third party.[117] For example, under the Civil Liability (Contribution) Act 1978, a tortfeasor who has been found liable to pay compensatory damages in a case of joint and several liability may obtain compensation for some or all of that payment from the co-tortfeasor(s). Section 2(1) provides that the sum 'shall be such as may be found by the court to be just and equitable having regard to the extent of that person's responsibility for the damage in question'. A co-tortfeasor has of course committed a wrong, but the wrong is against a third party, not the claimant seeking compensation. Similarly, under the *Fatal Accidents Act* 1976, the dependant of a deceased may recover against a defendant who wrongly caused the deceased's death in respect of losses suffered because of that death. Likewise, the *Contracts (Rights of Third Parties) Act* 1999 provides that, in certain cases, a third-party beneficiary of contract may recover in respect of losses suffered because of the defendant's breach of a contractual duty owed to the co-contractor. Analogous actions are also available under the *Congenital Disabilities (Civil Liability) Act* 1976 and the *Latent Damages Act* 1986. Non-statutory examples in this category include actions by disappointed legatees for losses suffered as a consequence of the defendant breaching a contractual duty owed to the (deceased) testator to revise or draw up a will,[118] as well as actions

[117] See Stevens (2007) 174–86. In the 1970s, English courts appeared to be moving in the direction of accepting that a wrong to a third party is, in general, sufficient to establish a breach of the duty of care in negligence: *Anns v Merton London Borough Councils* [1978] AC 728. They have since retreated: *Caparo Industries plc v Dickman* [1990] 2 AC 605; *Murphy v Brentwood* [1991] 1 AC 398.

[118] *White v Jones* [1995] 2 AC 207.

brought in respect of losses that were intentionally caused through unlawful means directed at a third party.[119]

In all of these cases, there has been a wrong, but it is not a wrong to the claimant. Given that the compensation must be paid to the claimant, not the victim of the wrong, it is difficult to see how these awards could qualify as wrong-based. They are clear examples of compensatory awards that cannot be explained as a response to a wrong.

Summary

The above examples demonstrate that courts frequently award compensatory damages in respect of non-wrongful actions. It is true that the vast majority of compensatory damages awards are issued in respect of wrongful actions. As I mentioned at the outset, it is therefore possible (though prima facie unlikely) that the cause of action for compensatory awards in cases where the defendant has committed a wrong is different from the cause of action in cases where the defendant is innocent. I explain below why this possibility should be rejected.

v. The Injustice-Based Theory

The preceding arguments are largely negative: they have sought to show that compensatory damages are not responses to either rights-threats or wrongs. But they have also pointed us towards a positive explanation of compensatory damages. The rules governing the assessment of compensatory damages are rules for determining when it is fair to attribute responsibility for the claimant's losses to the defendant. These rules respond, in other words, to the unfairness—the injustice—of the outcome of the parties' transaction. This conclusion is unsurprising. With rights-threats and wrongs out of the picture, the focus must turn to the outcome of the defendant's actions. And, it is difficult to think of any reason to reverse or undo an outcome that does not turn on the injustice or unfairness of that outcome.[120] As Arthur Ripstein noted (in commenting on Honoré's work on responsibility), the court's task, when it holds persons responsible for outcomes is 'primarily allocative, in the sense that assigning particular consequences to particular persons is a way of determining who will bear which costs'.[121] And, the question of how to make such allocations, as Ripstein notes, 'is ultimately one of justice'.[122]

[119] *OBG v Allan* [2008] 1 AC 1.

[120] As was true of restitutionary awards, compensatory damages are sometimes justified, instrumentally, in terms of the incentives they provide. I explain why instrumental theories are not competitors to an injustice-based theory in note 17.

[121] Ripstein (2001) 47.

[122] Ibid 38. In this essay, Ripstein appears to endorse Honoré's approach (see Honoré (1999)), which is broadly consistent with my interpretation of compensation. Ripstein writes that the victim's 'claim is that it would be unfair to her to relieve the defendant of liability, because the costs associated with this particular risk *properly* belong with the defendant rather than the [claimant]' (58). In his later work, Ripstein

But can anything more be said about the injustice that triggers compensatory damages? It can; however, as in the parallel case of restitutionary awards, there is not a great deal that needs to be said, at least for this book's purposes. The injustice-based interpretation of compensatory awards supposes that the basic question for courts is whether it is fair to hold the defendant responsible for the relevant losses (or, what amounts to the same thing, whether the relevant losses are fairly attributed to the defendant). The idea that individuals may be responsible for harms that they have caused others is familiar. If you carelessly drive over my bicycle, you would, I trust, accept responsibility for my loss. The same idea is assumed throughout the large and well-established theoretical literature devoted to responsibility and private law.[123] This literature focuses primarily on the law governing compensatory damages. And, it assumes, largely without argument, that the basic issue raised by compensatory damages is precisely the issue identified by an injustice-based interpretation, namely: 'under what conditions is it morally acceptable to hold a person responsible for the causal consequences of his or her acts?' [124]

What, then, are these conditions? When is it appropriate for courts to hold defendants responsible for a claimant's losses? It is not possible here to provide anything like a general theory of responsibility (though I will draw on such theories[125]). For present purposes, it is sufficient to show that the conditions under which compensatory awards are available align with a recognizable concept of responsibility.[126]

To begin, in both morality and law, we rarely hold individuals responsible for outcomes unless they are a factual cause of that outcome.[127] In the normal case, factual causation is established by showing that the relevant outcome would not have happened 'but for' the individual's action. If I had nothing to do with your injury, then, baring unusual circumstances (e.g. I am your parent and I neglected to look after you), I cannot be responsible for your injury. However, factual causation is clearly insufficient, standing alone: '[a]n extra element is needed to ground the legal sanction'.[128] My decision to open a store that competes with yours may be

defends the continuity thesis explanation of damages, in which 'fairness' and 'allocation' drop out of the picture: 'I mention both Honoré and Darwall not to dispute their accounts of responsibility and personal accountability, but because I think however important these aspects are in other domains of life, they do not figure in an account of the moral basis of the law of private wrongs': Ripstein (2016) 16.

---

[123] See e.g. Williams (1981); Nagel (1979); Honoré (1999), especially chs 3 & 6; Ripstein (1999) 269–70; Gardner (2001) 127; Perry (2001a); Cane (2001); Perry (2001b).

[124] Ripstein (2001) 38. 'In torts we are dealing with activities and their accident costs. The question is always who should bear these costs': Coleman (1980) 120–1. See also Prosser (1953) 17; Perry (2001a) 60; Honoré (1999) 78–9.

[125] See the work cited in note 124, especially Perry (2001a).

[126] My explanation broadly follows Honoré (1999) 78–9.

[127] On the significance of factual causation, see Honoré (1999) 14–40; Perry (2001a) 50.

[128] Honoré (1999) 27. See also Perry (2001a) 52 ('Outcome-responsibility [i.e. factual causation] is reason-affecting, but, as we have seen, there are no grounds for thinking that it is sufficient by itself to justify shifting a loss. The question to be asked, then, is whether there is some other factor that, together with outcome-responsibility, could serve as an appropriate justification for redistribution.')

a factual cause of your losing business, but no court would hold me liable for that loss. In any event, every injury has multiple factual causes. My carelessly driving into your parked car is a cause of the ensuing damage, but so too was your decision to park your car in that location.

What else is required? In both morality and law, the answer is that any one of a number of additional conditions may be sufficient.[129] The most obvious and practically important of these conditions is that the action that factually caused the loss was a wrong to the claimant. If you incur medical expenses as a consequence of my punching you in the face, it is fair to hold me responsible for those expenses because they are a consequence of something that I should not have done. By definition, if I should not have done the action, then you should not have suffered the consequences you suffered. And, since it was my choice to commit the wrongful action, it is fair to hold me responsible for those consequences. '[T]he duty to repair . . . wrongful losses is grounded not in the fact that they are the result of wrongdoing, but in the fact that the losses are the injurer's responsibility, the result of the injurer's agency'.[130] Responsibility for the consequences of one's wrongful actions is probably the most basic form of legal responsibility. But while some authors appear to assume, at least in their less guarded moments, that it is the only form of legal responsibility, authors who have considered the examples that I discuss below invariably accept that responsibility for bad outcomes is not limited to cases where those outcomes are a consequence of bad behaviour.[131]

A second sufficient condition, exemplified by employers' vicarious liability for the torts of their employees, is satisfied where someone commits a wrong while acting on another's behalf. Vicarious liability is often defended on the ground that it is fair for employers to bear the costs of their employees' actions, since they reap the benefits of those actions. However, while this defence is broadly of the right kind (i.e. fairness-based), it does not explain why vicarious liability only arises if an employee commits a tort. Further, this defence appears to support strict liability across the board. Most defendants benefit from the activities in which they were engaged when they harmed the claimant (why else engage in the activity?). A more plausible explanation is that it is fair to attribute an employee's actions to

[129] See Honoré (1999) 27–8. The closest that Honoré comes to offering a general statement of these conditions is the following: 'The argument for holding people responsible to others for harmful outcomes is that it is fair to make the person to whom the advantages will flow from an uncertain situation over which he has some control (or which he has chosen to enter into) bear the losses that may equally flow from that situation': Honoré (1999) 78–9. This proposition covers most, but not all, the conditions discussed below.

[130] Coleman (1992a) 443.

[131] 'Responsibility is not just a function of the quality of will manifested in conduct, nor of the quality of that conduct. It is also concerned with the interest we all share in security of person and property, and with the way resources and risks are distributed in society. Responsibility is a relational concept. Herein lies the key to explaining the justifying obligations of repair regardless of fault': Cane (2002) 109. See also Herman (1993) 97–9; Feinberg (1978) 102; Honoré (1999) 1–40; Gardner (2001); Ripstein (1999) 4.

the employer if the employee is acting in the course of employment.[132] If you have engaged someone to work on your behalf, it is fair to attribute their actions to you when they are engaged in that work. It follows that, if the employee's actions are tortious, the liability for the tort is fairly attributed to the employer.

A third sufficient condition, exemplified by *Rylands v Fletcher* liability, is that the defendant was engaged in an activity that is dangerous to others. Some dangerous activities are simply banned outright, for example, discharging firearms in public spaces. But others are permitted because their benefits are thought to outweigh the risks. Dams are inherently dangerous, but they are invaluable for controlling floods, providing irrigation, and so forth. At the same time, it is fair to hold individuals who choose to engage in dam building and other dangerous activities responsible for the harm that their activities may cause.[133] Individuals who engage in dangerous activities expose others to unusual risks, risks that go beyond the ordinary risks that are properly regarded as part of the ordinary vicissitudes of life (and for which there is ordinarily no liability without wrongdoing).

A fourth condition, exemplified by the liability in *Vincent v Lake Erie*, is that the loss arose from the defendant's decision to use the claimant's property to save its own person or property. The question of when such uses are permissible is difficult and controversial. One person's 'necessitous situation' (or 'emergency') is another person's ordinary circumstances. But, for present purposes, it is sufficient to accept that, however necessity is defined, it is fair to hold defendants responsible for damage that they have caused in a state of necessity. It is fair because the defendant chose to use the claimant's property. If I use your property to save my property (or my person), I should compensate you for your loss.

A fifth, closely related condition, exemplified by cases like *Dennis*, *Boomer*, and *Tito*, is that the loss arises from an act or omission that is normally wrongful, but that is not wrongful in the particular circumstances because its value far outweighs the harm that it causes. As with question of what circumstances qualify as a necessity, the question of when the costs and benefits associated with a normally impermissible activity make that activity permissible is difficult and controversial. But wherever the line is drawn, it is fair to make actors engaged in such activities pay for the harm that they cause. The explanation is the same as for *Vincent:* if the law allows you to do something that is normally impermissible (because it may harm others), and you choose to do that thing, it is fair that you compensate those whom the normal rule of impermissibility is meant to protect. *Dennis*, *Boomer*, and

[132] Robert Stevens also explains vicarious liability on the ground that the employee's actions are attributed to the employer: Stevens (2007) 257–74. However, while the examples Stevens offers in support of his position—such as attributing an individual's action to a corporate body (or to similar entities, such as sports teams) or to someone who has authorized the action—demonstrate that the law frequently attributes actions, they do not explain why the law attributes employees' actions to employers (and, further, attribute only some of those actions). My explanation is fairness.

[133] Fletcher (1972); Honoré (1999) 15.

Tito are milder versions of *Vincent*. The main difference between these cases and *Vincent* is that in *Vincent* it was too late for the claimant to request an injunction.

These comments fall far short of a comprehensive explanation of compensatory damages, much less of responsibility for loss in general. For the most part, I have merely asserted that the various situations in which courts award compensatory damages are consistent with ordinary intuitions about when it would be fair to attribute responsibility for the claimant's loss to the defendant. However, it is not clear that a great deal more can be said about responsibility for outcomes, at least if one's goal is limited to explaining the law. Writers on responsibility invariably test their accounts against ordinary intuitions about responsibility.[134] If the above description of those intuitions is unconvincing, it is doubtful that a theoretical account of responsibility would be more convincing. In any event, it is clear, I trust, that there is nothing unusual about saying that it is fair to hold defendants who committed wrongs, whose employees committed wrongs, who engaged in dangerous activities, or who used another's property for their benefit liable for the consequences of their actions. Courts, commentators, and ordinary individuals say these things all the time. This chapter's main contribution to the literature on responsibility is to fit this familiar idea into a general account of remedies.

D. Other Injustice-Responding Remedies

The awards available to necessitous interveners (discussed above), as well as those authorized under matrimonial property and contribution legislation, show that the category of injustice-responding remedies is not limited to restitutionary and compensatory orders. Other potential candidates are most likely to be found amongst those remedies conventionally described as orders to reverse unjust enrichments. Peter Birks and others have long assumed that the restitutionary orders discussed in this chapter are core examples of this broader category.[135] However, as strong doubts have recently been raised about this assumption,[136] I will limit myself to noting that, insofar as the orders that Birks assumed to be analogous to orders that reverse defective transfers are, in fact, analogous, their cause of action is the same.

The next most obvious candidates for inclusion in this chapter are remedies for actions that, as currently understood, appear to be neither contractual, tortious,

[134] 'The volitionist/distributive argument is an attempt to clarify our evaluative attitudes regarding actions that produce harmful outcomes, and to show why it is appropriate to conclude, in light of those attitudes, that under certain circumstances reparation is due. I do not think that anything more than this can be said': Perry (2001a) 55; '[P]ervasive and unshakeable features of human practical thought need no justification, though they call for an explanation': Raz (1986) 288–9. See also Williams (1981); Nagel (1979); Honoré (1999); Gardner (2001).

[135] Birks (2005) 4–19; Burrows (2011) 201–54.

[136] Stevens (2018); Penner (2018).

nor based on an unjust enrichment.[137] In closing, I identify two potential candidates, each of which illustrates this category's potential breadth.

i. Compensation for Detrimental Reliance (Equitable and Proprietary Estoppel)

In certain situations, claimants who have incurred expenses in reliance on another's representation may obtain a compensatory remedy, notwithstanding that the representation is neither contractual nor a tortious misrepresentation or other legal wrong.[138] If I erect a building on your land because your representation (or even your mere acquiescence to my actions) induced me to believe that you will transfer the land to me, I may be able to obtain an order directing you to compensate me for the cost of my improvements.[139] The scope of such relief varies amongst common law jurisdictions: in England, it is, in theory, restricted to representations involving property ('proprietary estoppel'),[140] while in the United States and Australia, it applies more generally (where it is usually described as 'promissory' or 'equitable' estoppel).[141] The basis of the doctrine is also a matter of dispute. Some writers explain these actions as, in substance, contract actions, the primary difference being that 'detrimental reliance' takes the place of 'consideration'.[142] For others, probably the majority, the doctrine's core role is protecting detrimental reliance; in this view, it does not matter, in principle, whether the defendant has made a promise, and the remedy may be more limited than a standard contractual remedy.[143]

I cannot resolve this long-running debate here (though I note that relief has been awarded in at least some cases where it is clear that the defendant did not make a promise and that this relief is less than what would have been awarded in a contractual action[144]). I only note that insofar as the detrimental-reliance interpretation explains some or all of the remedies in this area, these remedies appear to be injustice-based. In such cases, the claimant is compensated notwithstanding that

[137] See generally, McBride (1994); Muir (1990). Though outside this book's scope, various remedies for actions within Equity's historically exclusive jurisdiction (e.g. trust law) may also fall into this category. Possible examples here include Trustee Remuneration Orders (*Re Duke of Norfolk's ST* [1982] Ch 61 at 79; *Trustee Act* 2000, s 2); Variation of Trust Orders; and, where they are recognized, remedial constructive trusts (*Pettkus v Becker* [1980] 2 SCR 834).

[138] Closely related to the remedies discussed in this section are remedies available to claimants who, notwithstanding that they did not have a contract with the defendant, provide requested services or incurred a liability as a result of performing a requested action: see McBride (2004) 40–5.

[139] *Jennings v Rice* [2002] WECA Civ 159. See generally, Peel (2015) 119–35, 153–72.

[140] See generally McFarlane (2016). However, English courts appear to have awarded compensation for detrimental reliance on representations that did not involve property: see e.g. *William Lacey (Hounslow) Ltd v Davis* [1957] 1 WLR 952; Peel (2015) 134.

[141] *Restatement 2nd Contracts*, s 90; *Walton Stores (Interstate) Ltd v Maher* (1988) 164 CLR 387

[142] *Mea culpa*: Smith (2004) 233–45.

[143] See e.g. Spence (1999).

[144] See e.g. *Willmott v Barber* (1880) 15 Ch D 96.

the defendant neither committed nor threatened to commit a wrong. Consistent with this interpretation, the courts' explanations of what they are doing when they decide these cases are replete with references to 'injustice' and 'fairness'. In Deane J's words in the leading Australian decision of *Walton Stores (Interstate) Ltd v Maher*, the underlying issue in these cases 'is whether the appellant so contributed to the assumption that the exchange had taken place that it would be unjust or unfair if it were left free to ignore it'.[145]

ii. Property Transfer Injunctions

Certain orders to transfer specific property appear to be responses to injustices. Of course, most orders to transfer property are made in respect of property that is owned by the claimant. As we saw in Chapter 7, these orders, traditionally styled 'delivery up', are responses to rights-threats, specifically the threat that the defendant will not return the property. However, certain orders to transfer specific property appear to be responses to the same kind of injustice that ground compensatory damages.

One example is an order to undo or remove a wrong's consequences, such as an order a remove a structure that was constructed, unlawfully, on the claimant's land.[146] The mere existence of an unlawfully constructed structure is not itself a trespass or other wrong: trespassing is an action (it can only be committed through intentional action), not a state of affairs. Nor is an unlawfully constructed structure a nuisance: a structure that is located on the claimant's land cannot interfere with the claimant's use of that land. It follows that an order to remove an unlawfully constructed structure is, in substance, an order to undo the consequences of a wrong. Accordingly, its cause of action appears to be an injustice.

A second possible example is an injunction that directs the defendant to return property obtained through a wrong. In *Esso Petroleum Co Ltd v Kingswood Motors (Addlestone) Ltd*,[147] the defendant committed the tort of interference with contractual relations by purchasing a garage that was subject to a solus agreement (which precluded such a purchase) between the vendor and the claimant. Bridge J ordered the defendant to transfer the garage back to the vendor. Although the

145 (1988) 164 CLR 387, 461. See also Mason CJ and Wilson J at 495 ('Holding the representor to his representation is merely one way of doing justice between the parties'). *Walton Stores* includes forty-three references to 'injustice', 'fairness', and variations on these terms (e.g. 'unjust', 'unfair'). Although it refers to promises, s 90 of the American *Restatement 2nd Contracts* explicitly grounds its cause of action, and limits its remedial response, to what justice requires: '(1) A promise which the promisor should reasonably expect to induce action or forbearance on the part of the promisee or a third person and which does induce such action or forbearance is binding if injustice can be avoided only by enforcement of the promise. The remedy granted for breach may be limited as justice requires.'

146 *Kelsen v Imperial Tobacco Co (of Great Britain and Ireland) Ltd* [1957] 2 QB 334.

147 [1974] QB 142.

defendant had committed a wrong in purchasing the garage, its resulting ownership of the garage was not a wrong. The defendant had clear title to the garage. The purpose of the re-transfer, therefore, was not to end an ongoing wrong: the wrong was finished. Rather, the purpose can have only been to undo the consequences of the defendant's past wrong. As Bridge J observed, the order's effect was to 'enforce the personal liability incurred by a tortfeasor to undo the consequences of his tort which could have been restrained before it was committed'.[148] The injunction in this case appears to have had the same cause of action as an order to pay compensatory damages: an injustice.

[148] [1974] QB 142,156.

9
Defences

The core of remedial law is a set of rules that determine when, in what form, and at whose request, courts issue remedies. Unsurprisingly, the rules discussed in remedies textbooks typically have the same focus. However, what is surprising is that these textbooks are typically organized almost entirely around particular categories of remedies (e.g. 'rules about specific performance', 'rules about damages', and so forth).[1] If there is such a thing as 'the law of remedies' at least some of this law should presumably be about remedies in general. The decision to discuss specific performance, injunctions, damages awards, and so on within a single textbook implies that the laws governing these rulings reflect at least some common rules or principles. Yet, the way in which remedies textbooks are traditionally organized suggests that there are no such rules or principles.

As I hope is clear, this book takes a different approach. In Chapter 3, I argued that the creation, wording, and enforcement of private law orders are governed by general rules and principles. In Chapters 6 to 8, I argued that the availability and content of remedies are similarly governed by general principles. This final chapter focuses on the general rules and principles governing remedial defences.

I defend two general claims about remedial defences. The first is that the law of remedial defences constitutes a significant, though largely unrecognized, part of remedial law. Remedial defences are numerous and practically important. The second claim is that remedial defences are based on general principles—principles that cut across historical boundaries. Continuing an argument that I began in Chapter 3, I argue that it is unhelpful to classify, describe, and explain remedial defences—including so-called 'equitable defences'—in terms of their historical origins. There are exceptions, but in general, remedial defences, like remedial rules, are best understood by focusing on their substance. The same defences, and the same governing principles, could easily have developed in a unitary legal system.

Courts and commentators often criticize the defences discussed in this chapter. For the most part, these criticisms are tangential to this chapter's primary focus, which is to understand the specifically remedial nature of the rules governing remedial defences. However, the criticisms cannot be ignored entirely. My view that these defences reflect general principles turns in part on arguments about how they might plausibly be justified. Ideally, those arguments should explain not only why

[1] See e.g. Dobbs & Roberts (2018); Burrows (2004); Berryman et al (2016); Harris, Campbell, & Halson (2002).

Rights, Wrongs, and Injustices. Stephen A. Smith, Oxford University Press (2019). © Stephen A. Smith.
DOI: 10.1093/oso/9780199229772.003.0009

the rules in question exist, but also why they have been criticized and, in many cases, why their scope has been curtailed significantly in recent decades.

A final preliminary comment is that this chapter is undoubtedly incomplete. The discussion ranges across a large number of defences in a relatively short space. More importantly, my list of defences is almost certainly not exhaustive. A number of the rules discussed in this chapter are not typically associated with remedial law. In some cases, they ended up in this chapter only because I came across them while researching unrelated topics. Fortunately (at least for me), this book is not a treatise. This chapter's primary aim is not to describe the entirety of the law of remedial defences: it is to demonstrate that such a law exists at all.

A. Remedial and Substantive Defences

Broadly speaking, a defence is a reason for a court to refuse an order notwithstanding that the claimant has satisfied the relevant cause of action.[2] For example, proof that the defendant failed to pay for a sum due satisfies the cause of action for an order for a sum due; if nothing more is said, the court will issue the order. However, if the defendant establishes that the relevant limitation period expired, the court will refuse to issue the order. The expiry of the limitation period is a defence. In contrast, if the court refuses the order because the defendant introduced evidence that the sum was not in fact due, then the reason for the refusal is not a defence. The reason is that the cause of action was not satisfied.

It is often difficult to determine whether a particular reason for refusing an order is a defence as opposed to a denial of the cause of action. However, from the perspective of understanding remedial law, the most important distinction is not between defences and denials, but between two kinds of defences. Specifically, the most important distinction is between 'substantive' and 'remedial' defences. Only the latter are part of remedial law.

A defence is substantive if the reason it provides for refusing a remedy is that that the rights-threat, wrong, or injustice that the claimant asserts is not actually a rights-threat, wrong, or injustice (or it is a permissible rights-threats, wrong, or injustice[3]). For example, self-defence is a substantive defence to an action in battery

[2] See Goudkamp (2013) 5–7. The rules governing defences also inform potential claimants whether they are likely to obtain a remedy. Like much of remedial law, these rules are both directions to courts (telling courts when not to award remedies) and power-conferring rules for individuals (informing individuals of the circumstances in which they may obtain or be subject to remedies).

[3] For the purposes of distinguishing remedial defences from substantive defences (and, more generally, for distinguishing remedial-law reasons from substantive-law reasons for refusing relief), there is no difference between saying that a rights-threat, 'is not actually a rights threat' and saying that 'it is a permissible rights-threat'. In either case, the reason is substantive because in either case we are saying that the defendant should not feel bound to comply with her alleged substantive duty. In what follows, I will generally adopt the first locution. This terminology is more convenient, but it also reflects the core

because it establishes that an apparent battery was justified and therefore not actually a battery.[4] Another way of explaining this distinction is that self-defence is a substantive defence because it modifies the directions provided by the substantive law. The existence of this defence does not merely inform individuals that courts will not order them to pay damages if they injure others in self-defence: the defence also, and more fundamentally, informs individuals that it is permissible to injure other individuals in self-defence. Other substantive tort defences include consent, public necessity, recapture of land, and defence of another person. Substantive defences are a part of the substantive law; they are part of the law that stipulates how individuals should treat one another in day-to-day life.[5]

In contrast, a defence is remedial if the reason it provides for refusing an order is concerned exclusively with the desirability of the court issuing a judicial remedy or issuing a particular kind of judicial remedy (as opposed to the desirability of the actions or states of affairs that gave rise to the claimant's request). For example, the expiry of a limitation period is normally a remedial defence because limitation periods normally exist to avoid various practical problems that may arise if litigation is not brought in a timely fashion (e.g. stale evidence). The passing of six years since a debt was incurred is not a reason for the debtor to refuse to pay; however, it may be a reason to bar the creditor from receiving the court's assistance. The same reasoning applies in tort cases: the fact that a tort was committed twenty years ago does not make the tort any less wrong, but it may be a good reason for courts to refuse to get involved. Limitation periods and other remedial defences are a part of remedial law because they are fundamentally directions to courts: the expiry of a limitation period is (merely) a reason for a court to refuse a remedy. It is not meant to affect how the relevant parties act in day-to-day life.

Courts and legislatures sometimes explicitly classify defences as substantive or remedial. For example, the legislature in the United Kingdom has said explicitly that in most—but, interestingly, not all—cases the expiry of a limitation period has no effect on the parties' substantive rights.[6] However, with respect to many defences (e.g. illegality) the courts and legislatures are silent. Courts are occasionally required, in the course of litigation, to determine if a particular defence affects the existence or force of a substantive duty, wrong, or injustice (e.g. in cases involving

understanding of 'duty'. From the law's perspective, to state there is a legal duty to do X means that, all things considered, X should be done. The contrary view is defended in Gardner (2011) 42.

[4] See e.g. Goudkamp (2013) 106–7.

[5] The classification of the restitutionary defence of change of position is complex. My argument that the entirety of the law governing restitutionary orders is remedial suggests that change of position must be a remedial defence. However, the orientation of this defence is different from that of classic remedial defences, such as the expiry of a limitation period. Change of position resembles substantive defences (like self-defence) in that it goes to show that the injustice on which the claimant relies is not actually an injustice.

[6] The most important exception involves cases relating to rights in land: *Limitation Act* 1980, s 17.

conflicts of law or claims for restitution of money paid by mistake)—and, if they do this, they will effectively determine if the defence is substantive or remedial. But such cases are rare, and it is even rarer to find a reasoned analysis of the nature of the relevant defence. For their part, textbooks rarely consider how defences affect substantive rights except, sometimes, when discussing limitation periods.[7]

To determine if a defence is substantive or remedial in a case where the courts and legislature are silent it is necessary to ask why the defence exists and what the nature of the rights-threat, wrong, or injustice against which the defence may be raised is. Neither task is simple. Further compounding the difficulty is that remedial defences are inherently controversial. Where a remedial defence is established, the court will either refuse a remedy entirely (even if a rights-threat, wrong, or injustice is proven) or (in the case of 'partial defences') limit the claimant to a monetary remedy. Moreover, the underlying reason for the refusal is normally 'public policy', broadly understood—for example, the efficient operation of the court system. Not surprisingly, courts and writers frequently criticize such reasons or suggest alternative justifications for the rule. This feature of remedial defences helps to explain why the relevant law is often in a state of flux. It also explains why the classification of certain defences—illegality is a prime example—raises difficult issues.

As mentioned above, this chapter does not provide an exhaustive account of remedial defences. Rather, my more modest aim is to introduce and defend the general idea of a remedial defence. For this purpose, it is sufficient to illustrate the category by introducing some (I hope) relatively uncontroversial examples.

Three final preliminary points. As I have already indicated, the law governing remedial defences is complex, unstable, and frequently criticized. However, the idea of a remedial defence is in principal entirely valid. Throughout this book, I have argued that the question of how individuals should treat one another is different from the question of what courts should do when individuals ask for their assistance. Courts are publicly funded institutions, and it is natural and appropriate for them to consider 'public policy' when assessing requests for their assistance. It is not easy to determine when and in what degree such concerns should matter—which partly explains the state of the law in this area—but that they should matter seems incontrovertible.

Second, the distinction between general defences (this chapter's focus) and order-specific defences (examined in Chapters 6 to 8) could be drawn in different ways. Some remedial defences are specific to claims arising from particular substantive areas of law; for example, the *Limitation Act* 1980 distinguishes between actions 'founded on tort' and actions 'founded on simple contract'. Other defences are specific to particular claimants; for example, the defence of immunity applies

[7] Goudkamp (2013) is an important exception. He expresses the distinction between substantive and remedial defences as one between 'justifications' and 'public policy defences'.

(in varying degrees) primarily to the Crown, foreign diplomats, and defendants engaged in legal proceedings. But both the limitation and immunity defences are also general in the sense that (with certain exceptions) they apply to orders to pay damages, to pay a debt, to restrain from an activity, and so on. The classification of a defence as general or specific depends, therefore, on how orders are classified. As explained in Chapter 4 and illustrated in Chapters 6 to 8, the scheme adopted in this book focuses on the relationship between the cause of action and the parties' substantive rights. Within that scheme, the defences discussed below are general or largely general.

Finally, remedial defences are either 'full' or 'partial'. A full defence is a reason for refusing to issue a remedy entirely, while a partial defence is a reason for refusing to issue a particular kind of remedy (leaving open the possibility that the court will award a different remedy). In practice, partial defences are reasons for refusing specific relief and awarding damages instead. I begin by examining full remedial defences.

B. Full Defences

i. Absence of Formalities

The absence of a required legal formality is sometimes a remedial defence. For example, s 4 of the *Statute of Frauds* 1677 stipulates that 'no action may be brought' on a contract of guarantee unless the contract is in writing. Accordingly, the courts have consistently held that the absence of writing in a contract of guarantee precludes parties from bringing an action based on the contract, while leaving the parties' substantive rights unchanged.[8] It is because s 4 is a remedial defence that money paid under an oral contract of guarantee is not recoverable in an action for restitution: if the lack of writing prevented a contract from arising, restitution would be possible.[9] To similar effect, ss 22 and 24 of the *Marine Insurance Act* 1906 render a marine insurance contract that is not embodied in a signed policy 'inadmissible in evidence'—though the contract itself remains valid.[10]

In other cases, the absence of formalities operates as a substantive defence. The rule that an agreement for the sale or other disposition of an interest in land must be in writing was originally part of s 4 of the *Statute of Frauds*—and, as such, was

[8] *Leroux v Brown* (1852) 12 CB 801.

[9] *Thomas v Brown* (1876) 1 QBD 714.

[10] It follows that the rules stipulating that a contract will be enforced notwithstanding the absence of a required formality are also part of remedial law. Examples include the traditional rules that authorize a court to order specific performance notwithstanding the lack of a required formality if the contract has been 'partly performed' or if the defendant was guilty of fraud. Most of these exceptions have been abolished in England: Peel (2015) 221–2.

originally remedial—but in its current incarnation in s 2 of the *Law of Property (Miscellaneous Provisions) Act* 1989 it operates as a substantive defence. Rather than stipulating that 'no action may be brought' on a contract for the sale or other disposition of an interest in land, s 2 stipulates that such a contract 'can only be in writing'. The clear implication of this change in terminology is that an agreement that is not in writing is not a contract.[11]

It is not surprising that formal requirements sometimes operate as remedial defences and sometimes as substantive defences. Lon Fuller famously identified three functions served by formalities: evidentiary, cautionary, and channelling.[12] The first of these functions has a remedial focus because it reflects a concern for avoiding problems of proof that may arise in litigation. The second and third functions—the cautionary and the channelling functions—have a substantive focus because they are based on a concern for ensuring that, broadly speaking, contracting parties are aware of what they are doing when they enter contracts. In theory, a formal requirement could operate as a remedial defence in one case and as a substantive defence in the next, depending on which of these functions it served. However, in practice formalities cannot serve any of the functions identified by Fuller if courts must look beneath them to examine the substance of the relevant transaction. For this reason, lawmakers must decide, with respect to each formality, whether it serves a primarily evidentiary function or a primarily cautionary or channelling function. As discussed above, English lawmakers have decided that most, but not all, formalities serve a primarily evidentiary function.

ii. Immunity

The defence of immunity has been narrowed significantly in recent decades, but it may still be raised in certain circumstances by foreign states, the Crown, and individuals participating in legal proceedings. Briefly, foreign states enjoy a common law immunity in respect of actions in tort and other non-commercial transactions, with the important exception (introduced in the *State Immunity Act* 1978) that the immunity no longer applies where the relevant harm is death, personal injury, and damage or loss of tangible property.[13] The Crown, which formerly enjoyed sweeping immunities from civil actions, is presently immune only with respect to injunctions and orders for specific performance or for the recovery of land or property.[14] Special immunities to civil proceedings are also held by certain

[11] See Gray & Gray (2011); *Firstpost Homes Ltd v Johnson* [1995] 1 WLR 1567, 1571. Indeed, as the claimant must prove the writing, this requirement is arguably no longer a defence at all, but instead part of the cause of action.

[12] Fuller (1941).

[13] See Lewis (1990) 52–4.

[14] *Crown Proceedings Act* 1947.

Crown officials or in respect of particular Crown activities. For example, s 2(5) of the *Crown Proceedings Act* 1947 affirms the traditional rule that '[n]o proceedings shall lie against the Crown . . . in respect of anything done or omitted to be done by any person while discharging or purporting to discharge any responsibilities of a judicial nature'. Section 10(1) of the same Act exempts members of the armed forces from actions 'in tort for causing the death of another person, or for causing personal injury to another person, insofar as the death or personal injury is due to anything suffered by that other person while he is a member of the armed forces of the Crown'. Though not examined in this book, s 29 of the Act also prohibits so-called 'proceedings *in rem*' against ships, aircraft, or other personal property if the property belongs to the Crown. Finally, the common law traditionally held that any person taking part in a trial has civil immunity with respect to their participation: 'the court, judge and jury, and the witnesses including expert witnesses are granted civil immunity'.[15] In 2002, barristers' immunity was eliminated[16] and in 2011 the immunity of expert witnesses was similarly overruled.[17] At present, only judges, ordinary witnesses, and jury members enjoy this traditional immunity.

The Crown's now-obsolete general immunity in tort appears to have been a substantive defence as it was justified on the principle that 'the King can do no wrong'.[18] However, the immunities currently recognized by English law appear to be exclusively remedial. The opening provision of the *State Immunity Act* 1978 describes foreign states as enjoying immunities from 'the jurisdiction of the courts of the United Kingdom' (as opposed to immunities from the jurisdiction of United Kingdom 'law'). The remedial nature of this immunity is confirmed by the rule that proceedings may be brought against former diplomats with respect to torts or other actions that occurred while they were diplomats, as well as by the rule that foreign states lose their immunity if they are deemed to have submitted to a UK courts' jurisdiction.[19] The Crown's immunity is described in broadly similar language in the *Crown Proceedings Act* 1947 ('No proceedings shall lie against the Crown . . .'). The courts' willingness to issue declarations stating that the Crown has a substantive duty to the very things that, absent Crown immunity, would have been the subject matter of a specific performance order or an injunction further confirms that Crown immunity is a remedial defence. Finally, the remedial focus of the immunities afforded participants in legal proceedings is demonstrated by the courts' willingness to hold barristers liable in proceedings that, while focused on events that occurred prior to the abolition of barristers' immunities, were commenced after the date of abolition.[20]

15 *Arthur JS Hall & Co v Simons* [2002] 1 AC 615, 740 (Hobhouse LJ).
16 Ibid.
17 *Jones v Kaney* [2011] UKSC 13.
18 Blackstone (1765–69) Book III, Ch 17.
19 *Empson v Smith* [1966] 1 QB 426; *State Immunity Act* 1978, s 2.
20 *Awoyomi v Radford* [2008] QB 793.

It is not easy to justify even the limited range of immunities currently recognized by English law. However, such justifications as can be offered are consistent with treating immunity as a remedial defence. Immunities have nothing to do with the grounds for imposing substantive duties, the reasonableness of defendants' actions, or the justice of defendants' holdings. More broadly, there does not appear to be any reason that diplomats, the Crown, members of the armed services, or witnesses should not consider themselves bound to follow the same substantive rules as ordinary individuals. Diplomats should take care not to injure individuals, the Crown should perform its contracts, members of the armed services should not injure other members, and witnesses should tell the truth. However, there are reasons (or at least might plausibly be thought to be reasons) that such parties should not be subjected to legal proceedings. Allowing diplomats to be forced to defend their actions may harm relations with foreign states, specific performance orders cannot realistically be enforced against the Crown, judicially decided issues should not be re-litigated by suing witnesses, and the armed services have their own disciplinary procedures. These arguments are not reasons to grant the relevant parties license to ignore the substantive law. They are reasons for excluding these parties from the reach of remedial law.

iii. Statutory Non-Actionability

Many contemporary private law rights owe their existence to legislation. If such rights are threatened or breached, the right-holders can normally obtain a remedy in the usual way. For example, a claimant who has been injured from the breach of a statutory private law duty can obtain an order for damages from the breaching party. However, in some cases the legislation that creates a statutory duty stipulates that civil proceedings may not be brought for a breach of the duty. 'Non-actionability' provisions create remedial defences.

The *Health and Safety at Work etc. Act* 1974 provides an example. Section 2(1) states that 'It shall be the duty of every employer to ensure, so far as is reasonably practicable, the health, safety and welfare at work of all his employees'. Although many statutory duties are exclusively public law duties (i.e. duties owed to the public at large) and, as a result, are only capable of supporting public law actions and remedies, s 2(1) clearly creates a private law duty.[21] Yet by virtue of s

[21] In England, a statute creates a private law duty if, as a matter of statutory interpretation, it reflects such an intention. The courts have identified various indicia of such an intention, the most important of which are that the statute seeks to protect an identifiable class of persons and that a breach could lead to physical injury: Clerk & Lindsell (2018) [9-11]–[9-50]. Section 2(1) satisfies these tests: 2(1) protects an identifiable group—employees—and the harm it protects them from is primarily physical injury. Consistent with this interpretation, legislation promoting industrial safety is typically interpreted as giving rise to an action for breach of statutory duty (even when the statute provides for alternative

47(1) of the 1974 Act, no action is possible for breach of the employer's statutory duties: 'Nothing in this Part shall be construed . . . as conferring a right of action in any civil proceedings in respect of any failure to comply with any duty imposed by sections 2 to 7'. Section 47(1) creates a remedial defence: the section says nothing about the duties created in the Act; it merely precludes civil actions for the breach of those duties. In this respect, s 47(1) is similar to a statutory immunity or statutory limitation period. The only difference is that the statutory exclusion attaches to a duty created by the same statute that provides for the exclusion.

Most non-actionability clauses appear to have a similar effect as s 47(1). For example, the non-actionability clause in the *Guard Dogs Act* 1975 precludes civil proceedings for breach of an owner's failure to comply with its duty to control guard dogs 'on the premises'.[22] Another example is the statutory exclusion of civil proceedings for breach of a building owner's duty under the *Fire Precautions Act* 1971 to provide a 'means of escape' from 'the premises'.[23] Indeed, nearly all non-actionability clauses create remedial defences. The obvious reason to include such a clause is to preclude a liability that would otherwise arise for the breach of a statutory duty.

It might be thought odd that legislatures would create private law duties and, at the same time, preclude private law actions for the breach of those duties. Why bother to create a duty that cannot be enforced in the normal private law fashion? The short answer is that the legislature invariably provides other means of enforcing such duties (or, more strictly, of enforcing their public law parallels),[24] for example by quasi-criminal sanctions. The longer answer is that legislatures probably do not give much thought to whether they are creating private law duties. Legislatures need not consciously intend to create a private law duty in order to achieve this result: it is sufficient if they intend to create something that has the characteristic features of a private law duty (e.g. a duty that protects an identifiable class from physical injuries). Since legislatures often have this intention, they commonly create private law duties notwithstanding that they also commonly preclude the private enforcement of such duties.

means of enforcement: Clerk & Lindsell (2018) [9-17]; *Groves v Wimborne (Lord)* [1898] 2 QB 402; *Knapp v Railway Executive* [1949] 2 All ER 508.

---

[22] The duty imposed by the *Guard Dogs Act* 1975 is clearly a private law duty: it protects a particular group ('visitors on the premises') and its breach could result in physical injury.

[23] The building owner's duty is a private law duty: it protects a particular group ('persons on the premises') and its breach could result in physical injury. Under an earlier version of the Act (which did not include specifications for civil liability) visitors to premises were considered a particular class of persons in *Solomons v R Gertzenstein Ltd* [1954] 2 QB 243.

[24] Although the issue requires more analysis, it would seem that the availability of a public law remedy for breach of what appears to be a private law duty shows that the duty is both private and public. Theft is both a (private law) tort and a (public law) crime, but when the criminal law punishes theft, it is punishing the breach of the public law duty.

It is not strictly necessary to use a non-actionability clause to exclude statutory private law duties from private law enforcement. The legislature's intention to exclude may be established on other grounds. For example, in the appropriate circumstances such an intention may be inferred from the provision of alternative means of enforcement.[25] At the same time, it cannot be assumed that when judges deny liability for breach of a statutory duty on the ground that the legislature 'did not intend' that victims should be able to bring actions for damages that the legislature intended to create a private law duty.[26] It is true that the possibility of bringing an action for damages does not even arise unless the statute first creates a private law duty. However, it is likely that in many instances the reason courts focus on the legislature's intention vis-à-vis actions in damages is that they have assumed that an intention to exclude remedial rights is the same as an intention not to create substantive rights. This chapter is a warning against such an assumption.

iv. *Res Judicata*

The defence of *res judicata* may be invoked to bar re-litigation of an issue ('issue estoppel') or an entire claim ('cause of action estoppel') if that issue or claim has already been decided by a court: '[Once] the res—the thing actually or directly in dispute—has already been decided upon . . . by a competent court, it cannot be litigated again.'[27] *Res judicata* is a remedial defence because it is unconcerned with the existence or force of the rights-threat, wrong, or injustice on which the claimant's action is based: the doctrine's focus is the reasonableness of allowing the claimant to litigate the same matter a second time. This concern arises because re-litigation wastes judicial resources and may lead to inconsistent decisions. Re-litigation also makes it difficult for litigants to rely on decisions and, at the same time, leaves them vulnerable to vexatious litigation.[28] None of these reasons speaks to the merits of the claimant's action; they are merely reasons for refusing to give the claimant access to the courts.

v. Abuse of Process and *De Minimis*

'Abuse of process' is both a tort and a defence.[29] The tort is committed when a claimant initiates litigation for an improper or collateral purpose, for example to

[25] See e.g. *Lonrho Ltd v Shell Petroleum Co Ltd (No 2)* [1982] AC 173, 185.
[26] See *X (Minors) v Bedfordshire County Council* [1995] 2 AC 633, 748.
[27] *Ord v Ord* [1923] 2 KB 432, 439.
[28] Zuckerman (2013) 1239; *Lockyer v Ferryman* (1877) 2 App Cas 519, 530.
[29] The authority to strike out a claim for abuse of process is inherent in the court's jurisdiction, but it is also codified in *Civil Procedure Rules* s 3.4(2)(b), which provides that a court may strike out a claim

extort the defendant[30] or as a collateral attack on a criminal verdict.[31] The defence of abuse of process is broader: it may be invoked in any case where litigation is a 'disruptive, oppressive or otherwise inappropriate use of court procedures'.[32] For example, the defence has been established where claimants attempted to litigate an issue already decided in a sample case,[33] made factual allegations inconsistent with allegations in an earlier case,[34] or failed to consolidate joint claims.[35] In cases such as these (which need not involve an improper motive), the defence is traditionally called 'abuse of process estoppel'. Abuse of process estoppel is closely related to *res judicata* because it is used to prevent issues being raised that could have been raised in an earlier action and to prevent findings from an earlier proceeding being re-litigated by persons not party to that proceeding.[36]

The defence of abuse of process is clearly remedial. When the defence is used in the estoppel form, it is based on the same public policy concerns as *res judicata* (i.e. conserving judicial resources, avoiding conflicting decisions, and allowing parties to rely safely on decisions). When the defence overlaps with the tort (i.e. where it requires an improper motive), it is based on a concern for claimants abusing their right to access the court and, more broadly, on a concern for claimants undermining the court's authority. In both senses, the defence is unconcerned with the substantive merits of the claimant's action. Accordingly, the defence may be invoked notwithstanding that the court believes the defendant infringed (or is about to infringe) the claimant's rights. In Lord Phillips' words:

> An abuse of process is of concern not merely to the parties but to the court. It is no longer the role of the court simply to provide a level playing field and to referee whatever game the parties choose to play upon it. The court is concerned to ensure that judicial and court resources are appropriately and proportionately used in accordance with the requirements of justice.[37]

Like abuse of process, the concept of *de minimis non curat lex* ('the law does not concern itself with trifles')[38] has different meanings.[39] It is sometimes used as an

if it amounts to 'an abuse of the court's process or is otherwise likely to obstruct the just disposal of the proceedings'.

---

30 See e.g. *Grainger v Hill* (1838) 4 Bing NC 212.
31 See e.g. *Hunter v Chief Constable of the West Midlands Police* [1982] AC 529.
32 Zuckerman (2013) 618. Writers do not always distinguish the tort from the defence, with the result that the 'improper purpose' requirement is included in the definition of the defence. Zuckerman explains the difference at 618–26.
33 See e.g. *Ashmore v British Coal Corporation* [1990] 2 All ER 981.
34 See e.g. *Bradford & Bingley Building Society v Seddon* [1999] 4 All ER 217.
35 See e.g. *Bairstow v Queens Moat House plc* [2001] CP Rep 59.
36 Zuckerman (2013) 1253–69.
37 *Jameel v Dow Jones & Co Inc* [2005] QB 946 [54] (Lord Phillips MR).
38 *Taverner v Dominum Cromwell* (1594) 78 ER 601.
39 Veetch (1947).

interpretive tool, such as when a court holds that an apparent failure to satisfy a condition precedent or duty in a contract or statute is not in fact a failure if it is trivial.[40] In a similar way, *de minimis* is sometimes invoked to establish that a trivial infringement of riparian rights or a merely technical trespass is not a tort at all. When it is used in these ways, *de minimis* is part of substantive law. However, the concept may also be invoked as a remedial defence. This is the sense that was intended by Sedley LJ when he observed that a claim could be struck out on the ground that it was 'too trivial to merit court time and resources'.[41] Sedley LJ's statement assumes that a claim for trivial damages may be struck out notwithstanding its substantive merits, and the reason it provides for striking out focuses entirely on the cost of providing a remedy. When *de minimis* is used in this way, it is similar to the remedial defence of abuse of process, as judges have recognized.[42] It remains only to add that it is often difficult to determine if the concept is being used as a substantive or remedial defence because the triviality of an injury may show either that an apparent wrong was not in fact a wrong or that it was a wrong that does not merit getting courts involved.

vi. Limitation Periods

In certain circumstances, a claimant's failure to bring an action in a timely fashion may lead to the action being barred. The legal basis for this defence differs according to whether the claimant seeks a remedy that originated in the Royal Courts (e.g. damages, orders for a sum due) or a remedy that originated in the Chancery Court (e.g. specific performance, injunctions). In the former, the relevant law is statutory and primarily found in the *Limitation Act* 1980, while in the latter it is found in the judicial doctrine of 'laches'.[43] There are two main differences between the statutory limitation law and the doctrine of laches. First, while the statutory provisions normally specify that the relevant action may be barred simply on the expiry of a specified period (typically six years from when an action could first be

[40] See e.g. *Gillespie v Wells* [1912] 2 DLR 519.

[41] The full quotation reads 'I agree that as much of this claim as concerns trespass to goods and conversion cannot be struck out either as an abuse of the court's process or as a claim too trivial to merit court time and resources': *White v Whithers LLP* [2009] EWCA Civ 1122 (69). *De minimis* was understood in a similar way in the American case of *City of Bozeman Department of Transportation of State of Montana v Vaniman* 898 P2d 1208 (1995).

[42] In *White*, Ward LJ appears to have assumed that, at least when it was not used as a substantive defence, *de minimis* was an aspect of abuse of process: 'If such a trivial claim is brought, it is difficult to see anything more than nominal damages being suffered and I would encourage and expect such a claim to be struck out for being an abuse of the process.' (62).

[43] It appears that courts will not award specific relief if an 'analogous' statutory limitation period is expired: see note 121. Thus, the doctrine of laches is only invoked to shorten the period in which a claim may otherwise be brought. Remedies that owe their existence to statute typically are subject to limitation periods set out in the relevant statute.

brought), the doctrine of laches requires, roughly, that courts consider whether the delay is unreasonable given all the circumstances. Under the latter doctrine, the court is required to consider, in particular, whether the claimant acquiesced in the delay and whether the defendant was prejudiced by the delay. The second difference is that in cases where the doctrine of laches is invoked successfully the court will frequently exercise its authority under s 50 of the *Senior Courts Act* 1981[44] to award the claimant 'equitable damages' in lieu of specific relief.[45] In other words, the claimant in such cases is frequently awarded what I described in Chapter 6 as a substitutionary award. Strictly speaking, then, the doctrine of laches does not usually operate as a full defence—a reason for refusing an action entirely—but instead operates as a 'partial' defence. For this reason, the main discussion of laches appears in the discussion below of partial defences. For the purposes of this section, it is sufficient to mention that when laches operates as a full defence, it is a remedial defence for the same reasons that the expiry of a limitation period is a remedial defence.

The expiry of a limitation period is normally a remedial defence. With certain exceptions,[46] the expiry of a time period in the *Limitation Act* 1980 does not affect the defendant's substantive duty.[47] The Act states explicitly that the effect of the passing of a limitation period is that an action 'shall not be brought'.[48] Thus, a defendant who owes a debt prior to the expiry of a limitation period continues to owe the debt after the period has expired. The only legal significance of the expiring period is that a court will refuse to order the defendant to pay the debt.

The common law's understanding of the effect of limitation periods is understandable, although—as the exceptions demonstrate—it is not the only possible approach. The imposition of limitation periods can help avoid problems associated with delayed litigation, such as the risk of evidence going stale or the risk that the indefinite threat of a lawsuit may make it impossible for potential defendants to plan for the future and, more generally, to settle their affairs. Neither of these justifications is concerned with the substantive duty, wrong, or injustice underlying the claimant's action. These justifications explain, therefore, why limitation periods are normally remedial defences. However, they are not the only possible justifications. If a claimant has declined to take the opportunity to enforce a duty or remedy a wrong or injustice over a substantial period, it is arguable that the

[44] Formerly the *Chancery Amendment Act* 1858, s 2, popularly known as 'Lord Cairn's Act'. I consider awards under s 50 in more detail in the discussion of partial defences.

[45] See e.g. *Shelfer v City of London Electric Lighting Co* [1895] 1 Ch 287, 323; *Bracewell v Appleby* [1975] Ch 408, 419.

[46] The main exception relates to rights in land: *Limitation Act* 1980, s 17. Other exceptions include the extinction of title to personnel property for successive conversions, s 3(2), and the extinction of an advowson, s 25(3).

[47] It is '. . . trite law that English Limitation Acts bar the remedy and not the right': *Ronex Properties Ltd v John Laing Construction Ltd* [1982] 3 WLR 875, 879.

[48] 'An action founded on tort shall not be brought after the expiration of six years from the date on which the cause of action accrued': *Limitation Act* 1980, s 2.

claimant has implicitly waived the duty, wrong, or injustice, or at least should be treated as having done so. English law's general rejection of this argument reflects the high value it places on substantive rights.

vii. Illegality

In certain circumstances, courts will refuse to issue a remedy on the ground that the claimant's lawsuit is connected to an unlawful activity or to an activity that is against public policy (e.g. prostitution). For example, courts will refuse to award damages for breach of an agreement to commit a murder or for injuries that co-murderers cause to one another in the course of their crime. They will also refuse to enforce a promise to pay for the commission of a murder or to order the return of money paid for the commission of a murder that did not happen.

The conventional account of 'illegality' suggests that it is a remedial defence. According to the traditional and probably still dominant view, the doctrine of illegality is based on a principle—the '*ex turpi causa*' principle—that focuses explicitly on the courts' role in issuing remedies. In Lord Mansfield's oft-quoted words: '[t]he principle of public policy [underlying the illegality defence] is this: *ex dolo malo non oritur actio.* No court will lend its aid to a man who founds his cause of action upon an immoral or illegal act'.[49] To say that courts will not 'lend their aid' to wrongdoers is another way of saying that they will not award remedies to wrongdoers.

This characterization of illegality is broadly accurate: in most cases where illegality is successfully pled, it operates as a remedial defence. However, there are situations where illegality operates as a substantive defence and other situations where it is not a defence at all. I provide examples of each below. The discussion is not exhaustive. Although the English courts approach to illegality has been clarified, somewhat, following the Supreme Court's decision in *Patel v Mirza*,[50] the law in this area remains highly complex. Lawsuits may be connected to unlawful activities in myriad ways, and courts apply different principles to most of these ways. Further, there is little agreement over which distinctions are relevant; nearly every textbook adopts a different classificatory scheme. Against this background, the primary aims of this section are to demonstrate that illegality can operate in the different ways just described and, second, to explain the factors that must be taken into account to determine if illegality is operating as a remedial defence.

[49] *Holman v Johnson* [1775] 1 Cowp 341, 343. Lord Mansfield's '*ex dolo malo non oritur actio*' principle is more commonly expressed as '*ex turpi causa non oritur actio*'—hence the '*ex turpi*' principle. Contemporary affirmations include Beldam J in *Pitts v Hunt* [1991] 1 QB 24: 'Since the days of Lord Mansfield it has been a rule of public policy that a court will not lend its aid to a man who founds his cause of action on an illegal or immoral act'.

[50] [2016] UKSC 42.

It seems clear that illegality operates as a substantive defence when it is invoked as the basis for refusing to order specific performance of a promise to perform a legal wrong—for example a promise to commit a murder—or to award damages for the breach of such a promise. In both law and morality, a promise to commit a murder has no force: a legal duty to commit a murder would be an absurdity.[51] The *ex turpi causa* principle is therefore superfluous to the explanation of why such promises are unenforceable: notwithstanding that the claimants in such cases are almost certainly involved in wrongdoing, the question of whether the court should assist them does not arise since their action has no substantive basis. The claimant cannot point to a right that was threatened or infringed. The same reasoning explains why courts will not order defendants to perform promises to pay murderers their promised fees: the promise is only valid if the contract is valid. Though not strictly concerned with illegality, cases in which courts refuse to enforce promises to perform actions that are contrary to 'public policy' (e.g. promises to engage in prostitution) are explained by the same principle. A promise to engage in prostitution is ineffective from its inception. Consistent with this interpretation, it is orthodox law that an agreement to commit a legal wrong or to do something that is contrary to public policy is void *ab initio*, that is, the agreement fails to create a contract at all.[52]

Illegality also appears to operate as a substantive defence in cases where it is invoked to refuse an order to perform, or to award damages in respect of, agreements that, while not strictly requiring actions that are unlawful or contrary to public policy, facilitate such actions—for example, an agreement to sell locksmith tools to a thief.[53] In most cases, selling locksmith tools is morally and legally unobjectionable. However, assisting another to commit a wrong is a moral wrong and, in many cases, a legal wrong (to be an 'accessory and abettor'). Thus, just as a promise to murder is not binding, a promise to assist a murderer is not binding.[54] A similar explanation arguably applies to cases where enforcement is refused on the ground of illegality in the satisfaction of a contractual condition. The standard example is where insureds are denied recovery under insurance policies in respect of events that they wrongfully caused; for example, murderers who are denied recovery

[51] See Smith (2004), 249–51, 263–65.

[52] See *Arnhold Karberg & Co v Blythe, Green, Jourdain & Co* [1915] 2 KB 379, 388.

[53] See e.g. *Pearce v Brooks* (1866) LR 1 Ex 213, 217 (supply of a brougham to a prostitute for use in her business).

[54] What if the vendor is unaware that the buyer is a thief? In both morality and law, it is generally assumed that the wrong of assisting in a wrong is fault based: those who supply locksmith tools only act wrongly if they know of the buyer's improper purpose. In such cases, the contract should be binding so long as the vendor remains unaware of the buyer's purpose. Consistent with this interpretation, courts have permitted contracting parties who are unaware of the other party's unlawful intentions to bring actions for the contract price or to recover damages for breach of contract: *Mason v Clarke* [1955] AC 788, 793, 805. If a buyer brought an action in contract where the vendor had no knowledge of the buyer's unlawful purpose (e.g. because purchased locksmith tools were defective), the action would likely be refused. However, in such a case illegality would be a remedial defence (see below).

under their victim's life insurance policies.[55] The results in such cases can often be explained on the basis that the policy, properly interpreted, excluded beneficiaries in the claimant's position. But where such an interpretation is not possible, the principle that promises that promote wrongdoing are not binding explains the result. An explicit promise to pay a sum of money in the event that the payee kills another individual would clearly be void on the basis that it promotes wrongdoing. The result must be the same in the case where, though the contract does not contain an explicit promise to this effect, it is interpreted as implicitly requiring the payment. In the insurance cases, the courts are effectively invalidating an implicit promise to pay for harm caused by the insured's wrongdoing.[56]

As these examples suggest, illegality most frequently operates as a substantive defence when the claimant is seeking to enforce a contract. However, this category also includes some extra-contractual cases. A would-be thief presumably cannot recover for the tort of fraud against a defendant who intentionally misinformed him about the means to disarm a security system. The thief has no action because the defendant had no substantive obligation to tell the truth. Like the obligation to keep a promise, the obligation to tell the truth does not apply where the consequence of doing so promotes or facilitates wrongful acts.[57]

In the cases just discussed, courts sometimes invoke the *ex turpi causa* principle to explain why relief is denied.[58] However, while the claimants in such cases may be wrongdoers, the *ex turpi causa* principle is superfluous because the relevant contract is void *ab initio* or because no tort has been committed. The question of assisting wrongdoers does not arise (though the question does arise if the claimant is also, or alternatively, seeking restitution: see below). The same observation applies to two other categories of cases that, while typically discussed under the heading of illegality in tort textbooks, are not concerned with defences at all. In the first category, the claimant is denied recovery for harm that arises directly from his own unlawful act. For example, in *Vellino v Chief Constable of the Greater Manchester Police* the claimant was injured as a result of jumping out of a second-floor window while trying to escape the police.[59] The claimant's attempt to recover damages for

[55] See e.g. *Davitt v Titcumb* [1990] Ch 110.

[56] Cases in which courts refuse contractual relief because of illegality in the performance of a contract are more difficult (e.g. *Ashmore, Benson, Pease & Co Ltd v AV Dawson Ltd* [1973] 1 WLR 828). Suppose I agree to pay you to 'negotiate a house purchase' knowing that your negotiation technique invariably involves threatening and sometimes occasioning physical injury on the vendor. My promise to pay promotes your unlawful behaviour, and on this basis is arguably invalid for the same reason that promises that explicitly promote wrongdoing are invalid. However, given that our agreement can in principle be carried out perfectly lawfully, it may be simpler to explain such cases on the basis that, while the contract is perfectly valid, the claimant is a wrongdoer (in other words, on the basis of the *ex turpi* principle). If the latter interpretation is correct, then illegality operates as a substantive defence in these cases.

[57] Kant (1797b) appeared to disagree.

[58] Including Lord Mansfield in *Holman v Johnson* [1775] 1 Cowp 341, 343.

[59] [2002] 1 WLR 218.

the police's failure to take reasonable care to prevent him escaping was rejected on the ground that the injury was caused by his own act. The claimant in *Vellino* was unquestionably a wrongdoer and, moreover, his injury resulted from his own wrongful act (attempting to escape), but strictly speaking the reason for denying him relief is simply that his action of jumping out the window was deliberate and voluntary. On ordinary principles of causation, the claimant was the cause of his own injuries.

The second category is comprised of cases in which a joint wrongdoer is denied relief from the other wrongdoer, ostensibly on the basis that it is impossible to establish an applicable standard of care. Most of the cases in this category involve motor vehicle accidents. In *Pitts v Hunt*,[60] the claimant was injured as a result of joyriding on the back of a motorcycle that was driven carelessly—but with the claimant's full encouragement—by the defendant. It may be queried whether it is as difficult to establish a standard of care in such cases as some courts (but not all) appear to assume. However, it seems clear that in certain cases (of which *Pitts* is probably a good example) the difficulty is real. Nonetheless, the reason for the difficulty is not strictly that the activity was unlawful, but rather that the claimant agreed to participate in an inherently dangerous activity—in other words, that the claimant assumed the relevant risk.[61] The court would have found it just as difficult to establish a standard of care if the parties had decided to joyride legally on their own property. In the circumstances of *Pitts*, the claimant had probably assented to reckless driving short of deliberately crashing the motorcycle, and possibly even to that risk. It is unnecessary to invoke *ex turpi causa* or any similar principle to explain the results in such cases.

As these examples show, illegality often operates as a substantive defence or is simply not a defence at all. Still, in most cases illegality operates as a remedial defence, However, even in these cases the defence may have little to do with the *ex turpi* principle. Perhaps the clearest examples of illegality operating as a remedial defence are where claimants are refused damages for losses arising from their own punishment. In *Gray v Thames Trains Ltd*,[62] the claimant suffered post-traumatic stress disorder because of a rail accident caused by the defendant's negligence. While in this condition he killed a third party and was subsequently convicted of manslaughter. The claimant sought damages from Thames Trains with respect to losses he suffered because of the conviction. Lord Hoffman rightly rejected the claim on the basis that it would be inconsistent for a civil court to require the defendant to compensate the claimant for a loss of liberty that the criminal courts had imposed. Lord Hoffman did not explore this inconsistency further, but it seems

60 *Pitts v Hunt* [1991] 1 QB 246.

61 However, English judges cannot openly adopt this reason in motor vehicle cases because s 149(3) of the *Road Traffic Act* 1988 excludes the *volenti* defence.

62 [2009] UKHL 33.

clear that it is the same inconsistency that the remedial defence of *res judicata* seeks to avoid; indeed, Lord Hoffman's inconsistency principle is almost indistinguishable from the 'issue estoppel' version of *res judicata*. The only basis on which a civil court could find that Thames Trains was responsible for the consequences of Mr Gray's imprisonment was that Thames Trains was also responsible for the assault that led to the imprisonment. The latter finding would have been inconsistent with the criminal court's decision that Mr Gray was guilty of manslaughter, since that decision necessarily assumes that Mr Gray was responsible for the assault. In short, the issue of Thames Trains' responsibility for the assault, and so its responsibility for any consequent punishment, had already been decided by the criminal court: *res judicata*. As explained above, *res judicata* is a remedial defence. But its basis is a concern for the efficient administration of justice, not the *ex turpi* principle.

The *ex turpi* principle is the explanation for two other, related, categories of cases in which illegality operates as a remedial defence. The first category includes the relatively rare cases where relief is denied on the ground that the claimant's injuries, though clearly caused by the defendant (who was not a co-wrongdoer), were incurred while the claimant was engaged in wrongdoing. For example, in *Cross v Kirkby*[63] the defendant was not liable for injuring the claimant with a bat that the claimant (who was unlawfully protesting a hunt on the defendant's land) had been using to hit the defendant. The court held that the defendant acted in self-defence, but they also held that, even if self-defence could not be established, the claimant should be denied relief because he was engaged in wrongdoing. It seems reasonably clear that illegality operates here as a remedial defence. The courts presumably do not think that individuals should be at liberty to injure wrongdoers. Indeed, the principle that self-defence can only be invoked to justify proportionate responses shows that the law expects individuals to treat wrongdoers reasonably. Further, it seems reasonably clear that the basis of the defence in such cases is the *ex turpi causa* principle. Leaving aside the self-defence plea, the only reason to refuse to assist Mr Cross was that he was engaged in wrongdoing when he suffered his injury.

A second category consists of cases where claimants are denied restitution with respect to benefits that were transferred as part of an activity that is unlawful or contrary to public policy. In *Patel*, the Supreme Court significantly narrowed, but did not entirely eliminate, this defence.[64] For example, Lord Toulson suggested that a claimant who sought to recover a payment made in exchange for an unfulfilled promise to murder would be denied recovery.[65] The basis for such a denial is the

[63] [2000] EWCA Civ 426.

[64] *Patel v Mirza* [2016] UKSC 42. Lord Toulson suggested that the arguments for narrowing the scope of the illegality defence in claims for restitution apply equally to contractual claims. However, as I explained above, in contractual claims illegality often operates as a substantive defence. The reasons for restricting the illegality defence in restitution cases (see below) do not apply to such cases. Courts may rightly refuse to enforce an agreement to perform an unlawful act, yet, at the same time, order the return of payments made under that agreement (assuming that counter-performance has not occurred).

[65] Ibid [116].

ex turpi principle. The substantive principles according to which enrichments are deemed unjust, and thus should be returned, operate irrespective of the morality of the transferor's behaviour. The substantive law of unjust enrichment focuses on the justice of the parties' holdings, and as between the payor and the payee in an unfulfilled murder-for-hire agreement, the payor has the stronger claim.[66] The only possible reason to refuse restitution in such cases is that the courts do not wish to assist claimants who seek restitution of payments that were made in the course of their own wrongdoing.

As just mentioned, the *ex turpi* principle is only applicable, today, in a narrow range of cases. Still, it may be asked why wrongdoers should ever be refused the courts' assistance. Of course, judges should not help litigants to commit wrongs. However, that possibility only arises where a claimant seeks to enforce a promise to commit a wrong. In the cases where the *ex turpi* principle might conceivably be applied, the relevant wrongdoing has already happened or been abandoned. It might be thought that in such cases the wrongdoer deserves as much assistance as anyone else.

One possibility is that courts refuse to assist wrongdoers in order to punish them. However, refusing to issue a remedy is an arbitrary punishment (few wrongdoers seek remedies and the remedies they are denied often bear little relation to the seriousness of their wrongdoing) and the law already provides punishments for wrongs, punishments that it presumably regards as sufficient. The suggestion that granting remedies to wrongdoers somehow 'taints' the courts seems closer to the kind of explanation needed, but it leaves unanswered the question of why courts are tainted. The issue is difficult, but the most plausible explanation is that by assisting wrongdoers the courts may undermine respect for the substantive law. Although this book has stressed the distinction between substantive and remedial law, it has also stressed their close connection: remedies typically affirm, support, and complement substantive rights. This connection is implicitly denied by wrongdoers when they bring civil actions. Wrongdoers cannot, without contradiction, request a remedy to affirm, support, or complement their substantive rights since by their wrongdoing they have denied (or at least appear to have denied) that such rights matter or indeed that they exist at all. To make sense of a wrongdoers' request for relief it must be interpreted in a way that is consistent with such a denial. Such an interpretation is not impossible: for example, wrongdoers might justify their requests for damages on the ground that damages are a kind of licence fee.[67] If damages are licence fees, it is not inconsistent to request a fee and, at the same time, to proclaim a freedom to engage in the kind of behaviour that triggers such requests. However, this interpretation is inconsistent with the courts' explanation

66 But not where the promise is fulfilled. Notwithstanding that the agreement in such cases is invalid, a payee who has fulfilled the condition of payment is not unjustly enriched.

67 Oliver Wendell Holmes famously explained contract damages in this way: Holmes (1897) 462.

of what they are doing when they are awarding damages. The courts' explanation is that damages must be paid because the defendant committed a wrong. In short, the most plausible explanation of the *ex turpi* principle is that when courts assist wrongdoers they appear to be accepting the only grounds on which wrongdoers could coherently ask for such assistance—namely, that substantive rights do not matter or perhaps even exist.

This interpretation of the *ex turpi* principle explains why it normally only applies in cases of intentional wrongdoing: only intentional wrongdoers deny the existence or authority of substantive rights. It also explains why courts take into account the seriousness of the wrongdoer's wrongdoing, the relation between the wrong and the wrongdoer's request, and the seriousness of the wrongdoer's loss or injury when deciding whether to allow the *ex turpi* defence.[68] The more serious the wrong and the more closely connected it is to the action, the more likely it is that an award will send the wrong message. Lord Mansfield's partially successful attempt to limit the defence to cases where the claimants' actions are 'founded' on their wrongdoing reflects an obvious concern for the incongruity of issuing remedies to claimants who have publicly announced their infidelity to the law.

Finally, this interpretation helps to explain why the law in this area is both complex and controversial. The law is complex because there are infinite varieties of wrongdoing, infinite ways in which wrongdoing may be connected to lawsuits, and no obvious way to balance the harm of appearing to condone wrongdoing against the harm of refusing to permit a prima facie valid claim. The law is controversial because, on the one hand, it is not empirically established that granting remedies to wrongdoers undermines the substantive law and, on the other hand, wrongdoers may legitimately complain that whatever the intention, the effect of the *ex turpi* defence is to punish them twice for the same wrong. In principle, the courts' primary concern should be to see that duties are performed, wrongs are rectified, and injustices are eliminated. It is not clear that the existing law balances these considerations appropriately. In short, while a concern for undermining the substantive law is the most plausible justification for the *ex turpi* variant of the illegality defence, it is not clear that this concern ultimately justifies this defence.

viii. Settlements and Exoneration Clauses

Like the classification of illegality, the classification of settlements and of exclusion and limitation of liability clauses ('exoneration clauses') raises difficult issues. From one perspective, proof of a valid settlement or exoneration clause appears to be a remedial defence. Settlement and exoneration clauses preclude or limit potential

[68] See e.g. *Patel v Mirza* [2016] UKSC 42 [107]; Burrows (2004) 588–601.

defendants' liabilities to court orders.[69] It is true that if the common law recognized substantive duties to pay damages or restitution, then settlements and exoneration clauses might be regarded as waivers of the correlative substantive right to receive such payments (and so as substantive defences, if not denials). However, in the absence of such duties (as argued for in this book), the only effect of settlements and exoneration clauses is to preclude or limit the remedies a claimant can obtain from a court. Further, the explanation of this effect appears to have nothing to do with the substantive merits of the claimant's action: these defences operate regardless of whether a tort was committed, a debt owed, or an unjust enrichment occurred. From this perspective, settlements and exoneration clauses appear similar to, for instance, limitation periods: they are (merely) reasons for courts to refuse remedies.

However, viewed from another perspective, proof of a settlement or an exoneration clause is not a defence at all, let alone a remedial defence. In substance, settlements and exoneration clauses are promises by potential claimants not to bring legal actions or not to bring a certain kind of legal action. A court's decision to deny or limit a claim on the basis of a settlement or exoneration clause could therefore be interpreted as, in substance, specific performance of the claimant's promise. While the court does not strictly order the claimant to cease or limit the action, its decision to refuse or limit liability has the same result. Viewed from this perspective, settlements and exoneration clauses are contracts or parts of contracts that, like other contracts or parts of contracts, may be specifically enforced by the courts. The courts' treatment of these clauses is distinctive only in that specific performance is achieved indirectly, by courts refusing actions that are inconsistent with the claimant's contractual duty.

This second interpretation reflects the underlying reasons for giving effect to settlements and exoneration clauses better than the first interpretation. In general, a promise is legally binding in the common law if it is made in exchange for consideration (or in a deed) and if the parties intend to create legal relations. Valid settlements and exoneration clauses meet these requirements. Moreover, where a

[69] Settlements and exoneration clauses are different from waivers of substantive rights. Individuals are generally at liberty to waive their substantive rights. For example, I can waive my right not to be touched by you or (though the matter is more complex) my right to the payment of a contractual debt. Having waived these rights, the reason that I cannot later succeed in an action founded upon them is either that you did not infringe the relevant substantive right (in the case of you touching me) or that the right no longer exists (in the case of your right to payment). The rules governing such waivers are a part of the substantive law: waiver of substantive rights is a substantive defence. Settlement is sometimes confused with waiver because it is occasionally suggested, particularly in the context of negligence, that the substantive defence of consent is only a defence if the claimant had agreed 'to waive any claim': *Nettleship v Weston* [1971] 2 QB 691, 701 (Lord Denning). Such assertions arise from the failure to distinguish substantive rights from remedial rights. Denning's view is criticized, with counterexamples, in Stevens (2007) 17. The most that can be said for Denning's view is that claimants who purport to waive 'any claim' before the relevant injury occurred probably also intended to waive their substantive rights.

settlement or exoneration clause is invalid, the reason is normally one of the usual reasons for invalidating an apparent contractual promise (e.g. duress, mistake, unconscionability, and the like). Finally, it is difficult to think of any reason other than that settlement and exoneration clauses are contractual promises, and specifically contractual promises made by defendants to claimants, that courts should give effect to these clauses. An agreement between private citizens cannot bind a court; however, it is perfectly appropriate and normal for a court to hold citizens to the promises that they make to one another. In short, the law generally, and appropriately, treats settlements and exoneration clauses as simple contractual promises.

This conclusion is subject to one caveat. Although the validity of settlements and exoneration clauses is generally determined using the same rules that apply to other contractual promises, there are certain differences, particularly in respect of exoneration clauses. Some of these differences may simply reflect general contract law principles applied to the special circumstances in which exoneration clauses typically arise. For example, the rules that make it relatively easy for courts to set aside or limit exoneration clauses because they are unfair or do not apply to the event in question are arguably explicable on this basis.[70] However, certain differences appear to reflect specifically remedial concerns. The main example is the rule that invalidates entirely any attempt to exclude liability for death or personal injury resulting from negligence.[71] It is possible that this rule merely reflects the view that no one would freely consent to such an exclusion. However, the more natural interpretation is that there are certain wrongs for which an award of damages should always be available. If this book's position that damages awards create (not confirm) duties to pay damages is correct, then a rule that invalidates attempts to preclude parties' from seeking certain kinds of damages awards reflects remedial concerns, and so counts as a remedial defence.

C. Partial Defences

The remainder of this chapter examines a number of difficult-to-classify private law doctrines. The first three—adequacy of damages, supervision, and personal duties—are traditionally described as factors that courts take into account when deciding whether to issue specific relief. The other five doctrines—laches, impossibility, clean hands, hardship, and public interest—are traditionally described as 'Equitable Defences', and therefore as reasons for courts to refuse specific relief. In

[70] In the UK, the most important of these rules are legislative: see in particular the *Unfair Contract Terms Act* 1977 and the *Unfair Terms in Consumer Contracts Regulations* 1999.

[71] *Unfair Contract Terms Act* 1977, s 2. Similar provisions are found in the *Public Passenger Vehicles Act* 1981; *Defective Premises Act* 1972, s 6(3); *Law Reform (Personal Injuries) Act* 1948, s 1(3). Arguably, another example is the common law rule invalidating attempts to exclude liability for fraud: *In Re Banister Broad v Munton* (1879) 12 Ch D 131.

this book, I describe all of these doctrines as defences because in substance they are all reasons for courts to refuse specific relief notwithstanding that the cause of action for specific relief (a rights-threat) is satisfied. Stated differently, I argue that these doctrines provide reasons for courts to refuse the prima facie appropriate remedy.

I have added the qualification 'partial' to the description of these defences because, unlike the defences examined in the previous section, these defences typically operate as reasons for courts to refuse a particular form of remedy, rather than to refuse a remedy altogether. Courts that refuse specific relief because of a partial remedial defence ('partial defence') typically award substitutionary damages in lieu of specific relief. For example, where a court refuses specific performance because the order would be 'difficult to supervise' or 'intrusive of personal liberty' it will typically award damages in substitution for specific performance. Such an award is a response to a rights-threat (unlike other damages awards, which are responses either to wrongs or to injustices). Finally, I have not described any of these defences as 'Equitable' because, as I hope to show, this label is a distraction to understanding their rationale.

The label 'partial defence' nonetheless comes with caveats. To begin, courts traditionally present one of the doctrines discussed below—adequacy of damages—as an aspect of the claimant's cause of action. In principle, claimants seeking specific relief must show that damages are inadequate. It follows that while in substance adequacy of damages operates as a defence (or so I will argue), it is not a defence in the procedural sense.

Second, courts may invoke certain of the partial defences in cases where they do not merely refuse the requested remedy, but refuse to issue any remedy. For example, where a request for a *quia timet* order is refused on the grounds that the claimant has 'unclean hands' or has delayed unduly in requesting the order ('laches'), the court may also refuse to award damages in lieu of the order. In such cases, the claimant is able to bring an action for damages in the future if the defendant commits the threatened wrong. However, such an award is not a substitute for the original order, as the threat has passed (rather, it is a response to a past wrong or injustice).[72]

A third caveat is that while the partial defences are generally remedial defences, courts sometimes invoke them to refuse specific relief for substantive-law reasons. As we saw in Chapters 6 and 8 (and as I explain further in this chapter), courts sometimes refuse an injunction on the ground that it would cause 'hardship' or

[72] For similar reasons, these doctrines arguably do not operate as partial remedial defences where the amount of damages that are awarded in lieu of the requested order cannot reasonably be viewed as a substitute for that order. An example is a sum of damages awarded in lieu of specific performance, where the sum is far smaller than the cost of obtaining substitute performance. In the discussion of hardship and public interest below, I argue that in such cases the relevant doctrine is typically operating as a covert substantive defence: the court is using remedial law to modify substantive law.

that it would harm the 'public interest' in circumstances where the same hardship or harm to the public interest would arise had the defendant simply performed its substantive duty. I argue that in such cases courts use ostensibly remedial doctrines to modify the substantive law. Consistent with this interpretation, the quantification of damage awards in such cases shows that they are not intended as substitutes for specific relief.

A final caveat is that a further respect in which the defences examined in this section differ from those examined in the previous section is that they are 'cumulative' and 'discretionary'. They are cumulative because courts take into account all these defences, where applicable, when deciding on the appropriate form of relief. And they are discretionary because there is no formula for determining when these defences provide sufficient grounds to refuse specific relief. I discuss these features of partial remedial defences at the end.

Substantively, the main questions raised by the partial defences are why they exist and why they apply only to requests for specific relief. In broad terms, the position defended here is that the partial defences reflect largely administrative concerns and that they are restricted to specific relief because in practice these concerns only arise with respect to specific relief. There are exceptions and qualifications to this explanation, but they are consistent with its broader theme—which is that it is unnecessary to understand anything about the history or nature of the Chancery Court to understand why defences exist. These defences could have easily arisen in a unitary legal system. They reflect common sense, general remedial principles, principles that any court contemplating ordering a defendant to cease trespassing, deliver goods, provide services, or return chattels could be expected to take into account.

i. Equitable Defences?

The defences examined in this section are usually described as 'Equitable'. In part, this label is meant to remind readers that these defences are only applied to remedies that originated in the Chancery Court ('Chancery'), in particular, to specific performance orders and injunctions ('specific relief'). However, it is usually assumed that the label also tells us something important about the nature or foundation of these defences. In other words, the conventional understanding of these defences assumes that they did not merely originate in the Court of Equity, but also that they are substantively 'Equitable'.[73] One of this chapter's themes is that this way of understanding the partial defences is unhelpful. In principle, the questions that these defences require courts to ask should be asked in respect of all judicial

[73] See e.g. Spry (2014) 1.

orders: the only reason they are not asked universally is that, in practice, the answers are only significant with respect to orders that originated in the Chancery. In this (very) limited sense, these defences are Equitable. As I explain below, the principles that underlie the partial defence have little to do with Equity, regardless of how 'Equity' is understood. Similar doctrines could have easily arisen in a unitary legal system.

I examine the partial defences individually below. However, I begin with some general comments on their allegedly Equitable nature. Broadly speaking, there are four possible reasons it might be thought helpful to describe the partial defences as Equitable. The first is simply the historical fact that they originated in the Chancery, that is, in the Court of Equity.[74] The obvious rejoinder to this suggestion is that legal rules are rarely described in terms of their court of origin. There are no textbooks on 'Rules Originating in the Court of Appeal' or 'Rules Originating in Lord Atkin's Court'. So why have textbooks on 'Rules Originating in the Chancery'? Historical inquiries aside, there is no reason to describe legal rules according to their court of origin unless that description tells us something about those rules aside from their court of origin.

A second, closely related, possibility is that the defences discussed below are Equitable in the Aristotelian sense that they are exceptions, or at least that they apply to an exceptional type of remedy: specific relief. It is true, of course, that litigants seeking specific relief had to go to the Chancery because such relief was unavailable from the general courts, that is, the Royal Courts (see Chapter 3). However, the historically exceptional nature of specific relief does not justify describing it (or the applicable defences) as Equitable. Large parts of the contemporary law, whatever their origins, are exceptions to general rules or practices. Vicarious liability is an exception to the general rule that individuals are not liable for the acts of others. Exemplary damages are an exception to the general rule that damages are not meant to punish. The tort of negligence was at one time an exception to the general rule that tort liability was strict. None of this law is described as Equitable.

A third possible reason for describing these doctrines as Equitable is that the only explanation that can be offered for their existence is a brute historical fact—namely, that at a certain point in time they were recognized by the Chancery. This suggestion invites two responses. The first is that even if the argument's premise is accepted, the label 'Equitable' remains unhelpful. There are undoubtedly many rules for which the only explanation is that a particular court recognized them at such and such a time. However, jurists do not identify such rules by that court. The other response is that the premise is false: with rare exceptions, there are simple, non-historical explanations for these rules. I provide such explanations below. For

[74] See e.g. Meagher, Heydon, & Leeming (2002) 1.

the moment, it is sufficient to observe that it is unlikely that the only explanation for such a large, well-established, and generally well-accepted set of rules is historical. The common law evolves slowly, but it is not inert.

A final possible reason for describing the defences discussed below as Equitable is that they share a particular—and particularly Equitable—substantive foundation. Books on Equity often argue that Equitable doctrines share a common aim of preventing 'unconscionable conduct' (or, slightly more narrowly, of preventing the unconscionable insistence on rights derived from Royal Courts).[75] Such books invariably discuss 'Equitable Remedies' and, as part of those discussions, invariably examine the rules discussed in this section. The implication of this presentation is that the defences discussed below have a common aim: preventing unconscionable conduct.

The suggestion that the rules developed in the Chancery share the distinctive aim of seeking to prevent unconscionable conduct invites obvious objections. On the one hand, many of the rules relating to, for example, trusts and fiduciaries appear to have little to do with preventing unconscionable behaviour, notwithstanding their Chancery origins. Some of private law's strictest rules—rules that can impose severe penalties on parties who act in the utmost good faith—are found in fiduciary law (which originated in the Chancery). On the other hand, many of the rules that originated in the Royal Courts appear designed to prevent unconscionable conduct—for example, certain of the rules governing damages.[76] It is not surprising, then, that some Equity textbooks explicitly disclaim the suggestion that the rules they discuss share any common feature, aside from historical origins.[77] However, for present purposes the important point is that few of the partial remedial defences have anything to do with unconscionability. For example, 'adequacy of damages', 'supervision', 'impossibility', and 'public interest' have nothing to do with unconscionability. Further, even where the doctrines appear to have something to do with unconscionability, their concern is not so much to prevent unconscionable conduct as to ensure that the courts are not associated with such conduct, or so I argue below.

Finally, it is not possible to save the last suggestion by switching our focus from the partial defences to the rulings to which they apply. It is true that the defences discussed below are described as Equitable, not only because they originated in the Chancery, but, in addition, because they were only applied (and are still only applied) to rulings that originated in the Chancery. If the existence of those rulings

75 See e.g. Spry (2014) 1 ('Equitable principles have above all a distinctive ethical quality, reflecting as they do the prevention of unconscionable conduct'); Virgo (2018) 5 (' . . . Equity . . . restrains injustice by stopping the unconscionable conduct of a particular person'). Meagher, Heydon, & Leeming (2002) 3 disagree ('Equity can be described but not defined. It is the body of law developed by the Court of Chancery in England before 1873').

76 See e.g. Worthington (2006) 28–9.

77 See e.g. Meagher, Heydon, & Leeming (2002) 1.

reflects a concern for unconscionability, it would seem to follow that the partial defences are at least indirectly based on the same concern. However, the availability of specific relief does not reflect such a concern. Indeed, specific relief is perhaps the clearest example of a historically Equitable innovation that has nothing to do with unconscionability. An order to perform a contract or an injunction against trespassing directs the defendant to comply with a historically 'Legal' duty, that is, a duty that was first recognized by the Royal Courts. It is unnecessary to know anything about the history or (alleged) concerns of the Chancery to understand why a legal system might want to allow courts to order defendants to comply with their legal duties. Indeed, though they were originally not expressed literally as 'orders', rulings for the payment of a sum due under a contract or for the recovery of land—both of which originated in the Royal Courts—were in effect orders to, respectively, make the payment or quit the land. And in England today both of these rulings are expressed literally as orders. Aside from their historical origins, there is nothing Equitable about injunctions and specific performance orders. These orders simply direct defendants to comply with their legal duties.

ii. Internal Partial Defences

In the discussion below, I distinguish between 'internal' and 'external' partial defences. Internal defences focus on the content of the requested order, specifically on the nature of the actions it requires. For example, 'adequacy of damages' is an internal defence because its focus is whether the order's aim could be adequately fulfilled by a monetary award of damages. In contrast, external partial defences focus primarily on the context in which the order is sought, in particular, on the claimant's behaviour prior to seeking the order. For example, the 'clean hands' defence is external because it focuses on the propriety of the claimant's behaviour prior to litigation.

Precisely because they focus on the nature of the actions contemplated by the requested order, internal partial defences are most often invoked in cases where the claimant seeks specific performance of a contractual duty. It is because of these defences that specific performance is rarely available even where the claimant's contractual rights are under threat by the defendant.

Adequacy of Damages

The most important partial defence is 'adequacy of damages'. A judicial finding that damages are adequate is normally a sufficient reason to refuse a request for specific relief.[78] In addition, courts consider the extent to which damages are adequate when deciding whether to refuse relief for one or more of the other partial

78 There are relatively few reported cases where adequacy of damages is the primary reason for refusing specific relief. Laycock (1991) argues that American courts almost never deny specific relief on this basis. However, the explanation for the paucity of cases is no doubt primarily that few claimants

defences, such as difficulty of supervision or laches. Finally, courts sometimes invoke the concept of adequacy of damages in cases where they refuse relief for what are, in essence, substantive-law reasons. The discussion below focuses primarily on the first category of cases—where adequacy of damages is a sufficient reason to refuse specific relief—because they represent the most common and practically important use of the concept. However, it should be kept in mind that 'adequate' has a different meaning in the other cases.

In cases where adequacy of damages is the sole or main reason to refuse specific relief, damages are normally adequate if claimants can purchase equivalent or nearly equivalent performance of the relevant duty from a third party (or if claimants can perform the action at their own expense). Thus, damages are normally an adequate substitute for specific performance of a contractual obligation to deliver fungible goods or services because it is normally possible to purchase fungible goods or services from others. In contrast, damages are normally an inadequate substitute for specific performance of a promise to deliver unique goods or to convey land.[79] For similar reasons, damages are rarely an adequate substitute for a negative injunction, for example, an injunction against trespassing, because it is normally not possible to purchase a 'negative action' from others.[80] However, damages may be an adequate substitute for a mandatory injunction, as a third party (or the claimant) may be able to perform the relevant action (e.g. ensuring that the claimant's house does not collapse from soil erosion).[81]

Why do courts refuse specific relief where substitute performance is possible?[82] One possible explanation is historical. According to this explanation, the defence of adequacy of damages exists because specific relief originated in the Chancery and thus was only available when the remedies that originated in the Royal Courts, including in particular damages, were inadequate. In this view, the adequacy rule is one aspect of the general idea that Equity supplements the Law (see Chapter 2).

This explanation may well be historically accurate. However, it does not explain why courts recognize adequacy of damages as a defence today, nearly a century and a half after the merger of the Chancery and the Royal Courts. If the historical origins of specific relief were the only justification for such an important rule, it would have disappeared long ago. Perhaps for this reason, most contemporary

seek specific relief if damages are adequate. Further, as I explained in Chapter 6, in contract cases the rules governing termination effectively exclude this option in claims where, if the option had been pursued, the court would have held that damages were adequate.

---

[79] Or for an order for the recovery of unique goods: see e.g. *Falcke v Grey* (1859) 4 Drew 651.

[80] See e.g. *John Trenberth Ltd v National Westminster Bank Ltd* [1980] 1 EGLR 102.

[81] See e.g. *Hooper v Rogers* [1975] Ch 43.

[82] As we saw in Chapter 6, although specific performance, strictly defined, is not a common remedy, orders to perform contractual duties are common. In particular, courts regularly order defendants to pay contractual debts. Though not specific performance in the technical sense (because it originated in the Royal Courts), such orders are specific remedies in the sense that they direct claimants to comply with their substantive contractual duties.

writers attempt to explain the adequacy defence in non-historical terms. These explanations typically focus on the doctrine's application in contract cases. Perhaps the best-known contemporary explanation argues that the adequacy defence facilitates efficient breaches.[83] According to the 'efficient breach theory', the defence allows, and even encourages, contracting parties to pay damages rather than perform wasteful or 'inefficient' contractual promises.

Scholars have challenged the efficient breach theory's factual premises.[84] But as we saw in Chapter 6, the more fundamental objection to this theory (and to most other contemporary explanations of the adequacy rule) is that it is inconsistent with the law's recognition of substantive duties. The efficient breach theory views its task as explaining why the law leaves contracting parties free to pay damages rather than to fulfil their contractual promises. However, the substantive law does not leave contracting parties free to pay damages. The substantive law is clear that individuals should perform their contractual promises: a contractual duty is a 'duty' because it is meant to be fulfilled, and the failure to fulfil a contractual duty is a 'wrong' for the same reason.[85] If the law wished to leave contracting parties free to pay money in lieu of performing their contractual promises, the obvious way to do this would be to recognize that freedom in the substantive law. Rather than proclaiming that it is wrong to breach a contractual promise, the law would tell contracting parties that they are at liberty to pay damages in lieu of specific performance.[86] However, the law does not say this: it says that individuals have duties to perform their contractual promises.

A satisfactory explanation of the adequacy rule must explain not only why courts refuse to order specific performance when damages are an adequate substitute, but, at the same time, why the same courts affirm substantive duties to perform contractual promises, monetary and non-monetary alike. In other words, it must explain why the law regards adequacy of damages as a remedial, not substantive, defence. The best candidate for such an explanation focuses on the practical or administrative advantages of monetary awards. The 'administrative' explanation rests on two propositions. The first is that damages are often a reasonable, even if imperfect, substitute for specific relief. The second is that an award of damages typically imposes fewer costs on the legal system than specific relief. In combination,

[83] See Birmingham (1970).

[84] It is arguable that this view is now dominant, see e.g. Schwartz (1979); Posner (2003); Shavell (2006).

[85] 'Each promise that a promisor makes to a promisee by entering into a contract with him creates an obligation to perform it owed by the promisor as obligor to the promisee as obligee': *Moschi v Lep Air Services Ltd* [1972] 2 All ER 393, 400 (Lord Diplock). See also *Law Debenture Trust Corporation v Ural Caspian Oil Corporation Ltd and Others* [1995] 1 All ER 157, 173; *O'Brien v Robinson* [1973] UKHL 1.

[86] The most obvious reason that the law would do this is that at least some individuals treat the substantive law as a guide for action: see Smith (2011c). Further, judicial statements about substantive duties must be taken into account when making legal arguments. It is difficult to say anything about contract law without taking a position on whether individuals have substantive duties to perform their contractual promises.

these propositions suggest that courts prefer damages to specific relief because they are generally a less costly means of achieving the same or nearly the same result.

Damages are typically an adequate substitute for specific relief in the straightforward sense that claimants can often purchase identical or near-identical performance from a third party. Claimants can use awards of damages to purchase the same performance contemplated by specific relief. For example, a disappointed purchaser can purchase promised goods or services from a third party. Damages are typically an administratively cheaper remedy because it is a monetary ruling while specific relief, with rare exceptions (see below), is non-monetary. Monetary rulings are simpler to express than non-monetary rulings; more importantly, it is relatively easy for claimants and, crucially, for courts to determine if the defendant has fulfilled a monetary order.[87] Monetary rulings are therefore less likely to lead to further litigation. Finally, monetary rulings are typically easier and less costly to enforce than to non-monetary rulings. In most cases, the only practical way to enforce a non-monetary ruling is to punish the defendant, which requires an additional trial and, typically, incarcerating the defendant—and even then, the desired result may not be achieved.[88] By contrast, monetary rulings are enforceable through third party execution, for example by seizing and selling the defendant's property. As we saw in Chapter 3, execution against property typically does not require the court's further involvement; indeed, the enforcement of monetary awards is largely a private process. In short, monetary rulings have significant practical advantages.

It might be thought inappropriate for courts to concern themselves with the administrative advantages and disadvantages of their rulings. Specifically, it might be thought that courts should focus exclusively on whether their rulings are just. However, while achieving justice is certainly the courts' primary task, it is not—or

[87] The latter consideration would have been particularly important in the period during which the adequacy of damages principle developed, as there were few judges available to deal with follow-up disputes, particularly for litigants living outside London (Stein (1984) 36) and because there were limited enforcement mechanisms. Executing judgments was the business of sheriffs, and, as Lawson notes, 'Only the simplest tasks could be imposed on them, tasks that admitted of no discretion': Lawson (1980) 2. The Chancery Court had additional resources at its disposal: 'whereas the common law remedies were circumscribed by the refusal to employ the sheriff and his officers to do anything but operate on the defendant's property, the Chancellor was prepared to commit a disobedient defendant to prison for contempt of court. Moreover, since the Chancery was also an administrative department, the Chancellor could employ his subordinate officers to make inquiries, take accounts and so on': Lawson (1980) 3.

[88] An order to pay a debt is of course a monetary ruling. It is consistent with the above explanation, then, that litigants seeking such rulings do not need to prove that damages are inadequate. The other main category of ruling not subject to the adequacy of damages requirement, a ruling for the recovery of land, is also straightforward to administer though it is admittedly more difficult to enforce than a monetary remedy (since it may require force to remove a trespasser). The marginally higher costs associated with such rulings were, and no doubt still are, considered reasonable given the importance that the common law accords to property rights. Some rights are more valuable than other rights, and so are worth spending more to protect. Whether the common law correctly identifies such rights is another question.

at least should not be—their only concern. The courts are publicly funded state institutions. Providing justice through the courts is just one of the state's tasks: the state also builds hospitals, educates children, defends its borders, and so on. All of these tasks, including that of providing justice, are costly. The cost of providing justice explains why England has a limited number of courts. As I argued in Chapters 4 and 8, it would be irresponsible for courts to ignore the costs of the scarce services they provide, including the cost of providing and enforcing their rulings. Whatever arguments might be made for the irrelevance of economic considerations when determining how individuals ought to treat one another ('substantive law'), such considerations are clearly relevant when determining how judges and other state officials ought to act ('remedial law'). In particular, these considerations are undoubtedly relevant when courts contemplate whether and in what form they should assist individual claimants seeking to resolve private disputes.[89]

Of course, everything else being equal, courts should try to achieve as close to perfect justice as possible in their rulings. For this reason, the courts' willingness to award damages instead of specific relief should depend not just on the comparative administrative costs of specific and non-specific relief, but also on the extent to which the latter is an adequate substitute for the former. The positive law reflects this principle. The standard case in which courts hold that damages are inadequate is where it is not possible for the claimant to purchase or otherwise bring about the state of affairs contemplated by specific relief without the defendant's assistance. In such cases, damages are inadequate (notwithstanding their administrative advantages) because the claimant cannot purchase what specific relief is meant to achieve.

In theory, it is possible to obtain specific performance of a monetary obligation, but such awards are rarely sought or awarded in practice. Claimants who are owed money under contracts typically request, and are granted, orders for a sum due. Although orders for a sum due are not technically 'specific performance', in substance they are just that: an order for a sum due commands the defendant to perform a contractual duty. Not surprisingly, if claimants request specific performance of a monetary duty, the courts will normally refuse the request on the ground that an order for a sum due is an adequate substitute. As this explanation reminds us, it is more accurate to describe the 'adequacy of damages' defence as the 'adequacy of a remedy originating from the Royal Courts' defence. Orders for a sum due under a contract originated in the Royal Courts. In practice, the most common reason for ordering specific performance of monetary duties is to avoid

[89] Different considerations apply when the state seeks to punish individuals or otherwise interfere with their liberty. For example, punishing innocent parties cannot be justified on the ground that it will save taxpayers' money. The state should never act unjustly. However, the state may legitimately provide less-than-perfect assistance to individuals seeking a just resolution of a private dispute.

additional actions. For example, courts will sometimes order specific performance of duties to make periodic payments, such as under an annuity.[90] Similarly, in cases where courts order purchasers in contracts for the sale of land to complete the conveyance formalities, they also typically order the purchasers to pay the price.[91] Awarding specific performance in such cases is consistent with the above explanation of the adequacy of damages defence.[92] In the case of periodic payments, the order obviates the need for the claimant to bring a fresh action for a sum due every time a payment was missed, and in the case of conveyances, it obviates the need for the vendor to bring an action for a sum due following the conveyance.

In addition to reconciling the adequacy defence with the substantive duty to perform contractual promises, the administrative explanation explains why the adequacy defence's scope has evolved and, further, why the defence is often criticized. There is no obvious answer to the question of how much money should be spent on providing justice as opposed to building schools or other public expenditures. Moreover, the answer will undoubtedly change over time. In times of war, it is reasonable to give lower priority to providing judicial justice and higher priority to maintaining an army. The comparative cost of issuing non-monetary as opposed to monetary rulings will also change over time as the institutions of justice evolve. The cost of administering litigation is not constant. And wealthier societies can afford to provide better-resourced justice services. The adequacy of damages principle originated at a time when there were rarely more than fifteen judges assigned to the Royal Courts for the entire country.[93] Against this background, it is entirely appropriate that the scope of the adequacy defence continues to evolve and to be a subject of debate.

Thus understood, the adequacy defence is not tied to the history or particular concerns of the Chancery. All courts should worry about the costs associated with their rulings. The explanation for why, today, the defence only applies to rulings that originated in the Chancery is that, with rare exceptions, it is only with respect to these rulings that the defence could plausibly be invoked. There is no alternative to an order for a sum due or an order for damages that is easier to administer and that is an adequate substitute for such an order, or at least no alternative available in common law legal systems. With rare exceptions, orders to pay damages or for

[90] See e.g. *Ball v Coggs* (1710) 1 Bro PC 140; *Clifford v Turrell* (1841) 1 Y & CCC 138; *Beswick v Beswick* [1968] AC 58.

[91] See e.g. *Walker v Eastern Counties Railway Co* [1848] 6 Hare 594; *Johnson v Agnew* [1986] AC 367.

[92] However, the core order in such cases—namely, the order requiring the purchaser to complete the conveyance—is more difficult to explain. Arguably, damages might be inadequate for the vendor in the sense that they would be difficult to assess. If every piece of land is unique, then the vendors cannot be certain when, and at what price, they will find another purchaser. Nonetheless, in practice there are relatively clear market prices for many, if not most, parcels of land. The traditional explanation for such orders—namely, that the equitable principle of 'mutuality' requires that where one party can obtain specific performance the other party must have the same remedy (see Fry (1921) 219)—is not an explanation.

[93] See Stein (1984) 36.

a sum due are easily framed, enforced, and unlikely to lead to further litigation. There are exceptions, but they are invariably subject to special limitations.[94] The other main ruling to which the defence does not apply—a ruling for the recovery of land—can admittedly be difficult to enforce if the defendant refuses to quit the land voluntarily. However, damages are an inadequate substitute for such an order since the claimant cannot generally purchase an identical property and certainly cannot do so immediately.

Up to this point, my discussion of adequacy of damages has focused on the standard case in which this defence is the sole or main reason for refusing specific relief. As I mentioned earlier, courts sometimes invoke adequacy of damages in two other contexts. In each of these contexts, 'adequacy' has a different meaning from that discussed above.

In the first context, the main question before the court is whether it should refuse specific relief for a different remedial reason. In such cases, the courts sometimes mention adequacy of damages to support their decision on the main issue. For example, in *Ryan v Mutual Tontine Westminster Chambers Association*,[95] the court refused to order a landlord to comply with his contractual duty to provide a porter on the ground that the order would require constant supervision. But the court also stressed that a sum of £25 was adequate compensation for the claimant.[96] Adopting similar reasoning, in *North East Lincolnshire Borough Council v Millennium Park (Grimsby) Ltd*,[97] the court awarded specific performance of a building contract, notwithstanding that the contract raised supervision issues, because, inter alia, non-performance would cause a non-pecuniary injury ('an eyesore'), for which damages were not an adequate remedy.[98] Perhaps the clearest examples of this category are cases where courts refer to adequacy of damages when considering whether a claimant's request for a *quia timet* injunction is premature. For example, in *Litchfield-Speer v Queen Anne's Gate Syndicate (No 2) Ltd*,[99] the court refused the

[94] An exception—which proves the rule—is an order to pay damages in the form of a 'structured settlement', that is, an order to pay damages over an extended period of time in amounts that will vary depending on future events (e.g. the progression of an illness). Although some common law jurisdictions allow such orders in limited circumstances, the common law has traditionally been reluctant to award damages in forms other than a single sum to be paid. This reluctance is consistent with the above explanation of the adequacy defence since structured settlements raise many of the same administrative concerns as non-monetary orders. It also demonstrates that the concern for administratively efficient orders applies not just to specific relief but also to orders that originated in the Royal Courts.

[95] [1893] 1 Ch 116.

[96] See also *Pollard v Clayton* (1855) 69 ER 540, where the court refused specific performance of a contract for recurrent deliveries on the grounds of difficulty of supervision and laches. The court added that, while exact substitutes might not be available, damages could adequately compensate for the anticipated harm.

[97] [2002] EWCA Civ 1719.

[98] Similar reasoning supported the decision to issue an injunction in *Prophet plc v Huggett* [2014] EWHC 615. Although the court agreed that the defendant had 'somewhat' unclean hands, it noted the difficulty of assessing damages and the likelihood of repeated actions for damages.

[99] [1919] 1 Ch 407.

injunction, noting that the anticipated injury could be 'adequately remedied by a pecuniary payment'.[100]

In none of these cases was there an issue as to whether damages were adequate in the sense that they could be used to purchase substitute performance. If damages were adequate in this sense, there would be no need to consider whether the order would be difficult to supervise or whether the action was premature.[101] In cases of this kind, damages are adequate to the extent that they provide adequate 'compensation' for the anticipated injury. The test is one of subjective well-being: if awarding damages instead of specific relief award will leave the defendant worse off it is inadequate. When courts assess adequacy in this sense they consider the anticipated injury's magnitude, whether it is pecuniary or non-pecuniary, and how easy it is to predict and assess.

It is unsurprising that courts understand the meaning of adequacy of damages differently in this second category of cases. As discussed above, the normal reason that courts refuse *quia timet* orders is that it is not sufficiently certain that the order is needed to ensure compliance with the relevant duty. However, given that courts can rarely be certain that *quia timet* orders are unnecessary, they must balance the anticipated harm from an unnecessary order against the anticipated harm from failing to make a necessary order. And to quantify the anticipated harm from failing to make a necessary order, courts must consider whether that harm can be ameliorated, if it occurs, by an award of damages. If the anticipated injury is small, pecuniary, and easily quantified in monetary terms, then the potential harm that may arise from refusing a *quia timet* order is minimal.

Broadly similar considerations explain why the compensatory meaning of adequacy of damages is usually adopted where the primary reason for refusing specific relief is difficulty of supervision, laches, clean hands, or any other remedial defence. As mentioned above, remedial defences are inherently controversial: they authorize courts to refuse to order defendants to comply with their substantive duties even where there is clear evidence that the defendant is unwilling to comply with that duty and notwithstanding that it is not possible to purchase substitute performance. It should be no surprise, then, to find that courts that are

[100] See also Pearson J in *Fletcher v Bealey* (1885) 28 Ch D 688, 698 ('there must also be proof that the apprehended damage will, if it comes, be very substantial'). Where a request for a *quia timet* injunction is premature, the courts do not award damages in lieu, but instead leave the claimant the option of bringing a later action for damages if the anticipated injury occurs. Where courts award damages immediately in lieu of a *quia timet* order, the usual reason is that damages are adequate in the 'substantive' sense (see below). Because claimants typically request *quia timet* negative injunctions, it is rare for damages to be an adequate remedy in the first sense of the term.

[101] The complete story is more complex. The extent to which a substitute exists is a matter of degree. Where an identical substitute exists, courts normally refuse specific relief for that reason alone. But where the available substitutes are not identical, courts rightly take into account other reasons for refusing specific relief. In the cases discussed above, these other reasons dominate the court's reasoning. Accordingly, in these cases damages are a 'substitute' only in the weak sense that, for example, going to a play is a substitute for going to a concert.

contemplating invoking a remedial defence sometimes consider the potential impact of their decision on the claimant. And as in the case of *quia timet* injunctions, a large part of that assessment involves considering whether the anticipated injury is of a kind that can be ameliorated (even if not undone) by an award of damages.

The other context in which courts sometimes refer to adequacy of damages—and then give it a distinctive meaning—is where they refuse specific relief for 'substantive-law' reasons. As we saw in Chapter 6, a substantive-law reason for refusing specific relief is a reason that is unrelated to the form of the requested remedy. Stated in positive terms, substantive-law reasons focus on the intrinsic desirability of the action sought by the claimant, as opposed to the desirability of a court *ordering* that action. When courts refuse specific relief on these grounds they are saying that the substantive right on which the claimant's action relies is not actually a right. Of course, courts are not supposed to consider such reasons when they are contemplating remedial defences. By definition, courts are only supposed to contemplate remedial defences if they have already decided that the claimant's substantive rights are under threat. Nonetheless, it seems clear that courts sometimes do this. In such cases, the courts effectively employ remedial doctrines to modify the substantive law.

In the typical case of this kind, the court refuses specific relief because the benefit to the claimant of performing the relevant duty is minimal in comparison to the harm (or cost) to the defendant or the public from performance. For example, in *Miller v Jackson*[102] the court refused to order the defendant cricket club to cease operations, noting the significant public interest in playing cricket and the relatively small inconvenience that the claimants would suffer from the occasional ball landing on their property.[103] Similarly, in *Wrotham Park Estate v Parkside Homes*[104] the court refused to order houses to be torn down that were built in contravention of a restrictive covenant, noting that it would 'be an unpardonable waste of much needed houses' to tear down the houses and that '[n]o damage of a financial nature has been done to the plaintiffs'.[105] A final example is the American case of *Boomer v Atlantic Cement Co*,[106] where the court refused to order a factory to cease a nuisance (which would have led to its closure), noting that the ensuing harm—closing a factory that employed over 300 workers—was out of proportion to the inconvenience caused by the emissions.[107] I discuss some of these cases when examining the

[102] [1977] QB 966.

[103] They also mentioned that the claimants had bought their property knowing that it abutted the cricket club. I explain in the discussion of the 'hardship' defence why this factor is relevant.

[104] [1974] 2 All ER 321.

[105] Ibid 330.

[106] 26 NY 2d 219 (1970).

[107] Until recently, the courts' approach to injunctions for nuisance was in a state of flux: see Burrows (2004) 517. One line of authority, which includes *Miller*, supported a broad discretion to refuse injunctions The other line, perhaps best represented by *Shelfer v City of London Electric Lighting Co* [1895] 1 Ch 287, argued that injunctions should only exceptionally be refused. In *Lawrence v Fen Tigers Ltd* [2014] UKSC 13, the Supreme Court affirmed the first line.

'hardship' and 'public interest' defences below (and I discussed the general category of 'substantive-law reasons for refusing specific relief' in Chapter 6). For the moment, it is sufficient to note that in some of these cases the courts say that damages are an adequate remedy,[108] and when they do this, they understand the term in a different sense than the meanings discussed earlier. The conclusion that damages are adequate in cases like *Miller*, *Wrotham Park*, and *Boomer* is just another way of saying that performance is undesirable because its cost is disproportionate to its benefit. In these cases, adequacy of damages is effectively a substantive defence.

Supervision

Even where damages are inadequate in the usual sense (i.e. where substitute performance is not feasible), courts may award them in lieu of specific relief for either of two further reasons that are internal to the order. The first is that specific relief would be difficult to 'supervise'. Courts do not supervise rulings in the literal sense of watching over defendants to ensure that they do what courts ordered them to do. However, courts may be called upon to intervene when defendants fail to comply with rulings and, more generally, if disputes arise in connection with carrying out rulings. When courts refer to the difficulty of supervision, they are referring to their possible role in dealing with future disputes. Accordingly, the supervision defence reflects a concern for avoiding future litigation, and so for avoiding rulings that are especially likely to give rise to more disputes. Courts are rightly hesitant to issues orders whose satisfaction requires the litigants' future co-operation or—what usually amounts to the same thing—where it is not possible to state precisely the outcome contemplated by the order.

The supervision defence is most commonly invoked in cases where the claimant seeks specific performance or a mandatory injunction because these orders are most likely to lead to further litigation. For example, the supervision defence was the main reason that in *Co-operative Insurance Society Ltd v Argyll Stores (Holdings) Ltd* the House of Lords refused to order a supermarket to comply with its contractual obligations to stay open, serve customers, and so on.[109] As they invariably do in such cases, the House of Lords awarded the claimant damages in lieu of the requested relief.

It is arguable that the common law takes the supervision defence too seriously. The defence originated at a time when there were relatively few courts and when the public cost of litigation was high relative to other public expenditures. However, the defence remains justifiable in principle. The supervision defence is based on the same principle as the adequacy of damages defence. The courts' preference for monetary awards reflects the lower administrative costs associated with such awards.

[108] See e.g. *Wrotham Park Estate v Parkside Homes* [1974] 2 All ER 321, 341; *Jaggard v Sawyer* [1995] 1 WLR 269, 285.

[109] [1998] AC 1, 12.

One of the reasons that damages awards have lower administrative costs is that they are less likely to lead to further litigation. The justification for a distinct supervision defence is that some instances of specific relief raise special risks of re-litigation. An order to operate a supermarket raises a significantly greater risk of future litigation than an order to deliver goods. For the same reason that courts should worry generally about supervision—namely, that courts and other legal institutions resources are scarce, publicly funded goods—they should worry particularly about rulings that raise special supervision issues. And courts should worry about supervision even if damages awards are an imperfect substitute. How much weight this concern should be given in a modern legal system is debatable, but it seems incontrovertible that this concern should be given some weight.

As with the adequacy of damages defence, the supervision defence requires courts to balance competing concerns. It is not surprising, then, to find that even where supervision is potentially costly courts hesitate to refuse specific relief if damages are entirely inadequate. The clearest examples are the 'railway' cases in which claimants seek specific performance of contractual duties to build roads or bridges over land that the defendant (typically a railway company) has purchased from the claimant and which the claimant will not be able to access without a new road or bridge. Notwithstanding that construction contracts raise significant supervision issues and, for this reason, are not normally subject to specific performance orders, the courts routinely grant specific performance in railway cases.[110] The straightforward justification for this apparent exception is that damages are wholly inadequate because the claimants cannot purchase substitute performance from a third party. Only the defendants can build on their own land (or can authorize a third party to build).

Personal Duties

The final internal reason for refusing specific relief is that the relevant duty requires the defendant's non-trivial personal involvement. The 'personal duties' defence is the reason that courts refuse to order defendants to provide personal services, for example to work as an employee or to perform in a theatre.[111] Not surprisingly, this defence is invoked almost exclusively in cases where the claimant seeks specific performance of a contractual duty. The only exception is where the claimant seeks an injunction to enforce a negative contractual duty that, if fulfilled, would leave the defendant no practical choice but to perform a positive contractual duty.[112] As was true with respect to the supervision defence, courts invariably award damages where they refuse specific relief because of the personal duties defence.

[110] See e.g. *Wolverhampton and Walsall Railway Company v London and North-Western Railway Company* [1873] LR 16 Eq 433.

[111] See e.g. *Clarke v Price* (1819) 2 Wils Ch 158.

[112] *Warner Brothers Pictures Inc v Nelson* [1937] 1 KB 209.

It might be thought that the personal duties defence is a sub-category of the supervision defence because orders to perform personal duties invariably raise supervision issues. Yet courts and writers usually explain the rule on the basis that an order to perform personal services amounts to a kind of servitude.[113] This explanation is initially puzzling. A contractual promise to be another's slave is contrary to public policy and so is invalid as a matter of substantive law. However, few personal service contracts are invalid for this or any other substantive-law reason. Ordinary contractual promises to work as an employee are perfectly valid. On what basis, then, could an order to perform a valid promise to work amount to a kind of servitude? The order appears to do no more than to direct defendants to do what the substantive law says they should do.

The issue is difficult, but I suggest that the explanation lies in the different meanings conveyed by orders to perform personal services and rules that require the same action. A judicial order is an individualized directive, issued by an organ of the state. As we saw in Chapter 5, the duty to obey an order arises from the order itself (not from the parties' agreement), and, crucially, it is owed to the court, not the claimant. The only reason that an order provides to do what it requires is that a court issued it. From this perspective, an order to perform personal services indeed resembles a kind of servitude: the order is nothing less than a command from the state that the defendant perform personal services. Such orders might well be justified in certain circumstances. But given the importance that modern western societies place on the individual's freedom vis-à-vis the state, it is not surprising that the law regards orders to perform personal service with concern.

Thus understood, the personal duties defence is a remedial defence: its concern is the appropriateness of judicial orders that command defendants to perform personal actions, not the appropriateness of substantive rules that require the same thing. Further, like the supervision and adequacy of damages defences, the personal duties defence reflects a general remedial-law principle. It is not necessary to know anything about the particular history or alleged concerns of the Chancery to understand why contemporary courts might decline to order personal services. Indeed, the principle against ordering personal services is applied as strongly, if not more strongly, in civil law systems, which never had courts equivalent to England's Chancery.[114] It is true that in common law systems the personal duty defence is only available with respect to rulings that originated in the Chancery. However, there would be no point in asking whether an order that originated in the Royal Courts is too personal. Orders to pay damages for a sum due under a contract or to quit land never require the defendant's non-trivial personal involvement.[115]

[113] See e.g. Burrows (2004) 482; *De Francesco v Barnum* (1890) 45 Ch D 430 (where Fry LJ said that the courts were afraid of turning 'contracts of service into contracts of servitude': 438).

[114] See Zweigert & Kotz (1998) 474–5.

[115] The defendant does not strictly need to do anything in response to such orders because the only consequence of non-performance is that a third party may seize and sell the defendant's assets.

To conclude, the adequacy of damages, supervision, and personal duties defences could have arisen just as easily in a unitary court system. The historical fact that they arose in England's bifurcated system has influenced their operation in certain ways, but they are explicable without reference to that system. They reflect concerns that should matter to any court that issues remedies. It remains only to reiterate that explaining these defences is not the same as justifying them. The internal defences are controversial or, more strictly, their scope is controversial. This controversy is exactly what we should expect if, as I have argued, the internal defences require courts to balance the value of providing justice against the value of pursuing other public values.

iii. External Partial Defences

In addition to refusing specific relief for the internal reasons discussed above, courts occasionally refuse specific relief for reasons that are external to the order. In broad terms, external partial defences focus on the context in which the relevant claim was made, typically on an aspect of the claimant's behaviour. For example, specific relief may be refused (and damages awarded in lieu) because the claimant delayed unduly in bringing the application ('laches') or because the claimant took advantage of the defendant's ignorance ('clean hands'). These defences are external because their justification has nothing to do with the validity or force of the relevant substantive duty. Exceptional cases aside, these defences are merely reasons for refusing a particular kind of order.[116]

Even more than the internal defences, the external defences are usually assumed to reflect distinctively Equitable concerns. They are invariably described as 'Equitable defences' or as 'Equitable maxims' and, in contrast to the internal defences, there has been almost no attempt to explain them on grounds that do not refer to their historical origins.[117] Nonetheless, I argue that it is unhelpful to describe these defences as Equitable. As was true of the internal defences, it is unnecessary to know anything about the history or concerns of the Chancery to understand the contemporary application of these defences. With a few qualifications, these defences could have arisen in a unitary court system.

I will also argue that two of the (so-called) Equitable defences—'hardship' and 'public interest'—are substantive, not remedial, defences. The concerns that animate these defences are reasons not just for courts to refuse specific relief, but more

[116] 'Exceptional cases aside' because courts occasionally employ these defences to refuse relief for substantive-law reasons. For example, in the past the clean hands defence has been successfully raised in contract cases where, today, the court would probably hold that no contract was created.

[117] But see H. Smith (2018).

fundamentally are reasons for defendants not to perform the actions contemplated by such relief.

There is little agreement amongst courts or commentators about the number of (so-called) Equitable defences, their labels, or the borders between them. The discussion below focuses on five of the most important and widely accepted such defences.

Delay (Laches)

In practice, the most important external defence is delay or 'laches'.[118] Under the laches doctrine, courts may refuse specific relief if the claimant delayed unduly notwithstanding that the relevant statutory limitation period has not unexpired.[119] The principle that claimants may lose the right to judicial relief because they delayed is unexceptional and, as discussed above, is given effect more generally by the just-mentioned statutory limitation periods. However, laches differs from statutory limitation periods in that while the latter are triggered merely by the passage of a pre-determined period, under laches there is no set period. What counts as 'unreasonable' delay depends on the circumstances and, further, it is generally assumed that laches cannot be invoked unless the delay has prejudiced the defendant.[120]

The question raised by the laches doctrine is therefore whether there is any explanation, aside from history, for why claimants who delay bringing actions may be denied specific relief notwithstanding that the statutory limitation period has not expired? Why is specific relief subject to what is, in effect, a different limitation period? The answer, I argue, is that delays in seeking specific relief typically prejudice defendants more significantly than delays in seeking non-specific relief. The action sought in the standard suit for non-specific relief—the payment of money—rarely

[118] This defence is closely related to the defence of acquiescence: Burrows (2004) 573; Spry (2014) 457.

[119] The *Limitations Act* 1980 does not apply directly to requests for specific relief, but by virtue of s 36 (1) the Act may be applied 'by analogy'. While the issue is not conclusively settled, it appears that by virtue of this provision the Act applies to requests for specific relief (save for *quia timet* relief) insofar as they are not already barred by laches: see *Hovenden v Lord Annesley* (1806) 2 Sch & Lef 607, 630–1; Spry (2014) 431–2; Burrows (2004) 573; McGee (2010); cf (for specific performance) Burrows (2004) 501. In practice, the issue is largely moot as the laches defence is usually raised before the statutory period expires. The Act does not apply by analogy to requests for *quia timet* relief, but, again, this issue is moot in practice. Finally, the Act applies to orders for equitable damages in lieu of specific relief: *Cia de Seguros Imperio v Heath (REBX) Ltd* [2001] 1WLR 112. Consistent with my interpretation of laches, the Law Commission's Final Report on Limitation Periods in Civil Proceedings recommended that the Acts apply to specific relief (but without excluding the possibility of a laches defence): Law Com No 270.

In *P & O Nedlloyd BV v Arab Metals Co (No 2)* [2007] 1 WLR 2288, the Court of Appeal held that the *Limitation Act* did not apply by analogy to claims for specific performance. Moore-Bick LJ reasoned that no analogy could be drawn because the coercive nature of specific performance had no equivalent in an action for damages and because while a breach of contract must be established for damages, a breach of contract is unnecessary to obtain specific performance. Moore-Bick LJ went on to state:

> . . . whatever may be said about the undesirability of allowing a claim for specific performance to be brought more than six years after a breach of contract has occurred, the absence of a corresponding legal remedy makes it impossible in my view to say either that the remedy in equity is 'correspondent to the remedy at law' or that 'the suit in equity corresponds with an action at law' [48].

[120] Spry (2014) 449–51.

becomes more onerous through the passage of time. The cost of complying with a monetary order is relatively constant over time; indeed, the cost often decreases over time because of inflation. By contrast, the cost of complying with an order of specific relief may increase significantly with delay. For example, the cost of removing or repairing a structure may increase if the defendant has added to the structure or begun to use it for new purposes. Likewise, the cost of complying with an order to deliver goods may increase if the defendant has agreed to resell the goods or has put them to a particular use. To be sure, the burden of complying with specific rulings does not always increase over time. And in cases where claimants make clear that they have not relinquished their right to performance, defendants can hardly complain that the cost of complying with their duty has increased. It is appropriate, then, that the test for laches requires courts to determine if the cost of compliance has increased over time and, further, to determine if the claimant's actions implied acquiescence in the defendant's non-performance.[121]

In some cases, defendants subjected to non-specific rulings may be significantly prejudiced by the claimant's delay. The main example is where the claimant seeks an order to recover possession of land. Trespassers who are led to believe that the owner will not seek to eject them may well rely in significant ways on that belief, for example by improving the property. Because repossession orders originated in the Royal Courts, they cannot be set aside for laches. However, the unavailability of laches in such cases is explicable on non-historical grounds. As mentioned earlier, damages are rarely an adequate or even partially adequate substitute for a possession order. Further, insofar as landowners are unable to eject trespassers, their land will be effectively inalienable. Finally, the law already contains two doctrines—adverse possession and proprietary estoppel—that are intended to reconcile the interests of owners and non-owners. It would be anomalous if trespassers could attain greater protection by invoking laches.

Assuming that the statutory limitation period has not expired, claimants who have been refused specific relief because they have delayed may still obtain an ordinary damages award in respect of any wrongfully caused losses that they have suffered. In theory, courts can also exercise their authority under s 50 of the *Senior Courts Act* 1981 to award claimants substitutionary damages. However, in practice such awards are unusual because substitute performance is rarely possible.

Understood in this way, the laches defence reflects a concern for fairness to the defendant and so a concern for unconscionability in a broad sense. It is unfair to allow claimants to obtain specific relief in circumstances where their own tardiness or other actions have led the defendant to rely on an assumption that the claimant would not seek such relief. However, it is not necessary to refer to the defence's origins in the Chancery to understand why it is applied exclusively to specific rulings.

[121] Ibid 232–44.

The defence is applied only to specific relief because a delay in seeking such relief can prejudice defendants in ways that delays in seeking non-specific relief are unlikely to do. The defence of laches reflects the same principles that underlie limitation periods more generally.

Impossibility

Specific relief is ordinarily denied if it is impossible for the defendant to comply with the order.[122] For example, a court will not order defendants to deliver goods that they no longer own or possess. Specific relief is also ordinarily denied if the order would be futile or pointless. For example, specific relief is denied if the defendant can reverse the effect of the ordered actions by a subsequent non-wrongful act or if the harm that the order seeks to prevent has already occurred.[123]

The straightforward explanation for the impossibility defence is that there is no point in issuing an order if the order cannot be complied with, is futile, or pointless. Access to the courts is a limited resource: it should not be wasted on useless applications. It is not necessary to know anything about the Chancery to understand this principle. The explanation for the limitation of the defence to requests for specific relief is equally straightforward. An order to pay damages, a debt, or to quit land is never impossible, futile, or pointless. Of course, it is frequently the case that defendants are unable to fulfil monetary orders. But it can never be conclusively determined in advance that this is the case since it is always possible that the defendant may be able to borrow money or otherwise come into new funds.[124]

Clean Hands

In principle, specific relief may be refused if the claimant has 'unclean hands'. In broad terms, claimants have unclean hands if they have engaged in behaviour that—while not strictly a legal wrong or other reason to deny a substantive right—is undesirable and, further, is linked to the substantive right from which the claimant's claim arose.[125] For example, it has been held that a claimant's bad faith failure to disclose important information in the proceedings leading to a contract of sale constituted unclean hands.[126] In other cases, the concept of uncleanliness is interpreted more broadly, as where scientologists were denied an injunction

[122] Spry (2014) 419–21.

[123] See e.g. *Attorney General v Guardian Newspapers Ltd (No 2)* [1990] 1 AC 109.

[124] Where the defendant is insolvent, the order may be relevant to determining how such assets as the defendant has, or acquires, will be allocated amongst creditors.

[125] The traditional maxim 'he who comes to equity must do equity' is similar to clean hands—and raises the same issues—except that it looks to the claimant's future conduct. Broadly defined, the clean hands bar covers those cases, rare today, in which specific performance is refused because of the claimant's breach, the claimant's misrepresentation, the defendant's mistake, unfairness in the formation process, or (very rare today) unfairness in the contract's terms.

[126] See *Quadrant Visual Communications Ltd and Others v Hutchison Telephone (UK) Ltd and Another* [1993] BCLC 442; *Falcke v Grey* (1859) 4 Drew 651.

against defamatory publications because their own activities and beliefs were, in the judge's view, deplorable.[127]

As a consequences of the expansion over the last century of substantive defences such as illegality, duress, undue influence, unconscionability, mistake, and misrepresentation the clean hands doctrine is rarely invoked today. Indeed, it may be queried whether these defences leave any space for the doctrine. Nonetheless, the clean hands doctrine is defensible in principal. The doctrine is closely related to the general defence of illegality, in particular to that aspect of the illegality defence that allows courts to refuse relief to claimants whose behaviour, though lawful, is considered immoral or otherwise contrary to public policy. Under the latter doctrine, courts have refused to enforce prostitution contracts, notwithstanding that entering such contracts is lawful in most common law jurisdictions. By definition, the kind of behaviour at issue in cases of unclean hands is not sufficiently unclean to be contrary to public policy. However, it may be sufficiently unclean to invoke a narrower version of the 'public policy defence'.

As explained above, the most plausible justification for the invalidity of contracts that are illegal or contrary to public policy is that the courts do not want to be seen as even indirectly assisting or condoning immoral or otherwise undesirable behaviour (the '*ex turpi*' principle). In such cases, the courts are effectively saying to claimants what ordinary individuals often say in similar situations: 'I will not stop you from doing what you are doing, but I will not help you or get involved in any way'. The application of the *ex turpi* principle to particular cases turns on two factors. The first is the degree to which the relevant behaviour is contrary to public policy: the more serious the claimant's misbehaviour, the more reason courts have to refuse their assistance. The second factor is the extent of the assistance that the misbehaving party seeks from the state: the greater the assistance that is sought, the greater the risk that the state will be seen as supporting the claimant's misbehaviour. Taken together, these factors suggest that the test for disqualifying misbehaviour should be easier to satisfy in cases where the claimant is seeking a greater degree of assistance from the courts. The extent to which the claimant's behaviour taints the court depends on the extent of its involvement and the seriousness of the claimant's misbehaviour.

Claimants requesting specific relief are normally seeking more assistance than are claimants requesting payment of a debt, damages or the recovery of land. As explained above, specific rulings are often more difficult to draft than other orders, they may lead to further litigation, and crucially, they cannot usually be enforced other than by criminal prosecutions and criminal punishments. By contrast, rulings for the payment of a debt or damages or for the recovery of land are easy to express, rarely lead to subsequent litigation, and can be enforced with little or no

[127] See *Hubbard v Vosper* [1972] 2 QB 84.

involvement by the state. Against this background, it is not surprising that courts sometimes refuse requests for specific relief because of the defendant's undesirable behaviour even where that behaviour is not sufficiently undesirable to refuse relief entirely. The clean hands defence is an application of the general principle that courts should avoid being associated too closely with a claimant's undesirable—even if not strictly unlawful—behaviour.

This explanation of the clean hands bar is not meant to suggest that the courts apply the bar properly or even that the bar is on balance a good thing. Reasonable legal systems might well come to the view that the distinction between 'refusing all relief' and 'refusing specific relief' is too fine to be practically serviceable. However, the bar is not incoherent or patently unreasonable. Further, the clean hands bar is at most only indirectly related to a concern for unconscionability. One way of dirtying one's hands is to engage in unconscionable behaviour. However, as the Scientology case illustrates, it is not the only way. The clean hands bar is based on the same principles that underlie the traditional common law doctrine of illegality.

Hardship

Although 'equitable defences' are conventionally presented as reasons for refusing to issue specific remedies—and so as part of remedial law—there are at least two such defences that appear to be substantive. According to the first such defence—'hardship'—specific relief may be refused if it would cause undue hardship to the defendant. Broadly, undue hardship is established by showing that specific relief would place a burden on the defendant out of all proportion to its value to the claimant. A relatively recent, and rare, case in which this defence was invoked successfully is *Patel v Ali.*[128] The claimant sought specific performance of a contract for the sale of a residential property. Such requests are routinely granted (on the basis that land is unique and so damages are an inadequate remedy). However, in *Patel* specific performance was refused. Subsequent to the agreement to sell, the defendant's husband was sent to jail, one of her legs was amputated, and she bore two additional children. The combination of these events meant that she relied heavily on neighbours and nearby relatives for assistance. The court held that in these circumstances an order of specific performance would cause the defendant undue hardship. Accordingly, the claimant was granted damages in lieu of specific relief.

It might be thought that the hardship doctrine is based on a straightforward concern for unconscionability. Demanding specific relief in circumstances where it imposes a burden out of all proportion to its value appears to be unconscionable behaviour. However, this explanation must assume, implausibly, that the court's concern in *Patel* was solely over the kind of remedy sought by the claimant.

[128] [1984] Ch 283.

According to this explanation, the unconscionable behaviour that triggered the hardship doctrine was the claimant's decision to seek specific enforcement of his substantive right. In this view, the defendant's obligation to convey the property was fully binding. However, it seems clear that the court did not think that Mrs Ali should have felt bound to convey the property. The reasons that the court gave for refusing specific relief were concerned not with the form of specific relief, but with the content of the underlying substantive duty. The court did not want Mrs Ali to convey the property regardless of whether the reason she conveyed it was that she had a substantive duty to do so or because she was ordered to do so.

Where specific relief is refused because damages are adequate, supervision would be difficult, or the duty is personal, the court clearly believes that the defendant should have fulfilled the relevant substantive duty. The reasons for refusing specific relief in such cases are concerned entirely with the form of specific relief, not with the action that specific relief contemplates. In contrast, in *Patel* the court's concern is entirely focused on the contemplated action: the court clearly thought that the best result would be if Mrs Ali were able to keep her house. Yet according to the conventional explanation of the hardship defence, Mrs Ali had a legal duty to convey her house. In this view, if Mrs Ali had asked a lawyer, prior to the litigation, whether she had a legal duty to convey the property the answer would have been 'yes'. Yet the court in *Patel* clearly did not want her to convey the property. It is true that if Mrs Ali's lawyer also informed her that the courts were unlikely to order the performance of her duty to convey, she might well not have performed the duty. However, the courts cannot explain the hardship defence on this basis: the courts must assume that the duties it asserts should be treated as just that—duties.

The question, then, is whether it is possible to explain cases like *Patel* without assuming that defendants have legal duties to do what courts not only refuse to order them to do, but more importantly, do not think they should have done. Elsewhere in the law, the closest analogies to *Patel* appear to be 'necessity' cases (which I discussed in Chapter 8). For example, in the famous American case of *Vincent v Lake Erie Transportation Co*,[129] the court held that the defendant acted reasonably when he refused to untie his ship from the claimant's dock in order to save the ship from being destroyed in a violent storm. Yet the court also ordered the defendant to compensate the claimant for the damage caused to the dock. In *Vincent*, there was no opportunity for the claimant to seek an injunction against trespassing, but had such a request been made in time the court undoubtedly would have refused it. The reason they would have refused would have been the same reason that specific relief was refused in *Patel*: namely, the cost of performance was out of all proportion to its value. It follows that the justification for awarding damages in *Vincent* cases cannot be that the defendant acted wrongly: like Mrs Ali, the defendant in *Vincent*

[129] [1910] 109 Minn 456.

acted perfectly reasonably. Why, then, did the defendants in *Vincent* and *Patel* have to pay compensation? The answer, which I defended in Chapter 8, is that there are circumstances in which individuals must compensate for the harm they caused notwithstanding that they did no wrong.[130] Individuals in the position of the defendants in *Vincent* and *Patel* have what Francis Bohlen described in his analysis of *Vincent* as an 'incomplete privilege', meaning that they are allowed to do something that is normally not allowed, subject to the condition that they must compensate for any harm they cause.[131] Any other interpretation of cases like *Vincent* or *Patel* must suppose, implausibly, that individuals have legal duties to do things that the courts in such cases clearly did not think the defendants should have done.

Thus understood, hardship is a substantive defence: it is a reason for, in effect, modifying the defendant's substantive duty. The explanation for why courts refuse specific relief in cases like *Patel* is not that the claimant acted unconscionably in seeking specific relief, but rather that the duty that the claimant seeks to have performed does not exist.

Public Interest

The other equitable defence that appears to be substantive instead of remedial is 'public interest'. Like the hardship defence, the public interest defence is controversial, and has rarely been invoked successfully. One famous example is *Miller v Jackson*,[132] where the defence was invoked as one of the reasons for refusing an injunction to prohibit cricket on a field next to the claimant's property. The court held that an injunction would be contrary to the local community's interest in playing cricket on the village green.[133]

The controversy surrounding the public interest defence is unsurprising: it is relatively rare that the 'public interest' figures explicitly in judicial reasoning about private law disputes. However, for present purposes two other aspects of the defence are important. The first is that the defence has nothing to do with the prevention of unconscionable conduct. It may be petty and selfish to try to shut down a community cricket field, but it is not unconscionable. The second aspect is that whatever the defence's substantive merits or practical significance, it is substantive, not remedial. Insofar as the public interest should inform a court's reasoning in cases like *Miller*, it is a reason not merely to refuse specific relief but, more importantly, to deny the existence of the alleged duty. If the public interest is a sufficient reason not to order the cricket club to stop playing, it is also a sufficient reason for holding that the cricket club has no duty period to stop playing cricket. The court in *Miller* clearly did not think that the defendant should have stopped playing

[130] For a different (and in my view less straightforward) answer, see Gardner (2011) 42.

[131] Bohlen (1926) 313.

[132] [1977] QB 966. A more recent example, which I discuss in Chapter 8, is *Dennis v Ministry of Defence* [2003] EWHC 793.

[133] [1977] QB 989 (Cumming-Bruce LJ), 981–2 (Denning LJ).

cricket.[134] Yet if the public interest defence was only remedial, the fact that playing cricket was in the public interest would not have affected the defendant's legal duty to cease playing cricket.

iv. Discretion

According to the traditional and still conventional view, specific relief is never available 'as of right' but is instead only available in the court's 'discretion'. I discuss this view here because the discretion in question is a discretion to refuse specific relief because of one or more of the partial defences. For example, it is traditionally said that the determination of whether damages are an adequate substitute for specific relief or whether the defendant has unclean hands is a matter for the court's discretion.

The traditional view has been criticized on both descriptive and normative grounds.[135] The descriptive critique has two parts. First, it is claimed that in nearly all cases where specific relief is a prima facie possible remedy it is also possible to predict whether the court will grant such relief. For example, specific performance of an obligation to deliver fungible goods or to perform a personal service is almost never awarded. In contrast, injunctions against ongoing trespasses or infringements of negative contractual obligations are routinely awarded. More generally, there is an extensive body of law—a book-length corpus—governing the availability of injunctions and specific performance.[136] Decisions to refuse specific relief can be overturned on appeal. The second part of the descriptive critique points out that the application of the rules governing non-specific relief, in particular the application of the rules governing damages, is often difficult to predict. This unpredictability is incontrovertible in the case of punitive awards and awards for so-called intangible injuries (pain and suffering, loss of amenity, or loss of reputation). However, even the assessment of ordinary awards for consequential losses frequently requires courts to exercise considerable judgment, if not outright discretion. There is no formula for determining whether a loss is too 'remote' to be included in a damages award.

This critique is powerful, but it is not fatal to the traditional account. The fact that it is usually easy to predict whether specific relief will be awarded may show nothing more than that in most cases the factors that courts are meant to take into

[134] Lord Denning said as much by holding that the defendant had not committed a nuisance. This finding was of course a sufficient reason to deny the claimant's request. Lord Denning's further finding that specific relief should be refused was redundant, but it is less odd than it appears once it is understood that the basis for this second finding was, in substance, that the defendant was not committing a nuisance.

[135] See Burrows (2004) 457.

[136] See e.g. Spry (2014); Berryman (2013).

account when exercising their discretion point in the same direction. The traditional view does not suppose that courts have an unfettered discretion: it supposes that courts exercise discretion when considering the partial defences described above. This discretion is consistent with predictable results in most cases where claimants seek specific relief.

More importantly, the discretion that courts exercise when they are assessing requests for specific relief differs qualitatively from the discretion they exercise when assessing requests for non-specific relief. In the case of non-specific relief, courts go through a checklist of discrete questions. For example, in the case of orders to pay a sum due, the order will be issued if the debt is proven and the limitation period has not expired. In the case of compensatory damages, the checklist is longer, and some of the answers must specify relative magnitudes, but it is still a checklist (e.g. 'Is there a loss? Was the loss caused by the wrong? Was the loss reasonably foreseeable?'). In such cases, the court must consider, serially, a set of questions to which the answers are either 'yes' or 'no' (e.g. 'Did the defendant breach a duty owed to the claimant?') or quantitative (e.g. 'What sum fairly represents the claimant's suffering?'). Some of the latter questions arguably require the courts to balance, or at least weigh, different factors (e.g. the pain suffered by the claimant, the value of offsetting advantages, the egregiousness of the defendant's behaviour in the case of exemplary damages), but this balancing is done using a common metric—money—and it only happens at the stage when the court quantifies the award (not when it considers if the award is available at all).

The discretion that courts enjoy in regards to specific relief is different. As with non-specific relief, certain facts must be established before an order will be made—for example, the existence of a valid contractual obligation, the validity of title to land, or the existence of an actual or threatened trespass or nuisance. There are also certain facts that may clearly preclude an award, such as statutory immunity. But according to the traditional view, there are other facts that cannot be considered in isolation but must instead be weighed together, in a global or 'bundle-of-factors' fashion, to determine if specific relief should be awarded.[137] These facts are specified by the partial remedial defences; they include, therefore, the extent to which damages are an adequate substitute or supervision is difficult or the obligation is personal and so on.[138] In the traditional view, a court assessing a request for specific relief must consider all these circumstances at the same time, arriving at a decision by balancing them in a global fashion. It follows, in this view, that a

[137] 'All equitable remedies are, in the appropriate sense, discretionary. In the auxiliary jurisdiction of the court, for example, equitable discretions are exercised by taking into account all relevant matters that tend towards the justice or injustice of granting the remedy that is sought, such as hardship, laches, unfairness, the lack of clean hands, and so on, and by weighing them against each other in order to decide whether the particular relief that is in question should be granted in an absolute, partial or conditional form or else refused': Spry (2014) 4ff, 153–5.

[138] Ibid 10ff.

court might refuse specific performance of a valid contractual obligation on the basis that, while damages are an imperfect (but not wholly inadequate) substitute, supervision is moderately (but not insuperably) difficult, and the claimant acted somewhat (but not egregiously) in bad faith. The resulting decision is not arbitrary, and, in practice, it may be relatively easy to predict the result; nonetheless, this balance-of-factors reasoning process is different in kind from the checklist process that courts go through when contemplating non-specific relief. There is no formula to balance 'adequacy of damages' against 'difficulty of supervision' or 'cleanliness of the defendant's hands'. The court must simply consider the relevant factors and make a global judgment.

It is true that, in practice, courts assessing requests for specific relief typically focus on just one of the partial remedial defences. For example, a request for specific performance of a contractual obligation to paint a portrait or to work as a servant is typically refused simply on the basis that the courts will not order performance of a personal obligation. Similarly, a request for specific performance of a contractual obligation to deliver a unique good is normally accepted simply on the ground that damages are inadequate. This practice may explain why some judges and writers treat the remedial defences as serial tests.[139] However, this interpretation cannot explain the many cases in which courts balance or weigh different factors.[140] Further, there is a simple explanation for why courts typically only mention one factor: in most cases, the other factors are insignificant. Finally, the bundle-of-factors interpretation makes sense in principle. The partial defences identify reasons for and against specific relief. Difficulty of supervision is a reason in favour of damages, while inadequacy of damages is a reason in favour of specific relief. Neither reason excludes consideration of the other: each reason counts for or against specific relief to an extent that depends on the facts of the case. Like other reasons for and against particular actions, the reasons contemplated by the partial defences should be weighed against one another.

Judicial discretion is generally undesirable. The rule of law ideal requires that the law be clear and predictable. However, clarity and predictability are not the only virtues of good law. The values that underlie the partial remedial defences, such as the efficient administration of justice, are also important. Further, and significantly, a discretion to refuse specific relief is significantly less harmful to the rule of law ideal than a discretion to refuse to recognize a substantive right. Like other parts of remedial law, the rules governing remedial defences are directed primarily at judges, not citizens. They provide reasons for courts to refuse remedies. Although citizens consider remedial defences when contemplating litigations, they

[139] Spry notes various decisions in which judges have adopted, wrongly in his view, the serial approach: Spry (2014) 4–26. Burrows' textbook adopts the serial approach: Burrows (2004) 458–505, 569–75.

[140] See e.g. *Prophet plc v Huggett* [2014] EWHC 615, [39], [44]–[45]; *Scott & Another v Scott* [2012] EWHC 4186 [35], [37]–[38]; *Otuo v Brierley* [2013] EWHC 2869 [103]–[04].

are not meant to act on these defences when deciding how to behave in everyday life, for example, when deciding whether to fulfil a contractual promise or engage in a nuisance. Indeed, the vagueness of this part of the law might be thought useful insofar as it dissuades individuals from attempting to use remedial defences to guide their everyday behaviour.[141]

More generally, rights to judicial relief ('action rights') may legitimately be circumscribed in ways that substantive rights may not. As discussed above, part of the explanation for the partial defences is that providing 'justice services' is only one of the state's responsibilities. Further, the consequences of refusing specific relief are relatively minor in the vast majority of cases. In the typical case where courts refuse specific relief, the defendant is granted a substitutionary remedy in the form of an award of damages, quantified at the cost of obtaining substitute performance. Indeed, the most common reason that courts exercise their discretion to refuse specific relief is that damages are adequate, where 'adequate' means precisely that damages may be used to purchase or reimburse the cost of substitute performance. And even in cases where this reason is not the primary consideration, it is usually a secondary consideration. Finally, in the relatively rare cases where a substitutionary award is not possible or otherwise refused, the claimant retains a right to an award of ordinary compensatory damages.

The traditional view that specific relief is available only in the court's discretion is defensible both descriptively and normatively. However, the explanation for this discretion is not the traditional idea that the Chancery originally dealt with something other than the 'law' strictly understood. Rather, the explanation is that certain features of the rulings that, traditionally, were associated with the Chancery make it appropriate for courts to ask further questions before awarding them. These questions, in turn, do not present the courts with a check-list, but instead require them to weigh and balance a heterogeneous list of considerations.

[141] For a similar argument in the context of criminal law defences, see Dan-Cohen (1984) 639.

Bibliography

Allen, Sir C.K. (1931) *Legal Duties and Other Essays in Jurisprudence* (The Clarendon Press).
Arlidge, A. et al (2017) *Arlidge, Eady & Smith on Contempt* (5th edn) (Sweet & Maxwell).
Andoh, B. & Marsh, S. (1997) *Civil Remedies* (Ashgate).
Andrews, N. (2003) *English Civil Procedure: Fundamentals of the New Civil Justice System* (Oxford University Press).
Aristotle (reprinted 2009) *The Nicomachean Ethics*, W.D. Ross & L. Brown (trans.) (Oxford University Press).
Atiyah, P.S. & Cane, P. (2013) *Atiyah's Accidents, Compensation and the Law* (8th edn) (Cambridge University Press).
Atkins, J.R. (2014) (2015) (2016) (2019) *Atkin's Encyclopedia of Court Forms in Civil Proceedings* (2nd edn) (Butterworths).
Austin, J. (1832) *The Province of Jurisprudence Determined* (J. Murray).
Austin, J.L. (1979) *Philosophical Papers* (Oxford University Press) 233.
Baker, J.H. (2002) *An Introduction to English Legal History* (4th edn) (Butterworths).
Barker, K. (2013) 'Private and Public: The Meaning of Vindication in Private Law' in S. Pitel, J. Neyers, & E. Chamberlain (eds), *Tort Law: Challenging Orthodoxy* (Hart Publishing).
Barton, J.H. (1972) 'The Economic Basis of Damages for Breach of Contract' 1:2 *J Legal Studies* 277.Beever, A. (2007) *Rediscovering the Law of Negligence* (Hart Publishing).
Beever, A. (2016) *A Theory of Tort Liability* (Hart Publishing).
Bentham, J. (1970, reprint) *An Introduction to the Principles of Morals and Legislation*, Burns, J.H. & Hart, H.L.A. (eds) (Clarendon Press).
Berryman, J.B. (2013) *The Law of Equitable Remedies* (2nd edn) (Irwin Law).
Berryman, J.B. et al (2016) *Remedies: Cases and Materials* (7th edn) (Emond Montgomery).
Birks, P. (1997a) 'Harassment and Hubris: The Right to an Equality of Respect' 32 *Irish Jurist* 1.
Birks, P. (1997b) 'Definition and Division: A Meditation on the *Institutes*' in P. Birks (ed.), *The Classification of Obligations* (Clarendon Press).
Birks, P. (1998) 'Misnomer' in W.R. Cornish et al. (eds), *Restitution: Past, Present and Future: Essays in Honour of Gareth Jones* (Hart Publishing).
Birks, P. (2000a) 'Rights, Wrongs, and Remedies' 20:1 *Oxford J Legal Studies* 1.
Birks, P. (2000b) *English Private Law* (Oxford University Press).
Birks, P. (2000c) 'Personal Property: Proprietary Rights and Remedies' 11:1 *The King's College LJ* 1.
Birks, P. (2005) *Unjust Enrichment* (2nd edn) (Oxford University Press).
Birmingham, R.L. (1970) 'Breach of Contract, Damage Measures, and Economic Efficiency' 24:2 *Rutgers LR* 273.
Blackstone, W. (1979 reprint) *Commentaries on the Laws of England* (vols I–IV) (A Facsimile of the First Edition of 1765 – 1769) (University of Chicago Press).
Bohlen, F.H. (1926) 'Incomplete Privilege to Inflict Intentional Invasions of Interests of Property and Personality' 39:3 *Harvard LR* 307.
Bohlen, F.H. (1911) 'The Rule in *Rylands v Fletcher*, Part III' 59 *U of Pennsylvania LR* 431.
Burrows, A.S. (2002) *The Law of Restitution* (2nd edn) (Oxford University Press).

Burrows, A.S. (2004) *Remedies for Torts and Breach of Contract* (3rd edn) (Oxford University Press).

Burrows, A.S. (2011) *The Law of Restitution* (3rd edn) (Oxford University Press).

Burrows, A.S. (2015) *Principles of the English Law of Obligations* (Oxford University Press).

Calabresi, G. & Melamed, A.D. (1972) 'Property Rules, Liability Rules, and Inalienability: One View of the Cathedral' 85:6 *Harvard LR* 1089.

Cane, P. (2001) 'Responsibility and Fault' in P. Cane & J. Gardner (eds), *Relating to Responsibility* (Hart Publishing).

Cane, P. (2002) *Responsibility and Morality* (Hart Publishing).

Cappelletti, M., Kollmer, P.J., & Olson, J.M. (1989) *The Judicial Process in Comparative Perspective* (Clarendon Press).

Chambers, R. (2005) 'The Importance of Specific Performance' in S. Degeling & J. Edelman (eds), *Equity in Commercial Law* (Law Book Co)

Chitty, T. & Jacob, Sir J.I.H. (1965) *Chitty & Jacob's Queen's Bench Forms* (19th edn) (Sweet & Maxwell).

Clerk, J.F. & Lindsell, W.H.B. (2018) *Clerk & Lindsell on Torts* (22nd edn), M. Jones, A. Dugdale & M. Simpson. (eds) (Sweet & Maxwell).

Cohen, L. (1991) 'Holdouts and Free Riders' 20:2 *J Legal Studies* 351.

Coleman, J.L. (1980) 'Mental Abnormality, Personal Responsibility, and Tort Liability' in B.A. Brody & H.T. Engelhardt Jr. (eds), *Mental Illness: Law and Public Policy* 107 (Springer Publishing).

Coleman, J.L. (1992a) *Risks and Wrongs* (Cambridge University Press).

Coleman, J.L. (1992b) 'The Mixed Conception of Corrective Justice' 77 *Iowa LR* 427

Cook, W.W. (1915) 'The Powers of Courts of Equity' 15:1 *Columbia LR* 37.

Cooter, R (1989) 'Towards a Market in Unmatured Tort Claims' 75 *Virginia Law Review* 38.

Cooter, R. & Porat, A. (2019, forthcoming) 'Torts and Restitution: Legal Divergence and Economic Convergence' 92 *Southern California Law Review*.

Craswell, R (1989) 'Contract Law, Default Rules, and the Philosophy of Promising' 88 *Michigan LR* 489.

Dan-Cohen, M. (1984) 'Decision Rules and Conduct Rules: On Acoustic Separation in Criminal Law' 97:3 *Harvard LR* 625.

Darwall, S.L. (2013) *Morality, Authority, and Law* (Oxford University Press).

Davies, J. (2000) 'Tort' in P. Birks (ed.). *English Private Law* (vol II) (Oxford University Press).

Dedek, H. (2010) 'From Norms to Facts: The Realization of Rights in Common and Civil Private Law' 56:1 *McGill LJ* 77.

Dietrich, J. (1998) *Restitution: A New Perspective* (The Federation Press).

Dobbs, D.B. (1989) 'Ending Punishment in Punitive Damages Deterrence-Measured Remedies' 40:3 *Alabama LR* 831.

Dobbs, D.B. & Roberts, C.L. (2018) *Law of Remedies: Damages, Equity, Restitution* (3rd edn) (West Publishing Company).

Duff, R.A. (2001) *Punishment, Communication, and Community* (Oxford University Press).

Dworkin, R. (1986) *Law's Empire* (Belknap Press).

Edelman, J. (2018) *McGregor on Damages* (20th edn) (Sweet & Maxwell).

Ellickson, R.C. (1989) 'Bringing Culture and Human Frailty to Rational Actors: A Critique of Classical Law and Economics' 65:1 *Chicago-Kent LR* 23.

Elster, J. (1993) 'Some Unresolved Problems in the Theory of Rational Behaviour' 36:3 *Acta Sociologica* 179.

Elvin, D. & Karas, J. (2002) *Unlawful Interference with Land* (Sweet & Maxwell).

Essert, C. (2015) 'Legal Powers in Private Law' 21 *Legal Theory* 136.
Feinberg J. (1978) 'Voluntary Euthanasia and the Inalienable Right to Life' 7 *Philosophy and Public Affairs* 93.
Finnis, J. (1980) *Natural Law and Natural Rights* (Oxford University Press).
Fletcher, G.P. (1972) 'Fairness and Utility in Tort Theory' 85 *Harvard LR* 537.
Friedmann, D. (1995) 'The Performance Interest in Contract Damages' 111 *L Quarterly R* 628.
Fuller, L. (1941) 'Consideration and Form' 41:5 *Columbia LR* 799.
Fuller, L. (revised edition, 1969) *The Morality of Law* (Yale University Press).
Fuller, L. & Purdue W. (1936) 'The Reliance Interest in Contract Damages' 46 *Yale LJ* 52, 373.
Fry, Sir E. & Northcote, G.R. (1921) *A treatise on the Specific Performance of Contracts* (6th edn) (Stevens and Sons).
Gambaro, A. (1997) 'Abuse of Rights in the Civil Law Tradition' in A.M. Rabello (ed.), *Aequitas and Equity: Equity in Civil Law and Mixed Jurisdictions* (Hebrew University of Jerusalem).
Gardner, J. (2001) 'Obligations and Outcomes in the Law of Torts' in P Cane & J Gardner (eds), *Relating to Responsibility: Essays for Tony Honoré* (Hart Publishing).
Gardner, J. (2004) 'The Wrongdoing That Gets Results' 18:1 *Philosophical Perspectives* 53.
Gardner, J. (2011) 'What is Tort Law For? Part 1. The Place of Corrective Justice' 30:1 *L and Phil* 1.
Gardner, J. (2012) *Law as a Leap of Faith: Essays on Law in General* (Oxford University Press).
Gardner, J. (2018) *From Personal Life to Private Law* (Oxford University Press).
Glenn, H.P. (2014) *Legal Traditions of the World: Sustainable Diversity in Law* (5th edn) (Oxford University Press).
Goetz, C.J. & Scott, R.E. (1980) 'Enforcing Promises: An Examination of the Basis of Contract' 89 *Yale LJ* 7.
Goldberg, J & Zipursky, B. (1998) 'The Moral of *MacPherson*' 146 *U of Pennsylvania LR* 1733.
Goldberg, J.C.P. (2000) 'Duty and the Structure of Negligence' 10:1 *Kansas J of L and Public Policy* 149.
Goldberg, J.C.P. & Zipursky, B.C. (2002) 'Unrealized Torts' 88:8 *Virginia LR* 1626.
Goldberg, J. & Zipursky, B. (2010) 'Torts as Wrongs' 88 *Tex L Rev* 917, 980–983.
Goldberg, J.C.P. (2005) 'The Constitutional Status of Tort Law: Due Process and the Right to a Law for the Redress of Wrongs' 115:3 *Yale LJ* 524.
Goldberg, J.C.P. (2006) 'Two Conceptions of Tort Damages: Full v Fair Compensation' 55 *De Paul Law Review* 435.
Goldberg, J.C.P. (2016) 'The Strict Liability in Fault and the Fault in Strict Liability' 85 *Fordham L Rev* 743.
Goudkamp, J. (2013) *Tort Law Defences* (Hart Publishing).
Grantham, R.B. & Rickett, C.E.F. (2003) 'Property Rights as a Legally Significant Event' 62:3 *Cambridge LJ* 717.
Gray, K.J. & Gray, S.F. (2011) *Land Law* (7th edn) (Oxford University Press).
Great Britain, Court of Chancery. (1828) *Forms of Procedure in the Courts of Chancery* (J. Wilson & Son).
Halsbury's Laws of England. (2015) Volume 12A, *Civil Procedure* (LexisNexis UK).
Harris, D., Campbell, D., & Halson, R. (2002) *Remedies in Contract and Tort* (2nd edn) (Butterworths).
Hart. H.L.A. (1955) 'Are There Any Natural Rights' 64:2 *Philosophical Review* 175.
Hart, H.L.A. (1961) *The Concept of Law* (Clarendon Press).

Hart, H.L.A. (1982) 'Legal Rights' in H.L.A. Hart (ed.), *Essays on Bentham: Jurisprudence and Political Theory* (Clarendon Press).
Hart, H.M. et al (1994) *The Legal Process: Basic Problems in the Making and Application of Law* (Foundation Press).
Hedley, S. (2011) *Tort* (7th edn) (Oxford University Press).
Herman B. (1993) *The Practice of Moral Judgment* (Harvard University Press).
Hershovitz, S. (2012) 'The Authority of Law' in A. Marmor (ed.), *Routlege Companion to Philosophy of Law* (Routledge).
Hershowitz, S. (2014) 'Tort as a Substitute for Revenge' in J. Oberdiek (ed.), *Philosophical Foundations of the Law of Torts* (Oxford University Press).
Hobbes, T. (1994 reprinted) *Leviathan with selected variants from the Latin edition of 1668* Edwin Curley (ed.) (Hackett Publishing, first published 1651).
Hohfeld, W.N. (1913) 'Some Fundamental Legal Conceptions as Applied in Judicial Reasoning' 23:1 *Yale LJ* 16.
Hohfeld, W.N. (1917) 'Fundamental Legal Conceptions as Applied in Judicial Reasoning' 26:8 *Yale LJ* 710.
Holmes, O.W. Jr. (1881) *The Common Law* (Little, Brown, and Company).
Holmes, O.W. Jr. (1897) 'The Path of the Law' 10:8 *Harvard LR* 457.
Honoré, T. (1988) 'Responsibility and Luck' *L Quarterly R* 530.
Honoré, T. (1999) *Responsibility and Luck* (Hart Publishing).
Ibbetson, D.J. (1999) *A Historical Introduction to the Law of Obligations* (Oxford University Press).
Jaffey, P. (2000) *The Nature and Scope of Restitution* (Hart Publishing).
Judicial College (Guidelines) (2012) *Guidelines for the Assessment of General Damages in Personal Injury Cases* (11th edn) (Oxford University Press).
Kamm, F. (1985) 'Supererogation and Obligation' 82 *Journal of Philosophy* 118.
Kant, I. (reprinted 1996) *The Metaphysics of Morals*, M.J. Gregor (trans. & ed.) (Cambridge University Press) (original 1797).
Kant, I. (reprinted 1949) 'On the Supposed Right to Lie from Altruistic Motives'. *Immanuel Kant: Critique of Practical Reason and Other Writings in Moral Philosophy*, L.W. Beck (trans. & ed.) (University of Chicago Press) (original 1797).
Kasirer, N. (2001) 'Honour Bound' 47 *McGill LJ* 237.
Kay, M., Sime, S., & French, D. (eds) (2018) *Blackstone's Civil Practice* (Oxford University Press).
Kelsen, H. (1961) *General Theory of Law and State* (Russell & Russell).
Kimel, D. (2003) *From Promise to Contract: Towards a Liberal Theory of Contract* (Hart Publishing).
Kiralfy, A. (1949) 'The Problem of a Law of Property in Goods' 12 *Modern LR* 424.
Klimchuk, D. (2009) 'The Normative Foundations of Unjust Enrichment' in R. Chambers, C. Mitchell, & J. Penner (eds), *The Philosophical Foundations of Unjust Enrichment Law* (Oxford University Press).
Kortmann, J. (2005) *Altruism in Private Law: Liability for Nonfeasance and Negotiorum Gestio* (Oxford University Press).
Kramer, A. (2017) *The Law of Contract Damages* (2nd edn) (Hart publishing).
Lafferty, A. & Jarvis, K. (2008) *Commercial Enforcement* (2nd edn) (Tottel).
Landes, W.M. & Posner, R.A. (1987) *The Economic Structure of Tort Law* (Harvard University Press).
Law Commission & Scottish Law Commission (2010) *Damages for Late Payment and the Insurer's Duty of Good Faith* (Issues Paper No 6).

Lawrence, G.W. & Hunter, S.J. (1873) *An Elementary View of the Proceedings in a Suit in Equity: With an Appendix of Forms* (6th edn) (Butterworths).
Lawson, F.H. (1980) *Remedies of English Law* (2nd edn) (Butterworths).
Laycock, D. (1991) *The Death of the Irreparable Injury Rule* (Oxford University Press).
Laycock, D. (2010) *Modern American Remedies: Cases and Materials* (4th edn) (Aspen Publishers).
Levmore, S. (1985) 'Explaining restitution' 71 *Virginia Law Review* 65.
Lewis, C.J. (1990) *State and Diplomatic Immunity* (3rd edn) (Lloyd's of London Press).
Licht, A.M. (2008) 'Social Norms and the Law: Why Peoples Obey the Law' 4:3 *R of L and Economics* 715.
Littleton, Sir T. (1903) *Littleton's Tenures in English* E. Wambaugh (ed.) (John Byrne & Company).
Maine, Sir H.S. (1883) *Dissertation on Early Law and Custom* (John Murray).
Maitland, F.W. (1909) *Equity, also the Forms of Action at Common Law; Two Courses of Lectures* A.H. Chaytor & W.J. Whittaker (eds) (Cambridge University Press).
Markovits, D. & Schwartz, A. (2011) 'The Myth of Efficient Breach: New Defenses of the Expectation Interest' 97:8 *Virginia LR* 1939.
McBride, N.J. (1994) 'A Fifth Common Law Obligation' 14 *Legal Studies* 35.
McBride, N.J. (2004) 'Duties of Care—Do They Really Exist?' 24:3 *Oxford J Legal Studies* 417.
McBride, N.J. & Bagshaw, R. (2015) *Tort Law* (5th edn) (Pearson).
McBride, N.J. (2019) *The Humanity of Private Law* (Hart Publishing).
McCamus, J. (1979) 'Necessitous Intervention: The Altruistic Intermeddler and The Law Of Restitution' 11 *Ottawa LR* 297.
McGregor, H. (2003) *McGregor on Damages* (17th edn) (Sweet & Maxwell).
McFarlane, B. (2012) 'Unjust Enrichment, Rights, and Value' in Donal Nolan & Andrew Robertson (eds), *Rights and Private Law* (Hart Publishing).
McFarlane, B. (2016) Proprietary Estoppel (Oxford University Press).
McGee, A. (2010) *Limitation Periods* (6th edn) (Sweet & Maxwell)
McGhee, J., Baker, P.V. & Snell, E.H.T. (2000) *Snell's Equity* (30th edn) (Sweet & Maxwell).
McGhee, J., Bridge, S., & Snell, E.H.T. (2015) *Snell's Equity* (33rd edn) (Sweet & Maxwell).
Meagher, R.P., Heydon, J.D., & Leeming, M.J. (2002) *Meagher, Gummow & Lehane's Equity, Doctrines, and Remedies* (4th edn) (Butterworths LexisNexis).
Miller, C.J. & Perry, D. (2017) *Miller on Contempt of Court* (4th edn) (Oxford University Press).
Milsom, S.F.C. (1958) 'Trespass from Henry III to Edward III – Part II: Special Writs' 74:3 *L Quarterly R* 407.
Milsom, S.F.C. (1981) *Historical Foundations of the Common Law* (2nd edn) (Butterworths).
Ministry of Justice (2009) *Judicial Statistics England and Wales for the Year 2009* (Court Statistics (quarterly) Reports).
Moore, M. (1997) *Placing Blame* (Oxford University Press).
Muir, G. (1990) 'Unjust Sacrifice and the Officious Intervener' in P. Finn (ed.) *Essays in Restitution* (Law Book Co).
Murphy, J. (2010) 'The Nature and Domain of Aggravated Damages' 69 *Cambridge LJ* 353.
Nadler, J. (2013) 'Agency and Autonomy in Unjust Enrichment Law' in A. Brudner and J. Nadler (eds), *The Unity of the Common Law* (Oxford University Press) ch 5.
Nagel, T. (1979) *Mortal Questions* (Cambridge University Press).
Nicholas, B. (1992) *The French Law of Contract* (2nd edn) (Oxford University Press).
Nozick, R. (1969) 'Coercion' in S. Morgenbesser, P. Suppes, & M. White (eds), *Philosophy, Science and Method: Essays in Honor of Ernest Nagel* (St Martin's Press).

O'Hare, J. & Browne, K. (2017) *Civil Litigation* (18th edn) (Sweet & Maxwell).

Ogilvie, Sir C. (1978) *The King's Government and the Common Law 1471-1641* (Greenwood Press).

Oman, N.B. (2011a) Why There is No Duty to Pay Damages: Powers, Duties, and Private Law, 39 *Florida State University L Rev* 137.

Oman, N.B. (2011b) 'Consent to Retaliation: A Civil Recourse Theory of Contractual Liability' 96 *Iowa L Rev* 529.

Pearce, D. & Halson, R. (2008) 'Damages for Breach of Contract: Compensation, Restitution, and Vindication' 28 *Oxford JLS* 73.

Peel, W.E. & Goudkamp, J. (2014) *Winfield & Jolowicz on Tort* (19th ed) (Sweet & Maxwell).

Peel, W.E. (2015) *The Law of Contract* (14th edn) (Sweet & Maxwell).

Pekelis, A.H. (1943) 'Legal Techniques and Political Ideologies: A Comparative Study' 41:4 *Michigan LR* 665.

Penner, J.E. (2014) *The Law of Trusts* (9th edn) (Oxford University Press).

Penner, J.E. (2018) 'We All Make Mistakes: A 'Duty of Virtue' Theory of Restitutionary Liability for Mistaken Payments' 81(2) *Modern LR* 222.

Perillo, J.M. (1995) 'Abuse of Rights: A Pervasive Legal Concept' 27:1 *Pacific LJ* 37.

Perry, S.R. (2001a) 'Honoré on Responsibility for Outcomes' in P. Cane & J. Gardner (eds), *Relating to Responsibility* (Hart Publishing).

Perry, S.R. (2001b) 'Responsibility for Outcomes, Risk, and the Law of Torts' in G. Postema (ed.), *Philosophy and the Law of Torts* (Cambridge University Press).

Posner, E.A. (2003) 'Economic Analysis of Contract Law after Three Decades: Success or Failure?' 112:4 *Yale LJ* 829.

Priest, G. L. (1987) 'The Current Insurance Crisis and Modern Tort Law' 96 *Yale LJ* 1521.

Prosser, W.L. (1953) 'Palsgraf Revisited' 52 *Michegan LR* 1.

Rawls, J. (1971) *A Theory of Justice* (Harvard University Press).

Rawls, J. (1999) *Collected Papers* (Harvard University Press)

Raz, J. (1972) 'Voluntary Obligations and Normative Powers' 46 *Proceedings of the Aristotelian Society, Supplementary Volumes* 59.

Raz, J. (1977) 'The Rule of Law and Its Virtue' 93 *L Quarterly R* 195.

Raz, J. (1984) 'The Obligation to Obey: Revision and Tradition' 1:1 *Notre Dame J of L Ethics & Pub Policy*' 139.

Raz, J. (1985) 'Authority, Law and Morality' 68:3 *The Monist* 295.

Raz, J. (1986) *The Morality of Freedom* (Clarendon Press).

Raz, J. (1994) *Ethics in the Public Domain: Essays in the Morality of Law and Politics* (Oxford University Press).

Raz, J. (1999) *Practical Reasons and Norms* (2nd edn) (Oxford University Press).

Raz, J. (2004) 'Personal Practical Conflicts' in P. Baumann & M. Betzler (eds), *Practical Conflicts: New Philosophical Essays* (Cambridge University Press).

Raz, J. (2006) 'The Problem of Authority: Revisiting the Service Conception' 90 *Minnesota LR* 1003.

Raz, J. (2009) *The Authority of Law: Essays on Law and Morality* (2nd edn) (Oxford University Press).

Reid, E. (1998) 'Abuse of Rights in Scots Law' 2:2 *Edinburgh LR* 129.

Rendleman, D. (2006) *Remedies: Cases and Materials* (7th edn) (Thomson West).

Rendleman, D. & Roberts, C. (2011) *Remedies: Cases and Materials* (8th edn) (Thomson West).

Ripstein, A. (1999) *Equality, Responsibility, and the Law* (Cambridge University Press)

Ripstein (2001) 38 'Private Law and Private Narratives' in P. Cane & J. Gardner (eds), *Relating to Responsibilty* (Hart Publishing).

Ripstein, A. (2007) 'As If It Had Never Happened' 48:5 *William and Mary LR* 1957.

Ripstein, A. (2009) *Force and Freedom: Kant's Legal and Political Philosophy* (Harvard University Press).
Ripstein, A. (2016) *Private Wrongs* (Harvard University Press).
Risinger, D.M. (1982) '"Substance" and "Procedure" Revisited with Some Afterthoughts on the Constitutional Problems of "Irrebuttable Presumptions"' 30:2 *UCLA LR* 189.
Rogerson, P. (2006) 'Quantification of Damages – Substance or Procedure' 65:3 *Cambridge LJ* 515.
Rose, F. (2005) *General Average: Law and Practice. Maritime and Transport Law Library* (2nd ed) (Routledge).
Saprai, P. (2006) 'Restitution without Corrective Justice', 14 *Restitution L Rev* 41
Schwartz, A. (1979) 'The Case for Specific Performance' 89:2 *Yale LJ* 271.
Sharpe, R. (2017) *Injunctions and Specific Performance* (5th edn) (Thomson Reuters).
Shavell, S. (2006) 'Specific Performance v Damages for Breach of Contract: An Economic Analysis' 84:4 *Texas LR* 831
Simmons, J. (1979) 'The Principle of Fair Play' 8 *Philosophy and Public Affairs* 307.
Smith, H. (2004) 'Property and Property Rules' 79:5 *New York U LR* 1719.
Smith, H. (2012) 'On the Economy of Concepts in Property' 160:7 *U of Pennsylvania LR* 2097.
Smith, H (2018) 'Equitable Defences as Meta-Law' in P. Davies, S. Douglas & J. Goudkamp, *Defences in Equity* (Hart Publishing).
Smith, M.B.E. (1972) 'Is There a Prima Facie Obligation to Obey the Law?' 82:5 *Yale LJ* 950.
Smith, S.A. (2000) 'Taking Law Seriously' 50:2 *U of Toronto LJ* 241.
Smith, S.A. (2004) *Contract Theory* (Oxford University Press).
Smith, S.A. (2008) 'The Law of Damages: Rules for Citizens or Rules for Courts?' in D. Saidov & R. Cunnington (eds), *Contract Damages: Domestic and International Perspectives* (Hart Publishing).
Smith S.A. (2010) 'Rights and Remedies: A Complex Relationship' in K. Roach & R. Sharpe (eds), *Taking Rights Seriously* (Canadian Institute for the Administration of Justice).
Smith, S.A. (2011a) 'Rule-Based Rights and Court-Ordered Rights' in A. Robertson & D. Nolan (eds), *Rights and Private Law* (Hart Publishing).
Smith, S.A. (2011b) 'Why Courts Make Orders (And What This Tells Us About Damages)' 64:1 *Current Legal Problems* 51.
Smith, S.A. (2011c) 'The Normativity of Private Law' 31:2 *Oxford J Legal Studies* 215.
Smith, S.A. (2012) 'Duties, Liabilities, and Damages' 125:7 *Harvard LR* 1727.
Smith, S.A. (2013a) 'A Duty to Make Restitution?' 26:1 *Canadian J of L and Jurisprudence* 157.
Smith, S.A. (2013b) 'The Restatement of Liabilities in Restitution' in C. Mitchell & W. Swadling (eds), *The Restatement Third, Restitution and Unjust Enrichment: Comparative and Critical Essays* (Hart Publishing).
Smith, S.A. (2014) 'Remedies for Breach of Contract: One Principle or Two?' in G. Klass, G. Letsas, & P. Saprai (eds), *Philosophical Foundations of Contract Law* (Oxford University Press).
Smith, S.A. (2015) 'Duties to Try and Duties to Succeed' in A. Dyson., J. Goudkamp, & F. Wilmot-Smith (eds), *Defences in Tort* (Hart Publishing).
Smith, S.A. (2016) 'Form and Substance in Equitable Remedies' in A. Robertson & M.J. Tilbury (eds), *Divergences in Private Law* (Hart Publishing).
Spence, M. (1999) *Protecting Reliance: The Emergent Doctrine of Equitable Estoppel* (Hart Publishing).
Spry, I.C.F. (2014) *The Principles of Equitable Remedies: Specific Performance, Injunctions, Rectification and Equitable Damages* (9th edn) (Lawbook Co).

Stapleton, J. (1988) 'The Gist of Negligence' 104:3 *L Quarterly R* 389.
Stein, P. (1984) *Legal Institutions: The Development of Dispute Settlement* (Butterworths).
Stevens, R. (2007) *Torts and Rights* (Oxford University Press).
Stevens, R. (2009) 'Damages and the Right to Performance: A *Golden Victory* or Not?' in J.W. Neyers, R. Bronaugh, & S. Pitel (eds), *Exploring Contract Law* (Hart Publishing).
Stevens, R. (2018) 'The unjust enrichment disaster' 134 *L Quarterly R* 574.
Stoljar, S. (1989) *The Law of Quasi-Contract* (2nd edn) (Law Book Co of Australasia).
Summers, R.S. (1968) 'Good Faith in General Contract Law and the Sales Provisions of the Uniform Commercial Code' 54:2 *Virginia LR* 195.
Swadling, W. (2005) 'The Vendor-Purchaser Constructive Trust' in S. Degeling & J. Edelman (eds), *Equity in Commercial Law* (Law Book Co).
Swadling, W. (2011) 'The Fiction of the Constructive Trust' 64:1 *Current Legal Problems* 399.
Tettenborn, A.M. & Wilby, D. (2010) *The Law of Damages* (LexisNexis).
Treitel, G.H. (2000) 'Contract: General Rules' in P. Birks (ed.), *English Private Law* (vol II) (Oxford University Press).
Tyler, T.H. (1990) *Why People Obey the Law* (Yale University Press).
Varuhas, J. (2014) 'The Concept of 'Vindication' in the Law of Torts: Rights, Interests and Damages' 34: 2 *Oxford Journal of Legal Studies* 1.
Veetch, M.L. & Moon, C.R. (1947) 'De Minimis Non Curat Lex' 45:5 *Michegan LR* 537.
Virgo, G. (2006) *The Principles of the Law of Restitution* (2nd edn) (Oxford University Press).
Virgo, G. (2018) *The Principles of Equity and Trusts* (3rd edn) (Oxford University Press).
von Hirsch, A. (1993) *Censure and Sanctions* (Oxford University Press).
Waldron, J. (1995) 'Moments of Carelessness and Massive Loss' in D.G. Owen (ed.) *Philosophical Foundations of Tort Law Oxford* (Oxford University Press).
Walsh, W. (1930) *A Treatise On Equity* (Callaghan & Company).
Wasserstrom, R. (1963) 'The Obligation to Obey the Law' 10:4 *UCLA LR* 780.
Watts, P. (1995) 'Restitution - A Property Principle and a Services Principle' [1995] *Restitution L Rev* 49.
Webb, Charlie Webb, (2009) 'Property, Unjust Enrichment, and Defective Transfers' in R. Chambers, C. Mitchell, & J. Penner (eds), *Philosophical Foundations of the Law of Unjust Enrichment* (Oxford University Press).
Weinrib, E.J. (1995) *The Idea of Private Law* (Harvard University Press).
Weinrib, E.J. (2002) 'Corrective Justice in a Nutshell' 52 *U Toronto LJ* 349.
Weinrib, E.J. (2008) 'Two Conceptions of Remedies' in C.E.F. Rickett (ed.), *Justifying Private Law Remedies* (Hart Publishing).
Weinrib, E.J. (2012) *Corrective Justice* (Oxford University Press).
Weir, T. (1998) 'The Staggering March of Negligence' in P. Cane & J. Stapleton (eds), *The Law of Obligations: Essays in Celebration of John Fleming* (Oxford University Press).
Weir, T. (2006) *Tort Law* (2nd edn) (Oxford University Press).
Williams, B. (1981) *Moral Luck* (Cambridge University Press).
Williams, G. & Hepple, B. (1976) *The Foundations of Tort Law* (Butterworths).
Wilmot-Smith, F. (2016) 'Reasons? For Restitution?' 79 *Modern LR* 1116.
Witzleb, N. & Carroll, R. (2009) 'The Role of Vindication in Tort Damages' 17 *Tort Law Review* 16.
Woolf, Sir H. et al. (2011) *The Declaratory Judgment* (4th edn) (Sweet & Maxwell).
Worthington, S. (2006) *Equity* (2nd edn) (Oxford University Press).
Wright, C. (1942) 'Introduction to the Law of Torts' 8 *Cambridge LJ* 238.
Zakrzewski, R. (2005) *Remedies Reclassified* (Oxford University Press).
Zipursky, B.C. (1998a) 'Rights, Wrongs, and Recourse in the Law of Torts' 51:1 *Vanderbilt LR* 1.

Zipursky, B.C. (1998b) 'Legal Malpractice and the Structure of Negligence Law' 67:2 *Fordham LR* 649.

Zipursky, B. (2002) 'Philosophy of Private Law' in J.L. Coleman, K.E. Himma, & S.J. Shapiro (eds), *The Oxford Handbook of Jurisprudence and Philosophy of Law* (Oxford University Press).

Zipursky, B. (2003) 'Civil Recourse, Not Corrective Justice' 91 *Geo LJ* 695.

Zipursky, B.C. & Goldberg, J.C.P. (2001) 'The Restatement (Third) and the Place of Duty in Negligence Law' 54:3 *Vanderbilt LR* 657.

Zipursky, B.C. & Goldberg, J.C.P. (2016) 'The Strict Liability in Fault and the Fault in Strict Liability' 85 *Fordham LR* 743.

Zuckerman, A.A.S. (2013) *Zuckerman on Civil Procedure: Principles of Practice* (3rd edn) (Sweet & Maxwell).

Zweigert, K. & Kotz, H. (1998) *An Introduction to Comparative Law*, T. Weir (trans.) (3rd edn) (Oxford University Press).

Index

Note: *For the benefit of digital users, indexed terms that span two pages (e.g., 52–53) may, on occasion, appear on only one of those pages.*

abuse of process, *see* defences
abuse of rights 160–61
account of profits 214n96
acquiescence 270, 312–14
action rights, *see* rights
adequacy of damages, *see* defences, specific performance
aggravated damages, *see* damages
agreed sum, *see* sum due
assault 57, 77, 149–50, 244–45, 258–59
authority
  declaratory 114–17
  directive 117
  generally (in relation to orders) 114–26
  relationship theory of 122–23
  service conception of 120–22

battery 93–94, 149–50, 186–87, 208–9, 216–17, 219, 230–32, 260, 274–75
Birks, Peter 3n8, 6n16, 82n11, 88, 135–36, 144n29, 153n57, 179–80n4, 192n24, 204–5, 224, 230–31n19, 236n31, 238–39, 269
Blackstone, William 41, 42–43, 87–88, 177–78

causes of action
  classification of 87–96
  generally 80–96
  meaning 80–81
  see also injustices, rights-threats, wrongs
Chancery Court
  enforcement of rulings and 66–67, 71
  form of rulings and 2
  generally 10, 14n23, 20, 21–24, 27–28, 30–31, 32–39, 51–56, 66–67, 81, 141, 296–99
  legal effects of rulings and 59
  relationship to Royal Court 32–39
  see also equitable defences, equitable remedies
change of position 241, 245, 274–75n5
civil recourse theory 202n58, 251–52n69, 253
clean hands, *see* defences
compensatory orders
  damages and 222, 249–65
  detrimental reliance, for 269–72
  injustice, as a response to 225, 227, 249–72
  necessitous intervention and 225
  non-wrongs, for 225
  see also injustices
consequential loss, *see* compensatory orders
constitutive rulings, *see* rulings
constructive trusts 14–15n26, 114, 114–15n14, 171, 269n137
contempt of court 20–21, 32, 33, 62, 66, 70–71, 85, 302n88
continuity thesis 142n22, 163–64n84, 173–74, 181–99
contract
  duty to perform 3, 12–13, 14–15, 45
  history of remedial law and 35–36
  negative contractual duties 135
  primary remedy for breach of 22–23n40, 138
  termination of 164, 176
  see also efficient breach theory, specific performance, substitutionary damages, sum due
contributory negligence 188–89, 194n30, 227, 253–54, 255
conversion 79–80, 135
corrective justice 204–5n65
cost of cure (or performance), *see* damages
court-ordered rights, *see* rights
creative orders, *see* orders

damages
  aggravated 208, 209–10n73, 210, 219
  assessment of compensatory 188, 193–94, 197, 253
  collateral benefits and 188, 253–54
  compensatory 222, 249–65
  continuity thesis and 251
  cost of cure (or performance) and 165–66, 170n102, 174, 175, 189, 318
  diminution in value and 170n102, 189
  duty-confirming or duty-creating 179–99
  duty-creating view of 202
  equitable 172, 284–85, 312n120
  exemplary (punitive) 79–80, 88, 90–91, 92–93, 100, 126–27, 179, 198, 209
  foreseeability and 91–92, 188, 198, 253–54, 255n79

damages (cont.)
gain-based 214
injustice, as a response to 94–96, 101, 227–28, 265
innocent misrepresentations and 264
loss of amenity 182–83n7, 198, 219–20, 319
market-price 213, 215n100, 216
mental distress, for 219–20n132, 249
mitigation and 139, 188, 227, 253–54
necessity and 261
nominal 202–6, 208, 211
non-pecuniary 216
non-wrongs, for 227, 251
pain and suffering, for 218
pecuniary loss, for 223, 249, 252
pre-payment of 196, 199, 200–1
remoteness and 91–92, 188–89, 198, 227, 253–54, 255n79
restitutionary 214
rights-threats and 172–76
Rylands v Fletcher and 259
specific relief, in lieu of 172–76, 261
substantive duty to pay 3–4, 179–99
substitutionary 134, 138–76, 178–79, 184–85n12, 262–63n115, 295, 313
user 212, 213, 214
vicarious liability and 232
vindicatory 210
waiver 212
wrong-based 202–21
wrongs, for 202–21, 227, 251
wrongs to third parties and 264
see also continuity thesis, equitable compensation, injustices, wrongs
de minimis, *see* defences
debt, *see* sum due
declarations
against the crown 279
generally 14–15, 21, 82–83, 111–12, 114–15n14, 200–1
declaratory orders, *see* declarations
defamation 216–17
defences
absence of formalities 3–4, 5, 128, 277
abuse of process 282
adequacy of damages 38–39, 44–45, 99–100, 133, 141, 143, 145, 147, 148, 154–56, 167–68, 294–95, 299
clean hands 133, 294–95, 314
de minimis 148, 282
definition 274
discretion and 319
equitable defences 296, 311–18
exoneration clauses and 292
hardship 33, 40, 133, 157–58n72, 169, 294–96, 316
illegality 5, 275–76, 286
immunity 5, 278
impossibility 133, 294–95, 314
laches (delay) 133, 294–95, 312
limitation periods 5, 40, 45, 64–65, 76, 102, 275, 284
personal duties 133, 294–95, 309
public interest 133, 156–57, 161–62, 294–95, 318
res judicata 282
settlement 12–13, 112n9, 196–97, 236n33, 292
substantive and remedial, 274–77
statutory non-actionability 280
supervision 133, 294–95, 308
delivery up 144–46, 172–73
detrimental reliance 270
discretion, *see* defences

economic analysis of law 165–67, 229n17, 248–49, 265n120
efficient breach theory 165–67, 300–1
ejectment 142–44, 145
enforcement (of rulings)
direct 67
execution, by 67
fines and 70
functional explanation of 71
imprisonment and 70
indirect 70
meaning of 66
rights 66, 84
sequestration and 70
equitable compensation 54n25
equitable damages, *see* damages
equitable defences, *see* defences
equitable orders, *see* equitable remedies
equitable remedies 15–21, 25, 32–39, 51, 59
defences and 155
distinguished historically from legal 32–39
enforcement of 66–67, 71
form of 48–51
legal effects of 58–65
see also defences (equitable), delivery up, injunctions, specific performance
equity 32–39; *see also* defences (equitable), equitable remedies
estoppel, *see* proprietary estoppel
execution, *see* enforcement
exemplary damages, *see* damages
exoneration clauses, *see* defences

fairness 223, 228–29, 235, 246, 250–51, 254–56, 265–69; *see also* injustices

fiduciary duty, remedies for breach of 14n23
fines, *see* enforcement
foreseeability, *see* damages
formalities, *see* defences
free-standing orders, *see* orders

gain-based damages, *see* damages
Gardner, John 3–4n11, 157–58n74, 179–80n4, 181, 228n14, 229n16, 261, 274–75n3
Goldberg, John 130–31n36, 179–80n4, 202n58, 251–52n69, 259–60n102
good faith 233, 314–15, 320–21

hardship, *see* defences
Holmes, Oliver Wendell 2, 11–13

illegality, *see* defences
immunity, *see* defences
impossibility, *see* defences
imprisonment, *see* enforcement
injunctions
  definition of 146
  form of 49
  generally 146–56
  interim and interlocutory 19–20
  mandatory 50, 72, 97–98n24, 148–49, 155–56, 300, 308
  non-replicative 152
  partial defences and 154
  property transfers and 271
  quia timet 87–88, 112, 134–35, 143, 147, 149–50, 152, 153–54, 263, 305–6
  response to a rights-threat, as a 146–47
  response to an injustice, as a 271
  substantive law reasons for refusing 156
  to take care 149
  see also defences (equitable)
injustices
  meaning of 223, 228
  compensation for non-wrongs and 225
  compensation for wrongs and 227, 249–72
  detrimental reliance and 270
  necessitous intervention and 225
  no substantive duty to correct 232
  property transfer injunctions and 271
  responsibility and 250, 254–55, 256–57, 261, 265–69
  restitution and 224, 237–45
instrumental theories 229n17, 248–49, 265n120
interest awards
  classification of remedies and 12–13, 78–79n8
  duties to pay damages and 195
  form of remedies and 56–57
  legal effect of rulings and 60n36, 60n38, 64–65
  orders for a sum due and 140
  restitutionary orders and 241

judgments
  authority and 125–26
  distinguished from orders 32–39, 51, 59, 66–67, 125–26
  meaning 19–25
justice
  meaning 228–29
  remedial law and 13–14
  see also corrective justice, injustices

Kantian theories 27, 178n46, 245–46n54; *see also* Ripstein, Weinrib

laches, *see* defences
legal remedies
  distinguished historically from equitable 32–39
  enforcement of 66–67, 71
  form of 48–51
  legal effects of 60–65
  see also damages, delivery up, ejectment, equitable defences, equitable remedies, sum due, orders for
liability
  damages and 191–202
  distinguished from duty 192
  restitution and 238–43
limitation periods, *see* defences
liquidated damages, *see* stipulated damages
Lord Cairns Act, *see* damages (equitable)
loss of amenity, *see* damages

market-price damages, *see* damages
McBride, Nicholas 150n50, 150–51n53, 151n56, 209n71, 248n63, 253n71, 258–59n100, 259–60n102, 269–70n137
mesne profits, *see* damages (gain-based)
misrepresentation 92, 101, 226, 264
mitigation, *see* damages

necessitous intervention 225
necessity 92, 95–96, 237, 257, 261, 265, 268
negligence, tort of 150–52, 209, 217–18, 253n71
nominal damages, *see* damages
non-pecuniary damages, *see* damages
nuisance 89, 149–50, 152–54, 156–62, 262–63, 307–8

orders
  commands, as 113–26
  creation of 46–47

orders (cont.)
creative 98
distinguished from Judgments 32–39, 51, 59, 66–67, 125–26
distinguished from rules 110–13
distinguished from sanctions 106–9
enforcement of 66–71
form of 48–56
free-standing 101
grounds for 87–93
historical meaning of 32–39
kinds of orders 96–103
legal effects of 57–59
meaning of 14
obligation to obey and 114, 117
practical advantages of 124–25
replicative 97
rulings and 14–17
standing to obtain 129–31
substitutionary 98
terminological issues and 19
why courts issue 113–26
wrong-responding 100
see also damages, delivery up, ejectment, injunctions, restitutionary orders, specific performance, sum due
ostensuruas quare writs 42–43n27, 43–44, 196

pain and suffering, *see* damages
pecuniary loss, *see* damages
penalty clauses, *see* stipulated damages
Penner, James 171n104, 232n23, 247
personal duties, *see* defences, specific performance
policy arguments 64–65, 70–71, 160, 235–36, 254–55, 276, 283, 285–86, 315–16; *see also* utilitarianism
Posner, Richard 202n58, 204–5n63
powers (legal) 75
praecipe writs 42–43n27, 44, 196
pre-payment of damages, *see* damages
price, action for the, *see* sum due
proprietary estoppel 270
proximate cause, *see* foreseeability
public interest defence, *see* defences
public policy, *see* policy arguments, utilitarianism
punitive damages, *see* damages

quia timet injunctions, *see* injunctions

Rawls, John 120–21n25, 228n14, 233n25
Raz, Joseph 120–21n25, 181n5, 181
recovery of chattels, *see* delivery up
recovery of land, *see* ejectment
remedial law
definition of 6–7
remedies
definition of 2, 6–7
kinds of 9, 17
reasons for action and 8
terminological issues 17
see also equitable remedies, legal remedies
remoteness, *see* damages
replicative orders, *see* orders
res judicata, *see* defences
responsibility (for losses) 250, 254–55, 256–57, 261, 265–69
restitution, *see* restitutionary orders
restitutionary orders
change of position and 241
definition of 237
duty-confirming or duty-creating 238–43
generally 237–45
instrumental (economic) explanation of 248–49
interest and 241
no damages for failure to make restitution 240
property-law explanation 247
responses to injustices, as 224, 245
responses to unconscionability, as 246
Theft Act and 242
unknowability objection 243
see also unjust enrichment
rights
action 80
classificatory chart of 85
court-ordered 82
definition 75–76
enforcement 84
substantive 77
rights-based theories 26, 204–5n65, 251
rights-threats
definition of 133–34
wrongs and 134–36
see also delivery up, ejectment, injunctions, specific performance, sum due
Ripstein, Arthur 3–4n11, 111n5, 120–21n25, 179–80n4, 181, 190, 199n45, 218n120, 227–28, 265–66
Royal Courts
enforcement of rulings and 66–67, 71
form of rulings and 2
generally 32–39
legal effects of rulings and 59
see also judgments, legal remedies
rulings
classificatory chart of 17
constitutive 14–16, 17*f*, 112, 114, 115–16n14
criminal 16

declaratory 14–15
directive 1, 6–7
private law 14
procedural 16
public law 16
remedial 16
see also orders
Rylands v Fletcher, rule in 92, 95–96, 258, 259, 320

self-help 7–8, 68–69n57
sequestration, *see* enforcement
settlement
distinguished from performance 196, 200–1n54, 236n33
see also defences
specific performance
adequacy of damages and 295, 299
administrative explanation of 167–68, 301–3
availability of 164
damages in lieu of 172–76
definition of 162
efficient breach theory of 165–67
monetary obligations and 303–4
personal duties and 309
quia timet orders for 162–63
substantive-law reasons for refusing 168
supervision and 308
termination of contract and 164
vendor-purchaser constructive trust and 171
see also equitable defences, equitable remedies, substitutionary damages, sum due
specific relief, *see* delivery up, equitable remedies, injunctions, specific performance
standing 129–31
statutory non-actionability, *see* defences
Stevens, Robert 174n111, 179–80n4, 192n24, 202n57, 213–14n90, 216n101, 228n12, 249n66, 264–65n117, 267–68n132, 292–93n69
stipulated damages 18, 137–38
strict liability, *see* liability
substantive law
damages and 179–80
defences and 274–77
distinguished from remedial law 3–4, 7, 11–12
duties to perform contracts 166–67
historical development 39–46
meaning 1–2, 7
reasons to refuse injunctions 156
reasons to refuse specific performance 168
restitution and 238
rights-threats and 133–34, 136
see also substantive rights
substantive rights, *see* rights; substantive law
substitutionary damages, *see* damages
substitutionary orders, *see* orders
sum due, orders for 22–23, 48–49, 51n17, 137–41, 164, 303–4
supervision, *see* defences

tender 12–13, 196
termination, *see* contract
trespass 43–44, 133–34, 143, 144, 152–53, 157, 208, 313
trespass writs 196–97
trusts, remedies for breach of 14n23

ubi jus ibi remedium 5–6, 102–3, 223
undertakings (to a court) 135, 146–47
unjust enrichment 17–18, 23–24, 93, 94, 224–25, 228, 230–31n19, 237, 239, 245–46n54, 249, 269, 290–91; *see also* restitutionary orders
user damages, *see* damages
utilitarianism 25, 26–27, 204–5n65
utility, *see* utilitarianism

vicarious liability 259, 260, 267–68
vindicatory damages, *see* damages

waiver damages, *see* damages
Weinrib, Ernest 3–4n11, 160–61n80, 179–80n4, 181, 192, 204–5n65, 218n120, 229n15, 239n41, 245–46n54
White & Carter exception 139, 164, 164n86
Wrongs
Blackstone and 177
compensation for non-wrongs 225
compensation for wrongs and 227, 249–72
continuity thesis and 181
injustices and 229
rights-threats and 134–36
seriousness of 207–8
third parties and 264
wrong-based damages 202–21, 227, 251
see also damages, orders
wrong-based damages, *see* wrongs, damages
wrong-responding orders, *see* orders

Zipursky, Benjamin 130–31n36, 179–80n4, 202n58, 251–52n69, 259–60n102

www.ingramcontent.com/pod-product-compliance
Lightning Source LLC
Chambersburg PA
CBHW071824240926
52047CB00003B/26
9780199229772